Imperial Diplomacy

Imperial Diplomacy

Rosebery and
the Failure of
Foreign Policy

GORDON MARTEL

McGill-Queen's University Press
Kingston and Montreal
Mansell Publishing Limited
London

© McGill-Queen's University Press 1986
ISBN 0-7735-0442-7
Legal deposit first quarter 1986
Bibliothèque nationale du Québec
Printed in Canada

First published in Great Britain in 1986 by
Mansell Publishing Limited
6 All Saints Street
London N1 9R1
ISBN 0-7201-1734-8

This book has been published with the help of a grant
from the Social Science Federation of Canada using
funds provided by the Social Sciences and Humanities
Research Council of Canada.

Canadian Cataloguing in Publication Data

Martel, Gordon, 1946–
    Imperial diplomacy: Rosebery and the failure of foreign
    policy
    Bibliography: p.
    Includes index.
    ISBN 0-7735-0442-7
    1. Rosebery, Archibald Philip Primrose, 1847–1929.
    2. Great Britain – Foreign Relations – 1837–1901.
    3. Great Britain – Foreign relations – 1901–1910.
    I. Title.
    DA564.R7M37 1986   327.2'092'4   C85-099370-9

British Library Cataloguing in Publication Data

Martel, Gordon
    Imperial diplomacy : Rosebery and the
    failure of foreign policy.
    1. Great Britain – Foreign relations – 1837–1901. I. Title
    327.41   DA560
    ISBN 0-7201-1734-8

Contents

For Valerie

Preface

Archibald Philip Primrose, the fifth earl of Rosebery, is one of the most attractive and most perplexing figures in the landscape of modern British politics. In many ways he seems the quintessence of the Victorian ruling class: a large landowner of noble lineage with properties in Scotland and England; an improver of his estates, applying the new tricks of technology to increase his yield; a modern investor who carefully diversified his accounts in American mines, Latin American railways, eastern trade, and the Suez Canal; an Etonian and Oxonian trained in the classics; a traveller, a collector of china and tapestry, a keeper of journals. Nor are these similarities to the stereotype merely superficial; ideas and attitudes confirm the viewer's impression that here is one of those stalwart Victorians: his politics were pragmatic rather than ideological – Tories and Whigs alike sought him for their party when he came of age; he believed in the superiority of the Anglo-Saxon race and in the beneficence of British institutions; he strove to improve himself as well as his property; he married within his class and, when his wife died prematurely, continued to honour her memory by writing on black-bordered stationery and solemnly celebrating the anniversary of her death. But Rosebery transcended or, according to one's point of view, never lived up to the stereotype. Contemporaries regarded him as strangely idiosyncratic. He was sent down from Oxford; he married a Jewess; he collected pornography; he gambled and liked gamblers; he had few friends close enough to call him "Archie." His behaviour was unpredictable: he might invite acquaintances to spend the weekend at one of his country houses, greet them when they arrived, then disappear for the remainder of their stay. Most striking, and most bewildering to students of political history, was Rosebery's decision in 1896 to resign the leadership of the Liberal party – a bizarre act for which he has never been forgiven. Men are supposed to be forced out of power or step down when they have been worn out; they are not supposed to utter a few witty remarks and gladly step aside when they are young and have reached the height of their powers.

In one sense the amount of attention that has been paid to Rosebery is surprising, for he achieved very little in his political career. There are no great legislative acts, or even bills, associated with his name; it would be difficult to argue that the nature of social or political life in Britain was altered by his presence, or that the course of the nation's history would have been noticeably different had he simply tended to his estates and remained a private citizen. But Rosebery was a glittering creature. He gave wonderful speeches to enthusiastic audiences. The moment he entered politics he stood out from the crowd: Gladstone and Disraeli alike recognized that he was someone special, the kind of man to whom others instinctively looked for leadership. And this is what has attracted the attention of historians. How did a man of such great promise fail so dismally?

To speak of Rosebery, therefore, is to speak of personality and temperament – a necessity admirably suited to the tastes of the literate in the twentieth century, accustomed as we are to accept the fashionable precepts of psychoanalysis. Little serious attention has been given to what Rosebery actually did; more important – and more fun – to study what he said. No one has undertaken to study his foreign policy in spite of the fact that he was twice foreign secretary, in 1886 and 1892–4, and that such things as Rosebery did accomplish lay in this field. What we know of his foreign policy comes indirectly, in scattered articles or in monographs on specialized subjects. The best and most significant of these sources, G.N. Sanderson's *England, Europe and the Upper Nile*, deals with only one area of policy and was written without the benefit of access to the Rosebery Papers. By comparison, we have excellent and detailed treatments of the struggle of personalities within the Liberal party in 1893–4 in Peter Stansky's *Ambitions and Strategies*, and a full treatment of Rosebery's personality in Robert Rhodes James's superb biography.

To argue that an understanding of Rosebery's foreign policy is a gap that needs to be filled is a tedious and pedantic justification for writing a book – and the pages that follow may be regarded as tedious and pedantic. The intention, however, is more ambitious than gap-filling or hole-plugging. The central argument of this book is that it is impossible to understand Rosebery's career – or his decisions to enter politics and to leave it – without understanding the appeal that foreign policy had for him. Conversely, it is impossible to understand how he conducted the foreign policy of the empire without understanding his personality and the complex of relationships into which this led him. It will no longer suffice to dash off a few glib remarks asserting that all may be accounted for by Rosebery's prickly temperament or lack of sleep. Many men found Rosebery unusually easy to deal with when in office; for the most part he was amiable and polite and refused to interfere in areas of government for which he was not directly responsible. Moreover, because observers expect him to behave rashly, assertions are frequently made that he bludgeoned the cabinet into accepting unpopular policies by repeatedly threatening to resign. This was a myth. Rosebery never threatened to resign as foreign secretary; he once offered to resign, but this was quite different, coming in the aftermath of a crisis, not in the midst of it. The truth is that Rosebery was able to succeed in pursuing the policy in which he believed by a combination of persuasive arguments, hard work, and deception. The cabinet, even when overwhelmingly aligned against him, proved unequal to the task of controlling foreign policy.

Rosebery's policy was a personal one. Cabinet politics, the party, the press, and special interests were constantly threatening to intrude into the Foreign Office, but they never succeeded. While it has become the fashion to deride diplomatic history and assume that the structure of the state and underlying economic forces are all-important, this book argues that British diplomacy, as conducted by Rosebery, was relatively free of domestic constraints. Rosebery held steadfastly to the belief that it was his duty to stand above party politics and special interests. The duty of the foreign secretary was to construct a policy that served the interests of the entire empire, and only the man at the centre was able to correctly assess what these interests were, and how they were best achieved. Given this premise, it should not be surprising to discover what the documents reveal: that foreign policy in Britain was made by the foreign secretary and his professional advisers, not by the army, not by those benefiting from an increased navy, not by trading or manufacturing organizations, not by any cliques, cartels, or other conspirators.

To study foreign policy in the Rosebery era is, therefore, to study the diplomatic documents. Only the closest and most careful inspection of the day-to-day conduct of diplomacy reveals what British foreign policy really was. It is exceedingly dull to wade through mountains of drafts and dispatches but, unless this is done, the historian is unlikely to offer more than the usual trite references to imperialist rivalry among the great powers stimulated by economic competition. Those who made foreign policy in Britain had only the most rudimentary grasp of economics; they were more at ease with the classical world of Greece and Rome than they were with Malthus and Marx, Bentham and Ricardo. The documents reveal this ignorance. One searches in vain for sophisticated analysis of economic conditions and prospects in the areas of rivalry in the 1890s: Uganda, Siam, Morocco, Persia. One discovers instead that the diplomats often knew little about the businesses or the men they were supposed to be representing. Policy proceeded on the basis of a few simple assumptions about the nature of economic life: trade and commerce are good things, for natives and Europeans alike; London's position at the centre of international finance would assure Britain of a share of the profits in any large-scale economic enterprise; British manufactures are so good and cheap that they will continue to sell even in foreign colonies, even carried over foreign-financed railways. But the most simple assumption operating in the 1890s was that business should take care of itself. As long as there was no legal discrimination being applied against British subjects the Foreign Office saw no reason for becoming involved. Everyone imagined that the world would continue to develop along much the same lines as before, and that this was a good thing.

The threats posed to this beneficent world were traditional, political ones. Rosebery, his advisers, and his colleagues lived with one foot in the world of Alexander the Great, the other in the world of Napoleon Bonaparte; they felt more at ease with them than they would have with Lenin and Hitler, IBM and Exxon. What was seen as threatening was military conquest leading to the establishment of a new political order; everyone knew that economic prosperity followed from political power – the ruling class in Britain hardly required a sociologist to chart this for them. The Napoleonic experience had left no doubt of the consequences for Britain should the European continent come to be dominated by a single great power. Rosebery's first concern was always with the balance of power in Europe, which is surprising when one considers that almost all commentators have treated him as a great imperialist, concerned primarily with expansion, with "pegging out claims for the future." In fact, Rosebery liked the world he had inherited and saw little need for dramatic change. He was much more concerned with consolidating and defending what Britain already had than he was with grabbing more. And here the diplomatic documents can be misleading. For every hundred pages of documentation on some territorial dispute in central Asia or Africa we might find a paragraph on general political relations with European powers. This reveals how business was transacted, not what was important. The negotiations with Russia over the boundary to be drawn in the Pamirs, for example, dragged on for years and resulted in the production of tens of thousands of pages of documentation – yet the essence of these negotiations was Rosebery's ambition to improve British relations with Russia without appearing to make unnecessary concessions. There is hardly a word to reveal this aim in the "official" correspondence.

One major reason why historians who have treated Rosebery's foreign policy in the past have so often been misled is their necessary reliance upon official correspondence. The most significant material is to be found not in the Public Record Office, but in private collections: in the Rosebery Papers especially, but also in those of Harcourt, Kimberley, Morier, Dufferin, and others. The same might also be said of the Salisbury era, but the point must be made more forcefully in the case of Rosebery because he found himself dealing with a cabinet which he believed ignorant and obstructive. In his view, men like Gladstone, Harcourt, and Morley understood nothing of the nuances and subtleties of balance-of-power politics because they thought that Britain could take up a simple moral position and abandon the intrigues and dangers involved in foreign policy. He discovered that it was no good trying to explain to these men how British policy in Uganda or Siam was inextricably connected with politics on the European continent; he assumed that he would carry no weight if he argued that Britain must maintain good relations with the Triple Alliance in order to safeguard the British Empire from France and Russia. Thus some of the private cabinet correspondence can also be misleading, as Rosebery often recognized that to explain his true motives for undertaking a specific policy would only succeed in damaging his case.

A coherent and persuasive picture of Rosebery's foreign policy emerges only when all the pieces of the puzzle have been examined. Concentrating on his policy in a specific area will mislead because no area was treated as an entity unto itself. The impetuous act of a British officer on the North-West frontier could not only influence relations with Russia, it might also confirm the German assumption that Britain and Russia were bound to go to war over India; and this, in turn, might lead the Germans to some new initiative in their relations with Britain in Africa or the Middle East. The reason that Rosebery, like most foreign secretaries, had trouble with "men on the spot" is that he found their attention too narrowly focused on the situation confronting them; they could not view things from his lofty perspective. And understanding that Rosebery viewed his perspective as not only lofty but unique is absolutely vital to understanding his behaviour. He believed that he saw things in a way that no one else could, and this gave him a special responsibility, a duty which he alone could perform while in office.

This feeling of being above common affairs, yet being at the centre of events, exerted a tremendous force on Rosebery, and one that enabled him to overcome natural inclinations towards a private life of travel, horses, and reading. He felt that he was making a sacrifice in abandoning his privacy and entering the public arena, but as long as he believed himself to be successful, he was satisfied in performing his duty. Only when he became prime minister did he begin to regard himself as a failure, and that is when the sleeplessness, the bad nerves, and the sickness began. Rosebery abandoned public life when he realized that he was incapable of performing his duty effectively, when the contradictions inherent in his foreign policy began to be revealed. This is why he never returned; he knew he had failed and he could not see how to succeed.

Many colleagues and friends have contributed comments and criticisms in the preparation of this book. A few were asked to wade their way through one or more complete drafts, some were given the less burdensome task of reading a single chapter, while others were given the ultimate joy of an extended conversation. If the book is less than perfect, therefore, the critical reader should hold culpable: Gordon Craig, David Hamer, Barbara Jelavich, Ian Nish, Deryck Schreuder, Peter Stansky, and the late Cedric Lowe. But two men must be singled out as bearing even more responsibility than the rest: Edward Ingram, who was my honours supervisor while I was an undergraduate, and who then bitterly attacked every word I uttered, has continued to perform this invaluable service ever since; and Archie Thornton, who, as my PHD supervisor, first suggested Rosebery as a subject worth studying, and who has remained a benevolent ally ever since. If this book shows any vitality, any clarity, it is largely due to my good fortune in having had the opportunity to work with these two men.

The final years of preparing this book were undertaken while I was a member of the history department at Trent University in Peterborough, Ontario. As my colleagues there neither understood nor appreciated diplomatic history, I can hardly thank them for any direct contribution, but must admit that they provided a stimulating atmosphere in which to work; the chairman, Freddy Hagar, in spite of regarding all writing as egotistical self-aggrandizement, did his best to humour me in my pretensions. These years were also spent in the idyllic surroundings of Catharine Parr Traill College, where the members of the Senior Common Room provided wit and drink in equally liberal amounts. The benign countenance of our principal, Nancy Sherouse, shone on all those fortunate enough to dwell there, and without her patient good humour and marvellous dinner parties the tone of this book would have suffered appreciably. Finally, I wish to thank Peter Adams, dean of graduate studies and university research officer, without whose support this book would never have been finished.

Every author knows how difficult the preparation of a manuscript can be. My burden in this respect was eased by the assistance of five people. Shirley Hartwick transformed the wretched scratchings of my pencil into a legible rough draft; Dorothy Sharpe produced an impeccable manuscript from the revised version. I thank them both. I must also thank Peter Slade, who, in spite of his shabby appearance, admires clear writing; he drew my attention to many infelicitous phrases and vague references. I wish to express my sincere thanks to Charles Beer, who twice laboured through the text, and whose copy-editing improved it considerably. Valerie Martel, to whom this book is dedicated, proofread the manuscript with the same dutiful care and patience that she has always showed Rosebery and me. I owe her more than she will ever know.

Portions of this study which have appeared in the *Historical Journal*, the *Journal of Imperial and Commonwealth Studies*, and *Middle Eastern Studies* are reprinted by permission of the editors.

Rosebery Room, Rhodes House, Oxford

May 1985

Introduction

Rosebery, as a young man of the 1870s, seemed to have the path of greatness clearly laid out before him. Teachers predicted that he would succeed; family and friends expected it. He combined wealth, status, and intelligence, assets most likely to lead to political success. In spite of these expectations, however, Rosebery had not advanced far by the end of the decade. Nor was he particularly young; by 1880 he was thirty-three and he had not yet occupied a political office of any importance. These years should not be neglected, however, for they were a time of preparation, and it is difficult to explain Rosebery's political career without taking them into account. His attraction to public life was not straightforward: it is sometimes forgotten that his real career in politics lasted only slightly more than fifteen years. His career seems longer because observers before 1880 were wondering when he would step forward, while after 1895 they were bemused by the possibility that he might come back. A striking feature that runs throughout Rosebery's life, however, was the private turmoil that began in the 1870s and remained constant thereafter.[1]

Rosebery's greatest worry as a young man was a feeling that he lacked the moral strength to succeed in public life. He doubted neither his intellectual ability nor his capacity for hard work. He did doubt his ability to overcome what seemed to him a lamentable inclination to indulge himself in worldly, selfish pleasures. While most young aristocrats emerged from public school and university convinced of their ability to govern, Rosebery did not. "It is expected and assumed that a peer shall take to politics as a duck takes to swimming," he said. He denied that Eton and Oxford trained young men to govern. "I have grave doubts if Eton provided any special instruction for them in their future duties."[2] He devoted much of his time to the study of those subjects – political history and political economy – in which he felt his training to be inadequate. The real struggle in which he became engaged, however, was not to compensate for a deficient education, but to overcome the temptations of the sensual life. While he appeared to teach himself constitutional history and political economy, he was more actively engaged in persuading himself to devote his life to the service of the nation.

The journal in which he began to record his thoughts on history, literature, and current events reveals an obsession with what he considered a weak character. The notes he made were intended to remind him of what was admirable in human nature, and what was not. He noted, for example, that although he found Flaubert's *L'Education sentimentale* rather dull, it was not without merit. "There is one fine moral pervading every page," he recorded, "the emptiness of a life of pleasure."[3] This set the tone of the journal, which was intended to remind Rosebery continually that there must be a purpose to existence, and that it could not be found in a life of idle self-indulgence.

The desire for personal pleasure was something that Rosebery was determined to overcome. In another age he might have turned to psychoanalysis; other Victorians turned to their Bible. Rosebery turned to biography, to great men of the past who seemed, like himself, to have been torn between duty and pleasure. He noted of Alexander the Great that his passions for wine and women were predominant after his ambition. "They were spots in his character before they prevailed by the force of habit: as soon as they began to do so, the king and the hero appeared less, the rake and bully more."[4] Rosebery saw the same spots in his own character: he was too introspective and too honest to delude himself where his passions and ambitions were concerned. "It is encouraging," he assured himself, "for a reader who may be troubled with perpetual temptation to particular vices or laxities to remember that such vices are not in themselves absolute obstacles to success."[5] He surrendered. Because he could not eradicate the spots in his character, he proposed to recognize and suppress them instead. Were anyone to see this proposal, he noted, it would produce a great outcry; "but it must be remembered that I do not exclude the most Christian exertions to overcome such feelings."[6] The young Rosebery was struggling against his own nature. In public, he appeared able, confident, even arrogant; in private, he was uncertain and introspective.

If selfishness and principle beckoned to him simultaneously, Rosebery was uncertain which he would choose. "I sometimes think the Right would conquer, sometimes the wrong."[7] He believed it impossible to say with any certainty what his conduct would be under crucial circumstances. "Whence again I believe it to be true that the only foundation for strength in such a conflict is to have laboured steadily and blindly in the cause of what belief one may be possessed of."[8] Distrusting his own moral fibre, Rosebery attempted to create a mechanism within himself that would enable him to take the right course out of reflex action. If he laboured steadily for his beliefs, "then at any rate one of the strongest of the giants usually enlisted under the banner of selfishness – Habit – will be at hand to sustain the cause of principle."[9] Henceforth, Rosebery saw a challenge in every decision he faced: was he acting selfishly or on principle; was he reinforcing good habits or bad?

The young Rosebery exhibited the characteristics that later frustrated his friends and colleagues. Some of these characteristics seem to have been produced by this period of agonizing self-appraisal. Determined to make the right choice, to follow duty rather than selfishness, Rosebery created an inner conflict for himself over what appeared to others the most trivial and petty of matters. Once committed by a decision based on his moral code, however, Rosebery defended the choice even if it became apparent that it had been a tactical or political mistake. The pattern he established as a young man created an egotistic belief that most of those with whom he had differences were acting out of motives less worthy than his own. While others acted selfishly out of habit, he acted out of a conscious determination to do his duty – or so he often believed.

It was a short step from the belief that the highest purpose in life was the performance of one's duty to the belief that a perfunctory performance would in itself be an immoral act of selfishness. Vices and laxities he lumped together. Convinced that he had discovered, in habit, a way of encouraging the triumph of principle over selfishness, Rosebery looked for other methods to enable him to achieve his ambitions. To this end, he proposed that every man should write an account of his life each year. "What an inducement to improvement, what a reproof to the stationary, what a lash to those who have retrograded." Why do those who seek to know themselves neglect their own history? "Is it that to look back on the year is to look back upon a Golgotha, that our shrines are empty, that our memories are shadows: is it that we fear to look beyond them, that the end of the year does not resemble the happy close of a well-spent day but rather the uneasy waking from a disturbed slumber. Let us ask ourselves."[10] Rosebery was always asking himself, then and later, and his questioning was his greatest enemy.

While conducting this private war against selfishness and waste, Rosebery accomplished little in the world outside. He travelled, col-

lecting a hoard of tourist treasures; he raced, building one of the
better stables in England, and he never lost his fascination with either
travel or the turf. Publicly, he appeared gay, frivolous, and concerned
primarily with the pursuit of his own pleasures. Privately, he continued to search for more, trying to instruct himself in the cultivation
of habits that would remould his character. The cultivation of the
sublime would, he believed, "like the transfigured face of Moses reflect
the glory on which it gazes. For the intellect is capable of quickly
assimilating in some degree to what it contemplates."[11] This he wrote
while reading Macaulay, and fourteen years later he told a friend
that he owed everything to Macaulay's *Essays.*[12] His reading was
conscientiously didactic: "A wise man," he wrote, "should read and
meditate on some part of a masterpiece each day to give himself the
proper mental tone."[13]

Rosebery's appetite for the written word was voracious and eclectic: he read and appreciated novels, diaries, travel accounts, history,
the classics, but his greatest stimulation continued to come from
biography. The role of the individual in shaping the past fascinated
Rosebery, as it did many of his contemporaries. His later studies of
Pitt, Napoleon, and Chatham attest to this interest, but it was during
this introspective period that he explained what it was that attracted
him. "How wholesome and happy an occupation to plunge the dis-
secting knife into another subject," he wrote. "By standing face to
face with the dark shrine which discloses his mind and his main-
springs of action, we ourselves are led to place the finger on parts of
our own mechanism which we had ignored before but which we
know by finding them reproduced in the consciousness of another."[14]

Because it contributed to his knowledge of himself, biography
would also provide him with the impetus to succeed. An under-
current of fear always lay beneath Rosebery's ambition to pursue a
life dedicated to principle and the performance of duty – not a fear
that he lacked the ability to succeed but, rather, a fear that he did not
care enough for success. Biography was one of the things that was to
make him care. Biography, he exclaimed, "tells us what has been,
what virtue, what courage, what patience, what unselfishness. We
know the possible for we know what has been compassed through
her and we burn to emulate or exceed."[15] Not surprisingly, Rosebery's
friends found him intensely ambitious, but they also found it paradoxical that he should combine this ambition with a passion for
frivolous adventures and introspective solitude.

Inner turmoil disturbed Rosebery wherever he went, whatever he
did. On hearing the choir at St Mark's Cathedral in Venice, for example, he was moved to rapture, but the dreams into which he drifted

were filled with anxiety and uncertainty. "How many lives one can live in the long bursts of sound," he recorded, "lives almost always noble and energetic, seldom sensual and empty: how many ambitions one can construct: and how one can despise both life and ambition. The motive impulse which can make one project a lofty life and a pure ambition, and disdain mere life as such is not one surely to be disregarded or despised."[16] The young Rosebery was still dominated by confusion; he was not yet certain what he wanted, or why. He was certain only of what he should want: he should want to do his duty, to overcome the temptations of self-indulgence. He finally resolved to try, and in so doing he made a religion of duty. "The fulfillment of duty to the best of one's ability," he later confided to a friend, "would secure for one the favourable judgement of the Almighty."[17] Duty gave Rosebery not only a purpose in this life, but the promise of one hereafter.

These reflections might easily be dismissed as the confused, perhaps incoherent, ramblings of a young man, and certainly those entering public life are usually faced with some doubt and anxiety. Rosebery's reflections, however, tell us something about the career that followed. He expected public life to give meaning to his inner life, and therefore he always lived close to the edge of disillusionment. The pettiness that he discovered even at the top in politics hardly seemed to prove that this was the life to be chosen by those dedicated to duty and principle. When he was not questioning his own motives, he could usually be found examining those of his colleagues; whenever he became unhappy, the life of books, travel, and the turf beckoned. He never lost his taste for these pleasures, even when immersed in public responsibilities, and the uncertainty he displayed as a young man stayed with him throughout his career. His decision to follow the path of public duty needed reinforcement: he had to be shown that his sacrifice of worldly pleasures was worth the effort.

By the time he decided to enter politics Rosebery had arrived at a bargain with himself, a bargain that would prove most annoying to others. Although he had decided to sacrifice the life of pleasure in favour of the life of duty, he needed, and demanded, assurances that he had made the right decision. He needed to be told that he was indispensable, demanding that his contribution be acclaimed, that the nobility of his sacrifice be recognized. His legendary denials of ability and fitness for positions, the self-abnegation that irritated others, whether it be Aberdeen requesting Rosebery to act as godfather to his son or Gladstone offering him a position in the government, these were really no more than a demand that others keep their part of the bargain. Should the recognition he demanded be withheld or his motives impugned, Rosebery might tear up the contract and withdraw into solitude. Should he feel that he was supporting a cause that was ignoble or unworthy, he would grow contemptuous of himself and his colleagues. Others sensed that he was always on the edge of withdrawing, that he must be treated with care, and they resented him for it.

Rosebery's personality not only explains the difficulties that he would find in his future life in politics, but also suggests why certain questions attracted his interest. From the start he found it tedious to interest himself in questions that appeared less than momentous, and throughout his career he had to be forced or cajoled by the party managers into speaking out on issues that seemed to him to be of local or transitory interest. Even when he finally agreed to speak on local licensing, or the eight-hour day, he had seldom done his homework, and he could find interest in such questions only by relating them to the issues that he considered to be of real consequence. The noble and energetic life was not to be lived by devoting one's time to serving the petty aims of local or sectional interests. Questions affecting the future of the whole kingdom were the ones that appealed to Rosebery, and this facet of his nature was simultaneously a source of strength and weakness: it gave his politicking a sense of mission, which undoubtedly accounts for much of his popularity; but it also meant that he saw the larger questions not as political, to be settled by debate and compromise but as moral, to be settled by showing that one view was right, the other wrong.

Imperialism appealed to Rosebery's imagination from the beginning of his career, bringing all the diverse strands of national life into a coherent, unified whole, giving citizens of the empire a sense of purpose and duty. As befitted his station in life, he viewed questions from the top down. His first step in analysing any particular question was to see how it was connected with others, and how these together affected the future of the empire. Imperialism meant power and prosperity, and therefore all citizens ought to be prepared to agree that it was in the national interest to maintain and consolidate the empire, and that local or sectional interests could be advanced only if they did not conflict with national ones. This explains why Rosebery had so many problems playing the game of party politics: the task of the politician was to unite the kingdom, not divide it; politicians often seemed to him not only to be playing upon internal rivalries, but to be creating them.

Imperialism also explains the attention Rosebery paid to questions that may conveniently be placed under the headings of nationalism and education, subjects that seemed inextricably connected with the future power and prosperity of the empire. Education, compulsory and technical, would enable Britain to modernize and expand her industry and trade. Education in political economy would unite the "classes and masses" in the realization that their interests were mutual, not antithetical. Nationalism, its sources of inspiration recognized and properly handled, would prevent the empire from breaking down into its constituent parts.

Rosebery, as a practising politician, was never rigorous in his definitions, nor systematic in his philosophy. Commercial prosperity he sometimes saw as the cause of empire, sometimes the effect; empire was sometimes necessary to benefit all of mankind, at others to safeguard the British from the rest of mankind. In fact, just as public duty was to organize Rosebery's own life into a purposeful one, so was imperialism to organize the life of the nation. Later, when the complications and contradictions inherent in this formula became exposed, Rosebery retreated into the day-to-day management of affairs, dismissing any of his grand designs for positive reform as impractical for the present. At the beginning of his career, however, his political interests were well served by the causes he took up, especially as they were expressed in eloquent oratory that enabled him to stand out from the start.

In his first major speech, the presidential address delivered at the Social Science Congress held in Glasgow in 1874, Rosebery took up the cause of compulsory education. Although he had been sent down from Oxford when he refused to give up his stable, he nevertheless continued to prepare himself for public service by making a study of the role and effects of different educational systems.[18] At Glasgow, therefore, he was able to make a well-informed survey of educational practices in America and on the continent, concluding that he could not believe "that there ever was more clear necessity before any Government or any country than the imperative duty laid upon one to institute a directly compulsory education."[19] Britain was falling behind her competitors, all of whom were instituting radical measures of educational reform. Special technical training would "fit the producers for production and the distributors for distribution." Compulsory education, a humanizing education, would reduce drunkenness, crime, and pauperism. Education, he concluded, was the sole remedy for the deplorable state of the working classes.

Rosebery's support for education was neither brilliant nor original, and he admitted that his conclusion was hackneyed. But his proposal was striking in its advocacy of compulsory education, coming at a time when the Nonconformist National Education League was campaigning against even the moderate Education Act of 1870. One of the fundamental characteristics of his liberalism, therefore, was outlined at the beginning of his career. Those who argued that compulsory education would interfere with individual liberty, he said, needed Macaulay's schoolboy to remind them that a policeman, a tax, and a railway bill were all direct interferences with individual liberty. Liberal individualism was not to be his cause; some liberties had to be sacrificed for the sake of national prosperity and harmony, for his notion of educational reform went further than simply extending the technical expertise of the nation. Education was to heal the wounds inflicted by class warfare. Students would receive not only technical instruction but the instruction in political economy that would lead capital and labour to discover that their interests were "inseparably entwined." Rosebery proposed to use education to unite the empire into an organic whole. The state, he argued, must enable every man to obtain a general education fitting him to become a good citizen. Liberalism, to Rosebery, meant power. Educational reform, the extension of the franchise, imperial federation, were all things that he supported because they promised to provide the widest possible foundation of support for the state. "The true leverage of empire," he argued, did not rest in armies or fortresses, but in education. Knowledge meant strength, or, as Rosebery referred to it, "a peaceful method of supremacy."[20]

Rosebery's championship of educational reform placed him at the centre of liberal political culture. He espoused a policy that would unify community interests and transcend those of classes, regions, and sections. Reforms that increased the power and the prosperity of the empire would benefit everyone. Unfortunately, this initial campaign excited little enthusiasm; he needed a firmer base upon which to build a political career. He found that base in Scotland.

Although Scotland had been an important area of Liberal support for some time, it had usually been paid for its adherence in the various forms of patronage available. In the 1870s, stimulated by economic problems, and heightened by the Irish agitation, Scotland began to feel neglected. This gave Rosebery the opportunity to make the cause of Scotland his own. Although the greater part of his income came from his Scottish estates, at least until his marriage to Hannah de Rothschild, Rosebery had paid little attention to his Scottish heritage. Following the Liberal disaster at the polls in 1874, however, he deliberately set out to make himself an expert in the history and literature of Scotland. Within five years Rosebery had amassed an enormous and valuable library on Scotland; more important, he had established a reputation there.[21] He quickly became an intimate of the leading politicians, academics, and publicists of Scotland. He enthusiastically took up Scottish causes, involved himself in local affairs, and proclaimed Scottish triumphs in the arts and sciences. He also poured money into the Liberal machine in Edinburgh. Rosebery never took up a cause in which he did not see a principle at stake, however, thus reinforcing his belief that he was performing the highest duty possible by engaging in political life. He saw Scottish interests, as he did educational reform, in the light of Britain's imperial future. The successful union of England and Scotland had been accomplished by men who "had welded two great nations into one Empire and moulded local jealousies into a common patriotism."[22] Rosebery did not mean to suggest that regional interests, customs, and religions were to be sacrificed to an imperial uniformity. The strength of the empire developed out of the recognition of these differences, and throughout the early part of his career Rosebery consistently advocated giving control of local matters to local authorities.

When the Irish situation became critical, therefore, Rosebery had already constructed a framework of ideas in which he would interpret the situation. He regarded the problem as one between nations. In order to reconcile Ireland to the Union, he proposed that she should be given that degree of autonomy which would allow for her distinction as a national unity. This doctrine, he said, would strike many as a prescription for independence, and the cure more dangerous than the disease – a fear that might be reasonable if the Irish were to be given a special place within the empire. He would not grant them such a place; he emphasized instead the uniqueness of an empire that existed by the consent of its constituent nations, and not by the brute force of the strongest. Before he began to advocate a new kind of imperialism, therefore, Rosebery was already looking forward to a new kind of empire, one in which a structure could be established to allow for the adjustment of growing differences within it. Ireland was not to be a special case. If the empire were to survive, all the nations within it must be given greater control over their local affairs, and a voice in imperial ones.

Rosebery's policies arose partly from his personality, and the imperial outlook was the most important part of his political personality. Determined to make a place for himself in politics, he took some care in selecting the causes with which he would become associated. Both the issues he chose, educational reform and measures of autonomy for Scotland, established him firmly within the liberal tradition. His energy and devotion to principle and party succeeded in winning Gladstone over. Rosebery could not treat these questions modestly, however; to excite his interest he had to connect them with higher ambitions. Others might have seen this higher ambition in social justice or political right: Rosebery saw it in the British Empire. His interests bore the marks of this ambition; compulsory education would improve the abilities of the working class, and show capital and labour that their interests were inseparable; the successful union between England and Scotland might demonstrate the possibilities for a future imperial federation. Reforms in both these spheres were essential to the future prosperity and stability of the empire. Rosebery was becoming not only a man of the future, but also a man of the empire.

Educational reform had failed to excite the imagination of the public. It was fund-raising in Edinburgh, speeches on the past and future glories of Scotland, and support for Scottish issues in the House of Lords that had enabled Rosebery to assume a leading role in the Scottish section of the Liberal party. Until the Great Eastern Crisis of 1876, however, he had failed to establish himself as a figure prominent in national politics, and he remained on the fringes of power, impatient for success, yet unwilling to spend years labouring at small jobs, the course recommended by Gladstone. Travel and the turf continued to divert him from public life, and some admirers feared that these diversions, combined with his marriage to the shy Hannah de Rothschild, would lead him away from politics altogether. Gladstone's defeat at the polls in 1874, however, gave Rosebery the opening he needed, while Disraeli's new foreign and colonial policy fired his imagination in a way that education and Scotland had never done. Rosebery attacked Disraeli's new imperialism two years before Gladstone launched his campaign against the Bulgarian atrocities, and his attacks were seldom humanitarian in the style of Gladstone, but rather based upon his conception of the nature, and interests, of the British Empire. These attacks, which cost him Disraeli's friendship, enabled him to establish himself as the guardian of a somewhat peculiar tradition, Liberal imperialism.[23] The traditions enabling Britain to rise to a position supreme among nations, Rosebery proclaimed, were threatened by Disraeli. Instead of uniting the empire, as true imperialists must wish, Disraeli was dividing it: when he made the queen of England an empress in 1876, India was forever set apart from the rest of the empire. This new status for India, the Tories argued, would frighten off a Russian attack. Rosebery denounced the argument as feeble, and typical of the new departure, matching their claim that, by purchasing ten votes in the Suez Canal Company, they had secured the highway to India. Such conduct, Rosebery declared, was not dissimilar to that of the Chinese, "who with their Emperor at their head put their trust in wooden swords and ugly faces."[24]

Other Liberals attacked Tory management: the disasters in Afghanistan and South Africa made attack easy. Mismanagement, however, no matter how useful a weapon it might be to parties in opposition, is not the kind of theme likely to propel a young politician into the limelight, especially a politician who had no experience of management. Rosebery joined Gladstone and Harcourt in denouncing the immorality of Tory policies. The triumph of Britain throughout the century, he argued, rested on the extension of British liberties to other nations. This achievement, he proclaimed, had been the boast of men like Canning. Whenever the Tories had had the opportunity of helping other nations, however, "they had turned aside with a contemptuous smile." No longer could the Greeks, Bulgars, Serbs, and Armenians look to England in their distress. Instead, the Tories forced these nations, "the natural allies of Britain," to look elsewhere, "to a power which Her Majesty's Government had made the enemy of England."[25] Disraeli's new departure, Rosebery said, had resulted in debt, bloodshed, and complications of every kind.

Rosebery demanded a return to the old ways, to the traditions of liberalism and imperialism established by Canning and Palmerston. Later in his career, Rosebery denounced partisan attacks on foreign policy as threatening to the nation's security. Nevertheless, he was able to justify his own attack during the Great Eastern Crisis by maintaining that Disraeli's break with tradition was even more hazardous than the political debate it aroused. Disraeli, he said, was "harassing the four quarters of the globe." Disraeli's policy was "discreditable in its means and disastrous in its ends," his goal, a "will o' the wisp."[26] For the first time Rosebery was becoming known outside Scotland. His earlier speeches, mainly on education, had been ignored. His attacks during the crisis were reprinted in the national press; he regularly made the *Times*.

Because the purpose of Rosebery's performance was obviously personal and political, much of what he said can be disregarded. Twenty years later he would, for example, show what he thought of the Armenians as potential allies. Nevertheless, two things apart from his rhetorical success are noteworthy. First, he claimed to be guarding Liberal traditions, not creating a new kind of Liberalism; in his own mind, he was the logical successor of Canning and Palmerston. Naturally, there was a wing of the Liberal party with which he disagreed, as there was certain to be. Second, beneath the layer of political rhetoric, there lay another, more solid, one. Rosebery persistently attacked Disraeli for extending Britain's commitments without supplementing her power. The Tories, he said, had failed to recognize the wisdom of "the policy of reserve," in regard to the continent, that had been preserved by Liberals and Tories alike since Waterloo.[27] In this part of the attack, less flamboyant than the rest, Rosebery set out the principles by which he would be guided in foreign and imperial policy.

Three things, Rosebery argued, were never obtainable in Britain: absolute secrecy, silence in Parliament, and "that the Government should never be upset and be able to bind the country permanently to its policy."[28] Disraeli's government had, however, without consulting the British Parliament and the British people, incurred responsibilities of a vast and unknown kind. "To Parliament the policy of the Government had been a policy of obscurity enlivened by sarcasm."[29] Rosebery attacked the Tories for violating tradition: Disraeli's despotism would certainly lead to errors of judgment, while his policy was based on the illusion that it had the full weight of the British people behind it.

In office, Rosebery demonstrated what he thought of the British public as a guide to foreign policy; but for the moment he was content to imply that only a despotic regime would incur the commitments undertaken by the Tories. Their guarantee of Turkish territorial integrity in exchange for the sultan's promise of reform, for example, he denounced as a great mistake. If the Turks carried it out, it would mean no reform at all; if the British carried it out, it would mean virtual annexation. Annexation would extend British responsibilities to the breaking-point.[30] While some argued that eventual annexation was essential to preserve the Indian Empire, Rosebery argued that the annexation of Turkey was no more essential than the annexation of Spain for the preservation of Gibraltar.[31] If the British attempted to administer the Ottoman Empire, they would face a constant drain on their resources, resources already committed to Canada, Australia, India, and a large part of Africa. The British must learn to consolidate their empire.

Rosebery was one of the first to counter Disraeli's new imperialism. He quickly anticipated the political danger involved in the creation of a Conservative-imperial mythology. For fifty years the Liberals had enjoyed a virtual monopoly of the ideas behind foreign and imperial policy: the great ideas of free trade, national independence, and responsible government were intimately connected with Liberalism. If the Tories were permitted to pass themselves off as the party of national strength and imperial vigour, they would seriously damage the Liberal position in the country. Rosebery again acted as the guardian of tradition: he spoke, not against Liberal "Little Englanders," but against Tory imperialists. "Imperium et libertas," he said, was a noble watchword, but not one which was to be rashly arrogated to itself by any political party.[32] Besides, the Tories were not motivated by a new concept of national interest, but by a cynical assessment of their own political interests. They sought a distinctive foreign policy only because they had come to realize that all domestic policy, to be successful, had to be Liberal. They initiated their new departure simply to draw attention away from their failures in domestic policy.[33]

The debate during the Great Eastern Crisis signalled a new departure for Rosebery, as he enthusiastically established himself as the guardian of imperial tradition within the Liberal party. His speeches concentrated increasingly on the Liberal contribution to the origins of the empire. Attacked by the Tories for their neglect of the empire, the party was able to use a man like Rosebery to counterbalance the influence of the Cobdenites. Still, he was careful to attack the Tories and not his own party. The Liberal party, he announced, were as proud of the empire as any Tory could be, and they would maintain it "with their blood," if necessary.[34] After all, as he later said, "it is under us and under our party – under the guidance of our party for almost all the last fifty years of unparalleled power and unparalleled prosperity – that the Empire has reached its present position."[35] When someone finally used the phrase "Liberal imperialist" to describe Rosebery's political philosophy, he accepted the description, but added that it was accurate only if it meant that he was a Liberal who was passionately attached to the empire, intensely interested in the best means of sustaining and promoting the interests of that empire, and if it meant a Liberal who believed that the external policy of Britain was one that should be founded not on interference, but on reticence and independence.[36] Most definitions of Liberal imperialism ignore Rosebery's own, a curious omission when policy was an intrinsic part of the definition.

Liberal imperialism enabled Rosebery to make his name known throughout the country, while the election of 1880 enabled him to demonstrate how valuable he could be in the service of the party. He combined with W.P. Adam and J.J. Reid, Liberal organizers in Scotland, in persuading Gladstone to contest the seat for Midlothian. Rosebery's contribution to the success of the campaign, and his popularity throughout Scotland, at first surprised, then overwhelmed, Gladstone. "Rosebery has made a great impression, and is a hero not only in Edinburgh, but in Glasgow," he wrote to Granville.[37] Three months later he went further. Rosebery, he said, was not merely a clever man, but a remarkable one, and he predicted that the young man would be "the leader of the Liberal party in Scotland, and that in a sense beyond any, I should think, in which they have heretofore had a leader."[38] The triumph was impressive. Although Rosebery later exaggerated the costs of the campaign, claiming they amounted to £50,000, he convinced Gladstone that he was the "coming man" in Scotland, and his first bid for cabinet office was based largely on Scottish dissatisfaction and his ability to allay it.[39]

Pleased though he was with Rosebery's performance, Gladstone, following the election, refused to consider appointing him to the cabinet, preaching patience, hard work, and offering him minor administrative posts instead. Rosebery, he said, required experience. Rosebery, for his part, believed he had earned a place in the cabinet and became distressed when the offer was not made. In August 1881, after much misunderstanding and wounded sensibilities, he finally accepted an under-secretaryship at the Home Office. He did not last long. He found the work tedious and the company bad.[40] After bringing in the bill establishing a secretary of state for Scotland, he expected a promotion to the cabinet, and when none came, he resigned. It was not an auspicious start, and might, in fact, have been an abrupt end, but Rosebery was to make his place through the adversity of his own party.

The prestige of Gladstone's government had already received two stiff blows: first, the duke of Argyll had resigned in the spring of 1881 over Irish policy, and then John Bright resigned in July 1882 following the bombardment of Alexandria. Nevertheless, when Rosebery resigned from the government in June 1883, and then left the country in November for a six-month tour of Australasia, the government appeared to have the Egyptian situation well in hand. Wolseley had broken the Egyptian army at Tel-el-Kebir in September 1882, and in August 1883 the government announced its intention to bring the English garrison back to Alexandria and reduce it to 3,000 men. Although the government was involved in difficult negotiations with the French, the Egyptian situation seemed unlikely to upset domestic politics and thereby alter Rosebery's position. But, a few days after the Roseberys sailed for Australia, news of disaster reached England: a 10,000-man Egyptian force had been annihilated attempting to re-conquer the Sudan from the Mahdi. All of Egypt was in danger, and the British had no choice but to defend her from attack, making nonsense of their plans to withdraw from the country altogether. When Rosebery returned to Britain in March 1884, therefore, Gladstone was prepared to bolster the government's sagging popularity by bringing Rosebery into the cabinet. It took some months before a method to accomplish this could be found, and when Gladstone finally found what he believed to be an acceptable solution in November 1884, Rosebery turned him down.

Rosebery blamed the government's Egyptian policy for his refusal. "My view," he told Gladstone, "has always been that we must keep before us as our vital principle that we cannot leave Egypt without having established there a government stable and strong as regards the country itself, independent and respectable as regards other states."[41] The reply startled Gladstone, who claimed that this was the first he had heard of Rosebery's opposition to the government's Egyptian policy. Rosebery's declaration placed him in the group led by Hartington in the cabinet, who argued that a prolonged occupation of Egypt was now inevitable. The majority of the cabinet, however, continued to prefer an early evacuation. The Liberal party was in disarray over Egypt, and Rosebery was carefully weighing up the consequences of this for his political future: "my fear," he candidly admitted to Gladstone, "is this, lest I should be associated with the decisions to which the past acts and declarations of the Government tend."[42] A cabinet post, if it succeeded only in discrediting him, was hardly worthwhile; gaining power now might mean the risk of losing it in the future.[43]

Rosebery thought he saw a way out of his dilemma. "If our dealings in Egypt represented a fait accompli," he told Gladstone, "I should probably know how to accept it."[44] He would, in other words, join the cabinet only after questions of Egyptian policy had been decided, thus relieving him of any responsibility for the government's blunders. He found another way of avoiding responsibility. He had earlier assured Gladstone's private secretary that he would not take his case before the public, but in December he decided to speak out. There were, he announced, two sections in the Liberal party, one believing that the British should extricate themselves from Egypt at any moment and at any expense, and the other believing that, however disagreeable it might be to remain, they were not in a position to leave tomorrow. He left no doubt of where he stood. Where England interfered, he said, "it was not to weaken, but to strengthen; it was not to trample on, but to uplift."[45] The work of uplifting was the policy of bravery and humanity; to destroy and run was the policy of cowardice and selfishness.

When the next disaster struck, Rosebery was still wavering. In January 1884 the cabinet had dispatched General Gordon to evacuate the Egyptian garrison from Khartoum; but the Mahdists quickly cut off his expedition from Egypt, and Gordon himself became imperilled at Khartoum. Rosebery's first inclination was to "rally round the government," but he remained apprehensive.[46] The government had spent the better part of a year deciding how Gordon was to be relieved, when news reached London on 5 February 1885 that Khartoum had fallen and that Gordon was dead. Except for external defence, Gladstone had declared, the constructive work of the British in Egypt was over. To Rosebery, this seemed an "appallingly defective view of our Egyptian responsibilities." He might be out of the government in a week if he joined, as he had "no notion what stupendous act of folly the government may be contemplating."[47] The government was being attacked from all sides, but Rosebery, mostly through luck, remained free of criticism. If he joined the government and another disaster struck, "I should only wreck myself without saving them."[48]

Friends urged Rosebery in the opposite direction: such an opportunity might not come again. Everyone, they said, would honour him for abandoning his independence and joining a government on the verge of collapse. Everyone, they said, would interpret his joining as an act of self-sacrifice, not self-interest.[49] This was exactly what Rosebery liked to hear. He liked to think of himself as acting out of duty rather than selfishness. "The greatness of a nation," he declared, praising himself and the country in the same breath, "like the greatness of an individual, is shown not in moments of prosperity but in moments of adversity."[50] He submitted to the advice of his friends, but the day after he joined the government, he publicly declared his opposition to the government's past Egyptian policy. A bolder and clearer course, he told a cheering Epsom crowd, ought to have been adopted in Egypt. For the first time, he attacked the other, as yet unnamed, wing of the Liberal party, "those who say we should absorb ourselves in our own selfish concerns, and have neither a foreign policy, nor any colonies to have a policy about."[51]

Rosebery had decided to attack the Gladstonian wing of the party the day after joining Gladstone's government. Had Britain absorbed herself in her own concerns, as this wing desired, the recent disasters would not have been avoided. In fact, this government was more zealous for peace and nonintervention than any government in Britain's history. Rosebery drew the opposite conclusion from recent events. For several years he had been extolling the virtues of empire; at this point, however, he began to outline what should be the guidelines of a successful imperial policy. "What is really peaceful is firmness. There is nothing so warlike as indecision. There is nothing so certain to bring about war as the anxiety at all events, to avoid war."[52] The government he had joined had been drawn into a war against their will, because they were creatures of circumstance. The two great wars of the century, the Napoleonic and the Crimean, had been fought by the most peaceful of prime ministers, Pitt and Aberdeen. Gladstone, "who loves peace with an almost religious love," following the tradition, was being compelled to wage a bloody and perilous war.[53] The events of 1884–5 influenced decisively Rosebery's view of foreign and imperial policy.

The general point of his declarations was to make Rosebery appear to be the logical choice to conduct Liberal foreign policy in the future. Gladstone, relieved of the burden, could return to what he did best, domestic reform. The government had gone wrong, Rosebery argued, in failing to recognize the futility of shutting out British interests, by a hard and fast rule, from interests not strictly affecting her. A question of foreign policy could not be dealt with on its own merits, but had to be considered in the light of the influence it bore on other questions. The government had first to analyse its interests, then follow a defined and steadfast course. Only in this way was it possible to avoid interference, annexation, and war. As in all of his public statements of foreign policy, Rosebery managed to combine personal interest in creating a public image with sincere opinions on the conduct of policy.

Rosebery had, in 1885, little opportunity to put his principles into practice. The cabinet he had agreed to join devoted most of its energies to deciding on what time, and over which issue, it should resign.[54] This situation suited him; by the time it finally did resign, he had decided not to rejoin it. Nevertheless, his activities in what remained of Gladstone's second administration are useful in understanding the nature of his foreign and imperial policy. As lord privy seal his duties were light; he spent more time trying to disentangle the Sudanese and Penjdeh crises. Although he had little influence on policy, he faced, for the first time, a situation in which he was expected to give official guidance on questions of foreign policy. Ironically, the first record of this role came when he tried to convince Lord Hartington, the secretary of war, not to resign over the government's decision to hold in abeyance the advance on Khartoum.

One argument, Rosebery insisted, favoured the government and outweighed all others. With war impending with Russia and with the British army locked up in the Sudan, he argued, the British would be absolutely paralysed everywhere else. Questions of foreign policy could only be answered in the context of all Britain's imperial interests; they could not be considered in isolation. The French, Rosebery argued, were already instructing them in this lesson. "We have not a friend in the world (except Italy who would not stir a finger for us in Europe), and we have to recollect that if we have one hand tied down in Central Asia and another in Central Africa we may be practically danced upon in every other part of the world."[55] Control of the Sudan, he maintained, was not a vital British interest, while supremacy in Egypt was. In spite of any temporary disengagement in the Sudan, therefore, the government would be compelled to maintain a large army in Egypt, if only to maintain order among a population agitated by the success of the Mahdi. There was, he concluded, no easy solution: the best they could do was concentrate their forces and modify their plans as the situation developed.[56]

The dilemma Rosebery was trying to resolve was not new. He showed his natural inclination: consolidate; hold what was vital; allow the situation to develop; remain uncommitted; wait for an opening. His natural inclination was not to expand; in fact, he shied away from it. The Mahdi, however, posed a revolutionary threat to the international system. He aspired, Rosebery believed, to destroy the very foundation of Europe's relations with the East. His status as prophet depended upon ever-increasing victories, rendering him impossible to bargain with. His aspirations were dangerous to every Mohammedan power in the world, and the queen, Rosebery reminded his colleagues, was the greatest of the Mohammedan powers. At the same time, if he succeeded in setting Arabia ablaze, he would also reopen the Eastern Question. Upheaval, according to Rosebery, was contagious.

In Rosebery's opinion, there was no question of bargaining with an acquisitive, fanatical power, and the only alternative to bargaining seemed to be war. In a formula which was to become typical of his policies, however, he resisted this conclusion. The destruction of the Mahdi involved too many dangers: it would lead to complications with Russia, paralyse the British elsewhere, and, according to the commanding general, Wolseley, require Britain's greatest military effort since the Napoleonic Wars. While the Mahdi had to be prevented from expanding further, and while order had to be maintained in Egypt, achieving these aims need not entail the expense and dangers involved in reconquering the Sudan. Fewer men would be needed for this defensive policy, and besides, by preventing his continued expansion, the British could deprive the Mahdi of his status as prophet. Although Rosebery had little influence on policy, and the government was about to fall in any event, he did set out two fundamental principles: first, policy should be carefully coordinated to match British resources, and second, the effect of one question should not be allowed to endanger equally important interests elsewhere.

The same reasoning led him to the opposite conclusion in central Asia. The British, the Russians believed, might be "safely kicked," and this belief accounted for the difficulties the government faced during the Penjdeh crisis.[57] Rosebery dismissed the advantages of the settlement proposed by those who wished to minimize the dispute. Even if the government were to negotiate a sufficient frontier, the moral disadvantages would outweigh the practical advantages. When the government published the main features of the transaction, as they must, sooner or later, "we shall then have to reveal that for a considerable time past we have been enduring language and modes of treatment from the Russian Government such as no Great Power has ever endured."[58] Britain's status as an imperial power, Rosebery believed, hinged upon her conduct in disputes like this one, and no frontier settlement could be worth the resulting blow to British prestige.

Besides, their success at Penjdeh would only encourage the Russians in further acts of expansion, while shaking the foundations of British rule in India. Orientals, Rosebery maintained, worshipped success. The yielding of every point to Russia would be notorious throughout the East and the effect in the West would be as great. "All Europe is laughing at us. Our nose has been pulled all over the world."[59] If Britain were to dismiss the Penjdeh incident for the sake of a sufficient frontier, it would only lead other powers to draw dangerous conclusions concerning Britain's determination to defend her interests. Quiescence in this affair would entice Russia and the rest to challenge her wherever and whenever possible. Britain, Rosebery believed, would be unable to meet such challenges.

Rosebery began his analysis of foreign policy by demonstrating the connections between questions: the British had always to ask themselves how decisions taken in one area would affect their position in another; to be confronted in too many places by too many powers would permit their prestige to be damaged. Britain's only hope of avoiding repeated challenges and multiplying complications was to act quickly and firmly when challenged. He did not rule out negotiations and compromise, however; he had been prepared, after all, to allow the Mahdi, for a time, to go unchallenged. Instead of committing Britain to a policy of adventure all over the world, therefore, Rosebery proposed to commit British prestige only when the country was prepared to fight for it. The government, for example, had not committed itself to an immediate advance on Khartoum; it had only declared its intention to do so eventually. Strong words must be spoken only when the government intended to act; it could not take a firm stand only to step backwards when faced with difficulties.

Much of what Rosebery had to say concerning the imperial connection may be dismissed as political rhetoric, and properly so, but three or four general points stood out; and first among them was his view of the empire as a unit. He expounded this view for the first time in 1885, when his influence on policy was minimal, but it was to remain a consistent theme throughout his career, and those who look at his later policy in Uganda, without considering its connection with the Triple Alliance, or at Siam without considering its connection with the North-West frontier, would do well to remind themselves of the Sudanese-Penjdeh connection. His foreign policy was, as he later declared, a colonial policy.

Rosebery's first cabinet post lasted a mere six months, because the government fell in June 1885; but he did not regret the fall. In fact, had the Liberals won the election, he was not prepared to join a new government because he believed their management of foreign affairs to have been an unmitigated disaster. It is no small irony, then, that Rosebery was transformed from a relatively minor, and irritable, member of Gladstone's government in 1885 into the foreign secretary in Gladstone's new government in January 1886.

The transformation was remarkable. Gladstone had, after all, been arguing only a short time before that Rosebery lacked the experience necessary for appointment to a position of real governmental responsibility. The key to the change was Ireland. When Gladstone floated the idea of Home Rule in the "Hawarden Kite" he threw the party into disarray. This simultaneously removed some of the senior men from the party and made Gladstone eager to appoint men with some popularity in the country. Rosebery suited this requirement. Moreover, by a stroke of luck, his only real competitor for the job of foreign secretary, Charles Dilke, was removed from the running thanks to his relationship with Mrs Crawford – although Dilke doubted that this was simple luck. All were agreed – and the queen was adamant – that Granville could not return to the Foreign Office.

Rosebery seemed a logical choice because he had established a reputation as a man devoted to the defence of the empire. And he had demonstrated his statesmanship by rallying to the side of a government beset by foreign crises and internal squabbling. He had also been sent, while lord privy seal, on a secret mission to Berlin, where Gladstone hoped that he might heal the wounds supposedly inflicted on Bismarck by Granville's insensitivity to German colonial aspirations. This mission, which had some limited success, was really inconsequential in Anglo-German colonial relations; but it does appear to have contributed to Gladstone's belief in Rosebery's ability to manage foreign affairs.

What twentieth-century observers have noted as unusual in

Rosebery's appointment has been his youthfulness. But this misses the point. By the standards of the nineteenth century Rosebery was not particularly young for the Foreign Office: Grenville, Liverpool, Canning, and Derby had been younger when appointed; Castlereagh, Palmerston, and Salisbury had been in their forties. It was inexperience, not youthfulness, that made Rosebery's appointment unusual. What he lacked in experience he made up for in popularity. The earl of Kimberley, dismissing rumours that he himself might receive the appointment, cited the displeasure his appointment would have created in the public mind. "The best choice that could be made," he thought, was the one who would receive "universal approval" – Rosebery.[60] Similarly, Gladstone's private secretary noted that Rosebery's appointment was "the one which is by far most generally approved."[61] And yet Rosebery had done practically nothing other than give voice to some popular sentiments. If ever a career showed the importance of words, it was the rise of Rosebery.

CHAPTER ONE

Continuity in Foreign Policy: The Balkan Crisis of 1886

If there is one point on which history repeats itself, it is this: that at certain fixed intervals the Russian Empire feels a need of expansion, that that necessity is usually gratified at the expense of the Turk; that the other Powers, or some of them, take alarm, and take measures for curtailing the operation, with much the same results that the process of pruning produces on a healthy young tree.

Pitt (1891)

When he arrived at the Foreign Office in February 1886, Rosebery inherited from Salisbury a situation both dangerous and complicated. The complications arose from the aspiring nationalities of the Balkans. The inhabitants of Eastern Roumelia, calling themselves Bulgarians, had rebelled against the sultan in September 1885, demanding their right to be united with the rest of Bulgaria. The Serbs, in consequence, had attacked the Bulgarians in November, fearing that the creation of a big Bulgaria would give them a powerful opponent in the Balkans. The Greeks, appalled at the prospect of a big Slav state, had lined their troops up along the frontier, demanding Turkish territory that had been denied them at the Congress of Berlin in 1878. A few scholars and diplomats thought they understood these complications; most Englishmen judged them to be outside the pale of civilized interests. The dangers were easier to understand, arising from the aspirations of the great powers in the Near East that had driven Britain to the brink of war several times during the century and into her only major one since the Napoleonic era.[1]

The Balkans, however, had been kept quiet since 1881 by a system of informal partition: in the renewed Three Emperors' League of that year Austria-Hungary had recognized Russian paramountcy in Bulgaria, while Russia recognized Austrian paramountcy in Serbia. Bismarck arranged this settlement, restraining the two powers in the Balkans, and encouraging the Russians to look east, where, he believed, expansion would bring them into conflict with Britain, increase their reliance on Germany, and thereby safeguard Germany's eastern frontier. The Austrians feared that upheaval in the Balkans would lead to a war with Russia, a war they would lose if they could not rely upon the assistance of Germany. The Russians wanted a rest from the Balkan upheavals that had proved to be financially and militarily expensive. Their position in Bulgaria assured, the Russians could turn to domestic problems and Asiatic expansion. Besides, the Austrians were willing to guarantee them a bigger Bulgaria than the one created at the Congress of Berlin: a protocol of the Dreikaiserbund committed Austria to accept a union of the two Bulgarias if it occurred "by force of circumstances."

When the Russians evacuated Eastern Roumelia following the congress, they left behind 80,000 rifles with instructions for the inhabitants to practise with them and help themselves if they wished to unite their country. Their decision to support a united Bulgaria was primarily strategic: a large ally, but one dependent on Russian support, would make their road to Constantinople much easier, and, following the congress, they were certain that British designs for an aggressive policy in the Near East would necessitate the use of such a road. Salisbury's declaration that the British would respect only the "independent determinations of the sultan in regard to the closing of the Straits" convinced the Russians of the British intention to pass the Straits whenever it suited them.

In 1881 the Russians still assumed that Bulgaria was destined to be their perpetual client, as Disraeli had argued it would. They had good reasons for this assumption. The Bulgarians had achieved their independence by force of Russian arms, had adopted a constitution designed by a Russian commissioner, and had accepted as their monarch a nephew of the tsar, Prince Alexander of Battenberg, who had fought the Turks as a volunteer in the Russian army. By 1885, however, when the inhabitants of Eastern Roumelia arose in revolt, the Russians had come to regard Prince Alexander as a formidable opponent of their Balkan strategy. Russian generals and businessmen wanted a north-south railway to link Bulgaria and Russia for economic and strategic reasons, but Prince Alexander refused to build it, agreeing with Bulgarian businessmen that the east-west line linking Nish, Sofia, and Constantinople was the one that would benefit Bulgaria. In the spring of 1883 the Russians suspected the prince of attempting to arrange an anti-Russian alliance when he visited the other Balkan capitals and Constantinople. Their suspicions grew in the autumn when he dismissed the Russian generals, Kaulbars and Sobolev, and proposed marriage to Princess Victoria, the granddaughter of William II and Queen Victoria. Russian panslavists, already suspicious of Alexander's German background, regarded the proposal as an attempt to increase German influence, while strategists saw it as an attempt at alliance with Britain.

Tsar Alexander III never shared his father's affection for the prince, regarding him as an enemy of Russia, and objecting to anything that strengthened his position in Bulgaria, such as unification with Eastern Roumelia. N.K. Giers, the Russian foreign minister, met with the prince at Franzensbad in August 1885, to inform him of Russia's wish to maintain the status quo in the Balkans, and her decision, consequently, to oppose the unification of Bulgaria and Eastern Roumelia. The prince agreed, but he had little control of the situation: he could not hope to retain his popularity with Bulgarian nationalists if he refused to lead the movement. Consequently, when the rebellion broke out, the prince declared his approval and entered Philippopolis on 21 September, while the tsar repudiated unification and recalled all Russian officers serving in the Bulgarian army. Germany and Austria joined Russia in denouncing the rebellion, and declared their intention to uphold the settlement of the Treaty of Berlin.

Salisbury could have avoided the dangers of a Balkan crisis in 1885 had he followed his first inclination – to join the three emperors in upholding the Berlin settlement. This would have united the powers and made Bulgarian unification impossible. Most observers expected Salisbury to oppose the creation of a big Bulgaria: he had led the opposition to it at the congress in 1878. On 21 September Bismarck asked Salisbury to join in disavowing the movement, and even proposed a British naval demonstration to provide the sultan with moral support. The following day Salisbury ordered Sir William White, the minister at Constantinople, to join the powers in upholding the Treaty of Berlin. Two days later he reversed himself, declaring it to be his desire "to cherish and foster self-sustaining nationalities," and he proposed a "personal union" of the two Bulgarias under Prince Alexander, with each to retain its existing institutions.[2] Without Salisbury's sudden change, unification would not have occurred. Serbia would not have attacked Bulgaria, and the Greeks would have had no claim to compensation.

Salisbury's decision to abandon Turkey and support Bulgaria was a fateful one, and Rosebery's policy in 1886 cannot be understood without it. Salisbury had, as early as 1878, questioned the utility of continuing to use Turkey as a means of securing the road to India. As he saw it, the Turkish alliance was to enable the British Mediterranean fleet to pass through the Straits and attack Russia in the Black Sea. If the British were unable to pass the Straits, the Russians would be able to establish formidable naval power in the Black Sea and attack the British in the Mediterranean, thereby blocking their fastest, and cheapest, route to India. In its time this policy, Salisbury believed, had been wise enough, but the weakness of the Turks and their repeated refusals to follow British instructions convinced Salisbury of the necessity of finding an alternative. Besides, he did not really believe in the Russian maritime threat: the Russians had no naval history, their finances were never good, their social condition was critical, and they had no maritime population. The real threat to Britain, he argued, would come from a revived France, or a Germany determined to become a naval power, and in neither instance would Turkey be of use.

Had Salisbury been in the position of choosing for himself in 1877, he would have acquired Egypt or Crete as the best means of securing the road to India, and he would not have discouraged the obliteration of Turkey. This strategy would not have meant, of course, abandoning Constantinople and the Straits altogether. What Salisbury particularly objected to in the Turkish connection was its implication that Britain would uphold that empire everywhere and under any circumstances; the Crimean War had been a mistake because it had demonstrated that Britain would perform this role, and consequently the Turks felt they could mismanage their European territories, antagonize the Russians, and ignore British advice all at the same time. When Salisbury spoke of "obliterating" Turkey, therefore, he was not referring to Constantinople and the Straits; rather, he hoped to limit Britain's involvement in the Near East to those territories in which she was directly interested. He hoped to achieve this goal by acting with the Austrians, who were as interested as the British in keeping the Russians out of Constantinople, and who could use the Rumanian bottleneck to keep the Russians in the north. Austrian military power could not be used as a substitute for British naval power: if Russia could capture and control Constantinople by sea, then the Rumanian bottleneck was worthless. This formula added a continental complication to British policy at the Straits, as it was not, for the next thirty years at least, to be applied without taking the Austrian factor into account.

Salisbury's Balkan policy, first in 1878, then in 1885, was a part of his policy at the Straits. For the Straits to be useful to Britain, the sultan would have to permit British passage; if he chose to close them, the Black Sea would be safe from any British threat, while the Austrian connection would be lost. Therefore, in the Balkans, the

Russians had to be kept at a safe distance, allowing the sultan the freedom to make an "independent decision" when the question of permitting British passage arose. The new Slav state of Bulgaria, Salisbury assumed in 1878, would become the vassal of Russia, and consequently it had to be pushed behind the Balkan mountains, where it could not influence Turkish policy. The independence and integrity of the Ottoman Empire, he admitted, however, was something of a sham in 1856, and by 1878 had become a pure mockery. The Porte had to recognize itself as needing protection: Salisbury's keeping Russia at a distance in Europe was one way of providing that the protection would not come from her; his offering a guarantee of Turkey's Asiatic possessions seemed to hold out the best prospect for providing that it would come from Britain. This was Salisbury's policy in 1878, but by 1885 four factors had led him to alter it. First, the Bulgarians had proved to be anything but the vassals of Russia. Second, the ceding of Varna and the Sanjack of Sofia to Bulgaria in 1880 made it possible for an invading army to turn the defences, so the smaller Bulgaria of 1878 was still useful to the Russians if they chose to march on Constantinople. Third, the Turks had failed to garrison the Eastern Roumelian frontier, demonstrating their inability to withstand a Russian attack. Fourth, the British occupation of Egypt had antagonized the Turks, rendering them less likely than ever to follow British advice. The aim of Salisbury's policy in 1885 matched that of 1878, but events between these two dates convinced him that Bulgaria was now the best tool for defending Constantinople.

Upon entering the Foreign Office in 1886, Rosebery decided to uphold Salisbury's policy, despite the dangers involved. The Liberal government would, he immediately assured the Austrian ambassador, pursue the same policy as its predecessor.[3] Rosebery agreed entirely with the objects of Salisbury's policy in the east, and considered the prize of a big, stable Bulgaria, capable of acting as a bulwark to Russian expansion, worth the risk of a crisis. He did not, however, satisfy himself with simply picking up where Salisbury had left off, but attempted to establish continuity in foreign policy as a general principle. This idea has been explained in two ways. One explanation connects it with his youthfulness and sense of incapability; another explains it as a sign of instinctive Toryism.[4] Both are wrong. Rosebery did not doubt his ability to conduct foreign policy. His professions of incapability, when Gladstone offered him the Foreign Office, are not to be taken seriously: they were his customary way of wringing out of others the recognition that he demanded. When Rosebery espoused the doctrine of continuity, he intended it to represent the restoration of Liberal principles, not the continuation of Tory ones; the policy from which he intended no departure was "Lord Salisbury's *recent* policy in the east."[5]

Rosebery's Balkan policy was Gladstonian. He had been partly responsible for managing Gladstone's campaign on behalf of the Bulgarians during 1879–80, and he defended this campaign in 1885, when the new rebellion broke out against the Turks. Disraeli's main achievement, the separation of Eastern Roumelia from Bulgaria, had disappeared "like snow before the sun," and Gladstone's idea of a united Bulgaria had replaced it, "an idea which not only affords the best hope for liberty in the East of Europe, but the best security against Russian aggression."[6] Rosebery defended his foreign policy with a typically Gladstonian formula, showing how morality and British interests were really the same thing. Salisbury's support of Bulgarian unification, Rosebery argued, restored the principles on which British foreign policy had been conducted throughout the century.

Salisbury's conversion was not ideological. Prince Gorchakov, the late Russian chancellor, had predicted the conversion in 1878: as soon as Bulgarian unification could be turned to Russian disadvantage, he had argued, Salisbury would support it.[7] By 1885 Russia's attempt to dominate Bulgaria had failed, and she testified to this when reversing her policy and opposing unification. Britain reversed her policy accordingly. Nevertheless, ideas about nationalism and imperialism played an important part in the policies advocated by Salisbury and Rosebery. Throughout the century, Tories consistently underestimated the ability of nationalities to establish and retain their independence; Liberals, the ability of multinational empires to avoid dissolution. These natural inclinations, grounded in social and political philosophies, were overcome only when the evidence was overwhelming and the conclusion inescapable. In the case of Bulgaria, the Russians provided one important piece of the evidence while the Turks provided another.

When Liberals and Tories argued about nationalism in the Balkans, the practical side of their argument revolved around the question of which might be better able to withstand Russian influence, the empire of the Ottomans or new states in the Balkans. The Ottoman Empire was unreliable, Liberals argued, because its social decadence and political corruption guaranteed its eventual collapse. The Turks had proved they would not reform. The Balkan peoples, Tories replied, were too many and too weak to achieve political independence and stability. Evidence could be found to sustain both arguments, and Russia's admitted failure in Bulgaria was, by itself, unlikely to persuade Salisbury to reverse his position. The Turks themselves, by refusing to send troops to put down the Roumelian rebels, persuaded him: they lacked either the will or the strength to continue resisting Balkan nationalism. Whatever their motive, their inactivity proved to Salisbury that, in Europe at least, they were no longer capable of acting as a barrier to the Russians.[8]

Liberals made the most of Salisbury's conversion to the nationalist cause, claiming the virtues of their policy to have been recognized, even by the Tories. In the struggle between parties, this claim counted for a little; Salisbury's conversion counted for more in determining Rosebery's position within the Liberal party. Rosebery used the principle of continuity to raise foreign policy above party differences: "the more the Secretary of State for Foreign Affairs is considered as a non-political officer, the better for the country."[9] Controversy would be eliminated; both parties would apply the principles of foreign policy established throughout the century; the foreign secretary would speak "with the united voice of the English nation without distinction of party." Rosebery, of course, was to determine how these principles were to be interpreted and applied when he was in office. The Liberal party, having scored a political victory, was satisfied; Gladstone, seeing the possibility of removing foreign affairs from the realm of political controversy, was satisfied. If Rosebery could keep things quiet he would be given a free hand in conducting foreign policy. "No other important issue of a disturbing character should be raised," Gladstone told him, "while we have this big Irish business on hand."[10] If Rosebery could keep things quiet, he would have a free hand in the conduct of foreign policy; he hoped Gladstone would remain fully occupied with Irish affairs.[11]

When Rosebery thought of controlling foreign policy, he was concerned less with the Balkans than with Egypt: Liberals were not likely to quarrel with him over the issue of Bulgarian unification, but they were always prepared to fight over Egypt. "My policy," he confided to the commissioner for Egypt, "would be to leave things alone for the present and shield Egypt from the intolerable nightmare of new Commissioners, Projects, Reports, and Conventions."[12] Gladstone hoped to extricate Britain from Egypt more quickly by assisting in political and financial reforms; Rosebery intended to leave Egypt alone and he used continuity to do it. Salisbury had already shown some desire to evacuate Egypt by sending Drummond Wolff to Constantinople, so the two parties, Rosebery could argue, were agreed on the principle of Egyptian evacuation, as they were on Bulgarian unification. The exact terms of evacuation could be worked out later. Gladstone, having more important business to transact, was prepared to forget Egypt once the principle of evacuation had been recognized.[13]

To keep England in Egypt, Gladstone from meddling with foreign policy, and the Liberal party from splitting any further, Rosebery had to keep the Balkans quiet, but in the winter of 1886 this was no easy task. Salisbury, after declaring his support of Bulgarian unification, had made no progress in achieving it. When Rosebery took office in February, Bulgaria and Turkey were no closer to agreeing on terms of unification. Bulgaria and Serbia, after agreeing to a cease-fire in November, were no closer to settling their differences, and appeared ready to renew hostilities. Greece, despite the opposition of the great powers, continued to demand territorial concessions from Turkey. Gladstone's return to power added a further complication: Salisbury's policy, the Greeks and Russians were encouraged to believe, might be reversed.[14] Rosebery's first official task as the new foreign secretary, therefore, was to convince everyone concerned that nothing new would be attempted.

The Greeks, Rosebery discovered, were difficult to convince: they expected Liberals to be more helpful than Tories when it came to assisting nations struggling to be free. This was a not unreasonable expectation: Gladstone publicly prided himself on furthering the cause of the Greek nation; Rosebery was president of the Philhellenic League.[15] Nevertheless, Rosebery refused to assist the Greeks while they remained lined up, armed and threatening, along the Turkish border. Although he did not particularly dislike the Greek territorial demands – hinting that they might win through diplomatic channels what they sought by force of arms – he was determined to prevent them from bankrupting the Turks and causing further upheavals in the Balkans.[16] Besides, the Greeks, he was convinced, had to be saved from themselves; he did not believe them capable of beating the Turks. Left alone, "the Turks would be at Athens in four days, the King would be at Claridge's hotel in a fortnight, and it would not be altogether a simple matter to get the Turks out of Athens again."[17]

The new Balkan states seemed a reasonable instrument for safe-guarding Britain's principal interests in the eastern Mediterranean. The British believed that they could be well defined, along lines of nationality, thereby avoiding the previous risk of the Porte conceding pieces of territory to the powers in exchange for concessions else-where. They would, Liberals expected, guard their independence more jealously than an imperial state, and would eagerly undertake the social reforms necessary to political stability. The British could supply advice, loans, even arms; they would not have to supply an army. Unfortunately, defending Britain's interests by means of these new states created new difficulties; usually, it meant having to choose among those states. Greece, Bulgaria, Serbia, and Montenegro disliked one another at least as much as they did Austria and Russia, and perhaps more. Moreover, the rulers of these new states sometimes proved as unreliable, as intractable and aggressive, as the oriental potentates who so outraged Gladstone and other Liberals.

In spite of these difficulties, however, the Liberals, led by Gladstone, continued to hold on to their optimistic view of the Balkan future. In the face of the war between Serbia and Bulgaria, the rebellion in Eastern Roumelia, and the mobilization along the frontier of Greece and Turkey, Gladstone continued to work for the creation of one large Graeco-Slav country. He had a simple explanation for these difficulties: the Balkan states were being led astray by selfish rulers who were pursuing their own petty interests. "King Milan," he wrote after Serbia attacked Bulgaria, "is a pest," and he considered using the ultimate weapon – his tongue – against the defenceless king.[18] Nationalism, in Gladstone's view, was of no use without democracy, because despots and special interests would use their position to distort the wishes of the people. The British ambassador to Greece, Sir Horace Rumbold, contributed to this view of the situation: "Athenian lawyers and place-hunters," he reported, were behind the current crisis with the Turks. "The Greek people," he argued, sustaining Gladstone's argument, "are not in this movement and don't care about it."[19] Rosebery agreed, and stated his intention to separate the Greek government from the Greek people in this affair.[20] Liberal talk about constitutionalism and democracy was, therefore, more than idle rhetoric: Liberals sincerely believed that despotic, unconstitutional regimes distorted the true wishes and interests of the people. Nor did they regard constitutional regimes as ends in themselves; Liberals believed these regimes would act in the best interests of Great Britain. The confederation of the five "Free States" envisioned by Gladstone "would more than anything else stay the hands of Russia and put an end to Austria's sinister designs."[21] Balkan nationalism, in this view, was a more attractive instrument than the Ottoman Empire for the safeguarding of British interests in the eastern Mediterranean.

Nationalism, Rosebery concluded, in order to triumph, had to be restrained. Fortunately, he found Gladstone equally anxious to restrain the Greeks. Restraint suited the foreign, as well as the political, requirements of the prime minister. Two things were necessary if Gladstone's Balkan solution were to be realized: neither Austria nor Russia could be permitted to intervene in the affairs of the Balkan states, and conflicts between the Balkan states could not be permitted to obscure the interests these states shared. The problem of restraining the Balkan states reminded the British of why they were necessary in the first place. Military weakness necessitated an ally, but without military influence it was difficult to restrain anyone from acting. Restraining the Greeks appealed to Rosebery and Gladstone partly because they were the only ones over whom the British could exercise any authority.

Restraining Greece had simplicity to recommend it. Despite their mobilization along the frontier – perhaps because of it – the Greeks realized their army was no match for the Turkish, and they depended instead on their navy, leaving them vulnerable to the influence of British sea power. Although unable to restrain Serbia or Bulgaria, the British Mediterranean fleet could easily neutralize the Greek navy.[22] Rosebery's problem was to find some way of using naval power, the only strategic advantage Britain enjoyed, to keep the Balkans quiet, and secure the unification of Bulgaria. Unfortunately, the British ambassador at Athens, the man who should have known best, doubted that neutralizing the fleet would keep the Greeks from attacking. Their warlike spirit, Rumbold argued, would not be broken until the Serbo-Bulgarian and Eastern Roumelia questions were settled. "As long as the negotiations at Bucharest and the arrangement between the Porte and Prince Alexander are not finally concluded," he reported, "the Greeks may claim that the chapter of acccidents is still open to them."[23] If this were true, Rosebery might, by neutralizing the Greek navy, succeed only in alienating Britain's most likely ally in the eastern Mediterranean. In the meantime, the Balkans would continue to be an armed camp, and Bulgarian unification doubtful.

Had Rosebery been looking for guidance, he would not have found it among his ambassadors – not that they did not offer it. Neutralizing the Greek fleet would accomplish nothing, according to Rumbold, writing from Athens; expecting the Serbian question to be settled before the Eastern Roumelian and the Greek was hopeless, according to Sir Frank Lascelles, writing from Sofia; disarming Serbia and Greece was the first priority, according to Sir William White, writing from Constantinople, for it would not be possible to obtain concessions on Bulgaria from the sultan until he felt secure on these other matters.[24] These warnings, if they meant anything to Rosebery, showed that his ambassadors preferred avoiding unpleasant negotiations; they preferred to give the responsibility to colleagues elsewhere. Fortunately for Britain's foreign policy, her foreign secretaries usually disregarded the advice of her ambassadors. Rosebery, following this tradition, conducted his own foreign policy, in spite of his youth and inexperience. Early in February 1886, he categorically told the Greeks that the Liberal government had found engagements entered into with regard to Greece from which they could not recede, and that these engagements were for the best interests of peace and of Greece herself.[25] Rosebery might, of course, have been following where Salisbury had led; he used the fear that he might not do so to bring Germany and Austria-Hungary into line. Continuity, which to the Greeks was made to appear categorical, was made to appear tenuous when placed before the Germans and Austrians.

A recalcitrant cabinet, Rosebery hinted to Berlin and Vienna, might resist the doctrine of continuity and refuse to restrain the Greeks.[26] The hint was immediately effective, causing Bismarck and Kálnoky, the Austro-Hungarian foreign minister, to point out that he held the key to the situation: if he restrained Greece, and she were denied compensation for Bulgaria's unification, the apparent legitimacy of Serbia's demands would disappear.[27] Throughout the crisis, Rosebery assumed that the Germans and Austrians were as interested as the British in preventing any further upheavals, and he also assumed that the Austrians were as capable of controlling Serbian actions as the British were of controlling Greek. The talk of legitimate demands did not interest him. But if upheaval were to be avoided and Bulgaria given the opportunity to grow strong, Serbia had to be restrained, and Britain had no way of restraining her. Therefore, Rosebery promised to restrain the Greeks only if Kálnoky restrained the Serbs, gambling on the Austro-German fear of a change in British policy igniting the Balkans and leading to the Austro-Russian conflict that Bismarck had been trying to avoid for more than a decade. The gamble succeeded. In mid-February Kálnoky urged the Serbs to conclude arrangements for peace, insisting that they drop most of their demands. The Austrian chargé d'affaires at Belgrade was conveniently discovered to have been encouraging King Milan's pretensions, and was sent on a long leave.[28] The Serbs had no choice but to submit, the threat of Austrian intervention on their behalf having saved them from being overrun by the Bulgarians in the autumn of 1885. Their resistance disappeared, and the situation existing before the war was restored. Rosebery had settled the first part of the Balkan question by threatening the Germans and Austrians with discontinuity in foreign policy.

The Serbian part of the Balkan problem was so easily settled because it required nothing of Russia. The Austrians, when Rosebery posed them the alternative, had preferred peace in the Balkans to promoting the interests of their client. They refused, for the same reason, to participate in negotiations between Bulgaria and Turkey. Kálnoky, although favouring the creation of a large, independent Bulgaria, preferred to have Russia resume paramountcy there, if the alternative was an armed struggle for control of the Balkans.[29] While

Britain, France, and Italy were prepared to accept an arrangement recently worked out between Turkey and Bulgaria, Austria and Germany were prepared to accept it only if it met with "general agreement."[30] This meant bringing in the Russians. Neither Britain nor France nor Italy was capable of fighting Russia in the Balkans. If Bulgarian unification were to be purchased by force of arms, it would be paid for in Austrian blood and treasure, so the question of unification, Kálnoky and Bismarck insisted, had to be solved by Britain and Russia.

The arrangement recently concluded by Bulgaria and Turkey provided for Prince Alexander's appointment as governor general of Eastern Roumelia, the "personal" solution to the question of Bulgarian unification. He was to be renewed in this position every five years, at the behest of the sultan. In return for this appointment, the prince promised to provide military assistance to the sultan in time of war. The Balkan question, once the Serb and Greek parts appeared to be under the control of the Austrians and British, began to turn on these intricacies of diplomatic negotiation. Sir William White, largely responsible for negotiating the arrangement, recognized the arrangement to require toning down "to suit the Russian autocrat's palate and to be cooked again 'à la sauce Muscovite'."[31] Therefore, in mid-February 1886, an arrangement for Bulgarian unification satisfactory to both Prince Alexander and the sultan had been reached; the British approved of the arrangement, and the Austrians and Germans, while remaining aloof from the negotiations, were prepared to accept it if the Russians did. The next stage of the Balkan question, lasting for two months, concentrated on working out the details of unification acceptable to the Russians. For this reason the diplomats on the spot, in Constantinople, St Petersburg, and Belgrade, began to play a more important role.

Before Rosebery could attempt to solve the second part of the Balkan question, he had to overcome the obstinacy of his ambassador at Constantinople. White considered himself to be personally responsible for inducing the sultan to agree to the proposed terms of unification, and he resisted any changes tending to impair his personal influence at the Porte, proposing instead to modify the terms at the expense of Bulgaria. The Russians had initially objected to the reference to "Prince Alexander," instead of the "Prince of Bulgaria," and to the renewal of his nomination as governor general of Eastern Roumelia without the sanction of the powers first being obtained. While White proposed that Rosebery give in to these objections, he refused to contemplate giving in to a third, Prince Alexander's pledge of military assistance to the sultan in time of war.[32] The sultan, he said, had drafted this article of the arrangement himself, because he needed to maintain the illusion that the prince was his vassal. The provision for military assistance had been publicized throughout the empire, and to retract it now would strike a further blow at the sultan's prestige.[33]

White, who has been proposed as a hero of Balkan nationalism, actually advocated the cause of the Ottoman Empire.[34] He had personal reasons for his choice: Constantinople was a temporary appointment; he actually held the less lofty position of minister at Bucharest. In a very short time, however, he had established a personal influence with the sultan – or so he argued, and so London believed. White faced enough obstacles in the diplomatic service: he had started in the consular service, regarded as menial by professional diplomats; his wife was unsuitable, and he was old. Any chance he had of rising in the service depended on the position he had recently established at Constantinople. If Rosebery forced him to reverse his position on the military arrangement, his personal influence, and therefore his hope of promotion, might be forever lost.[35]

Sir Robert Morier, White's colleague at St Petersburg, adopted the opposite argument, trying to persuade Rosebery to give up the military arrangement. Although Prince Alexander's independence of Russia had incurred the enmity of the tsar, Morier argued, he had remained a hero of the Russian Slavs nevertheless; if he now pledged himself to fight on behalf of the Moslem Turks against his fellow Christians, he would unite all parties in the desire to see him deposed.[36] Morier believed Rosebery to be a supporter of the prince, and therefore tried to induce him to give up the military arrangement by showing him how it endangered the prince. His argument, like White's, was misleading: although Alexander's personal position was a critical one in the Balkan situation, and although policy, to a certain extent, depended on how diplomatists assessed his strengths and weaknesses, Morier worried less about the prince's future than about the danger Britain faced in supporting him. Morier's role, throughout the Balkan crisis of 1886, lay in persuading Rosebery to subordinate the Balkans to the greater cause of improving relations with Russia, thereby safeguarding British India.[37]

Rosebery might reasonably have been expected to require little persuasion. As one who had advocated closer imperial ties, who had portrayed Britain's foreign policy as colonial policy, and who had proposed to subordinate Sudanese policy to Indian in 1885, he might have been counted upon to see the question of Prince Alexander's position in a unified Bulgaria as trivial when placed alongside the momentous one of the defence of India. Morier hoped that this would be the case, but he was forced to recognize that Rosebery's promise to continue Salisbury's policy when added to Gladstone's commitment to Bulgarian unification complicated matters somewhat. To meet these complications he constructed a three-part argument: first, Prince Alexander's position could not be made secure without Russian consent; second, Salisbury's policy in 1885 had been risky and mistaken; third, a defensible North-West frontier, currently in the process of being constructed by a joint Anglo-Russian Commission, was worth more to Britain than was Bulgaria, whatever its size and shape. Within his first two months in office, therefore, Rosebery was forced to decide how he could assist liberal nationalism in the Balkans, how such assistance would fit the doctrine of continuity in foreign policy, and how these two factors could be reconciled with the traditional requirement of defending British India. In deciding as he did, Rosebery demonstrated the importance of political assumptions and the insignificance of the doctrine of continuity in formulating foreign policy.

Rosebery's policy combined elements of both the Bombay and Punjab schools of Indian defence.[38] Like adherents of the Bombay school, he believed that a clearly defined, defensible Afghan frontier was a useful device in preventing attack, and he gave the clearest demonstration of this belief in his Pamirs policy of 1892–5. But he had already, during the Penjdeh crisis, shown himself to prefer diplomacy to frontiers, arguing that the frontier offered by Russia was not worth the loss in prestige, and suggesting, in the manner of the Punjab school, that threats of general war were more effective. Britain's military weakness in Asia could, he believed, be compensated for by naval strength in the Mediterranean. The argument between advocates of the Asiatic and the Near Eastern defence of India went back at least as far as the Napoleonic Wars; lately, Britain's two leading military strategists, Lords Roberts and Wolseley, had renewed the argument, the first arguing in favour of defending India in Afghanistan, the second in favour of defending it in the Black Sea. Before Rosebery committed himself to one of these strategies, and before showing how his decision would affect the diplomatic questions at issue, Morier attempted to persuade him to the Roberts view.

India, Morier argued, could be defended only in Asia. Since the Russians had agreed, in 1884, to delimit the Afghan boundary, Morier had come to see himself as engaged in erecting the defensible North-West frontier that the British had been seeking throughout the century.[39] Rosebery would be foolhardy to hazard its achievement by alienating the tsar over Bulgaria, a process of alienation initiated by

Salisbury when, in the autumn of 1885, he had used the Bulgarian situation as a reprisal for Penjdeh. Excellent and delightful though this reprisal might have been from "the artistic side of diplomacy," wrote Morier, it was heartbreaking "to one who was conscious the whole time of the possible recoil out in Asia."[40] Rosebery should go in for substance, not artistry: it was impossible for Britain to pose any lasting threat to Russia in Europe, whereas erecting a defensible frontier in Asia would provide a permanent barrier against Russian expansion.

Morier had, therefore, both immediate and permanent reasons for persuading Rosebery to oppose the Turco-Bulgarian military arrangements: immediate, because it would enable the Afghan Boundary Commission to reach a speedy solution, once the tsar's irritation had been removed; permanent, because it would remove the temptation for the British of interfering in the Balkans, where they should realize their inability to contain the Russians.[41] These elements in the Bombay school's arguments were isolationist. Containing Russia in Europe, Morier maintained, was possible only by relying on an ally in Europe, reliance that would weaken Britain by drawing her permanently into the affairs of Europe; it was far better to retain control of the seas, build defensible frontiers, and remain self-reliant.

Adherents of the Bombay school had little confidence in the willingness of the great powers to assist Britain, but they had even less in the ability of small states to retain their independence. Afghanistan and Persia existed only to be dominated, and if the British did not dominate them, then the Russians would. Morier extended this thinking to the Near East, where, he insisted, Bulgaria could not remain independent of Russia; if Prince Alexander "builds all his hopes on the Porte and ignores the huge heave of the Slav ocean behind him of which Bulgaria represents but the breakers on the opposing shore he will certainly go wrong."[42] To Morier, the strategic distinction between the small Balkan states and those of central Asia seemed obvious: while Britain might hope to dominate Afghanistan or even Persia, she could never hope to dominate Bulgaria or Serbia. India, in this view, could be defended only in Asia; trying to defend it in Europe was bound to fail, which was why Morier was so determined to have Rosebery drop his support of Prince Alexander.

The Russians, Morier argued, did not believe in the independence of small states, and their disbelief added a further complication to the British position in Bulgaria. Prince Alexander, who had earlier listened to Russian advice, had recently come to rely on British, and his intimacy with the British minister convinced the Russians that he was merely a puppet who had changed hands. This was dangerous,

Morier urged, because it was wrong. Under no circumstances would Parliament go to war to keep the prince on his throne, no matter how much the British public sympathized with him. Moreover, seeing the prince as a British puppet would induce the Russians to believe they could recapture Bulgaria by removing him. If the British desired to keep the prince in his place, therefore, they must resist the temptation of acting as his guardian. While Morier claimed to be fully sensible of the advantages of a strong Balkan principality, all his arguments demonstrated the impossibility of establishing one. Assuming the British to be engaged in a struggle to keep the Russians out of India, he was prepared to surrender Constantinople to Russia if it strengthened the position of the British in Asia.[43] Giving up Prince Alexander came more easily. It is against the background of the long argument over how India was best defended that Rosebery's policy during the Balkan crisis of 1886 came to be designed.

Ironically, Rosebery appeared to share Morier's pessimistic view of small states because, on 11 February, before his ambassador's arguments arrived, he instructed White to learn whether the Porte could be induced to drop the military arrangement. The defensive purpose of mutual military assistance should, he said, "be sufficiently secured by friendship based on common interest, and by the natural action of the constitutional relations between the Porte and the Principality, without the necessity of a formal and specific stipulation."[44] Rosebery's instructions echoed one of those maxims upon which Britain had conducted her foreign policy throughout the nineteenth century. Common interests, not signatures on paper, led to common action in time of war. In fact, Rosebery appeared to welcome the contest over the military arrangement as a way of testing future relations between Bulgaria and Turkey. He was prepared to urge its abandonment because he hoped to convince the Turks and their former Balkan subjects of their common interests. As the *Times*, possibly primed by Rosebery, phrased it, "it is for Turkey so as to order her policy as to win the confidence of the independent nationalities of the Balkan peninsula, and thus dispose them spontaneously to rally round her in times of trouble."[45] If this cooperation could be achieved, the traditional purpose of the Ottoman Empire, to serve the interests of British foreign policy by blocking Russian expansion, could be achieved through a new, perhaps more reliable, form. Splitting up into national states might finally end the internal dissension that, to British liberals at least, had seemed to paralyse Ottoman policy; if the new states could then be drawn together in common fear of Russia, Britain's position in the Near East might be made stronger than before. In part at least, Rosebery saw the crisis of 1886 as a test of the practicability of this new design.

Rosebery's policy was too daring for Sir William White, who, instead of executing his instructions, sent in a long argument against them. Rosebery, who assumed that his instructions would be obeyed, had informed the German ambassador that White would advise the sultan to abandon the military arrangement. He had asked for German support of this representation; Bismarck agreed, White objected, and Rosebery was embarrassed.[46]

Youth and inexperience placed Rosebery in an awkward position. His principal ambassadors, at least twenty years his senior, had laboured long enough in the diplomatic service to make him appear a novice. Aware of the difficulties this situation might cause, he had, soon after assuming office, written personal letters to his ambassadors. "My inexperience will make private and personal communications from you especially valuable," he told White; "I know that for many reasons I may count upon your kind assistance."[47] "I am writing to receive information," he told Sir Augustus Paget, the ambassador in Vienna, "and not to offer opinions which cannot have much value in view of my inexperience in this office."[48] This elaborate self-effacement, the product of Rosebery's personality, might have convinced White that he really felt unprepared for the task of conducting foreign policy. Rosebery's manner must have appeared obsequious to the bombastic and domineering White, who replied as if he were instructing, not serving, his master.

White's imperious dispatches threatened to disrupt Rosebery's management of foreign policy, adding a personal reason to the political one for keeping him quiet. Rosebery's position in the government depended on the faith of Gladstone: he had promised, through continuity, to keep foreign affairs quiet, thereby permitting the prime minister to concentrate on Ireland. Gladstone, though participating less than he had during Granville's time at the Foreign Office, continued to see all the important dispatches. If he saw an ambassador dominating his foreign secretary, he might reconsider his appointment of an inexperienced man, especially as he habitually distrusted career diplomats. The dispute with White over policy in the Near East provided the first opportunity for Gladstone to judge Rosebery's talent as a manager of men.

Rosebery tailored his manner to suit his political requirements, and the dispute with White proved to be the first of many occasions on which he demonstrated this talent. Later in his career he allowed his temper to flash out when he wanted his colleagues to think him too temperamental to tamper with. In 1886, when his requirements were different, he determined to demonstrate his capacity for controlling his subordinates, but in such a way as to show Gladstone, who already suspected him of unnecessary prickliness, his ability to control them through the firm and judicious exercise of authority, not through loss of temper. Accordingly, Rosebery chose to ignore White's arguments, and simply issued new instructions, explicit and direct, for White to take the initiative and induce the sultan to drop the military arrangement with Prince Alexander.[49] He did not lose his temper; he did not even issue a reprimand. A week later, Morier repeated White's performance, and, by delaying to act on his instructions, managed to upset another manoeuvre arranged beforehand at Berlin. Rosebery remained calm, leading the senior clerk at the Foreign Office to describe his new master as "thoroughly goodnatured and tolerant."[50]

Rosebery's problems with White and Morier, handled as they were with tact and grace, cannot be attributed to sharpness of temper. They arose, in fact, because the three differed on the question of how the Balkans and the eastern Mediterranean fitted in with the defence of British India. The difference with White had arisen because Rosebery's first goal in the Near East was to guarantee British paramountcy in Egypt. Like Palmerston, Rosebery would have preferred to leave Egypt alone, its occupation being costly and troublesome. However, the Suez Canal, once opened, gave the French access to the most direct route to India, and, if the British left Egypt without first establishing a stable and secure government and guaranteeing their paramountcy there, the French would intervene at the first opportunity and pose a permanent threat to India. The British had difficulties enough defending India against the Russians; adding the French to those difficulties might make the burden too heavy to bear. The prospect of Russia dominating the sultan of Turkey or the prince of Bulgaria paled by comparison with the threat of two great powers causing trouble in India whenever they chose. In 1886, when the British still believed themselves able to force the Straits and threaten Russia in the Black Sea, the balance had already swung from the Ottoman Empire to Egypt. Rosebery preferred not to choose between the two if this could be avoided, but Turkish friendship, while providing the obvious means of avoiding the choice, was not to be purchased at the price of British paramountcy in Egypt.

White's mistake was in failing to appreciate this change in British thinking. He continued to put good relations with the sultan ahead of Britain's position in Egypt, thinking of Egypt only in terms of its effect upon his influence at Constantinople.[51] White believed that cooperating with the sultan in the Balkans, which, in February 1886, meant upholding the sultan's view of his arrangement with Prince Alexander, would lead the way to an Egyptian settlement. Once Egypt was settled, Britain could resume her customary role as guardian of the

Ottoman Empire – and Sir William would be responsible for this momentous achievement. The sultan, unfortunately, spoiled this plan by reversing the order of priorities: he would cooperate in the Balkans only after being assured of an Egyptian settlement, and he had already indicated as much to Rosebery when White refused to follow his instructions on the military arrangement.

At Rosebery's first reception of the diplomatic corps, the Turkish ambassador, suggesting that the past be forgotten, proposed to settle the Egyptian question.[52] But the Turks had little to offer in exchange, except their cooperation in the Balkans. Thus their manoeuvre produced an effect opposite to the one they intended: Rosebery inclined to rely more on Bulgaria and less on Turkey. If Turkish enmity would be the price Britain had to pay for paramountcy in Egypt, then it made no sense to take the sultan's side in his negotiations with Prince Alexander. The military arrangement worked entirely in the sultan's favour, Alexander having agreed to it as a concession. The Bulgarians did not want the arrangement, and neither did the Russians; if Russian consent to unification could be purchased by giving up, temporarily at least, the hope of a Turco-Bulgarian military alliance, then Rosebery was prepared to give it up. When, on 16 February, White finally obeyed his instructions and announced Britain's opposition to the military arrangement, the Turks acquiesced. In spite of White's warnings, they had little choice: no power could be found to support them, and they had to satisfy themselves with the vague hope that Britain and Germany would induce Russia not to raise new objections.[53]

After a month in office, Rosebery, who was receiving conflicting reports from Sofia, Constantinople, Berlin, and St Petersburg, was still not certain what the Russian objections to the Turco-Bulgarian arrangement really were. Having first decided to restrain the Greeks in return for Austria's restraining the Serbs, and then to oppose the military arrangement, he quickly found himself to be negotiating in the dark, and for this reason it is easy to lose sight of his object, hidden as it was in a mass of detail. His first object in the Balkans was to keep things quiet, but this could have been accomplished simply by falling in with the Russian view. His second object was to establish a big Bulgaria, stable and independent of Russia, but this had to be accomplished without a general upheaval. Therefore, from mid-February on, Rosebery was forced to decide how far he could go in achieving the second object without jeopardizing the first. The resulting diplomatic situation was made even more complicated than it need have been, because Rosebery preferred to continue working in the dark.

Sir William White proposed, quite reasonably, to ask the Russians for precise counterproposals.[54] Before the British made more concessions, he suggested, Rosebery ought to commit the Russians to a bargaining position, as they would otherwise be likely to keep asking for more. Rosebery, however, chose once more to ignore the advice of his ambassador. Acting upon liberal assumptions about the nature of despotism, Rosebery disregarded White's proposal. "The mind of an absolute monarch," he declared, "develops in all sorts of subterranean directions." He offered this aphorism as explanation of the current difficulties over Bulgarian unification. "My own conjecture is that the Russian Emperor, though perfectly honest in wishing for peace, cannot bring himself to definitely ratify the establishment of a state of things which leaves Prince Alexander in possession of the tricks and honours of the game."[55] Rosebery preferred, therefore, to avoid insisting on precise counterproposals to the Turco-Bulgarian agreement as he believed that they would only commit the tsar firmly to his own proposals by making the negotiations more obviously a battle for prestige. As his next diplomatic manoeuvre, Rosebery attempted to reduce the appearance of Prince Alexander's victory in exchange for the tsar accepting the substance, and this effort gave form to the complex negotiations from the middle of February to the end of March.

Ironically, Rosebery proved less willing than Salisbury to stand by the hero of Bulgarian nationalism. Acting upon liberal assumptions about the nature of nationalism, he decided to mollify the tsar at the risk of endangering Prince Alexander. "Nations are never obliterated," he had earlier declared;[56] only their "national development" could be impaired. He believed that Bulgaria needed time: a crisis over Prince Alexander's personal safety might precipitate Russian intervention and impair national development. Monarchs, as the Russians were to demonstrate a few months later, could be changed overnight, and Britain, without military influence in the area, could not hope to intervene. If the Bulgarians were to play the part assigned to them by the British, their independence must transcend the abilities and policies of one man. Given time, Rosebery believed they would. In this instance ideology played a critical role in the development of foreign policy.

Because Rosebery believed the position of Prince Alexander to be of secondary importance, he was able to persuade the Russians to agree to Bulgarian unification. Bismarck and Kálnoky had insisted that they would agree to unification only if it met with general, meaning Russian, agreement. Rosebery's problem, therefore, was to find an arrangement to which the Russians would agree, and, had it not been for his faith in liberal nationalism, and the tsar's in despotism, it is unlikely that such an arrangement could have been found. Assuming that their problems in Bulgaria were personal and monarchical, the Russians still preferred a big Bulgaria if it led to the establishment of a new, pro-Russian, monarchy. If the prince could be changed, they believed, Bulgaria would change with him. Russia insisted, therefore, on referring to the "Prince of Bulgaria" and not to "Prince Alexander" in the agreement naming him governor general of Eastern Roumelia, and on limiting his appointment to five years, thereafter to be subject to the approval of the powers. The sultan, however, refused to make an unlimited appointment of an anonymous prince, while Prince Alexander refused to accept a limited appointment. In mid-March, Rosebery prepared to remove the prince's name from the agreement, gambling that all Bulgaria needed was time; but he argued that if the prince were to remain anonymous there should be no stipulation regarding time, which would only guarantee another crisis five years hence.[57]

When Rosebery decided to gamble on the strength of Bulgarian nationalism, he removed most of the differences between Britain and Russia. A diplomatic blunder on the part of the Bulgarians removed the only remaining one. The sultan believed that he would have some control over the prince if his appointment as governor of Eastern Roumelia were to be reconsidered after five years, and a formula to this effect was arrived at between Russia and Turkey. Tsanow, the Bulgarian representative at Constantinople, agreed to this formula on 22 March.[58] He was immediately recalled to Sofia and disavowed by Prince Alexander. "Is Tsanow a knave or a fool or a scapegoat? or all three?" Rosebery wondered, but he decided, nevertheless, to accommodate himself to the arrangement. "If the Prince can keep on the throne five years," he argued, "he is safe for an unlimited period. If he cannot, what is the use of a longer term?"[59]

Prince Alexander, Rosebery feared, might prove less fatalistic: Russian agents in Eastern Roumelia, together with Bulgarian conservatives, were already proclaiming the presence of Prince Alexander to be the only barrier to real, permanent unification. If they were successful in propagating this idea, Alexander might come to be regarded by the Bulgarians themselves not as an instrument of national unity, but as an impediment to it. If Alexander authorized the formula incorporating a time-limit, to which Tsanow had agreed, he would confirm the accusation of creating a temporary, and fragile, Bulgarian unification. Alexander might, therefore, choose to disregard the powers and proclaim an absolute union with Eastern Roumelia. Rosebery urged the prince instead to yield under protest, showing up Russia as the sole enemy of the union under a governorship without term. Alexander, believing he had no choice, yielded, and on 5 April the powers sanctioned the Turco-Bulgarian agreement, thus ending the crisis.[60]

The most dramatic acts in a diplomatic crisis are seldom the most important. The great powers of Europe, insisting that the Greeks demobilize their army and stop threatening the Turks along the frontier, blockaded the Greek fleet during May and June, but by this time the real crisis had passed. The crisis had centred in Bulgaria, and Rosebery had consistently refused to undertake measures coercing the Greeks until a Turco-Bulgarian settlement had been reached. The powers fought for the future of Bulgaria because they believed that the control of the Straits lay with her, and neither Britain nor Russia would befriend Greece while both continued to believe that a big Bulgaria might become an ally. For the moment, the powers were determined only to avoid war, and without their assistance the Greek government could not hope to succeed against Turkey. The Greeks remained obdurate, however, for the sake of domestic politics. Their only hope for a "welcome and honourable excuse for yielding" was direct European coercion: it was dishonourable to yield to the Turk.[61]

The naval blockade of Greece, therefore, launched on 27 April, was performed as a charade for the benefit of the Greek government, and only after repeated but less visible diplomatic threats had failed. As Rosebery phrased it, "I do not myself see much use in the Allied fleet cruising about to prevent the Greek fleet coming out, when, as a matter of fact, the Greek fleet has no intention of coming out."[62] Beset with legal complications, the blockade provided numerous opportunities for any of the five powers to withdraw. None of them did. None of them wanted to upset the delicate balance recently established in the Balkans. The Greeks were forced to give in and the blockade was raised at the beginning of June. The diplomatic contest appeared to be over. In fact, it had scarcely begun: the Serbs and Bulgarians remained antagonistic; the Greeks devoted the next decade to preparing an army to fight the Turks, an army that would relieve them of their reliance on the British fleet; the Russian panslavists began making immediate plans for the removal of Prince Alexander from the throne.

Diplomatic crises usually end when one side, through the exercise of will or power, has triumphed over the other. The Balkan crisis of 1886 was unusual, because no one triumphed. Neither the Serbs nor the Greeks could claim to have triumphed, although Prince Alexander could reasonably claim to have succeeded in uniting Bulgaria. Rosebery could, and did, claim responsibility for the success of the prince.

The appearance of victory went to Bulgaria and Britain. The Russians, who had permitted this, did so because they did not believe that they had lost, but that a united Bulgaria might yet become the client of Russia. Both sides were buying time. Rosebery believed that time would bolster Bulgarian independence; the Russians, that time would destroy it.

While Rosebery's early career partly explains his behaviour at the Foreign Office, his management of the Balkan crisis explains much of his later career. He was applauded by everyone: by Tories for continuing Salisbury's policies; by Liberals for upholding the freedom of small states; and, most important, by Gladstone for keeping things quiet. "I do not remember an instance of such an achievement carried through in the *first quarter* of a Foreign Secretaryship," Gladstone told Rosebery, "and it is one to which your personal action has beyond doubt largely contributed. It is a great act and a good omen."[63] Rosebery's argument, that what is really peaceful is firmness, appeared to have proved itself. His promise, that continuity in foreign policy would end political squabbling, appeared to have been fulfilled. Henceforth he was regarded, and came to regard himself, as a man above party.

The applause that greeted Rosebery's first performance as foreign secretary should not obscure the fact that his triumph was based on an illusion. He appeared to have reestablished the Concert of Europe in acting with the great powers to blockade the Greek fleet, cooperating in a manner that had not been seen for a generation. He could claim to have kept the Russians out of the Balkans, to have stopped Turks from killing Greeks, and to have assisted a nation struggling to be free. He could claim that his policy of firmness and his principle of continuity had enabled him to achieve his objectives with no expense in British blood and only a little treasure. In fact, his policy was neither firm nor continuous, and his success was the result of a gamble on the ultimate triumph of liberal nationalism. He had first given way on Russia's opposition to the military arrangement, then on Prince Alexander's personal position, and finally on the duration of the agreement. Salisbury would never have gone so far, and in fact Rosebery's concessions amounted to a reversal of the policy he had inherited in January. In their haste for relief from the disasters that had plagued British foreign policy for several years, few noticed the differences between Salisbury and Rosebery, or the concessions on which Rosebery's success had depended.

Rosebery was incapable of continuing Salisbury's policies because he was incapable of thinking like Salisbury. The assumptions by which he was guided were those of nineteenth-century liberalism: he believed in reform, education, and, most of all, the strength and vitality of nationalism. The policies he advocated in domestic politics did not disappear when he entered the Foreign Office; when they were applied to foreign politics, they led him to conclude that a strong, united, and independent Bulgaria was in the best interest of Britain. Britain, however, could do little to assist Bulgaria, either now or in the future. If Bulgaria were to survive, she had to be strong enough, and resolute enough, to do so on her own. The unification established in the agreement of March 1886 gave her the opportunity to succeed; if she failed, then she was of no value to Britain as a future ally. Rosebery was optimistic but fatalistic. Salisbury, by way of contrast, had demonstrated a firmer attitude to the terms of Bulgarian unification. Having no particular faith in the enduring characteristics of national states, he had determined to safeguard Prince Alexander's position and to draw him as close to the sultan as possible. Although Rosebery and Salisbury shared the same objectives in their eastern policy, they differed fundamentally in their application of it.

Statesmen dislike even the appearance of defeat in diplomacy, and British diplomatists began to anticipate retribution from the Russians as the price of Bulgarian unification. Paget feared that the Russians, in agreement with the French, might choose to champion the cause of Greece.[64] The Greeks, after all, considered themselves to have been betrayed by the British for the sake of the Bulgarians, and might become willing allies of Britain's opponents. Morier, in contrast, feared retribution for the Balkan settlement would come in Asia, and with the approval of Germany and Austria-Hungary.[65] For a moment it appeared as if both predictions might be wrong, that the Russians would instead react in the Black Sea. At the end of May, the mayor of Moscow, with the tsar sitting next to him on the platform, spoke in favour of reviving the Black Sea fleet; its revival would, he declared, soon result in the reappearance of the cross on St Sophia.[66] The Turks were struck with the similarity between this declaration and the one with which Alexander II had committed himself to war in 1876. Paget was also struck by it.[67]

Morier discounted the possibility of Russia reacting in the Black Sea; the new fleet, he pointed out, would not be ready to fight for several years. In his opinion, the mayor's speech was not the signal of imminent attack, but an indication of Russia's long-term strategy. The tsar's failure to disavow the mayor's statement, however, signalled to Morier that Giers, the Russian foreign secretary, was in trouble. The "western and pacific element," he reported, was under attack for its feeble inactivity during the Balkan crisis, and he expected the Russians to respond in Asia.[68] Morier, of course, was simply repeating the position he had advanced since the beginning of the crisis: the British could not expect to score diplomatic triumphs in the Near East without paying for them in Asia. While the Germans and the Austrians might be prepared to assist the British in preventing Russian expansion in the Balkans, they would always encourage Russian expansion in Asia. His conclusion was always the same: British India could be defended only in Asia, where European allies were of little use. Russia's taking revenge in Asia for Bulgarian unification should teach Rosebery to rely on Morier who could, he claimed, feel "a Siamese connection" between the Eastern and Western twins; "I can as it were touch and press the living limb with my hand, feel the pulse, or perceive the nerve tissues connecting the one with the other."[69]

The Balkan settlement of April 1886 had created a situation in which the Russians were anxious for some kind of diplomatic victory, and Bismarck was prepared to assist them to achieve one if doing so did not lead to complications with Austria. They might not have acted, however, if Prince Alexander had not violated the recent agreement and, declaring the union of the two Bulgarias complete, promised, in mid-June, to call together a Great National Assembly. His action negated the concessions that Giers had won through negotiation, and Giers, to save his position, was forced to respond.

The Russian blow, when it was finally delivered on 3 July, struck Rosebery "not like a thunderbolt in a clear sky, for the sky is far from clear, but like a thunderbolt in a November fog," because Giers responded in an unexpected way.[70] He issued only a mild remonstrance against the prince and continued to negotiate the Afghan boundary – the obvious place for Morier's "recoil in Asia." Giers, however, announced that the port of Batum, on the Black Sea, was no longer to remain unfortified and free to the commerce of all nations, as the tsar had declared in 1876.[71] Not one of Rosebery's advisers had predicted this response, which immediately became confused in a legal problem. The tsar's declaration had been attached to Article 59 of the Treaty of Berlin. Giers, arguing that the declaration had been spontaneous, maintained that Batum's freedom could be abrogated should the tsar or his successors so desire. The tsar's declaration, Rosebery replied, had been an integral part of the treaty, for which the British had relinquished other claims.[72] The legal argument, however, was beside the point: Giers selected Batum because of its symbolic significance, and Rosebery responded accordingly.

Prince Alexander's declaration of complete unity for Bulgaria amounted to a unilateral modification of the Treaty of Berlin, and Giers's Batum declaration amounted to the same thing. Everyone but the Russians considered the termination of Batum's freedom to be an infringement of the spirit, if not the letter, of the treaty, but Count Kálnoky curtly replied that "the Treaty of Berlin had already undergone a good deal of ill-treatment."[73] No one acted against the prince and no one would act against the Russians. None of the powers cared for Batum: not the Russians, not the British, certainly no one else. The port was of little strategic significance because its exposed harbour made it unfit for either a great arsenal or a naval stronghold.[74] The Russians had been quietly fortifying it for some time, and the British had chosen to avoid a wrangle and pretended not to notice. The Russians had made no attempt to bargain for British approval beforehand; they acted, as Rosebery said, almost "as if they wished it to be considered an outrage."[75] If Russia had confidentially approached the powers and pointed out the inconvenience of Batum's status, he claimed, they would have met the Russian government half-way. Giers, he concluded, had deliberately chosen to violate the treaty for the sake of violating it.

A quick survey of Europe by Rosebery made it clear that no other signatory of the Treaty of Berlin would respond unfavourably to the Batum declaration; it appeared to him almost as if there had been a prior arrangement to this effect.[76] When someone suggested a conference be held to legalize the transaction, in the manner of the London Conference of 1871, Rosebery dismissed the idea as sanctioning what he considered an illegal act. More to the point, such a conference would not have suited his political requirements. His response was conditioned by considerations of domestic politics; he was determined to prove that a Liberal government, with himself at the Foreign Office, was as capable of acting with strength and firmness as a Tory one. He was convinced that there would be no fight over Batum; the crisis would be one of words, and a little Russian annoyance would be a cheap price to pay for the purchase of Liberal prestige. A gentle rebuke, he told Morier, would cause intense annoyance in England. Her voice must be heard in an incontestable note: "such a course moreover while satisfying the national sentiment, can have no worse effect than a mild remonstrance. It is all the more necessary from a Gladstone Government."[77] Gladstone, with his reputation as a russophile, might have been expected to demur, and Rosebery did not pretend, even with him, to be acting in defence of treaty obligations, or out of moral considerations. The Russian declaration, he told Gladstone, quite simply, "is a slap at us." "That," he admitted, "is its main importance."[78] He proposed to pretend, however, that the blow was aimed at the Treaty of Berlin, and not at Britain. Rosebery could defend the sanctity of treaties, uphold British dignity, and, most important, take no risk. He proposed a reply that would "elicit support and respect and not contempt at home and abroad." After careful consideration, and a few minor changes in Rosebery's original draft, Gladstone approved of what became known as the Batum Dispatch.[79]

Morier was the only one to oppose the dispatch; he preferred collective action. If Britain acted alone, he said, she would only play into Bismarck's hand by setting herself at loggerheads with Russia. He might have realized that, if he were right, collective action was impossible. He proposed a "gentle but collective snub."[80] Perhaps he hoped to manoeuvre Rosebery into a less acerbic reply; only the month before, he had warned him that the Germans and Austrians "would not move a finger to help us in Asia." Good relations with Russia was the essential aim of Morier's mission in St Petersburg.[81] Rosebery suspected that Giers had squared Germany, Austria, and France beforehand, and he refused to consider a mild remonstrance. Morier agreed: "the moment you tell me any and every combined action was impossible then there was no course but the very energetic one you have taken."[82]

Rosebery's vigorous reply to the tsar's declaration on Batum was grounded primarily in the sanctity of international engagements. The declaration, he said, obliterated a distinct stipulation of the Treaty of Berlin. The British plenipotentiaries to the congress had stated that the constituting of Batum as a free port was the condition on which they assented to its acquisition by Russia. He refused to admit that the commercial inconvenience of Batum's status furnished "a justification for a peremptory declaration of the Russian Government on its own sole authority that this portion of the Treaty is to be regarded as no longer valid." Although Britain had no material interest in the matter, the dispatch declared, "one direct, supreme, and perpetual interest" was at stake: "the binding force and sanctity of international engagements." The British government refused, therefore, to recognize or associate themselves with the proceeding of the Russian government, which "must rest upon the sole responsibility of its authors."[83]

Because the words of Rosebery and Giers were intended for their publics, and not for each other, the Batum affair came to nothing. On 18 July Morier reported that, when he communicated the dispatch, Giers entirely lost his self-possession, exclaiming that it was "the most wounding communication that has ever been addressed by one power to another. It has gone straight to my heart and will remain there till I die."[84] Rosebery thought this was overdoing it. The performance, he suggested to Morier, must have been theatrical.[85] Giers, by the time his conversation with Morier ended, was hinting at the possibility of an Anglo-Russian understanding, to "take in hand" the Turkish Empire, when it collapsed. A minor affair like Batum, he said, would not be allowed to interfere with this possibility.[86] Russia's formal reply, ending the affair, was courteous and moderate.[87] A few days later Gladstone's government fell. Rosebery did not return to the Foreign Office for six years.

Rosebery left office receiving praise from all sides. His colleagues in government were especially grateful for the respite from the ordeals of the Granville regime. Anthony Mundella, president of the Board of Trade, thought Rosebery an ideal foreign secretary.[88] Bryce claimed that he could better write the history of the last government after having seen Rosebery "make it so well."[89] Rosebery had promised that steadfast adherence to the principle of continuity would bring tranquillity abroad, and events proved him right. He had, Hamilton noted, "the complete confidence of his colleagues and the country."[90] Gladstone proclaimed publicly that Rosebery would one day lead the Liberal party. Khartoum, the Balkan crisis, and the Batum dispatch had transformed Rosebery from an isolated young politician, who felt he had been tried and found wanting, into a man who was considered by his party to be an essential part of any Liberal government.

The professionals at the Foreign Office and in the diplomatic service were pleased with the performance of their new master. Mostly old and Tory, they seem to have expected little of a young Liberal. The "recent administration of affairs" by the Liberals, wrote Sir Augustus Paget in February 1886, "was characterized with more bungling, disaster, bloodshed, disgrace, financial ruin, and humiliation than ever fell to the lot of any previous administration."[91] He made an exception of Rosebery; within a few years he was shouting "bravo Rosebery," and wishing that the young man did not belong to that "infamous crew."[92] Continuity in foreign policy had a particular appeal for career civil servants who regarded the machinations of party politics with disgust.

They were also pleased when Rosebery proved himself to be a capable manager of men. Morier and White, both of whom disobeyed instructions, did not suffer as a result. Rosebery spoke highly of White, and was searching for a way to send him back to Constantinople when the government fell.[93] The elderly Lord Lyons, the ambassador at Paris, was impressed with Rosebery, as was Sir Frank Lascelles, the young minister at Sofia.[94] Two years later, a rising young clerk in the Foreign Office wrote to Rosebery that he had seen "a black Tory of this office who said that since Lord Clarendon's time none had been anything like as popular in the office as you have been."[95] The permanent under-secretary, Sir Philip Currie, classed him with Salisbury.[96] The assistant under-secretary, Sir Villiers Lister, called him "the best Foreign Secretary in my time."[97] This praise, coming after Rosebery had been in office a mere six months, shows how great was the sense of relief that he gave; but it also shows that his admirers may have been expecting too much.

Rosebery's tenure of office in 1886 was so brief that it has received little attention, yet it is essential in understanding how contemporaries regarded him. His popularity in the country, when combined with the trust of his colleagues and the admiration of his subordinates, provided him with a place unparalleled in the Gladstonian Liberal party. He made his reputation on the basis of two phrases: "continuity in foreign policy" and "peace through firmness." As closer examination has shown, he did maintain the broad outlines of Salisbury's policy, continuing to support the unification of Bulgaria and the blockade of Greece. On specific measures, however, he differed substantially from Salisbury, and these differences arose from judgments he made concerning the strength and vitality of movements for national independence.

Rosebery's first six months at the Foreign Office showed that he adhered to many of the same traditions as Salisbury. He resisted any commitment to go to war and he retained a "free hand" for British diplomacy; he would certainly have avoided entering an alliance in time of peace, had anyone offered it. In fact, he was even less willing than Salisbury had been to run risks. He knew the Greek blockade to be a charade, even though it was a necessary one, and he was certain that the Batum affair would amount to no more than a few harsh words. He managed to establish a reputation for firmness, but, in 1886 at least, only his words were firm. Avoiding commitments was to become a far more important part of Rosebery's foreign policy than any determination to be firm.

CHAPTER TWO

The Essential Diplomatist: Uganda and the Control of Foreign Policy

... this mania for cutting and carving ... produced a moral effect which was disastrous to the new Empire. The founder of such a dynasty should have attempted to convince the world of the stability of his arrangements. He himself, however, spared no exertion to prove the contrary. Moving boundaries, shifting realms, giving and taking back, changing, revising, and reversing, he seemed to have set before himself the object of demonstrating that his foundations were never fixed, that nothing in his structure was definite or permanent. It was the suicide of his system.

Napoleon: The Last Phase (1900)

Politicians are often haunted by disasters over which they had little control. The careers of Aberdeen, Gladstone, and Asquith were all transformed – or ruined – by events in the Crimea, the Sudan, and on the Western front. Rosebery, whose fate was more unusual, was haunted by success. Expectations were high when he entered the Foreign Office and higher still when he left. "His short tenure of office has certainly placed the political ball at his feet," Edward Hamilton concluded, "and he has got the *nous* to kick it the right way."[1] Neither Hamilton nor Gladstone considered that Rosebery might not care for the prize. No one took seriously his statements that he had already attained the summit of his ambition at the Foreign Office: these bore too striking a resemblance to the statements of unfitness he had made before joining the cabinet, before taking the Foreign Office. They neglected the fact that this time he gave a reason other than incapacity or indifference. "I doubt if a peer can ever lead the Liberal party again," he told Gladstone.[2] Wishful thinking led them astray; as critics underestimate the importance of the situation for the success of policy, so do admirers overestimate the importance of the man.

After the fall of Gladstone's government in the summer of 1886, Rosebery returned to the unusual combination of activities that he had enjoyed before taking office. He continued putting together a most bizarre assortment of treasures: worthless, even fake, memorabilia, particularly of Napoleon; Goya tapestries purchased at incredibly low prices; china and silver; and, of course, books – literary, historical, and pornographic. He resumed his travels, alone or with Lady Rosebery, notably to India and Egypt. He accepted an invitation to contribute a study of Pitt to John Morley's series on "Twelve English Statesmen," and the book, which occupied much of his time, became an immediate best-seller. His passion for the turf continued unabated, and he flourished in the afterglow of his release from office: "it would be glad tidings of great joy if I knew that I should never have to fill a post or make a speech again. I am too happy with books and horses to make public life anything but a sacrifice for me."[3]

Notwithstanding his habitual declarations of preference for life outside, Rosebery continued to immerse himself in politics. He took up the cause of reforming the House of Lords. He was elected chairman of the Imperial Federation League. He was elected alderman to the first London County Council and quickly became its first chairman, receiving praise from all sides for his energy, fairmindedness, and even temper. In fact, in the four years after the fall of Gladstone's government Rosebery betrayed no intention of removing himself from political life. Whenever he was touted as the next leader of the Liberal party, however, he assiduously denied having any such ambition, and his denials are the more credible because he freely admitted the Foreign Office to have been his goal.[4] "I do not wish for the leadership; even if I felt fit for it I should not wish for it."[5]

One reason why he continued to be highly regarded in the leadership stakes was the belief that he occupied the middle ground as far as the Irish question was concerned. A minor political incident demonstrated this belief, and some of the difficulties to which it led. The rectorship of Glasgow University became vacant early in 1887, and the selection committee, searching for a Liberal candidate, found itself in difficulty. The Unionists refused to accept the Gladstonian proposal of John Morley, while the Gladstonians refused the proposal of Lord Hartington. "A Conference was held and it was unanimously agreed that you were the only candidate for whom both parties could vote *heartily*," one of the participants wrote to Rosebery.[6] The compliment of being regarded as above party squabbles appealed to Rosebery's nature, and he agreed to run for the rectorship, believing that Morley and Hartington had agreed to step aside. When this proved not to be the case, Hartington running against him and winning, a breach was opened between the two which lasted until Winston Churchill, during one of his abortive efforts to establish a new party in 1902, reconciled them. The incident was exactly the kind most likely to embitter Rosebery, causing him public embarrassment by making him appear to have sought distinction, when it obviously had sought him. After this incident his statements in support of Home Rule became stronger than before.

Although he continued to complain of political life, Rosebery displayed no intention of deserting it. His succesful tenure in 1886 had reinforced his confidence, while the public and private acclaim he received suited the needs of his character. During this interval between Liberal governments, he was as busy as other leaders in speech-making and planning for the future. He was prepared to serve in a Harcourt administration, but believed the best solution upon Gladstone's retirement would be for Spencer to lead – with Rosebery returning to the Foreign Office.[7] He was prepared to keep a hand outstretched for Chamberlain, though there seemed little chance of its being grasped, and he tried to avoid becoming too pronounced a partisan, fearing it might injure the two questions he was most concerned with, reform of the House of Lords and imperial federation. He continued to deny having any desire to lead the party. "He was more than content," he told Hamilton, "to serve his country as Foreign Secretary whenever the opportunity offered."[8]

Rosebery believed he had a duty to perform at the Foreign Office and felt he had proved himself capable of performing it. His idea of continuity seemed to have caught on; officials at the Foreign Office were keeping him privately informed of events. Part of his plan for reforming the House of Lords involved arrangements that would make continuity easier to achieve: he favoured the appointment of the foreign secretary and the heads of the military and naval departments for terms of years, with spokesmen in the House of Commons. "Rosebery is all for as little Parliamentary interference as possible with the Executive Government."[9] He did his best to conceal differences on foreign policy during Salisbury's administration, but Gladstone's natural inclinations made this difficult. The Triple Alliance, which was receiving much publicity in Britain during the winter of 1888–9, worried Gladstone, who wanted to make it clear that Britain would not be drawn into it. While he regretted its formation altogether, as violating the principle of free intercourse among nations, he was particularly determined to warn Italy of the evils of such an arrangement. Rosebery was as determined to keep Gladstone quiet. He told Gladstone that offering Italy advice, even considering his past services to her, would be an interference: "how should we relish it in England if a foreign stateman were to offer us advice or remonstrances about their alliances?"[10]

Rosebery's debates with Gladstone always revealed an interesting combination of principle and self-interest. Fearing that the principle of noninterference might not carry sufficient weight to induce silence, Rosebery hinted at more practical consequences. First, he raised the spectre of the Irish question. Reminding Gladstone of his instruction in 1886, when he had told Rosebery that the important matter was to keep foreign affairs from disturbing England, "where we had a great enterprise on hand which would fully occupy our energies," he asked if this instruction did not now apply with equal force. Besides, if Gladstone spoke out he would divide the Liberal party; "there are many Liberals I think who would be of an opinion that Italy had acted wisely in entering upon this alliance, and could not well otherwise have secured her own safety."[11] This was the first skirmish in what was to be a long campaign fought over the Triple Alliance and Britain's relationship with it. Rosebery believed that good relations with Germany were the only thing saving Britain from French aggression, and that Gladstone's great weakness was his failure to admit the continuing enmity of France.[12] This different view on the Triple Alliance therefore came to be mixed in with their differences on Egypt until the two questions became inseparable, Gladstone explaining French enmity by Britain's refusal to evacuate Egypt as promised, Rosebery explaining Britain's refusal to evacuate by French enmity. Gladstone regarded Britain's good relations with the Triple Alliance as a guarantee that French enmity would continue; Rosebery regarded them as the only guarantee Britain had that French enmity would not result in war.

The debate on Egypt and the Triple Alliance was also part of a larger debate on the nature and function of the late Victorian Liberal party. Most party leaders had welcomed Home Rule because it simplified party politics; before 1885, sections and pressure groups were tearing the party apart through their promotion of special interests. The heyday of the party, when Nonconformity had offered a coherent political program, had passed, and Nonconformist politics became increasingly diversified, resulting in a series of worthwhile causes, none of which appeared to have preeminent importance. To substitute for lost unity, some party leaders advocated program politics, and Joseph Chamberlain initiated the National Liberal Federation to provide an institutional umbrella for fixing priorities. Others, like John Morley, favoured a single issue which would unite the party because of its overriding importance. Gladstone's great ability as leader was his ceaseless arranging, ordering, and assessing of the relative weights of political subjects. More than anyone else, he was able to define the relationships of various questions, and, therefore, when he espoused a great cause, it was to "illuminate the surroundings."[13]

The government of 1880–5, however, was elected on a great negative issue. Concentrating on Disraeli's foreign policy, while it united them, had left the Liberals without a program, and the imperial and Irish crises that developed served to aggravate, rather than create, the disorder and confusion that already characterized the party leadership. There was no longer fundamental agreement on the meaning of progress, even among Radicals: "Constructive" Radicals wished to use the machinery of the state to promote social reform; "traditional" Radicals wished to minimize state interference. It was in this situation that Gladstone began to regard the Irish question as having such force and magnitude as to assert precedence over everything else. When certain sections of the party, notably the Whigs and Chamberlain Radicals, opposed Home Rule to the point of schism, Gladstone was convinced that it was better for the party to split on an issue of political conscience rather than remain united. Great national causes, he believed, needed the Liberal party for fulfilment – the Tories constituting the party of repose – while the Liberal party needed to devote itself to great national causes, if it were to subdue the divisive forces within itself.

Rosebery had welcomed Home Rule as a way of uniting the party enthusiastically behind a great principle. He had also welcomed it because Gladstone maintained that its importance made it impossible to decide questions of priority among other questions. As long as Ireland dominated domestic politics, in other words, Rosebery would be permitted to retain control of foreign policy in any Liberal government. The first skirmish on the Triple Alliance question was a preliminary sign that this formula was disappearing. First, as the details of Home Rule came in for more discussion following 1886, the party leaders found themselves increasingly divided on matters of detail. In Rosebery's imperialist conception of Home Rule, it was essential that Irish MPs should continue to sit at Westminster; others, determined to avoid Irish obstruction in the future, wished to exclude them. Second, the party was increasingly disenchanted with the Irish preoccupation, and most of the leaders were forced to associate themselves with the Newcastle Programme, containing a wide variety of measures designed to appeal to non-Irish voters. Third, the Parnell divorce case in 1880, which split the Irish party itself, dealt a blow to Home Rule and consequently removed the "Irish obstruction" as an excuse for concentrating entirely on the Irish question.

The return of disorganization in Liberal politics, the reemergence of rampant and uncontrollable sectionalism, reached its peak with Gladstone's retirement in 1894. Before that, however, beginning with the new Liberal government in August 1892, Home Rule had already lost its usefulness in controlling Gladstone, so far as Rosebery was concerned. As it was obvious that the new Home Rule bill was certain to be defeated in the House of Lords, Gladstone was less willing to ignore other questions in which he was interested, like Egypt and the continental alliance system. Moreover, as Ireland receded and other questions moved to the front, the leadership of the party began to contest the control of future policies. Local option, land reform, Welsh and Scottish disestablishment, workmen's compensation, were some of the measures espoused by party leaders who regarded one or more as their special cause. Rosebery, who continued to regard foreign policy as his specialty and was determined to retain control of it, and Harcourt, equally determined that the party, not an individual, should control policy, briefly confronted one another in an affair that indicated the manner in which this contest was to be fought.

Lord Salisbury, in May 1890, announced that Britain had agreed to give Heligoland, a tiny island in the North Sea forty miles from the German coast, to Germany. In exchange, Britain was to receive much of the Nyasa-Tanganyika plateau to add to its sphere in East Africa. James Bryce, Rosebery's under-secretary for foreign affairs in 1886, had been looking for a foreign policy issue on which to attack Salisbury. Earlier in the year he had warned Rosebery that the Radicals were complaining that they did not "go for" Salisbury sufficiently on matters of foreign policy. "It is all very well," Bryce complained, "but he hasn't given us much chance. Opposition can't always have the luck of 1876–1879. Hadn't we better concoct something to attack him about when the session opens?"[14] Continuity in foreign policy clashed with control of the party, and continuity was to suffer. When the Heligoland agreement was announced, Bryce and Rosebery prepared to ask critical questions of the government. Harcourt disagreed. He approved of Salisbury's policy as "the most effectual reversal of the Beaconsfield policy of 1879."[15] Bryce was able to buy Harcourt's silence only at the price of absenting himself from the House when the question came up. "The odd state of the party in the Commons," he warned Rosebery, "will give the next Liberal Ministry some trouble."[16]

Harcourt was fighting to establish the principle that the party, meaning Liberal members of Parliament, controlled foreign policy. "I cannot admit the right of a single member of the party to appear to commit us at this crucial moment to an opposite opinion," he told

Gladstone. "I fear we are fundamentally at issue with Rosebery on these questions, and if it is so I think the sooner we make up our minds the better."[17] This foray presaged Harcourt's strategy for the next five years. His strength came from his position in the Commons, where he was second only to Gladstone. If Rosebery, isolated in the Lords, could be represented as conducting a policy of his own, and thereby alienating the party from the leadership, effective control of policy might be given to Harcourt, who would then become the obvious successor to Gladstone. But a meeting of the former cabinet showed that the tactic was a failure. Rosebery came to the meeting prepared to speak his mind, "and give it straight to Harcourt," but, when Harcourt sensed that his colleagues would fail to support him, he shut up completely, showed no sign of fight, and tried to make out that there had been no difference of opinion.[18]

Harcourt's strategy might have been a reasonable one, but his fumbling tactics always destroyed any advantage that he enjoyed. In the case of Heligoland, Rosebery had not even expressed an opinion; Harcourt had flown into a rage over the question Bryce had proposed to ask, assuming that he had been acting on Rosebery's behalf. All Harcourt had achieved in the Heligoland incident, however, was to warn Rosebery of his strategy and irritate his colleagues.

Rosebery responded with a strategy of his own. He called the earl of Spencer and John Morley, the two members of the former cabinet most devoted to Home Rule, to a meeting to discuss Ireland and Harcourt. He showed them Harcourt's letter to Gladstone, in which Harcourt had stated that "compared with this issue the Irish question is one of insignificant importance."[19] Harcourt, with characteristic abandon, had claimed this to be Morley's view. Spencer and Morley agreed that a thorough understanding and communication on essential points would give the next government that validity and consistency which it was otherwise likely to want, "otherwise Harcourt would lead the Cabinet such a dance as would discredit us."[20] By way of contrast with Harcourt, who appeared ready to abandon Home Rule, Rosebery appeared steady, and prepared to act in accord with Spencer and Morley. Rosebery's strategy was to act quietly, remain a good colleague, and resist the temptation to infringe on matters more closely connected with other departments.

Control of foreign policy was never far from Rosebery's mind, and in fact it was a consideration intrinsic to his strategy on political matters. The more Rosebery considered the future, Eddie Hamilton noted, "the more he is convinced that the real rub ahead will be between him and Harcourt holding such directly contrary views as they do on foreign and colonial matters." He was anxious, therefore, to try and make "a sort of small ring by way of protection against Harcourt, out of such men as Morley, Spencer and Fowler." The secret of success at the Foreign Office, Rosebery was convinced, was "to act off your own bat and to carry your Ministerial life in your hand in the event of the disapproval by the Cabinet of your acts."[21] Foreign policy was an essential element in late Victorian Liberal politics, and as long as Rosebery was determined to control policy, he was involved in political intrigue.

In the midst of these manoeuvres and calculations for the future, Lady Rosebery died, and the dark side of Rosebery's nature immediately began to take control. Before 1890 his character was complex and often puzzling. At one moment he would appear gay, energetic, and witty, entertaining small groups of friends and keeping large audiences on the edge of their seats. Then he would retreat into the solitude of his Scottish castle, or invite friends to one of his houses and then disappear from view. Before the death of his wife, while he stated that he would prefer to live outside politics, he increasingly immersed himself in its inner workings; after her death he resolved to leave politics altogether. Lady Rosebery's love and devotion had provided the foundation that enabled Rosebery, never the object of much personal affection, to enter the public arena. Her death removed his support, and part of his motive. Naturally melancholic, he became morbidly so, using black-bordered paper for the rest of his life, and fasting alone on the anniversary of her death. He had always had difficulty sleeping, but in his agony it became a medical problem, tormenting him whenever public life added to his misery.[22]

Rosebery's closest friends feared the effect of his retirement and urged him to remain in public life, if only for the sake of his mental health. They feared, quite reasonably, that he would withdraw into himself, doing nothing and seeing no one, and they hoped that politics would gradually draw him back into the open. For more than a year Rosebery avoided all political activity and practically all social engagements. Randolph Churchill, with troubles of his own, urged Rosebery to return.[23] James Bryce declared that he did not care to make "any further effort either for the Liberal Party, or to secure a seat in the House of Commons, unless I feel sure that the ideas for which I care have some place in Liberal Councils." "My action," he said, "in its humble way, depends upon yours."[24] Rosebery responded to these, and to other pleas, by fleeing the country: "in England, it seems, I cannot be left alone. I only ask to be ignored and forgotten: for a time at any rate."[25]

Rosebery, almost against his will, and certainly against his judgment, could not keep himself from holding out the hope that he might return to politics. He did nothing to stop the flow of information on inner politics, especially the flood produced by his young Scottish ally, Ronald Munro-Ferguson, and he continued tutoring Gladstone on the proper attitude to be taken with respect to the Triple Alliance.[26] He reflected in his biography of Pitt, written about this time, that "men who pine for unofficial repose dread the painful process of quitting office – the triumph of enemies and the discomfiture of friends and the wrench of habit – as men weary of life fear the actual process of death."[27] During the general election held in the summer of 1892, he convinced himself that he could assist his friends and perhaps defeat his enemies, by making some speeches on behalf of the Liberal party, but he maintained at the same time that he would not return to office. To those who insisted that "the management of Foreign Affairs can be trusted to you &. to you alone," he replied that there was Lord Kimberley, who would do "very well."[28]

Kimberley, however, who reflected the attitude of many of the party's leaders, feared Rosebery's absence would weaken the Liberal government, not only because he was the most acceptable person for the Foreign Office, but because he was, next to Gladstone, "by far the most influential man in the country of our party."[29] When a Liberal victory in the election appeared to be imminent, Kimberley joined Spencer in trying to persuade Rosebery to come into the government as foreign secretary. Their pleas undoubtedly moved him and served to reassure him of the position he held in the party, but still more flattering to his vanity were the attempts of the queen, the prince of Wales, the editor of the *Times*, and Salisbury to convince him of the country's need.[30] As it has been shown, from the beginning of his political career Rosebery had seen himself as a man above party, a man who served the interests of the whole empire, regardless of region or class. Moreover, he preferred to think of himself, not as a career politician, but as someone who responded to the needs of his country. In August 1892, therefore, Rosebery was torn between his wish to retire from politics and his desire to do his duty. "Is there not a call of duty, of friendship, of affection which is stronger than your own will ...?" Spencer asked.[31]

Rosebery's hesitation in accepting office in 1892 has led some to see him as carrying out a calculated political manoeuvre, using his strong political position to extract from Gladstone the promise of a free hand in foreign policy.[32] This view, based on a mistaken interpretation of the characters of both Gladstone and Rosebery, is false. Rosebery would undoubtedly have liked a free hand: he always believed the disasters of the Granville regime to have been caused by the cabinet's interfering, while his own success in 1886 would not have been possible had he contended with the same degree of interference. Nevertheless, he realized that there was no possibility of his being given a free hand, as such an arrangement would violate Gladstone's deepest beliefs in the constitutional roles of the prime minister and his cabinet. If Rosebery joined the government he had to be prepared for bitter disagreements: Gladstone and Harcourt had already demonstrated that their views on the Triple Alliance, Egypt, and parliamentary control of foreign policy differed from his own, while Sir Charles Dilke had announced, during the summer election campaign, his intention of raising the Egyptian question in Parliament. Without an agreement that would give him a free hand, and without the assurance that the Irish question would lead Gladstone to ignore foreign affairs, Rosebery would face a much more difficult situation at the Foreign Office, with respect to the cabinet, than he had in 1886. Already less enthusiastic about politics following the death of his wife, it is not surprising that he should hesitate to resume office in 1892, given the obvious difficulties that lay ahead.

When Rosebery overcame his reluctance and finally, after much prodding, agreed to return to the Foreign Office on 18 August 1892, he was prepared for trouble, and, as a result, questions of foreign policy immediately assumed a new meaning. The questions arising in the early months of the new government's life were not debated strictly on their merits: Rosebery, Gladstone, and Harcourt were competing for control of policy, and the method by which a decision was reached might be more important than the decision itself.

Gladstone wasted no time demonstrating his interest in foreign policy, and proving that Rosebery was not to have a free hand. On 26 August he seized upon a dispatch from the ambassador in Rome as an opportunity to complain of not being informed as to Salisbury's Mediterranean policy, his Egyptian policy, and any agreements or engagements that Italy had entered into concerning the Mediterranean.[33] This single note, written in the government's first week, probed more deeply into foreign policy than anything Gladstone had done in 1886. He opposed the Triple Alliance because he believed it increased the likelihood of war by dividing Europe into armed camps. The British should certainly stay out of it, he argued, because it would commit them in advance to war in Europe, and they should encourage the Italians to stay out of it too. The alliance was obviously aimed at the French, but the proper way to forestall French enmity, according to Gladstone, was to remove its cause, not to build up a league against France. Gladstone's attitude to the Triple Alliance was directly linked to his attitude to the occupation of Egypt, as he believed that evacuation would restore good relations with the French and make unnecessary an agreement with the Triple Alliance. At the same time, if the British drew closer to the alliance, they would increase French enmity and make the evacuation of Egypt more difficult. In raising this question, Gladstone gave notice to Rosebery of his determination to pursue his policy of evacuating Egypt and restoring friendly relations with France.

Rosebery was equally determined to have the British remain in Egypt, or, if they left, to do so with the right to reenter, should the Egyptian government prove unstable.[34] In other words, his attitude had remained unchanged since 1885-6, when he had defined British paramountcy in Egypt as a primary aim of his foreign policy. At that time he had portrayed the French as the most important rivals of the British, and the increased naval program that they had undertaken in the Mediterranean did nothing to dissuade him from this view. Therefore, after one week in office, he had to develop a scheme to forestall Gladstone's plan for leaving Egypt, accommodating the French, and rejecting a working relationship with the Triple Alliance.

Rosebery began by passing over Salisbury's relations with Italy as if they had formed an inconsequential part of his diplomacy. Salisbury, he said, had assured him that he had promised no material assistance to the Italians, and besides, whatever promises Salisbury might have given could only have been personal ones.[35] In any case, other matters were certainly more pressing, Rosebery said. He took this line knowing that Salisbury regarded Italy as the key to Britain's relations with Europe, because it connected Britain with the Triple Alliance. If the British gave any indication of preferring the French to the Italians in the event of a conflict, the Italians would very likely abandon the Triple Alliance and go over to the French. This being the case, the Austrians and Germans would feel themselves too weak to withstand a Franco-Russian attack, so the Germans would offer themselves to the Russians by acquiescing in their designs on Constantinople; the Austrians would likely receive the rest of Turkey-in-Europe, as far as Salonica. Having the French and Italians allied in the Mediterranean, the Russians established in Constantinople, and the Austrians controlling the Balkans was not a prospect likely to induce optimism in British official thinking. Salisbury believed that Italy, if she felt certain of British protection, would remain in the Triple Alliance, maintaining simultaneously the status quo in both Europe and the Mediterranean.[36]

Unlike Salisbury, with whose formula he agreed, Rosebery had to deal with Gladstone, and therefore found himself in the awkward position of carrying out a policy while attempting to hide the reasons for it. The Liberals had not governed for six years, so no one in the cabinet was officially committed to a particular policy when it came to relations with the Triple Alliance. Nevertheless, of the senior members of the government, Gladstone, Harcourt, and Morley were publicly committed to evacuating Egypt at the first opportunity. Evacuating Egypt, however, meant improving relations with France, which, according to Salisbury, meant the end of the Triple Alliance and all kinds of new problems for Britain. During the first months of the new government, therefore, Rosebery said very little about grand strategy, but tried to demonstrate to the members of the Triple Alliance his determination to follow Salisbury's lead. At the same time, he tried to gauge where individual members of the cabinet stood on questions of foreign policy, in order to anticipate from which directions support for, and opposition to, his policies was likely to come, and how strong each was likely to be.

Rosebery is often accused of having been more fervently anti-French than Salisbury, an accusation certainly at the bottom of the distrust of his policy felt by Gladstone, Harcourt, and Morley. In fact, he was no more a francophobe than Salisbury, who had constructed his European and Mediterranean policies on the assumption of continuing French enmity. "The popular prejudice is too strong," he told Rosebery in August 1892, for France ever to be agreeable to England.[37] At the moment, he said, she was most aggressive in West Africa, and would probably become so in Morocco; she was as troublesome as she could be in Egypt, while hindering Britain as much as she could at Constantinople; she was also hostile in Uganda and Zanzibar.

Rosebery concurred in Salisbury's judgment and accepted his conclusion that France required constant vigilance, but he seldom committed this view to paper. In order to achieve his objectives Rosebery had to act as if distrust of the French had nothing to do with his policy, and consequently his letters and memoranda to the cabinet are full of the kind of reasons he thought they were likely to accept; we should not be misled into thinking that these documents reflect his real views. More revealing was the attitude he expressed privately to those within the inner circle of diplomacy. French colonial adventurers like Mizon, who was about to embark on a mission to West Africa, were troublesome, he told Dufferin, because "Mizon is an intractable, coarse-grained, determined man, and I shall be surprised if there is not a row."[38]

The immediate problem confronting Rosebery in mid-August 1892, then, was how to find a way to reassure Italy and the Triple Alliance of his intention to follow Salisbury's lead in continuing to work with them against the French, yet at the same time allow Gladstone to continue to believe in the possibility of evacuating Egypt and restoring good relations with the French. To convince Gladstone, he attempted to pass lightly over Salisbury's promises to Italy, pretending they were inconsequential; he combined this with a manoeuvre designed to overwhelm Gladstone with a series of other questions that he made out to be of the greatest significance. The attempt failed, and Gladstone continued to demand that Rosebery tell him exactly what Salisbury had promised the Italians. Rosebery, who avoided telling him for two weeks, decided, on 31 August, that it was more dangerous to leave him in the dark than to tell him. He probably would have decided differently had Salisbury's assurances to the Italians not been ambiguous.

Salisbury had not committed Britain to provide the Italians with material assistance; he had, however, agreed with Italy to maintain the status quo in the Mediterranean and to consult her if circumstances arose that threatened it.[39] Gladstone could hardly object to this agreement, as it committed Britain to nothing and was predicated upon her friendship with Italy. This part of the contest for the control of policy, therefore, went undecided. What the agreement with Italy meant for the future course of British policy had to wait upon events; Rosebery continued to use it as an arrangement against France, while Gladstone saw no reason why it should forestall his attempt to restore good relations with her.

Rosebery did what he could to assure the Triple Alliance of his intention to adhere to Salisbury's connection, undertaking to consult the Italians in the event of the Mediterranean status quo being threatened. But with the Triple Alliance, as with the cabinet, Rosebery faced a more difficult situation than had Salisbury. Because the members of the Triple Alliance generally, and the Germans particularly, distrusted the intentions of Gladstonian Liberals, they wanted, ironically, a greater commitment from them than they had received from the Tories.[40] Rosebery refused to give it. While he agreed to uphold the principles of the Mediterranean agreement with Italy, he refused to offer assistance to the Italians unless the French attacked them "groundlessly," and, like Salisbury, he would not commit the government in advance. The Italians, he argued, because they would have to rely on the sympathy of the British people, must understand that the circumstances in which a collision took place would be critical.[41] Rosebery, in other words, was prepared to offer Italy protection against France only if Italy behaved like a defensive power, upholding the status quo.

In refusing to commit himself any farther than Salisbury had done, Rosebery demonstrated an added complication in Britain's relations with Italy and the Triple Alliance. His first aim in the Mediterranean was to uphold the status quo, but doing so required the cooperation of Italy, who was commonly regarded as an acquisitive, aggressive power. Any outright guarantees of forthcoming assistance, therefore, might have the opposite effect to the one desired: Italy might take the initiative in provoking a war with France. Rosebery wanted to avoid war, especially in the Mediterranean, where, the Admiralty now believed, France would soon be in a position to challenge Britain. Although the Admiralty was divided on the question of relative naval strength, and consequently on the strategy to be followed, most experts believed that it might be necessary, for a time at least, to abandon the Mediterranean to the French, if the French had the assistance of Russia.[42] There were, therefore, practical reasons for the refusal of Rosebery and Salisbury to commit themselves to Italy in advance of the event of war: they both believed the Italian connection to be critical to the British position in the Mediterranean and Europe, but the Italians were useful only insofar as their taste for acquisitions could be controlled; and forcing them to rely on British public opinion was the best instrument that could be devised for exerting control.

The members of the Triple Alliance were not pleased with the position taken by Rosebery, and for the next three years they attempted, through a series of controversial, and sometimes contradictory, measures, to have him commit Britain more clearly to the side of the Triple Alliance. Rosebery's policies, both when he was foreign secretary and later when he was prime minister, must be considered against this background. The scene of his policies shifted continually from Africa to central Asia to the Far East; nothing very striking occurred in Europe, yet his policies in Uganda and Morocco, the Pamirs and Persia, Siam and China, hinged on the state of European relations, particularly on Britain's relations with the Triple Alliance. The form these relations took varied considerably over the next three years, but the objective, on both sides, remained substantially the same. Rosebery was satisfied with the way things stood in Europe, and intended, by continuing to work with the Triple Alliance, to see that they remained the same; the Triple Alliance, however, grew increasingly suspicious of the British attitude, and attempted to force her into joining the alliance as a full partner.

At the centre of the competition between Britain and the Triple Alliance over the terms of the connection between them lay the developing Franco-Russian alliance. The Germans, fearing that this relationship was aimed against them, tried to protect themselves by drawing Britain into the Triple Alliance. They tried to do this by

showing Rosebery how the French and the Russians were cooperating against the British in Africa and Asia. Rosebery, however, believing the Franco-Russian accord to be aimed at Germany, felt he need
not fear it as long as the Triple Alliance remained intact; what he did
fear was a state of affairs in which one alliance would lead to a
breakdown of the other and a consequent realignment of European
diplomacy, in which Britain would likely suffer. To keep Britain out of
the alliance, Rosebery attempted to demonstrate to its members her
ability to proceed without their assistance, and at the same time he
tried to demonstrate his continuing desire to work with them.

France and Russia, as a matter of fact, were themselves competing
to determine the nature of their alliance, and, in August 1892, the
outcome of the competition had not yet been decided. Although a
military convention had been drafted in that month, committing
Russia to the French view of the alliance as one aimed at Germany in
Europe, the tsar had not yet approved the convention, continuing to
hope it could be used against Britain.[43] Therefore, in the months
following August, every diplomatic question took on an added significance, as the great powers of Europe tried to decipher what it really
meant and convince others of the validity of their interpretation.
Rosebery knew little of the actual state of negotiations between France
and Russia; his ambassador in St Petersburg, Sir Robert Morier,
seemed unaware that anything was afoot.[44]

The first issue to arise that diplomats tried to decipher came to be
known as the Pamirs question. During the summer of 1892 reports
reached London of a Russian military expedition to the headwaters
of the Oxus, a small piece of extremely mountainous terrain, apparently belonging to Afghanistan but also claimed by the Chinese, which
separated the British and Russian empires in central Asia. The reports
received from this remote land were confusing, and, when Rosebery
took office, the only thing of which he could be certain was that an
unknown number of Russians had fired some shots at an unknown
number of Afghans. What caused the incident, who had the right to
be where, and what the incident implied for Anglo-Russian relations
remained to be seen.[45]

Rosebery's first reaction demonstrated his preoccupation with
cabinet politics: he tried to use it in distracting Gladstone's attention
from the Mediterranean. On 30 August, when Gladstone admitted he
had never heard of the Pamirs, Rosebery began swamping him with
information. Reports of missions, maps of prior agreements, and
detailed information on conversations with Russian officials were
dispatched from the Foreign Office with increasing frequency, while
reports on Italy and the Mediterranean were kept to a minimum. At

the same time, Rosebery attempted to place events in a setting familiar to Gladstone. The Russians, he said, send an expedition, then deny they have sent it, but claim circumstances have changed and that they will send a small one; it then clashes with the Afghans and the expedition turns out to have been a large one.[46] Rosebery, by portraying the situation in this hypothetical way, was able to create a bleak picture without relying on evidence; the acting minister at St Petersburg estimated the size of the Russian expedition to be between fifty and one hundred men; Rosebery told Gladstone that the figure was closer to two thousand. In fact, Rosebery admitted privately, the situation was not alarming, but he did his best to alarm Gladstone, mainly by making events appear to be leading to a repetition of the Penjdeh crisis of 1885.[47] If he could convince Gladstone of his ability to save the government from another humiliation, he might be left alone to conduct his own diplomacy elsewhere, as had been the case in the Balkans in 1886. And, as in the Balkans in 1886, Rosebery attempted to have his policy appear to be Gladstone's, in this case by proposing a joint commission of inquiry, always a favourite with Gladstone. The tactic succeeded, and Gladstone was soon involved in drafting instructions and considering Rosebery's proposals.[48] The Mediterranean was almost forgotten.

While Rosebery manoeuvred to draw Gladstone's attention away from the Mediterranean, where he could cause great difficulties, to the Pamirs, where he could do little, another manoeuvre, equally complicated, was also going on. Those men directly involved in defending India were competing to win Rosebery's support for their policy. Men like Lord Lansdowne, viceroy of India, Lord Kimberley, secretary of state for India, Sir Robert Morier, ambassador to St Petersburg, and General Brackenbury, formerly director of Military Intelligence and now a member of the Viceroy's Council, did not regard the Pamirs question as a minor, local affair whose main importance lay in diverting attention from the Mediterranean. Instead, they regarded the situation as one more piece in the century-long puzzle of trying to defend India. The Pamirs question, therefore, in which Rosebery had sought refuge from discussions concerning British relations with the Triple Alliance, soon became caught up in considerations of grand strategy.

Sir Robert Morier minimized the consequences of the Russian expedition. He discounted the report of Colonel Swaine, the British military attaché in Berlin, who had categorized the Russian expedition as a tremendous one. Swaine, he assured Rosebery, was "the most inveterate fly gobbler and flyer of canards on the planet."[49] According to Morier, the Russians had no intention of invading India at the moment, especially as they were on the verge of bankruptcy.[50] What the Russians wanted, he said, was the southeast corner between Wakhan and the Chinese frontier, to enable them to sweep into Hunza.[51] Morier believed that the way to improve Anglo-Russian relations was to establish a defensible frontier in India; he had proposed such a policy to Salisbury at the beginning of the Pamirs affair, but Salisbury had rejected it; Morier now turned to Rosebery in the hope of convincing him that such a policy could lead to a permanent improvement in relations.

A defensible frontier was possible only if the required force was available to the British, and Morier believed that the section of the frontier from Chitral to Hunza was one of the few where Britain enjoyed a military advantage.[52] He was not deterred by the opposing view of experts. General Brackenbury dismissed Morier's assessment as unwarranted optimism. Britain's military superiority in the area was not only questionable: Russia probably enjoyed a decided advantage.[53] Russia's game, according to Brackenbury, was to draw Britain beyond the Hindu Kush, stretch her communications, and leave her to occupy an indefensible frontier. This interpretation of Russia's intentions fitted into a wider view of foreign policy proposed by Brackenbury. A Russian invasion of India, he argued, was not imminent. Forward movements on the part of the British in India, by making conflict more likely under less advantageous conditions, assisted the Russians, who could then use the situation in India to win concessions elsewhere. The Indian government, which, he said, was led by Lord Roberts to favour a forward policy in Afghanistan, "cannot look beyond their own immediate horizon. They think of Russia as if she had no European frontier, no Triple Alliance to consider, no Eastern Question in Europe present to her eye and as if her one aim and object was the conquest of India."[54] Brackenbury and Morier, who were agreed on Russia's intending no immediate invasion, disagreed on how the Pamirs question was related to long-term strategy.

Rosebery, obviously, was going to be forced to choose between the assessments of Morier and Brackenbury, but the choice, at this stage, was not between a policy of firmness and a policy of conciliation, but between areas where the Russians might be stopped. Morier proposed to stop them along the frontier, employing superior military force, while Brackenbury proposed to stop them by threatening repercussions in Europe, because the Russians enjoyed a military advantage along the Indian frontier. This debate, on where Russia might best be stopped, had been going on at least since the time of the Napoleonic Wars, and had most recently been the subject of bitter debate between Britain's two leading military men, generals Roberts and Wolseley. Roberts, advocating a forward policy, believed Russia had to be stopped in Asia, and he saw Afghanistan as the best place to do it. Wolseley, in contrast, believing Russia would always be stronger than Britain in Asia, envisaged a British attack through the Straits and into the Black Sea, where Russia was both accessible and vulnerable.[55] If Rosebery were to take a firm line in responding to Russia's move into the Pamirs, he could then use the Indian army on the frontier, or threaten Russia with naval action in the Black Sea.

By September 1892 Rosebery regarded the Wolseley-Brackenbury strategy as no longer a practical possibility. Russia's new Black Sea fleet had transformed the Eastern Question, as Britain had now to consider the likelihood of a Russian attack on Constantinople. The Admiralty, which argued that the Mediterranean fleet could not prevent such a catastrophe, was still willing, should an attack occur, to force the Straits. Unfortunately, it was prepared to do so only given certain conditions: Britain could not force the Straits and attack Russia in the Black Sea if she had, simultaneously, to defend herself against the French Mediterranean fleet. Thus the Franco-Russian alliance transformed Britain's strategy in the Mediterranean, and, along with it, her ability to defend India.

Brackenbury's successor at the War Office, General Chapman, assured him on 8 September that, "if we wished it we *can't* undertake anything against Russia through the Black Sea: her fleet has steadily increased and until after a naval action in which the naval power of France has been paralysed we cannot move a man."[56] Additionally, a war with France would render the Mediterranean useless for communications with India; the troop-ships would have to go by the more costly and slower Cape route.[57] Thus the possibility of France and Russia cooperating in the Mediterranean necessitated a new strategy, or at least a new variation of the Wolseley strategy, if that of Roberts was not to be adopted.

Rosebery had already portrayed the situation as a dangerous one, and had thereby succeeded in focusing the attention of Gladstone on the Pamirs. He had succeeded by taking a moderate line and creating an Anglo-Russian commission of inquiry. Rosebery believed, in fact, in the opposite: the advance placed Britain in no immediate danger, but it would be most difficult to bring the Russians to negotiate. Thus, while appearing to advocate moderation, he had hinted, as early as 26 August, at the possibility of a British expedition to parallel the Russian. The new situation in the Mediterranean meant that there was no alternative to the threat of a local response, forcing Rosebery into a position where he had to rely on the government of India if the Russians were to be compelled to negotiate.

Relations between the Foreign Office and the government of India were usually strained, since they saw the problem of defending British India from different perspectives. Men at the Foreign Office had always to consider how India's frontiers would influence the European balance of power, and, for Rosebery, in August 1892, this consideration meant that a crisis with Russia would play into the hands of the Triple Alliance by showing the Franco-Russian alliance to be aimed at British interests in Asia, Africa, and the Far East. The most alarming reports of the size and aims of the Russian expedition to the Pamirs came from Berlin. Rosebery, therefore, tried to keep the Pamirs question a local one, not only because Britain could no longer threaten Russia in Europe, but to demonstrate to the Triple Alliance his ability to settle imperial problems without European assistance. The viceroy and his council, however, thought British interests in Europe were secondary to those in India; the European balance of power was, in fact, for them, a device for defending India, although not necessarily the best one. In this situation it was not surprising to see London and Calcutta become embroiled in one of those disputes that characterized British foreign and imperial policy throughout the nineteenth century.

Before the Liberal government took office in August 1892 the government of India had made preparations to send a mission, led by General Roberts, to the amir of Afghanistan. The amir had, during the past year, encroached upon Indian territory in Wano, Chageh, and Asmar, and repeatedly refused to be controlled by the government of India in his relations with Russia.[58] Roberts was to give the amir the guidance he needed: Afghan troops were to evacuate the contested areas while Calcutta resumed control of Afghan foreign policy. The Liberal government, with Rosebery at the Foreign Office and Kimberley at the India Office, feared that Roberts would succeed only in driving the amir into the arms of the tsar so they insisted that the mission be postponed.[59] The viceroy, Lord Lansdowne, immediately threatened to resign.

Lansdowne regarded Afghanistan as the most crucial element in the defence of India. Like earlier adherents to the Bombay school, he believed that India should be defended as far away as possible from the centres of population because the real threat posed by Russia was that of inciting rebellion. A Russian attack, coming as it must through Afghanistan, was best met far to the north, along the Oxus, which in 1873 had been agreed upon as Afghanistan's northern frontier. Afghanistan would, however, fulfil her purpose only if she agreed to be guided by the British and, to Lansdowne, guidance meant control. Thus, when the Liberal government insisted that he postpone indefinitely the Roberts mission, he regarded the decision as an attack on a fundamental policy, and his threat to resign was less a fit of personal pique than an attempt to force the government to change its mind.

Rosebery gave no indication of seeing the possibility of political difficulties in the Pamirs question and, in fact, Lansdowne backed down before the matter reached the cabinet, thereby postponing a political controversy over policy in central Asia. Kimberley handled Lansdowne tactfully but firmly, refusing to allow Roberts to proceed, but agreeing to send a mission sometime in the future.[60] Lansdowne reluctantly agreed to the compromise, using the amir's evacuation of Wano as a sign of good faith. But, while an immediate political crisis was avoided, the contest between London and Calcutta for control of policy in India became more devious and more difficult.

The Liberals agreed to compromise on the mission to Kabul because they believed that time would enable them to control the danger; properly conducted, the mission might not drive the amir onto the side of the Russians. The danger, as they saw it, was personal. Roberts, the foremost advocate on a forward policy, would, they assumed, treat the amir as a British vassal rather than as an ally. For this reason Lord Ripon, former viceroy of India, now colonial secretary, advised Kimberley, on 26 August, to remove Roberts at once.[61] Kimberley agreed. When Lansdowne requested to have Roberts stay on for another term in India, Kimberley responded by asking Henry Campbell-Bannerman, the secretary for war, to find some excuse of military protocol to refuse the request. Roberts, he said, "is the very powerful representative of a foward policy which has gone very far already and if it goes on, may involve us in serious dangers."[62] The Liberal government, which was to divide on almost every issue of foreign policy over the next three years, stood united on India and Afghanistan. Rosebery, Gladstone, Kimberley, Ripon, and Campbell-Bannerman opposed anything resembling a forward policy when they took office, and set out to destroy it by removing its most outspoken advocate. Removing Roberts proved easy; removing his influence proved impossible.

Lansdowne, who would not give up his control of Indian defence policy without a fight, decided to use the incident in the Pamirs to demonstrate the validity of his policy. India had to exert more direct control on Afghanistan, he argued, because the amir was too weak to be relied on and too devious to be trusted.[63] Instead of worrying about making a contented ally of the amir, the British should be seeking to add permanently to their political and strategic strength on the frontier. The government of India had warned the amir not to advance north of the Oxus, but he had refused their advice, and the Pamirs incident was the result. Moreover, the amir's actions displayed his weakness: he was driven to such extremities by the need to demonstrate his power to his subjects.[64] Therefore, according to Lansdowne, relying upon the amir as an ally meant relying on someone too weak to be useful, someone whose weakness would succeed only in embroiling the British in unnecessary conflicts with the Russians. Opposing the Roberts-Lansdowne policy would, in this view, land the British in even more serious difficulties: the amir would try to expand his territories, and the British would be reluctantly drawn into defending him against the Russians.

This argument, although it carried a certain amount of weight, failed to convince Rosebery. The Pamirs affair, which was to drag on for more than two years, was useful to him in the first instance because it diverted attention from the Mediterranean. Furthermore, anticipating greater political difficulties ahead, he had good reason to welcome the unanimity of Liberal opinion on the subject. Lastly, and most important in understanding his relations with Lansdowne and the government of India, he was determined to show the Triple Alliance that he could, without relying on its assistance, and without Britain becoming a member of it, take a firm stand against the Russians in Asia, and yet improve relations with them. To do this, Rosebery had to force the Russians to sit down and negotiate a settlement in the Pamirs by threatening them with a parallel expedition.[65] The whole incident would then be used to display Britain's strength in Asia, and her ability to get on amicably with the Russians.

Ironically, then, Rosebery and Kimberley found themselves in the position of forcing a forward policy on the government of India, because Lansdowne, on 1 September, refused to authorize a British expedition to the Pamirs. Using the government's arguments against them, he dismissed such an expedition as too dangerous and too costly. "I am," Lansdowne declared, "altogether averse to gratuitous extensions of our territory, or our liabilities."[66] Rosebery and Morier, who had already given hints to the Russians of their intention to respond with an expedition, never suspecting the government of India might oppose such an advance, were incensed. "If at this early date their teeth begin to chatter and they already see ghosts," Morier declared, "the chances of a successful negotiation at St Petersburg are cast to the winds."[67] Few incidents demonstrate so strikingly the connections between European and Asiatic policies, between domestic and foreign politics, as the difficulties involved in conducting a clear and consistent policy in an affair as apparently distant from Europe, and British domestic politics, as that in the Pamirs.

With the threat of a parallel expedition removed, Rosebery sought another method of preventing a Russian advance. The Russians and the Chinese had agreed to a protocol in 1884, which had drawn the frontier between them directly south from Uzbel giving the Chinese possession of the strategic passes. If the Chinese could be induced to hold this line, then Britain's position in the north could be safeguarded without relying on the Afghans, and perhaps without sending a military expedition. Rosebery therefore undertook a third initiative, but this time one more diplomatic and perhaps easier to control.

Indian officials, however, were no more enamoured of this manoeuvre than they had been of the first two. Even Kimberley, who had stood with Rosebery against Lansdowne on the question of the mission to Kabul, was dismayed by the prospect of relying on China, which was, he said, a "broken reed."[68] Her armed forces in the Pamirs were practically nonexistent: a small force of Afghans had easily turned them out of Somotash. This event was hardly surprising, as the region was of little strategic value to the Chinese: the Russians and the British controlled better routes by which they might invade China, should they wish to invade. Economically, the region was worthless. Kimberley had good reason for supposing that the Chinese were not to be counted on.

Reports from India confirmed Kimberley's suspicions. The British agent at Gilgit reported that China had withdrawn her forces from the disputed territory, and this action, he believed, was simply a prelude to ceding the whole of the territory to Russia.[69] China, he argued, was not prepared to risk a conflict with Russia. Lansdowne suggested that the Chinese, even if some backbone could be put into them, were not really a significant improvement on the Afghans. "I have been constantly impressed," he told Kimberley, "by the inability of the Chinese to control their outlying dependencies; their hold over their local officials is very slight ... they are inconvenient neighbours."[70] His estimate suited his policy: the only reliable element in the situation was the military strength of the British Raj. The only convenient neighbours were vassals; independent allies might just as well be considered enemies. China, bigger than Afghanistan, and with a centre of power farther away, was impossible to control from Calcutta.

All of Lansdowne's arguments in the early days of the Pamirs affair were designed with a single purpose in mind. He was resolved to show Rosebery and Kimberley how foolish their refusal to reduce the amir's pretentions to independence had been. In other words, Afghanistan really was the most reliable element in the defence of the northeast frontier; the buffer principle still operated. But, in Lansdowne's view, the buffer had to be strictly controlled; the amir had to act as the vassal, not the ally, of Britain. Thus Lansdowne pointed to the expenses and difficulties involved in sending a parallel expedition to the Pamirs, but at the same time pointed to the awkwardness of substituting a Chinese alliance for the requisite military force.

These manoeuvres on the part of the viceroy made life at the Foreign Office rather difficult for Rosebery. He could not act too decisively against the Russians without antagonizing the russophiles in the Liberal party, which partly explains why he wanted to threaten a parallel expedition but why he had no intention of actually sending one. The manoeuvre was to be strictly diplomatic, but its success depended on the compliance of the government of India. At the same time Rosebery could not concede too much too soon to the Russians without lending credence to the argument of the Triple Alliance that Britain's weakness outside Europe would finally compel her to become a member. The question, "who faces the greater danger from France and Russia?" was at the back of every diplomatic tangle arising in these years. In the Pamirs, Rosebery had to show that Britain was entirely capable of meeting the Russian threat on her own. Better still, he would like to go farther and show that the two Asiatic powers might settle their differences; if such a settlement could be accomplished, it would be clear that the Triple Alliance faced the greater danger. Britain could then continue in her informal partnership with the alliance: she would enjoy the benefits of its existence without running its risks.

The ideal solution to the Pamirs question, as Rosebery saw it then, consisted of an amicable settlement arrived at through firm diplomacy. There was no hurry; the danger was not immediate – time was available in which the Chinese manoeuvre might, in spite of the misgivings of Lansdowne and Kimberley, be attempted. The fact that Chinese policy was controlled from Peking did not disturb London as it did Calcutta. The fact that the Chinese had more important interests outside central Asia gave the British an advantage, as far as Rosebery was concerned. As the Chinese had to worry about the Russians in Manchuria, the French in Indo-China, and the Japanese in Korea, it might prove useful to them to have a friendly Britain. Moreover, the Chinese were currently negotiating a settlement of the Burmese frontier, a region of some economic value when compared with the barren Pamirs. Thus Rosebery had good reason to believe that the Chinese might be induced to cooperate on the Pamirs question.

As Rosebery saw it, the Chinese combined two advantages; a strong legal position and a weak military force. Although weak, the Chinese possessed sufficient force to harass forward movements. As Kimberley remarked, "the example of Tonking shows what serious power of annoyance they can exercise on a frontier without any open quarrel."[71] Yet, as even Lansdowne conceded, they posed no threat to India.[72] Their legal position in the Pamirs was strong: the protocol of 1884 with Russia had conceded to them the strategic passes, and the Russians gave tacit recognition of the strength of this position when they promised to overlook the amir's violations of the 1872–3 agreement if the British would, in exchange, permit them to settle their frontier with the Chinese free of British interference. Rosebery took the cue. He promised to support the Chinese in their negotiations at St Petersburg. The Chinese promptly disavowed any intention of abandoning their claim to the disputed territory.[73]

Rosebery's difficulties with the government of India were not to disappear so promptly; they persisted, in fact, until the Liberals fell from power in the summer of 1895. For a time, Rosebery and other Liberals hoped the difficulties would end when Lansdowne was replaced with a Liberal viceroy, but the cabinet was in the process of discovering how arduous was the task of finding a suitable replacement. When they finally did appoint the earl of Elgin they discovered, in the Chitral affair of 1895, that having a Liberal viceroy was no guarantee of his cooperation. This was hardly surprising. The world viewed from Calcutta was quite different from the one seen from London.

Particularly different was the view of turbulence on the frontier. Men in Britain wished to avoid difficulties by acting as if India too were an island, hence their zeal for the principle of the buffer state: as the channel had protected Britain from attack, so might a desert or a barren mountain range do the same for India. Such a creation would avert the possibility of coming face-to-face with the enemy, a possibility that might precipitate hostilities. Men in India, by way of contrast, saw the Raj as a continental power that could not solve its problems by acting as if it were an island. They too subscribed to the buffer principle, but with a difference: buffers must be controlled and kept quiet. Afghanistan, Persia, and Burma were not like the English Channel, because they contained unruly inhabitants who had to be guarded against, who might provoke rebellion within India, or who might fall under the spell of a foreign government.

These differing views of the frontier explain an additional complication that arose once Rosebery had decided on his Chinese
manoeuvre. The territory at issue between Britain and China in their
Burmese negotiations, Kochin, had never been a part of the kingdom
of Burma. The Chinese undoubtedly hoped that cooperating with the
British in the Pamirs would result in their recognition of China's right
to it. The government of India, however, regarded Kochin as a strategically valuable piece of property, and one whose unruly tribes could
not be managed properly by the weak government of China. Although
the government of India had no legal right to the territory as Burma's
successor, they subscribed to the political principle that no territory
should be omitted from British control unless its omission was consistent with the safety of the frontier.[74] In accordance with this way of
thinking, they dispatched a military expedition to occupy Sadon, in
the heart of the disputed territory. This was not a move calculated to
improve relations with China. "It is a misfortune," remarked the head
of the eastern department at the Foreign Office, "that territorial claims
within the narrowest limits result only in fresh discoveries of their
officers of tempting districts which it is absolutely necessary to
grab."[75] Rosebery protested against further filibustering operations by
the government of India while he was attempting to negotiate with
the Chinese.[76] If his Chinese manoeuvre were to succeed, he would
have to find a way to control the government of India, a task that
many before him had found impossible.

Rosebery's principle of continuity, so useful in 1886, did not help,
and actually favoured Lansdowne, since the expedition to Sadon, like
the Roberts mission to Kabul, had been endorsed by Salisbury and
the secretary of state for India.[77] The Indian authorities were, as Sir
Philip Currie, permanent under-secretary at the Foreign Office, complained, determined to carry out their policy of "Grab" whether the
Foreign Office liked it or not.[78] Kimberley was enlisted in the attempt
to restrain Lansdowne: he agreed with Rosebery that China had the
ability to do great mischief along the frontier, and great good in the
Pamirs. He instructed Lansdowne to send no more missions and to
define the minimum requirement for a defensible frontier. This
Lansdowne refused to do; he would not admit that such a frontier
existed, not while territory remained beyond his control. Refusing to
define what frontier was necessary meant that the Liberal government would be forced to take the responsibility for any settlement.
The Tory party in general, and Lansdowne in particular, would be
relieved of the responsibility for future difficulties, while they could
claim that any success in the area was due to their earlier initiative.
But the conflict between Rosebery and Lansdowne ran deeper than

party politics: political compatibility had not prevented clashes between London and Calcutta in the past. Political differences succeeded only in increasing the tension. At bottom, the view of the frontier depended more on the vantage-point of the witness than on his politics.

Rosebery, it was becoming clear, was not going to find any quick solution to the problem of the Pamirs, and negotiations with Russia had scarcely begun by the end of 1892. Differences with the government of India had slowed the process, and, while diplomats complained of the meddling of Indian authorities "with the International business of which they don't know the ABC," there was little they could do to prevent it.[79] Irritating as this was, it did not cause Rosebery any great difficulty in 1892. As long as he managed to avoid an open confrontation with Russia, he would not have to abandon his principal objective – showing Germany that he could deal with the Russians without their assistance. The Pamirs question, after a few moments of fear in September, was settling into a tedium that removed it from the realm of cabinet politics; it dragged on for more than two years before it was resolved.

Rosebery's diplomacy during his first months back at the Foreign Office was a curious business. Most of his difficulties, and most of his negotiating, concerned not foreign governments, but the government of India and his own cabinet. The Foreign Office documents for the final months of 1892 reveal little of Rosebery's foreign policy; the main evidence of that policy is to be found elsewhere.

Equally curious, looking elsewhere has produced the myth that has enveloped Rosebery's foreign policy at least since 1895. Historians have followed the lead of many contemporaries in regarding cabinet conflict as the essential element in Rosebery's policy. The Cobdenites of the cabinet – Gladstone, Harcourt, and Morley – are supposed to have given Rosebery so much difficulty that they succeeded in enervating whatever policy he might have chosen to follow. Certainly the years 1892–5 were ones of bitter cabinet disputes, especially during the contest for leadership of the party produced by Gladstone's resignation. Historians who assume that men are incapable of fighting and working at the same time, who assume that politicians are unable to concentrate on four or five things at once, are mistaken. In the years 1892–5 Rosebery won every debate on foreign policy that reached the cabinet. How he won makes a fascinating, complicated story, but his having to play the game of cabinet politics should not mislead; he played for high stakes – control of Britain's foreign policy – and the result was a consistent and largely

successful diplomacy. But success in diplomacy brought with it failure in politics, and it has been the story of failure that has been told
ever since.

The first and most notorious problem in foreign and imperial affairs
that confronted the government was Uganda. The Imperial British
East Africa Company, which had recently gone bankrupt, had
declared its intention to evacuate Uganda. In an earlier financial
crisis, Salisbury had bolstered the company with a loan, but in 1892
he refused to do anything more for it. Consequently, the company
proposed to evacuate the country by 31 December. If the Liberal
government intended to intervene in this affair then they must do so
quickly, as communications took three months to reach Uganda. But
intervention seemed unlikely as Gladstone, Harcourt, and Morley
approved of the plan to evacuate.[80] The affair seemed settled, as
Rosebery's doctrine of continuity suggested that he would simply
follow Salisbury's lead.

Rather than follow this simple course, however, Rosebery undertook a campaign to reverse the decision to evacuate. He began by
arguing that the statements of Salisbury and Balfour had been misinterpreted. "It cannot be doubted that they would have held to
Uganda had they held on to office; but uncertain of their tenure, they
... preferred to leave this embarrassing question to their successor."[81]
He tried to avoid the appearance of contradicting the principle of
continuity, which was rather difficult under the circumstances. Fortunately, Tory statements on Uganda were sufficiently ambiguous to
allow Rosebery to reopen a question that had seemed to be closed.
And, in order to win this first contest in the cabinet, he was prepared
to cheat. Through Sir Philip Currie, who maintained his close relationship with Salisbury throughout the life of the Liberal government,
he arranged to have Salisbury issue a public statement to the effect
that he had not intended to give up Britain's position of paramountcy
in Uganda, whatever he may have said about the company.

The first issue in the debate on Uganda was whether or not it was a
matter open to discussion. No one was prepared to argue the merits
of the case. Gladstone clung to the doctrine of continuity, even after
Morley had assured him that Salisbury's statements were indeed
open to several interpretations. Obviously, Gladstone hoped to avoid
a wider debate on imperialism by treating the Uganda affair as a
matter of settled policy.

On 16 September Rosebery circulated, without comment, a Foreign Office memorandum on all aspects of the Uganda question.
Written by Sir Percy Anderson, head of the African department, the

document drew an unmistakable connection between Uganda and Egypt. The retention of Uganda, Anderson argued, was essential to Britain's position in Egypt.[82] Those members of the cabinet who wished to evacuate were not favourably impressed. "I thought it was a pleading from a missionary society or from the Company," commented Gladstone, who did not realize the extent to which Rosebery himself was responsible for the document.[83] Rosebery had instructed Anderson to stress the "dangers that would result from its abandonment to trade and missionaries, and the political dangers of letting the French and Germans in."[84]

Rosebery, when he saw that the political dangers would not move the cabinet, fell back on an argument more likely to appeal to the sensibilities of politicians. Evacuation, he warned, would result in the massacre of Christian converts; more to the point, such a massacre would lead to a public outcry in Britain. He denied that continuity and imperialism were the issues confronting the cabinet. "The pressing point before the government is not now the expediency of an East African Empire, nor is it the question of assisting the East Africa Company, nor of maintaining a sphere of influence, nor of the Mombassa railroad, nor of the intentions of the late government." The only question, according to Rosebery, was "whether, in view of the fact that a Company has been allowed to interfere, with a royal charter granted by the executive for that purpose, we are content to face the consequences of leaving the territory, the inhabitants and missionaries to a fate which we cannot doubt."[85]

Rosebery argued that although the Tories had created the situation, the Liberals would nevertheless be blamed by the public if a massacre were to occur in Uganda. The claim was not entirely without foundation. All reports from Uganda did point in the direction of civil war, but these reports, as Gladstone and Harcourt quickly pointed out, came from those convinced of the need to remain there.[86] Although Rosebery's most determined opponents discounted the predictions of disaster, others in the cabinet were not so eager to risk the consequences of their being wrong. Memories of Khartoum and Majuba hung over the cabinet discussions of Uganda like a thundercloud.[87] The Liberals had been out of office for six years, and some were less than anxious to risk public displeasure so early in the life of the new government. The *Times* warned, on 1 October, that "public opinion will have the opportunity of declaring itself in ways more impressive to the tremulous politician than the most convincing argument."[88] Rosebery was beginning to succeed in turning the larger question of imperialism into one of temporary political expediency;

the trick was to convince enough of his colleagues that a political crisis could be avoided by at least delaying evacuation while they gathered more information about the state of affairs in Uganda.

But why did Rosebery risk his position and his prestige so soon in the life of the government? He does not appear to have been convinced by his own argument of an impending massacre, which appears only in his correspondence with colleagues in the cabinet. The usual answer, simple but vague, is that he was an imperialist. This is certainly true. Rosebery always believed that without the empire Britain would become a second-rate state. But his imperialism, in the Uganda affair at least, had become inextricably bound up with his famous declaration that what Britain was doing was "pegging out claims for the future." This is certainly not true. Every sign indicated that Uganda was a bad business venture; even those most determined to remain admitted this – in private. In public, those who were going to foot the bill for a continued British presence had to be given some hope that they would receive returns on their investment. "Pegging out claims" meant there was no hope of returns in the foreseeable future, but if the British remained in Uganda they could continue to hope, Micawber-like, that something might turn up.[89]

If a massacre of Christians failed to move Rosebery, and if he had no hopes of a profitable East African empire, why should he endeavour to remain in Uganda? Because (to borrow Bismarck's phrase) his map of Africa was in Europe. Immediately upon his return to the Foreign Office Rosebery had been pulled in two opposing directions. Gladstone had questioned Salisbury's promise to Italy and Britain's relations with the Triple Alliance. He proposed to evacuate Egypt as soon as possible, which would improve relations with France and end Britain's dependence on the Triple Alliance. At the same time, the Germans were trying to draw the British even closer to the alliance. Rosebery rejected both alternatives, although he did believe that Germany was the only possible ally of Britain in Europe.[90] French enmity would not end with a British evacuation of Egypt; it would only be made more dangerous. The Triple Alliance, by pinning down so much French and Russian manpower and by causing them so much expense, was the best guarantee Britain had that the two states would refrain from confronting Britain in Africa or Asia. Becoming a member of the Triple Alliance was unsatisfactory because it meant that Britain might end up fighting a war in Europe for the sake of German or Austrian interests. Rosebery, therefore, had to resist the arguments of both Gladstone and the Germans. Uganda was the first line of resistance. To remain with, but not of, the Triple Alliance, Rosebery had to remain on the best possible terms with its members.

His relations with the alliance were going to be personal and concealed. For the Germans to accept him, then, they had to be convinced that, Gladstone to the contrary, Rosebery's power within the cabinet and his reputation in the country were such that his personal and private guarantees to continue working with them could be relied on. When Rosebery boasted of his power to the German ambassador he did so to allay Germany's understandable suspicions of a Gladstonian government. When he launched his campaign to remain in Uganda, he knew there could be no more striking display of the power he wielded in the government than to overturn the apparent decision of the Salisbury government, and to overcome the objections of Gladstone, Harcourt, and Morley, the three most powerful men in the government.

Suppose the scheme failed, suppose the Germans were not reassured and the informal working arrangement with the Triple Alliance fell apart; how would Uganda look then? Much the same. The Germans almost certainly would demand Britain's formal adherence to the alliance. The more vulnerable the British were in Egypt – and it was widely believed within the Foreign Office, at least, that the loss of Uganda would make them more vulnerable – the more difficult it would be to escape commitment to the alliance. If the worst happened and the British lost the assistance of the alliance at Cairo and in the Mediterranean then they would become even more dependent on their own resources. Every line of logical argument led Rosebery to the conclusion that Uganda must be retained; it would be troublesome and expensive to do so, but general diplomatic calculations necessitated retention.

In at least one way, the more resolute were Rosebery's opponents in cabinet, the more he stood to gain if he won, because the Germans and the French would have to conclude that, in spite of the strongest opposition, he was powerful enough to have his own way. Sir William Harcourt was certainly resolute. "All the forces of Jingoism are at work to compel us to administer their *damnosa hereditas* and to annex the whole of Equatoria," he wrote to Morley.[91] What Salisbury had promised or intended was, Harcourt maintained, quite beside the point: the Liberal party operated on different principles. He rejected the warnings of a massacre of Christians, which was "leather and prunella to cover the Jingoism."[92] Harcourt decided that imperialism was going to be the issue fought out in the debate on Uganda.

Assessing the role of domestic politics in foreign policy is a difficult task. Zara Steiner has recently demonstrated that, while *Innenpolitik* may have accounted for much of Germany's policy, it accounted for less of Britain's. The politics of leadership, however, at least in the period 1892–5, was more important than the politics of special interests or pressure groups. Certainly leadership was one of the issues at the back of the Uganda debate. It was obvious to everyone that Gladstone, about to turn eighty-four, was not going to last much longer, and Harcourt and Rosebery, as the only men in the cabinet with any substantial following in the country, were the obvious candidates to succeed him.

Of the two Rosebery was better liked by those in the cabinet. He conducted himself quietly, seldom interfering in the business of other departments, and had kept the travails of foreign politics out of the forefront in 1886, a great relief to those who had suffered through the government of 1880–5. Harcourt, by contrast, was provocative.[93] He loved a quarrel, no matter what the issue, and his quarrels often took him far from the domain of his own department, and usually into someone else's. When he went to the Exchequer where interference in departmental affairs was routine, he became still more quarrelsome. Campbell-Bannerman, by no means an "imperialist," found Harcourt's attacks on War Office expenditure a constant irritant.[94] If the leadership question became a popularity contest Harcourt would lose. Uganda offered the opportunity of transforming the question into a matter of principle: Rosebery would be shown up as a jingo-imperialist, Harcourt would establish his credentials as an outspoken opponent of imperial expansion.

Political calculations were never far from the surface during the Uganda debate. To say this is not to argue that the positions taken by Harcourt and Rosebery were entirely disingenuous, but their tactics and their rhetorical flourishes were certainly influenced by politics, which was also resposible for the way that some decisions, apparently inconsequential, were made. Harcourt, as leader of the House of Commons, tried to exploit Rosebery's position in the House of Lords: "Nothing shows how completely these Peers are up in a balloon ... there is not a man on the front bench in the House of Commons who could or would stand up to defend it [the retention of Uganda] and if he did he would be howled down by the whole party."[95] In other words, someone so far removed from the realities of politics could not be entrusted with the leadership of the party.

Most of the cabinet were inclined to see Uganda in the way Harcourt predicted. In spite of his attempt to distinguish between an anti-imperialist House of Commons and an imperialist House of Lords, however, lords Ripon, Herschell, and Kimberley were no more enthusiastic retentionists than commoners Morley, Asquith, and Fowler. But none of them was prepared to disregard the potential for political disaster. Something, they argued, ought to be done to avoid a massacre. Even Ripon, whose memorandum on Uganda had been drafted at the inspiration of Lewis ("Loulou") Harcourt, Sir William's son, believed in the possibility of a massacre.[96] Cabinet records show that Rosebery was practically alone on the question of retention, and that he knew himself to be alone. Harcourt had successfully demonstrated the cabinet's opposition to imperialist ventures and he had placed himself, at the very beginning of the Uganda debate, at the head of the opposition.

Perhaps Harcourt decided that, having won the ideological debate with Rosebery, he should be magnanimous in victory. A moderate line on the actual policy to be followed would certainly go far to demonstrate his ability to lead. As far as the contest for leadership was concerned, Harcourt needed only the appearance of victory. Rosebery, by contrast, needed the substance of victory if his diplomacy were to succeed.

Fortunately for Rosebery, he did not need the substance immediately; for the moment he had only to delay the decision to evacuate. Such a delay would make clear how strong was his position in the cabinet and, at the same time, emphasize his commitment to British paramountcy in Egypt. Rosebery and Harcourt were, therefore, prepared to compromise if a suitable arrangement could be found. Each appealed to the other's vanity in the hope of colouring the compromise in his favour. Harcourt had Rosebery proposed for the Order of the Garter; Rosebery had Harcourt invited to be minister-in-attendance at Balmoral.[97] The results were laughable, showing how little the two men really understood the other. The honour irritated Rosebery because it reminded him it should have come in 1886, when it would have secured Lady Rosebery's entry into the highest reaches of European society. Harcourt left Balmoral convinced that the queen "was not at all a keen Ugandaite ... Our African difficulties will not come from *that quarter.*"[98] This failure of each man to understand the character of the other would later cause serious problems, but in 1892 it counted for little.

What the situation required was not good temper, for both men were for the moment amiable enough, but a good compromise. The kind of compromise that was eventually found was determined by the nature of Harcourt's anti-imperialism. He did not find repugnant the idea of ruling other races; what he really objected to was the expense. He regarded the empire as a business venture. A precursor of J.A. Hobson, he thought a balance-sheet could be drawn up that would demonstrate that the benefit to the whole nation was not worth the expense. The purpose of government was to maximize the profits of the nation and minimize the losses. He looked at Uganda in this light. The experience of the Imperial British East Africa Company showed that no profits were to be made in Uganda. If the British were to remain, and here Hobson would echo his words a decade later, it would be to protect certain special interests, not to benefit the nation as a whole.

Economic prospects in Africa as a whole were bad, according to Harcourt. Those who thought the continent could be turned into another India were mistaken. English settlers could not work in Africa, "or get these savages to work for them. These natives are not like the mild Hindoo with whom you can do as you please."[99] If the government were going to spend the taxpayers' money, it should go to improving the lives of the British people, who would question whether the millions needed to retain Uganda might not be better spent on themselves. The movement for retention, he said, was "like a restless land owner who having already a dozen Estates which he can with difficulty look after mortgages their income to buy an immense dilapidated property for fear his neighbour should acquire it."[100] Nothing would have suited Harcourt more than to apply the principles of good estate management to the empire.

On Uganda, therefore, Harcourt was prepared to compromise, but, whatever form this compromise might take, it had to be cheap. For a moment, it seemed as if Cecil Rhodes would save the situation when he proposed to administer Uganda on the government's behalf – for a fee of £24,000 a year. Harcourt smiled at this plan. "Rhodes is a great Jingo, but then he is a cheap Jingo."[101]

Rosebery had a different plan. The Tories had earlier contemplated turning over the administration of Uganda to the sultan of Zanzibar, and now Rosebery renewed this idea so quietly that it hardly seemed to be his own. Harcourt liked the idea so much that he credited himself for having thought of it.[102] "If that amiable black man would only render us this service," Harcourt promised, he would "everlastingly bless him."[103] The compromise began to take shape, because the Zanzibar proposition promised to relieve Britain of the expense of direct intervention that Harcourt objected to. Rosebery claimed to be satisfied because the proposition would provide for the sphere of influence he desired to establish. The Zanzibar proposition established the background against which a commissioner was chosen to investigate the situation in Uganda.

The selection of Gerald Portal as commissioner has been a mystery. Some have argued that he was a known retentionist, and therefore certain to recommend the course desired by Rosebery, while others have argued that his appointment left the question open, as otherwise Harcourt would never have agreed to his being selected.

The solution to the mystery lies in the Zanzibar proposition. Harcourt thought the proposition solved the problem: the investigation would simply find the best way of doing what he and Rosebery had already agreed on, turning Uganda over to Zanzibar. Thus the question of who was sent out to investigate mattered little, Harcourt objecting only to a "lunatic" like Lugard. Rosebery, who assumed that Harcourt had failed to grasp the implications of the Zanzibar proposition, was determined to establish a protectorate, and had resorted to the proposition only as a temporary expedient to quiet Harcourt's fears and to induce him to accept a commissioner who would turn in the report Rosebery wanted.

The Zanzibar proposition was, in fact, Gerald Portal's brainstorm. He told Rosebery that it might work as a "deus ex machina" to maintain Britain's position along the coast and the interior up to Lake Victoria, or perhaps to the Nile.[104] It was not surprising that the proposition should have come from Portal, because he was determined that Britain should maintain its hold on Uganda. Portal had for several years been in Zanzibar, where he had saved the sultan from bankruptcy. He assured Salisbury that Zanzibar would remain the chief centre and trading depot in East Africa. In fact, Portal envisioned precisely that "vast Equatorial Empire" that Harcourt and Gladstone found so disturbing. "I am fighting like a wild cat to prevent the Government from giving up Uganda," he wrote; "if they do, it will spoil a brilliant and possible future for English Africa."[105]

Portal was an ambitious man, a point that has been overlooked because he died young, before much of his ambition could be realized. In 1892 he envisioned himself at the head of the equatorial empire that he sought to create. Cromer, it was rumoured, would soon be leaving Cairo in order to take over the embassy at Rome. Portal hoped that the rumour would prove false because he needed another two or three years before he could hope to replace him in Cairo, by which time English Africa would stretch from Alexandria to Mombasa.

Portal's ambition partly explains his views on Uganda, and it also explains the instructions that were issued to him by Rosebery.[106] Although Portal had already assured him that "no one will regret more than I shall, to see English authority withdrawn from Uganda," Rosebery seems to have feared that Portal's ambition might overcome his desire for retention. He might take too literally the words of the cabinet's directive to find "the best method of dealing with that country." Rosebery countered this possibility by making it clear that Portal's future lay in the hands of the foreign secretary, and not in those of the cabinet. "You are acting wisely in your own interest with regard to your future," he assured him. Portal's main duty, Rosebery said, was settled; he was to arrange the "best means of administering Uganda." The saving clause inserted by the cabinet, Rosebery went on, was "mainly one of form."[107] While closer inspection of the country might lead Portal to modify his views, it should not change them. Rosebery suggested that there were three possible conclusions to Portal's investigations: to administer Uganda under Zanzibar, to place it under the direct protectorate of Great Britain, or – a possibility not to be contemplated – to evacuate it. The retention of Uganda was a foregone conclusion, not from the moment at which Portal was selected to act as commissioner, but from the moment Harcourt jumped at the Zanzibar proposition. All that remained were, indeed, questions of form.

Rosebery had succeeded in consolidating his position within the cabinet and at the Foreign Office as a result of his handling of Uganda. The decision to create the Portal mission left the general impression that he had "conquered the Cabinet on Uganda."[108] Officials at the Foreign Office had no doubt concerning the conclusion of the mission. Portal would, Currie confidently remarked, "take care that our occupation of Uganda will be a permanent one."[109] As a result of the victory, Rosebery, his parliamentary secretary told him, would "be backed up by [his] office after this as no one was ever backed before."[110] Some members of the cabinet anticipated that Rosebery's victory might cause trouble in the future. Ripon, the colonial secretary, who saw himself as "not a troublesome person about foreign affairs," nevertheless feared "that if Rosebery gets his way about Uganda he will be very difficult to manage."[111]

The impression of being firmly in control of policy was precisely what Rosebery had tried to create during the debate on Uganda. His relations with the Triple Alliance were going to be awkward, and if his diplomacy were to succeed, then its members must believe that his word counted when he told them that he would work with them but that there could be no formal alliance. Rosebery's diplomacy was going to be a personal one. Given the cabinet's opposition to imperial ventures, its distrust of the European system of alliances, and the inclination of some to abandon Egypt and restore the liberal alliance with France, Rosebery's task was not a simple one.

In their attempt to explain the essence of the Uganda debate, historians have overlooked one of the characteristic tactics employed by Rosebery to succeed in his aim of establishing a personal diplomacy. Even Gladstone remarked, in the midst of the controversy, that Rosebery's "tone was excellent."[112] In spite of the legend to the contrary, Rosebery did not threaten to resign – he did not even use extravagant language – although the possibility that he might pick up and leave the government was forever in the minds of his colleagues. According to the standard interpretation of Rosebery's character when in office, this should be surprising – he should have shown his prickly temper. Instead of lashing out when others told him what he should do, however, Rosebery responded to them with courtesy and good nature. The Uganda debate was the first instance in which he used his temper as a tool, a tactic he would apply many times before the government fell. His amiability seemed to signify to the cabinet a desire for harmony, a willingness to bridge the gaps created by differences in principle. In fact, Rosebery was prepared to be magnanimous because he regarded any sort of compromise on Uganda as a moral victory; the nature of the compromise promised, if it did not guarantee, that it would be a real victory as well.

Rosebery's careful conduct during the Uganda debate forms a striking contrast with his actions in Egypt where, instead of assuming a conciliatory and good-natured pose, he became pompous and bombastic. The explanation of the contrast is simple: Rosebery regarded any compromise on Egypt as a defeat.

Rosebery knew from the start that Egypt would be a problem. Gladstone was publicly committed to evacuation, and, immediately the government was formed, he began to prepare evacuation programs. Rather than immersing himself in the Irish question, and rather than permitting Rosebery a free hand in foreign affairs, Gladstone had asked for summaries of the Egyptian situation and the particulars of what had passed while the Liberals were in opposition. He had used these materials to draft a memorandum on evacuation and he was preparing to bring the question before the cabinet when Morley stopped him. "My strong impression," Morley said, "is that it would be best to let the matter rest until the Cabinet is face to face with an actual and present necessity for taking a line."[113] Certainly, Morley argued, it would be wiser to allow the Uganda storm to subside before arousing fresh susceptibilities at the Foreign Office. Morley recognized that raising the Egyptian question was certain to divide the cabinet, and his fear on this point showed one of the essential features of the new government: the cabinet were prepared to delay applying their principles, or even abandon them, for the sake of remaining in power.

Nevertheless, a manoeuvre on the part of the French ambassador suggested to Gladstone that an opportune moment had arrived for discussing the Egyptian problem. W.H. Waddington had decided to retire from diplomacy and return to politics; he had been an elected deputy for some time, but had not taken up his seat in the Senate. The political situation in France was not stable – even for France – and anyone with a good reputation had an opportunity to achieve a high place in the next ministry, or even to form it. The man who secured the British evacuation of Egypt would certainly achieve great popularity.[114] Waddington knew, however, that evacuation was not going to be accomplished by going through Rosebery. Waddington, Rosebery remarked, "piques himself on never mentioning the word Egypt."[115] The ambassador chose, therefore, to reopen the question not with the foreign secretary, but with the prime minister.

Waddington asked Gladstone if the British government was prepared for a "friendly conversation" on Egypt.[116] If so, he thought the French government would be prepared to indicate a possible basis of settlement. To Gladstone, this seemed the perfect opening. Waddington lamented the interruption of "the old Granville arrangement," as, Gladstone supposed, "all do."[117] At a stroke, Gladstone imagined Egypt evacuated and harmonious relations restored with France. Glowing with the expectation of a settlement, he reported the conversation to Rosebery. Instead of responding favourably, however, Rosebery exploded in a fit of temper. Waddington, he replied, had no right to go to Gladstone about foreign affairs. So far as Rosebery was concerned, Waddington's procedure "has rendered the transaction of business with him almost if not quite impossible."[118] He refused to bring the question before the cabinet: "as to my negotiating now for the evacuation of Egypt it would be in my opinion a pernicious waste of time and energy."[119]

Rosebery's explosions of temper were nothing if not timely. This one came at the very moment that a compromise on Uganda was reached. Gladstone, in contrast, had badly timed his approach. The moment the cabinet began to look forward to an end of the debate on foreign policy, Gladstone seemed determined to initiate a new debate. Gladstone appears to have misconstrued Morley's advice: "an actual and present necessity" was the situation that the Irish secretary had envisioned as creating the conditions necessary to act in Egypt. Waddington's proposition, however seductive, did not make a necessity of the question, and if the cabinet could avoid a debate on Egypt they would. Gladstone, who began by insisting that the French had every right to open the question with him, soon realized his mistake. He tried to save something from the initiative by turning the question of a reply over to Rosebery.[120] Had it been a matter of soothing sensitive feelings, this tactic might have worked. But Rosebery refused to take up the question in any form. "I suggest," he wrote unpleasantly to Gladstone, "that you send him what answer you please about Egypt with a subtle reminder that the most convenient course is to treat foreign policy thro' the F.O."[121] The reminder was, in fact, directed at Gladstone himself. Rosebery seized upon Waddington's blunder as an opportunity to stifle, temporarily at least, any discussion in London of Egypt's possible future.

In Paris, Rosebery used the blunder as an opportunity to demonstrate his control over foreign policy. The British ambassador, Lord Dufferin, explained to Alexandre Ribot, the minister of foreign affairs, "that a Cabinet was a thing unknown to our Constitution and that the Secretary of State held his Commission direct from the Queen, and was himself solely and individually responsible to Her Majesty, to Parliament and to public opinion for the conduct of foreign affairs."[122] This interpretation might have surprised Gladstone – had he ever seen it – but whether it was constitutionally correct was of little importance because, when Gladstone was forced to drop the matter, after he had first assured Waddington that he would bring the French proposal before the cabinet, he demonstrated that Dufferin's interpretation of the constitution was politically correct. Rosebery assured Dufferin that if Ribot "thinks to deal over my head he is greatly mistaken. Under that system I can assure him that Austrian or Chinese procedure will seem electrical compared with mine."[123]

Had Gladstone not been so easily tempted by the prospect of conciliation with France he might have waited upon events before raising the Egyptian question. Had he waited, he might have had a better chance of success, for a crisis in Egypt was beginning to unfold. The young, impressionable khedive, it was reported, was being worked upon by the anti-English pashas to dismiss his "too-English" first minister, Mustapha Pasha Fehmy. The dismissal, wrote Arthur Hardinge, the first secretary at Cairo, "would mean friction with the English officials and would stimulate French and Turkish intrigues."[124] Although this particular alarm proved false, Cromer warned that the danger had not passed.[125]

Egypt, apparently at the edge of affairs in 1892, was actually at the centre, for it was on Egypt that relations with France, Germany, and even Russia were seen to hinge. In Gladstone's opinion the occupation of Egypt was the only obstacle on the path back to the old Anglo-French liberal alliance. Restoring harmony with France would relieve Britain of her dependence on Germany and the Triple Alliance. With Britain and France cooperating in the Mediterranean, Italy would abandon her ill-advised partnership with Germany and Austria-Hungary. Britain would be safe in the Mediterranean, she could cut back on her program of naval spending, and the possibility of becoming involved in a continental war would be diminished.

Harcourt agreed. He argued that occupying Egypt had transformed Britain from an insular state into a continental one.[126] As an insular state with a big navy to protect her (and Harcourt always supported a big navy), Britain had little to fear from Europe. Once she had territory to protect in Egypt, however, she laid herself open to every sort of political intrigue, as she depended on the support of the Triple Alliance.

Rosebery simply turned this argument on its head. The British were in Egypt because of French animosity; if the British left, the French would use the opportunity of local upheaval to step in. Once in Egypt, the French would be better placed to threaten British interests; they could prevent the British from using the faster and cheaper Suez route to India and the east; they could more easily influence the Turks and cooperate with the Russians at Constantinople and the Straits. As far as Rosebery was concerned, evacuating Egypt would increase French animosity, not end it. This outcome would make Britain dependent on the Triple Alliance, as the less able the British were to meet the French threat on their own, the more they must rely on the Germans to meet it for them. The more they relied on the Germans, the more likely the possibility that they would end by engaging in a continental war.

This debate could not be resolved, and Liberals believed in either one argument or the other. While both sides offered proof in support of their propositions, no proof would be regarded by the other as conclusive. The only possible way of getting agreement would be for the French to give prior evidence of their good intentions by acceding to the British position in Egypt. During the years 1892–5 there was no likelihood of this happening, so the debate went on, permeating the discussion of every foreign question that arose.

It is easy to see that there were differences of opinion on Egypt, but it is easier not to notice that these differences obscured a more fundamental agreement. Both sides of the argument were grounded in an insular outlook: men on either side maintained that following the policy of the other meant increasing British dependence on the Triple Alliance, and consequently increasing the likelihood of becoming embroiled in a continental war. Such thinking is usually seen as implicit in the Gladstone-Harcourt program, but it was equally so in Rosebery's. As he saw it, Britain's occupation of Egypt gave a strategic advantage over France, and one that reduced her reliance on Germany. But Rosebery's policy was more complicated than this imperial formula, because he regarded the Triple Alliance, by its very existence, as Britain's best guarantee of security outside Europe. By pinning down the bulk of Franco-Russian military resources, the alliance relieved Britain of threats that would otherwise be much more perilous. Rosebery wished to keep the Triple Alliance alive, if he could.

Increasingly, however, the Germans would argue that the British must join the alliance if it were not to die. Their argument took two forms. They sometimes argued that British promises of support for Austria at the Straits and in the Balkans were not sufficient, and that the Austrians might therefore come to an arrangement with Russia. More frequently, and more plausibly, they argued that the Italians were not certain enough of British assistance in the event of war with France. This uncertainty might lead the Italians to join France and Russia in favour of the irridentist program against Austria. In a paradoxical, roundabout way Egypt came to function as another Roseberian tactical device.

As long as the Germans continued to believe that they could use Bismarck's Egyptian *bâton* to beat the British, they would continue to believe in the possibility of directing British policy. If the British were to evacuate, then the Germns would lose this sense of control. When the Germans finally lost the *bâton* with the signing of the Anglo-French entente in 1904, they accelerated their naval program in a futile attempt to find a substitute. But this is to anticipate. In 1892 Britain was still with the Triple Alliance though not of it, and Rosebery worked to maintain that state of affairs.

The two issues that absorbed Rosebery's attention in 1892 were parts of this wider strategy. Clearly, the retention of Uganda was designed to increase the security of Britain in Egypt; it would also show the Germans that Rosebery, who favoured the Triple Alliance, controlled policy and that Britain would remain in Egypt, thus continuing to antagonize France. Less clearly, Rosebery's policy in the Pamirs was designed to show Germany that Britain could handle a threat from Russia without relying on German assistance. He never accepted the argument that Russia in the Pamirs posed a direct threat to British India. He had to act firmly on the frontier, but more for diplomatic than strategic reasons. The ideal solution to the Pamirs question, as Rosebery saw it, was a negotiated settlement that would display both British firmness and the possibility of an accord with Russia.

In undertaking this program, Rosebery was carrying the heaviest of burdens. He had to conduct a personal diplomacy. The Germans, who naturally distrusted Gladstonian foreign policy, were going to be more difficult to deal with than they had been while Salisbury was in power. They were going to require assurance that Britain was to be relied upon, and so were the Austrians and the Italians. Rosebery was prepared to assure them that their understanding would continue to operate, but he could promise them nothing. They were going to have to rely on his good intentions and his ability to control policy. Rosebery tried to substitute himself for the alliance the Germans wanted and, as a result, his personality and his policy automatically became the focal point of any discussions with the Germans. Moreover, taking personal responsibility for the successful management of foreign policy meant that his colleagues would blame him for anything that went wrong.

One of the questions that remained unanswered was whether or not Rosebery's temperament could stand up to the treatment it received as a result of his personal diplomacy. Thus far his public life had been an unmitigated success, with the result that he had never been forced to weather the storms of a public outcry or even strong opposition from his colleagues. In 1886 the cabinet, and especially Gladstone, had stood behind him while he negotiated a settlement of the Near Eastern crisis. When the party split over Ireland, those who watched him stay with Gladstone felt little rancour, refusing to believe he could be a sincere Home Ruler. Yet friends and enemies alike recognized him to be of a delicate temperament. When he agonized over apparently trivial matters and demanded repeated displays of approval for his actions, observers might reasonably wonder how committed he was to continuing in public life. After the death of his wife his behaviour became even more idiosyncratic: he dined alone, working while he ate, and took solitary drives through London in the early hours of the morning. It was reasonable to wonder, then, how he would stand up if things began to go wrong.

CHAPTER THREE

The Near East in World Policy: The Struggle for Supremacy

... foreign policy necessarily varies with the varying importance of states. There is, indeed, no such thing as a traditional foreign policy in the sense of its being necessary and inevitable, any more than, in conditions of the atmosphere, a ship carries the same traditional sails, or a man wears the same traditional clothes. The instinct of self-preservation guides the European powers with the same certainty as weather moves sheep in the hill.

Pitt (1891)

Average men, as Joseph Conrad once remarked, try to control events; wise men, recognizing the control of events as beyond their abilities, try to create systems through which the unexpected may be turned to their advantage. Rebellions in faraway places will, they know, occur periodically; their citizens will be imprisoned, kidnapped, or murdered; commercial or industrial concessions will be unfairly awarded to others; new developments in technology or agriculture will suddenly transform a worthless piece of property into one hotly competed for by the great powers of the day. Diplomatic responses to these unexpected events depend on circumstances so varied, so subtle, that they are almost impossible to describe, except in detail. But the responses do share a common characteristic, no matter how peculiar the circumstances of the individual case: diplomatists always respond according to the effect the case will have on the general pattern of diplomacy.

Rosebery was not an average man. He did not confuse power with omnipotence. He knew that the control of African tribesmen and Asian warriors lay beyond his authority, that the foresight necessary to predict the unfolding of events in Asia and Africa was an ability that even the imperial Anglo-Saxon race had yet to acquire. He did not attempt to impose on events his vision of how the world ought to be, but he did attempt to see that events did not destroy the world as it was.

The world of the 1890s was a British world, and Rosebery saw no need to change it. Foreigners, of course, would always try to change things, would always cause trouble for the British – as they always had. Their role was to complain: the lower orders everywhere had difficulty recognizing their own interests. The role of a British foreign secretary was to see that these complaints did not get out of hand. Rosebery expected trouble; he did not expect Frenchmen, Russians, and Germans to behave with impeccable manners – few foreigners had acquired the British characteristic of losing with style and grace. He did expect that what H.G. Wells would soon call "the politics of complaint" could be managed, that the framework of the world system – the foundations of which had been laid by British engineers – could be maintained, and that London could continue to settle disputes about politics just as Greenwich could about time.

To maintain the system by which the world worked required that Rosebery continue to act as if he had all the strings in his hands. What men believed to be true was more important than what was. Therefore, because the diplomats of Europe believed that the loss of Uganda might enable the French to control the headwaters of the Nile and thus threaten Egypt by damming up the river or sending down an expedition to invade, Rosebery had to act. These fears, given modern geographical knowledge, now appear ludicrous. Almost as difficult to imagine is the British fear of a Russian invasion through the difficult, barren Pamirs, thousands of miles from supply depots and requiring vast expenditure on rail lines and fortifications. But men believed that this too was a real possibility, and in both cases Rosebery was forced to take a firm line in order to show the diplomats of Europe that the calculations upon which they had based their politics still held good, that no rearrangement of the world system was going to occur as a result of Gladstone's return to office.

Rosebery operated on this premise because he believed the international system worked to Britain's advantage. Two things protected the British Empire – a big navy and the balance of power in Europe – and Rosebery wanted to maintain both. Of the two, the second is the more difficult to understand because in the 1890s the balance of power meant the alliance system. Rosebery believed that as long as France and Russia were faced with the united opposition of the Triple Alliance, they would not be able to muster sufficient force to threaten the British Empire. Behind his diplomacy in the Pamirs, and even in Uganda, lay this assessment of the political and military situation in Europe. A War Office report on "Twenty Years of Russian

Army Reform and the Present Distribution of the Russian Land Forces" showed how the European situation affected Britain's relations with Russia.[1] Circulated in January 1893, the report drew attention, not to the figures of total strength, which were always awesome, but to the changes in distribution that had occurred during the last decade. Whereas in the St Petersburg, Finland, Odessa, Moscow, Caucasus, and Don military districts (that is, in those districts not bordering on the European land frontier) the numbers of troops had remained almost stationary, in those bordering on Germany and Russia there had been a startling increase. The Vilna, Warsaw, and Kiev districts had been augmented with 124 battalions of infantry, 148 squadrons of cavalry, and 61 batteries of field artillery. "Can it be wondered at," the authors queried, "that the German and Austrian Governments regard with ever increasing uneasiness this piling up of troops on their frontiers?"

One obvious effect of the change in military planning, reflected in the wider political situation, was to make Germany and Austria more anxious for a good understanding with Britain. Austria, in particular, needed Britain's support at the Straits and in the Balkans, and the Mediterranean agreements of the late 1880s arose from their mutual interests there. Austria also needed Britain to keep Italy on her side in order that she would not be faced with a repetition of the disaster of 1866 by being compelled to fight on two fronts. It was through Italy, in fact, that the naval power of Britain came to be connected with the military power of Germany and Austria. Through Italy, Britain acted with the Triple Alliance, but Rosebery steadfastly refused to make Britain a part of the alliance.

The other effect of the military situation in Europe, and the one that made possible Rosebery's Pamirs policy, was the deployment of Russian forces in central Asia. Here, the War Office report noted, there had been no increase in military power, and thus it concluded that "no great events are expected in this quarter." In other words, Russia, by concentrating the bulk of her forces in Europe, made India safe for the British. Playing the role of guardian to British India, however, was not particularly attractive to the Triple Alliance. The Anglo-Russian frontier in central Asia should, as they saw it, set Britain and Russia at odds, and thus draw Britain into the Triple Alliance. Therefore, Rosebery's Pamirs policy had been designed with two things in mind: to show the Triple Alliance that Britain was capable of acting firmly without its help, and, if the alliance went too far in its demands on Britain, that Rosebery might be prepared to settle his differences with Russia.

In the diplomacy of Europe between 1892 and 1895, therefore,

Russia occupied a pivotal position. Sometimes the Germans, sometimes the Austrians, would threaten to abandon their informal
arrangement with Britain in favour of a settlement with the Russians.
Both sides would argue that a settlement with the Russians was
impossible for the other: the Germans would argue that the situation
in central Asia guaranteed perpetual Anglo-Russian animosity, while
the British would argue that the situation in Europe made Russia
peaceful in central Asia. Every troop movement, every new fortifica-
tion or rail line that was built, every speech, every rumour was carefully analysed for signs of Russia's intentions, and just as carefully
moulded into the shape suited to diplomatic requirements.

The central question for Rosebery in these years, then, was
whether or not he could keep Britain in the favourable position she
occupied, enjoying the advantages of the continental system of alliances without running the risks of becoming a fully integrated
member of the system. For him this question formed the background
of every event in diplomacy between 1892 and 1895. No event was too
trivial to overlook. Sewers in Morocco might be as reliable a guide to
relations and intentions as battleships in the Mediterranean. Events
in the east, however, were likely to be more interesting than most, for
only at Cairo and Constantinople did the great powers come together.
More to the point, Egypt was the one spot where Germany could,
because of her position on the Caisse de la Dette, directly influence
Britain. Bismarck had used the Egyptian *bâton* before in order to
extract concessions from Britain, but so far Rosebery had remained
free from its blows. On 7 January 1893, however, the German consul-
general in Cairo informed Lord Cromer, the British commissioner,
that he must no longer look to Germany for assistance in English
projects in Egypt, and Rosebery's first lesson in the uses of the bâton
began.[2] Sir William White, British ambassador at Constantinople from
1886 to 1891, used to complain that while the Triple Alliance was
useful to Britain elsewhere, notably in Egypt, it did her no good at
Constantinople where it did not exist. The Germans, he argued, were
determined to maintain the Three Emperors' League of Germany,
Russia, and Austria, and in practice this meant not offending the
Russians at Constantinople. He thought the Germans were able to
take this position because they had no direct interest in the Near
East. When the sultan proposed to German bankers in September
1888 that they undertake a substantial railway concession in Anatolia, White therefore welcomed the proposal as an opportunity to
drive a wedge into the Three Emperors' League.[3]

The wedge took the form of a railway concession in Anatolia.
Working together, the British, Germans, and Italians had secured

from the sultan the right to build a railway from Ismidt to Angora. The concession, given to Alfred Kaulla of the Württembergische Vereinsbank and Dr Georg von Siemens of the Deutsche Bank, was to include secret British participation through a group led by Vincent Caillard, president of the Council of the Ottoman Public Debt.[4] A French group had unsuccessfully opposed the concession, marking the first serious defeat of Franco-Russian interests since the British occupied Egypt. More important, White assured Salisbury, it would mark the beginning of a split between Germany and Russia "and bids fair to become a new departure for Germany at Constantinople which it will be interesting to watch."[5] The Kaulla affair, which in 1893 would appear to drive Britain and Germany apart in the Near East, began in 1888 with the promise of bringing them closer together.

By 1890 Caillard's participation in the railway had fallen through, and the Anatolian Railway Company became an entirely German enterprise, a state of affairs equally suited to the political and financial interests of the sultan. Unlike the British and the Russians, the Germans appeared to have no territorial ambitions in the Ottoman Empire.[6] Further, if a Russo-German rivalry should develop in the Near East, and end in war, the war would, logically, be fought in Poland rather than Asia Minor. Cooperating with the Germans, then, offered the possibility of long-term political advantage, but it also offered financial rewards: the sultan's immediate motive for granting the concession of 1888 had been the promise of a loan. In 1892 the sultan, who again needed money, proposed to Kaulla that the Anatolian Railway should extend its line from Angora to Baghdad, realizing this would stimulate a bidding war from which he could extract another loan.[7]

When Kaulla, joining with a German commercial company, responded favourably to the sultan's proposal in December 1892, he did not bother to inform the British, their participation in the venture having disappeared some time ago. When the British Foreign Office heard of the proposed arrangement, the initial reaction was to regard the affair as strictly commercial. The Germans, after all, had not approached them to arrange things politically. When British commercial interests expressed opposition to Kaulla's concession, therefore, the British government prepared to intervene on their behalf and saw nothing extraordinary in doing so.

Explaining the relationship between British commercial interests and the government has never been easy: the British, never sure what the relationship was, or what it should be, were themselves confused. Rosebery's diplomacy during the Kaulla affair can be understood only if this confusion is taken into account. When Rosebery decided to intervene on behalf of British commercial interests in the Ottoman Empire, he knew practically nothing about them. He thought he knew enough because, at the end of December 1892, Edgar Vincent, another Englishman who had served as president of the Council of the Ottoman Public Debt, and who was now president of the Imperial Ottoman Bank, had assured him that the extension of the Anatolian Railway Company would result in a loss to British interests of two million pounds sterling.[8] Ironically, in view of later developments, Rosebery did not object to Germany's extending the railway from Angora to Baghdad, as he assumed it would stabilize the Turkish economy and thereby contribute to Britain's political interest in maintaining the Turkish state. Besides, he realized the sultan would refuse to award the concession to Britain, because to do so would look like a preliminary to declaring a protectorate over Asia Minor.

What Rosebery instructed his ambassador to object to, on the basis of information provided to Vincent, was not the Angora to Baghdad line, but a second, smaller, politically and strategically less significant one. Because the line to Baghdad would run through difficult terrain, it would be extremely costly and take years to build. Therefore Kaulla had proposed that, in exchange for undertaking to build this line, he should be given the concession to extend the Hidar Pach–Ismidt line south to Konia. This line, which could be built quickly and which would terminate in Turkey's prime agricultural area, would conflict with the designs of two other lines, the Smyrna to Aidin and the Smyrna to Cassaba, whose owners hoped to extend them into the interior around Konia. Excluding them from this area, they claimed, would bankrupt them. Rosebery, on 25 December 1892, instructed his ambassador to try to delay the granting of the concession to Kaulla, in order to take their claims into account.

When the German foreign minister, Marschall von Bieberstein, heard of the British intervention, he erupted. On 6 January 1893 he called in the British ambassador to tell him that if the information he had received was correct, "he must regard it as an inimical act towards Germany." It would, he declared, "render impossible the continuance of the cordial cooperation which had been of so much benefit to both countries."[9] Rosebery, he said, had delivered a blow to the Triple Alliance; the French were already jubilant. Marschall no doubt assumed that Rosebery knew what he was doing – an unwarranted assumption. The German government, which for a decade had been balancing domestic agrarian, industrial, and trading interests, each having its own view of a proper foreign policy, regarded commerce and politics as two sides of the same coin: neither could be considered apart from the other.[10] Assuming the British thought in the same way, the government concluded that Rosebery's action in opposing their railway must have been motivated by wider political considerations.

The Germans were particularly sensitive to actions like Rosebery's in opposing the Kaulla concession because they regarded them as indicating how the British connection with the Triple Alliance worked, and under what conditions.[11] Nevertheless, had it not been for the "new course" *(neue Kurs)* in German foreign policy instituted after the fall of Bismarck, this particular controversy would have amounted to little. Essentially, the new course meant breaking the old defensive and conservative arrangement with Russia, and substituting for it an aggressive policy of commercial expansion, particularly in the Near East. The Triple Alliance, in the hands of William II, was to be transformed into an offensive arrangement assisting the growth of German economic and political power; Bismarck's fear of Russia, and his defensive arrangement with her, would be shown to have hindered her growth.[12] Rosebery's action in January 1893 therefore threatened a fundamental assumption of the new course, since it appeared to prove that the British, who regarded their connection with the Triple Alliance as a political and defensive one, would refuse to assist German commercial expansion. Henceforth, Marschall aimed to use the affair to show Rosebery why the British were bound to assist them in the future.[13]

The telegram announcing Marschall's reaction to the British representations at Constantinople arrived on Rosebery's desk on the morning of 6 January 1893. The next day a second telegram arrived, this time from Cairo. Lord Cromer reported that the German consul-general had called on him to recite Marschall's complaints against the attitude of Britain in Constantinople. The German, he said, had laid particular stress on the British actually having supported French interests over German. Given the British attitude at Constantinople, the German Foreign Office had instructed its representative to inform Cromer that he "must no longer look for German assistance in English projects in Egypt."[14] Cromer, naturally, was upset: the Austrians and the Italians would follow the German lead, the British would be isolated, and only the French and Russians would benefit. "A good understanding," he assured Rosebery, "is very much to be desired."[15]

Rosebery, who had never before experienced the sensation of having his knuckles rapped with the Egyptian *bâton*, was startled by Marschall's action. The German explosion, he told Cromer, was "quite unexpected," but he promised to try his best to arrange it amicably.[16] Britain's problem in the Kaulla affair, however, did not arise so much from Rosebery's inexperience, as from the general, haphazard way of dealing with questions of commercial interest customary at the British Foreign Office. Rosebery had undertaken to act against Kaulla entirely on the information provided him by a private individual, Edgar Vincent. The first hint that this information was possibly suspect came from the Germans, via Cairo, when they complained of being disregarded for the sake of a French interst. Rosebery, in acting to defend the interests of the Smyrna-Cassaba and Smyrna-Aidin lines, did not realize that the former, originally a British venture, had fallen under the control of the French; a subordinate interest in the line had been maintained by a British group, however, a group that included Edgar Vincent.[17] Only the Smyrna-Aidin line could be considered a proper British interest, and its representatives had never approached the Foreign Office.[18] Rosebery had, through ignorance, managed to do precisely what the Germans had accused him of doing: he had taken the side of French interests at Constantinople.

For a few days in January British ignorance succeeded in compounding the original error. Sir Edward Malet, the ambassador at Berlin, began with a moderate defence of his government's action by arguing that the question of constructing a railway from Angora to Baghdad was a vital one for Britain, raising as it did "the whole question of our communication with India."[19] The Germans, he assumed, would appreciate how delicate the situation was if they were given to believe that the British had acted out of a concern for the defence of India. In this situation it could be understood how the British might find it necessary to take some steps at Constantinople to prevent a concession being given without obtaining guarantees to safeguard their interests. But in fact, the possibility that a German railway to Baghdad might have political consequences damaging to British interests had never occurred to Rosebery, nor, apparently, to anyone in the Foreign Office. So far, the political consequences had arisen as the result of Britain treating the affair as entirely commercial, not as the result of a concern for India.

Malet's attempt to defend the British action succeeded only in convincing Marschall that he had been right from the start, that the British judged the situation by its political ramifications, and that they had to be made to see that their policy in political affairs had to be arranged with the Germans beforehand. The British should recognize it as being in their interests to have the line to Baghdad built by the Germans rather than by anyone else. Germany, he said, "could never have any political designs in the East," and her support for British policy must be of some value.[20] Marschall was, quite clearly, attempting to use the Kaulla affair for the purpose of establishing a formula to guide future Anglo-German relations in the Near East: the

British, politically suspect at the Porte, could hope for few commercial concessions in the future, and, as the Germans were friendly while the French and Russians were not, they should assist the Germans in securing whatever concessions became available. If the British were not prepared to yield to the simple logic of this argument, then the Egyptian *bâton* could be wielded to drive the lesson home.[21]

The British came closer to accepting the argument than might be imagined. When the affair began in December, they saw no reason to treat German interests in any special way; the concession threatened existing British interests to the amount of two million pounds sterling, and these interests were to be defended, no matter who threatened them. The head of the eastern department at the Foreign Office, Sir Thomas Sanderson, later noted having had misgivings that the Germans would be offended, but he appears to have been alone, and even he "did not anticipate their flying out like this."[22] By the time the affair ended, the British were prepared to accept the basis of the German argument, although Rosebery attempted to deny their contention that it applied automatically, suggesting instead that they should arrange affairs first in London – not an inconsequential modification.

Rosebery began his rather awkward attempts to appease the Germans by denying that he had done what they accused him of. He had, he said, merely instructed his ambassador to delay while the government decided whether, or how, the concession would injure British interests.[23] In fact, he had gone much farther, instructing Sir Clare Ford "to prevent the concession being granted as being prejudicial to British interests," and the Germans were quite correct in believing that Ford had done his best to act against them.[24] Rosebery had acted too rashly, but this he was not prepared to admit. Instead, he blamed the Germans for not asking for an explanation from him before they acted at Cairo; and for not, from the start, coordinating their policy with the British. Rosebery, in January 1893, was paying the price for refusing to commit himself to the Triple Alliance. Informal, friendly arrangements depending on national sympathies and personal understandings, the German actions during the Kaulla affair implied, were an imperfect substitute for clear working agreements.

In spite of his arguments, Rosebery backed down from his original position, instructing Ford to arrange his next moves with his German colleague; but backing down turned out to be more difficult than he realized, and the process revealed his ambassador to be among the factors making a complicated situation more so.[25] Sir Clare Ford was not one of the great ambassadors of the nineteenth century. All his diplomatic experience had been in the west, where he had worked hard at quietly encouraging British trade, and where he had steadily, if slowly, risen in rank. At Constantinople he was controlled by the officials he was supposed to command, he never appeared able to grasp the political situation, and he had never made any attempt to consult the German ambassador, Radolin, on the concession, though reporting that he met with him frequently. He thought it his duty as an ambassador to protect British interests, and in his zeal to do so had gone farther than Rosebery intended.

Ford wanted to reserve the Angora to Baghdad railway for Britain. He had not, it turned out, awaited instructions from Rosebery before intervening in the Kaulla affair. When Rosebery first instructed him to delay the concession, Ford reported that he had already brought "to the serious consideration not only of the Porte but of the Palace as well the great prejudice which would be inflicted on British interests were new railway concessions ... given to a German Company."[26] When Rosebery reported the German complaints, Ford could not see that he might have made a mistake: "all I asked for was fair play," he complained.[27] Nothing could be more traditional, or more praise-worthy, but it was precisely this tradition of which the Germans complained: in the east the British continued to compete with German trade even while they received German diplomatic support.

When Rosebery, on 9 January, instructed Ford to arrange his policy with his German colleague, he did not yet realize how zealous his ambassador was in protecting British interests. Ford continued to oppose the concession, even after receiving his new instructions, and reported, on 13 January, that he had sent a pro-memoria to the grand vizier pointing out "the injuries which the German concessions now contemplated would inflict" on the British companies.[28] He also complained that the Porte had neglected the proposals of a Mr Stani-forth, who wanted the concession of the line to be built to Baghdad. Three days later he asked Rosebery to take a firmer line at Berlin, suggesting that such a stance would induce Kaulla to be more rea-sonable in satisfying the claims of British interests.[29] The British, Rosebery replied, no longer cared about the Smyrna-Cassaba line, nor did they desire to press too strongly the claims of the Smyrna-Aidin; Ford should try to find some concession, "not necessarily great," that would, to some extent, satisfy the Smyrna-Aidin people. Ford's obduracy, his determination to protect British interests and his conviction of being right in asking for no more than fair play were forcing Rosebery into a position where he had to make explicit the nature of the new relationship with Germany that was developing in the Near East.

In Berlin, Marschall continued to impose his version of the Anglo-German relationship on the events of the Kaulla affair. When Malet tried to defend British actions as a legitimate defence of existing interests, dropping the argument that the Baghdad line was politically important because it affected communications with India, Marschall dismissed the contention as irrelevant, given the Anglo-German friendship. That a German application was detrimental to British interests did not mean the British should protest, "as it brought the British government into play as against the German government."[30] Germany helping Britain politically at Cairo, in other words, henceforth meant Britain giving Germany unqualified support for her commercial program in the Near East. Malet tried his best to resist the conclusion, but Marschall, who had by this time completely receded from his angry attitude, seemed convinced that he had gained his point by the action he had taken.

In London, Rosebery showed himself to be well aware of the implications of the Kaulla affair. But, like his ambassador, he was powerless to do more than hint at the possibility that German action might have consequences not entirely agreeable to that nation. If the good understanding between Britain and Germany were to be translated into Englishmen standing aside at whatever sacrifice of their interests whenever a German financial agent applied for a concession, Rosebery told the German minister, then "it would have to bear a very severe strain."[31] If the Germans wanted to arrange for mutual action, they should do so in advance; had they informed Rosebery of the true state of affairs concerning the Kaulla concession, he would, he assured them, have followed a different course.[32] The Anglo-German understanding, as defined by Rosebery, implied nothing automatic; he was prepared to offer help when circumstances requiring it arose, but it was something to be negotiated.

As far as the Kaulla concession was concerned, Rosebery had no alternative to accepting the German position, and Ford was instructed to work closely with his German colleague and avoid any appearance of working with the French.[33] When Ford continued to misconstrue his instructions, he compelled Rosebery to be more explicit: it was important to work "in complete accord with Germany as regards railways in Asiatic Turkey."[34] No matter what Rosebery suggested concerning the future ramifications of the Kaulla affair, the Germans had made their point decisively and dramatically, and Rosebery had been forced to accept it. He was forced to accept it because, as long as Britain needed Germany's help at Cairo, minor interests like railways in Turkey had to be subordinated to the major one of safeguarding Britain's position in Egypt. Precisely how precarious that position was became apparent in the aftermath of the Kaulla affair.

The German demonstration of the connection between railways in Turkey and politics in Egypt might have lost some of its dramatic impact had not the British already been expecting trouble in Cairo, and had it not precipitated a crisis in Egyptian domestic politics. Over the past few months, the young khedive, Abbas Hilmi, had repeatedly indicated his determination to act independently of Cromer's advice. By the end of 1892 the Egyptian prime minister, Mustapha Pasha Fehmy, had fallen seriously ill, and Abbas was proposing to replace him with an anglophobe, Tigrane Pasha.[35] Simultaneously a number of important financial questions were about to come before the Caisse, where, Cromer assured Rosebery, the German representative would virtually control the decisions, since the Austrian and Italian representatives were certain to follow his lead.[36] Marschall could not have chosen a more opportune moment to instruct Rosebery in the uses of the Egyptian *bâton*.

Cromer was particularly upset when the Germans, on 9 January, threatened to stop helping the British in Egypt, because he had finally reached the point in his administration of Egyptian finance where he felt able to undertake some positive action of his own. After ten years of financial reforms, Cromer had succeeded not only in balancing the budget, but in producing a surplus of revenue. He proposed to use this revenue to increase the Egyptian army. The European powers, naturally, interpreted the proposal as designed to tighten Britain's hold on the country, since the army would continue to be commanded by British officers. France refused to agree to the proposal, but before the Kaulla affair exploded, Germany had promised to agree to it. When the German consul-general called on Cromer on 7 January, telling him he must no longer count on German assistance in Egypt, he withdrew the earlier promise of support for the increase of the Egyptian army. Cromer feared his management of Egyptian affairs was threatened by British opposition to the Kaulla concession at Constantinople.

Cromer's fears soon proved correct. The khedive, as Sir Clare Ford had discovered in September, had been corresponding with his grandfather, the deposed Ismail, who lived in Constantinople. Abbas appeared to be listening to his grandfather's advice, while relations between Ismail and Sultan Abdul Hamid appeared to be "very friendly."[37] On 3 January, Cromer, anticipating trouble, warned Rosebery of the khedive's inclination to grasp the first opportunity to show his independence and strength of character. When the Kaulla affair threatened to end Anglo-German cooperation at Constantinople and Cairo, it must have seemed to Ismail and Abbas that the opportunity to oppose Britain had arrived.[38] On 15 January the khedive dismissed Mustapha Pasha Fehmy and replaced him with Fakhry Pasha, described by Cromer as a close friend of Tigrane's, the anglophobe he had expected to receive the appointment, and an "incapable man of bad character." What began as an apparently harmless competition for railway concessions in Asiatic Turkey had precipitated a political crisis in Egypt.[39]

Cromer welcomed the crisis. Abbas, he told Rosebery two days before Mustapha's dismissal, "will have to receive a sharp lesson sooner or later – and the sooner the better."[40] He wanted Rosebery to authorize him to take whatever steps were necessary to prevent the change in ministers. If English influence in Egypt were to be maintained, he argued, the khedive had to be forced to yield "at whatever cost."[41] He proposed to take military possession of the ministries of finance, justice, and the interior, and the Egyptian telegraph office. In place of the deposed ministers, Cromer would put Englishmen who would act under his instructions until Abbas submitted names of ministers acceptable to the British.[42] "If the Khedive is allowed to win the day," he telegraphed to London, "English influence will be completely destroyed."[43]

Cromer presented Rosebery and the cabinet with a simple choice: they could go either backward or forward, the Egyptian situation having reached the point where it was impossible for the British to go on as they had been. According to Cromer, when the khedive had decided to assert his independence, he had destroyed the system that had hitherto prevailed. Under the previous khedive, Tewfik, Cromer had managed to stay out of sight, pulling the Egyptian political strings as seldom as possible, but pulling them nevertheless. He had disliked this system because it was artificial and unsatisfactory, but it had one advantage: it worked.[44] Abbas Hilmi, complained Cromer, wished not only to appear to govern, "but to do it actually." By refusing to listen to advice, Abbas forced Cromer out of hiding, made apparent the reality of British management, and shattered the old system. If they were to remain in Egypt, the British had no choice but to assert themselves more vigorously. "I would take the present opportunity of bringing matters to a head," he declared.[45]

Cromer's decision seemed certain to lead to a cabinet crisis in Britain and perhaps to the fall of the government, by bringing Rosebery and Gladstone into renewed conflict. In 1884 Rosebery had refused to join Gladstone's government because of its Egyptian policy, and changed his mind only after the fall of Khartoum convinced him that it was his duty to "rally 'round the government." Nevertheless, he was careful to dissociate himself from the government's previous policy, clearly aligning himself with those who believed that British must remain in Egypt for some time to come. If the British evacuated Egypt prematurely, he argued, the French would come in, threatening Britain's strategic position in the Mediterranean, her trading relations, and her route to India. Before evacuating, therefore, a stable and independent Egyptian government had to be established, and, in case something went wrong, Britain must be given the right to re-enter. Although Rosebery consistently declared himself opposed to annexation, many contemporaries found it hard to appreciate how his policy differed from one of annexation.

During Rosebery's first term as foreign secretary, in 1886, his difference with Gladstone on Egypt had been kept hidden by the Irish question. At that time Home Rule had, according to Gladstone, precedence over all other issues, so his instructions to Rosebery were simple: keep foreign affairs quiet. Rosebery, who was determined to avoid giving any sign of impending evacuation, was happy to oblige. The system worked well: Gladstone ignored Egypt, Rosebery cooperated with Bismarck at Constantinople and Cairo, and a crisis in the Balkans, which had seemed likely to involve Turkey, Greece, Serbia, and Bulgaria in war, was settled peacefully by the great powers, who demonstrated their cooperation in a blockade of the Greek fleet. Gladstone, praising Rosebery for his management of policy, began to predict that he would succeed him in the leadership of the Liberal party. In his enthusiasm, Gladstone forgot that they were divided by a real difference of opinion on Egypt.

In 1892 Rosebery realized that the difference still existed, while the solution no longer applied. Home Rule having come in for more discussion following 1886, Liberal leaders found themselves increasingly divided on matters of detail. Moreover, the country had become disenchanted with the Irish preoccupation, so that party leaders had to return to the questions they had managed to ignore, and the Parnell divorce case, having split the Irish party itself, had removed obstruction in Parliament as an excuse for concentrating on Ireland. Gladstone recognized that his new Home Rule bill was certain to be rejected by the House of Lords, and he was no longer prepared to ignore other questions involving important principles, such as the British occupation of Egypt. In the winter of 1893 Rosebery faced the prospect of heated battles in the cabinet if he was to keep Britain in Egypt.

Not surprisingly, the majority of the cabinet preferred to avoid vigorous action in Egypt; but, if forced to choose, they were more inclined to go backward than forward. The three most prominent members of the government, excluding Rosebery, considered the occupation of Egypt to have been a mistake and were anxious to end it at the first opportunity. Gladstone, Harcourt, and Morley agreed to reject Cromer's proposal. "This amounts to the annexation of Egypt," cried Harcourt, "a claim to our right of exclusive possession."[46] Morley declared he would not be a party to active intervention in Egypt.[47] Gladstone feared that Cromer's "large words" might include the use of force, "a breach of the dual understanding that the British were in Egypt to support the government."[48] Cromer anticipated difficulty with the government, arguing that the khedive had acted because he believed the government would not support its representative in Egypt.[49] Knowing Rosebery's views on Egypt, however, he felt he could count on his support. Loulou Harcourt, an enemy of Rosebery, thought it likely that both Rosebery and Cromer would resign over the issue.

That Rosebery did not resign – that he did not even come close to resigning – is an interesting feature of the January crisis. Given Rosebery's desire to establish British paramountcy in Egypt and his reputation for bad temper, the Kaulla affair and its aftermath should have led him to demand that the cabinet support Cromer and threaten to leave if they refused. Only three days before Cromer asked for his support Rosebery had assured Eddie Hamilton that he was having his own way at the Foreign Office, his colleagues having seen "that he must take his own line or else they [would] have to get on without him."[50] Cromer's request suddenly revived the cabinet's interest in foreign policy, and whereas they had neglected the Kaulla affair and recent developments in Morocco, they were now preparing to tell Rosebery what policy should be. Here was a classic situation for a fit of Roseberian temper, but none came. To everyone's surprise, Rosebery agreed to tell Cromer that the course of action he had proposed was unacceptable.[51]

Rosebery's reaction to Cromer's request seemed inexplicable. Cromer immediately complained to the queen of Rosebery's failure to support him, suggesting the cabinet must have been too strong for him. He did not realize Rosebery had given in without a fight. To Cromer, looking at the situation from the perspective of an administrator, the question facing the government was simply one of who was to govern Egypt: he or the khedive. If the government answered that it was to be the khedive, the British might as well pack up and leave tomorrow. He guessed, incorrectly, that forcing the government to choose between extremes would strengthen Rosebery's hand.[52] It did the opposite. Given a simple choice between annexation and evacuation, the government would choose evacuation. "Having his own way" at the Foreign Office did not mean Rosebery was in the position of being able to annex Egypt. On the contrary, having his own way practically depended on avoiding the issue altogether. The Kaulla affair embittered Rosebery's future relations with the Germans partly because their actions, by precipitating an Egyptian crisis, threatened to upset his control of foreign policy, an ironic result when it is remembered that one of his aims in controlling policy was to maintain a close connection with the Triple Alliance.

Rosebery's hands were tied, not freed, by Cromer's extremism. "It would have been impossible to get the cabinet to agree to the occupation by force of the public offices, and more especially to the seizure of the telegraph wires." Nor did Rosebery agree with the alterantives posed by Cromer: the vigorous measures "should be reserved as a fifth act, and not as a second."[53] The best diplomatists recognize steps of intermediate action where others see only a dichotomy. Cromer, Rosebery said, might have refused to receive any communications from the new government. If this move failed, the British might announce an increase in their garrison. Next, Cromer could have agreed to the sultan's proposal to have the khedive come to Constantinople for investiture, reminding him that he was a vassal of the sultan. All these steps, Rosebery argued, would have gradually increased the pressure on Abbas, while the cabinet would not have been forced to choose between annexation and evacuation. Possibly, if all these measures had failed, it might have been necessary to take the ones proposed by Cromer, but this last step, Rosebery felt sure, would never have been reached.[54]

Cromer, misled by his own stake in the situation, saw none of the possibilities envisioned by Rosebery. Instead, he saw ten years of hard work and administrative reforms about to be thrown away overnight by an impetuous boy. He welcomed the crisis over the ministerial changes because he saw the opportunity of safeguarding his work in the future. When Rosebery asked him to suggest less extreme measures, he refused: "I can suggest nothing less violent than the measures which I have already proposed," and complained that Rosebery's telegrams gave "little indication of your intention to act vigorously in support of any representations I may make here."[55] Rosebery responded calmly to the impertinence, explaining it away as a result of the stress and strain under which Cromer had been labouring. "I can well understand," he wrote privately to Cromer, "that under those circumstances telegrams are not so calmly studied as in the sylvan seclusion of Berkeley Square."[56] He asked Cromer to remember that telegrams not marked "private" would be seen by the cabinet, and that there might be features of the situation better seen only by Rosebery.

Events proved Rosebery's view of the situation to be the right one. Without resorting to the extreme measures proposed by Cromer, the British managed to frighten Abbas, who gave way, removed Fakhry

Pasha, and promised to follow British advice on all important matters. Rosebery successfully rejected both Cromer's measures and his conclusions. "My own view," he concluded, "is that we must affect to go on as before," precisely what Cromer had claimed to be impossible.[57] Rosebery realized that there was no easy way out of the Egyptian situation: Britain could not evacuate because France would step in, but she could not annex because the cabinet would not allow it. The situation made her depend on German help more than ever, and the Germans had demonstrated, in the Kaulla affair, that the price of their help was going up.

Going on as before in Egypt did not necessarily mean standing still, and one of the consequences of the Kaulla affair was that it convinced Rosebery of the necessity of strengthening the British position in Egypt. Ironically, then, just as Rosebery appeared to acquiesce in the cabinet view of Egyptian policy, and thereby avoid a ministerial crisis, he produced the crisis he appeared determined to avoid, when he agreed to a new proposal of Cromer's. Before the January crisis, Cromer had agreed to replace a British infantry battalion in Egypt with more cavalry. On 19 January he proposed, instead, to have the infantry battalion remain, to have the cavalry sent out anyway, and to have an additional infantry battalion accompany it.[58] Rosebery agreed. The settlement of the day before, he told Gladstone, was only a respite.[59] "The snake," he told the queen, "is scotched and not killed."[60]

Gladstone was enraged. In the autumn of 1892, soon after the formation of the government, he had responded favourably to Waddington's attempt to begin negotiations on the evacuation of Egypt.[61] As we have seen, Rosebery had managed to avoid the negotiations only because of Waddington's violation of protocol in approaching the prime minister rather than the foreign secretary.[62] Gladstone had accepted Rosebery's stand, but sending reinforcements to Egypt went too far in the other direction. "I would as soon put a torch to Westminster Abbey as send additional troops to Egypt," he declared. "I can see nothing for it but for Rosebery to resign."[63] His reaction, along with the cabinet's, was made the more intense because Cromer's recent demand for vigorous action raised the possibility of the additional force being used for offensive purposes. The war secretary, Henry Campbell-Bannerman, and the colonial secretary, Lord Ripon, felt the reports from Egypt contained "a strong tinge of Cromerism," suspecting that Cromer was trying to force them into annexing Egypt.[64] English troops and residents could not be imperilled, Campbell-Bannerman thought, or Cromer would have said so.[65]

Rosebery, who had decided to support Cromer's request from the start, recognized the cabinet's decision would turn on the question of immediate danger. Cromer's unfortunate expressions at the beginning of the crisis, he complained to the queen, had bred irritation and suspicion in the cabinet.[66] The English in Egypt must, as he said, affect to go on as before. A massacre of residents, a Dervish invasion, another Arabist uprising, because they would create a political crisis in Britain, were the kind of threats to which the government would respond. After some hints from Rosebery, Cromer discovered a threat to the garrison and the residents.[67] Rosebery did not resign, nor did Gladstone put the torch to Westminster Abbey. Cromer received his additional troops, and Rosebery, announcing the increase, claimed it indicated no change of policy or modification of the assurances Britain had given on the subject of the occupation.[68] The English, as Rosebery said they must, were affecting to go on as before.

The Kaulla affair and its aftermath demonstrated, as clearly as any incident could, the dilemma in which the British found themselves in the 1890s. Naval strategists, although they did not agree on all the features of the situation, were convinced that Britain had lost her naval superiority in the Mediterranean. In fact, they were generally agreed that if Britain faced a war with France and Russia, apparently a logical conclusion of the Franco-Russian alliance, she would have to withdraw her fleet from the Mediterranean. This made the control of Egypt even more important than it had been, for, it was believed, if France controlled both the Mediterranean and Egypt, she would not only force Britain to rely on the slower and more expesive Cape route for trade and communication with India, but she might use her control of Suez to mount an attack on Britain in the Indian Ocean. Therefore Rosebery, who had opposed evacuation in 1885-6, was more determined than ever to retain control of Egypt. The opposition of the Gladstonians to continuing the occupation, however, meant he could do little to strengthen the British hold on Egypt: at best he could, by conjuring up the threat of a disaster, send a few more troops.

These considerations made the British in general, and Rosebery in particular, more dependent on Germany than they had been in the days when Bismarck first used the Egyptian situation to secure colonial concessions. Germany tried to use this dependence to force Britain into the Triple Alliance. The reason the British found German methods so irritating – there was little difference between Rosebery's complaints and the later ones of Lansdowne and Balfour – was that the Germans had to demonstrate their dominance. Given the ambitious designs of the new course, it did the Germans no good to negotiate quietly and amicably for commercial and colonial agreements with the British, and permit British participation in the Triple Alliance to remain informal. Germany could expand only by transforming the Triple Alliance, and Britain's role in it, into an offensive arrangement. To this end, the British had to be made to realize that their position in Egypt, which made them dependent on German help, could be maintained only by acquiescing in German commercial expansion in the Near East, and in Germany's political leadership of the Triple Alliance. The Kaulla affair had offered the perfect opportunity for demonstrating the logic of this reasoning.

The aftermath of the Kaulla affair seemed to show that Rosebery had no alternative to accepting the German argument. At the first sign of trouble between Britain and Germany at Cairo, a crisis erupted, and Rosebery, with the connection between German commerce in Turkey and the British political position in Egypt demonstrated so forcefully, immediately reversed his position on the Kaulla concession. The reaction of the cabinet to Cromer's proposals for solving the Egyptian ministerial crisis showed, at the same time, that the apparent alternative to evacuating Egypt, annexing it, did not exist. Britain must, in Rosebery's words, "go on as before," which seemed to mean continued dependence on Germany at Cairo. It seemed, therefore, that when Rosebery accepted the logic of the German argument, he would be forced to accept its conclusion as well, and Britain would be drawn into the Triple Alliance, the terms and purpose of which would be determined by Germany.

Rosebery's policy in the period following the Kaulla affair showed, even under circumstances most favourable to Germany, that Britain would make every effort, and undertake a number of risks, to avoid joining the Triple Alliance. When Marschall, in the midst of the affair, claimed that the transaction had dealt a blow to the good understanding between Germany and Britain, Rosebery agreed, "but not in the way Baron von Marschall intended it."[69] He was disgusted with the German outburst: although he was a leading advocate of the good understanding with Germany and the Triple Alliance, they, in turn, had treated him with contempt and embarrassed him in cabinet by making the foundation of his foreign policy seem shaky. Rosebery, who would not evacuate Egypt, but who could not annex it, had to continue working with the Germans, but, partly as a result of the Kaulla affair, the relationship became awkward and irritating, with each side distrusting the other, and each trying to assert control.

The Kaulla affair set the tone of Anglo-German relations until the collapse of the Liberal government. Germany persisted in trying to drive Britain into the alliance, using the same methods she had used during the affair. Rosebery, determined to resist, developed a program that would allow him to continue to work in accord with Germany, but would also allow him the freedom to remain outside the Triple Alliance. In this program, he acquiesced in German economic expansion only after negotiation and when it suited his purpose: "our understanding is not altogether one-sided."[70] The first part of the program saw Rosebery try to lessen the danger from France by establishing better relations with Russia, a policy that resulted in the Pamirs agreement of 1895. In the second part, he aimed to overpower France in the Mediterranean by an increase in naval building, a policy that resulted in the Naval Act of 1893, Gladstone's resignation, and Rosebery's becoming prime minister. The third part of the program was less straightforward. "There is a considerable section in the Liberal Party that would gladly see a close understanding with France," Rosebery declared during the Kaulla affair. "It would greatly facilitate their views if they knew of this sort of proceeding."[71]

Grand diplomatic programs, such as the one designed by Rosebery, are easy to conceive but difficult to execute. In the months that followed the Kaulla affair, few opportunities arose that would enable Rosebery to show the Germans his determination to resist the conclusions they had drawn from the affair. Besides, there seemed no reason for haste. As soon as the affair ended, the Germans restored the old policy of the good understanding in the Near East. At Cairo, Cromer received the support he needed for his financial and military measures. At Constantinople, the Germans advised the sultan to come to terms with the British on the occupation of Egypt; French advice, Marschall told the Turkish ambassador, should be disregarded.[72] The Germans, having scored a diplomatic triumph in the Kaulla affair, seemed prepared to wait before renewing their efforts to bring the British into the alliance.

No doubt the Germans believed they could wait because events appeared to be moving in the direction they desired. Although nothing particularly dramatic occurred in the aftermath of the Kaulla affair, the few diplomatic questions that appeared to be developing seemed destined to work to Germany's advantage. What the Germans wanted, of course, were clear signs that Russia and France intended to work against Britain outside Europe. Reports from the Pamirs, Persia, Morocco, and Siam suggested that the Germans were going to get what they wanted.

The Pamirs, frozen solid and encased in snow, were quiet but worrying. The Russians, it was feared, were simply biding their time until spring, when they would occupy by force the strategic territory they desired.[73] In January the anglophobe *Novoe Vremya* published a long article on the value of the Pamirs, arguing that their occupation by Russia would enable her to hold Afghanistan in awe "and to annihilate that ring of robber states with which the English have engirt India on the North." Moreover, "when once the mighty hand of the White Tsar rests on the summits of the Hindu-Kush, it is to be supposed that the intrigues of the English will cease, and their policy in Europe will become much more accommodating."[74] With these threats in the air, Rosebery had little choice but to continue conjuring up the possibility of a British counter-expedition, even though the government of India had told him this was out of the question.[75] At the same time, he continued to try to arrange mutual action with the Chinese at St Petersburg. Both of these manoeuvres were designed to forestall a new Russian expedition in the spring.

If Rosebery were to succeed in resisting the German argument that Britain's parlous condition outside Europe forced her to depend on the Triple Alliance, then he had to do what he could to keep things quiet in Asia. Thus the threat of a counter-expedition to the Pamirs did not suggest an inclination to move the frontier forward; rather, it was part of Rosebery's policy of forcing the Russians to negotiate. In this way the Pamirs were also becoming a touchstone of Anglo-Russian relations. If Rosebery's calculations were right, then the Russians, facing the Triple Alliance in Europe and turning their ambitions to the Far East, should seek to avoid a quarrel in central Asia. Russian activities on the Hindu Kush were watched carefully, not only for their local ramifications, but also for what they revealed of the state of the balance of power in Europe.

For the time being, however, the Pamirs question appeared more likely to lead to trouble than to an understanding, and it was not alone in creating a diplomatic scene pleasing to German taste. The domestic situation in Persia had been deteriorating for some time, and British agents feared that it would soon lead to Russia dominating the country. The Russians were demanding that Persia, in return for her failure to meet some financial obligations, cede to them the Khorassan village of Firuzeh in the north of the country.[76] The British minister at Teheran, Sir Frank Lascelles, who was alarmed by the decaying condition of Persian politics and finance, reported that it would be an arduous task if Britain were to attempt to arrest the process of decay.[77] Here then was another situation far removed from Europe, which seemed likely to create more fear and suspicion of Russian designs and thus move the British closer to the Triple Alliance.

Rosebery's policy in Persia reflected his general diplomatic program. Lascelles could see no alternative to Persia's ceding Firuzeh to Russia, so – anticipating Curzon's scheme of partition – he proposed that Britain should demand a village in Seistan, in the south of the country, in exchange. Rosebery, who later appointed Lascelles ambassador to St Petersburg, respected his judgment. He nevertheless rejected his proposal. Britain, he argued, could no longer bear the burden of the whole world: Persia must be placed in the second rank of British interests. "All we can do," he told Lascelles, "is to do our best to keep the rickety concern going."[78] Given the gloomy portrayal of Persia's future provided by Lascelles, this meant, in effect, allowing Russia to dominate her eventually. Rosebery refused to contemplate a struggle over Persia.

Persia was, curiously, the one spot where Rosebery's plan of Indian defence did not clash with that of Lansdowne and Roberts. Lascelles, who had hoped to be supported in his partition plan by the viceroy of India, received no more encouragement from Calcutta than from London. "The question," Lansdowne said, refusing to bestir himself, "is an imperial, not an Indian one."[79] He accepted the Roberts view that India was best defended by the Indian army, ideally along the Kabul-Kandahar line. If Indian communications and lines of supply were to be stretched as far as Persia, this defensive strategy might be ruined. Besides, buffers were not to be counted on unless there were some means of exerting influence over them, the history of the last century having shown that eastern states were incapable of real independence. Thus the government of India readily accepted Rosebery's decision to reject the Lascelles partition project.

Rosebery's reasoning, however, differed markedly from that of Lansdowne and Roberts. The first line of Indian defence, in his view, was the balance of power in Europe. As long as Russia had to contend with the Triple Alliance, she was not likely to be troublesome in Asia. The danger lay in provoking Russia to the point where she would seek an accommodation with the Triple Alliance in order to concentrate her efforts in Asia. Rosebery therefore avoided even the appearance of competing with Russia in Persia, and attempted to arrange for mutual action, should the shah be deposed and a crisis of succession erupt.[80] Whereas Rosebery's Asiatic policy was inseparable from his European, Roberts saw no connection between the two: "Whatever help we may derive from continental alliances and complications in other parts of the world," he told Lansdowne, "it is not reasonable to suppose that foreign nations will fight our battles for us in the east."[81] Rosebery, of course, never imagined that the Triple Alliance would fight in the east. In his view it did not have to: it satisfied his Asiatic requirements simply by pinning down millions of Russian troops in eastern Europe.

On the surface of diplomacy then, affairs appeared to be working in Germany's favour: new military expeditions might be sent to the Pamirs in the spring, while a competition for the future of Persia might develop if the shah were deposed. But these advantages would prove superficial if Rosebery succeeded in his intention of avoiding a confrontation with Russia on either front. Although this policy was still in the first stage of development, Rosebery was quietly working at improving relations with Russia, the first tactic in his program of remaining outside the Triple Alliance while continuing to work with it and use it to his advantage.

The Germans continued to assume, almost until 1914, that the possibility of a British accord with the Russians in Asia was bound to fail. In the 1890s the possibility of an improvement in Britain's relations with France seemed even more remote. Everywhere one looked, Britain and France appeared to be quarrelling. Although the quarrel was most obvious in Egypt, it was also evident in West Africa and Indo-China. But at the time of the Kaulla affair it was in Morocco that trouble seemed most likely to develop, thereby lending substance to Germany's argument concerning the value of the Triple Alliance to Britain.

Like most diplomatic questions that arose outside Europe, that of Morocco might be told as a story in itself. Peculiar characteristics, especially her location and geography, distinguish the Moroccan from other affairs, and the story there cannot be fully understood without taking these into account. When Rosebery returned to the Foreign Office in 1892, he inherited a situation in Morocco that had been complicated by the ambitious designs of the British minister. Sir Charles Euan Smith had conducted a foreign policy of his own, on the one hand using bribes and threats at the Moroccan court, while on the other proposing to the French that they should partition the country, with Tangier to go to Britain.[82] The policy failed, as it was bound to fail, because Britain lacked the power necessary to frighten the Moors and the French simultaneously. Smith's bombast succeeded in destroying the position of Britain at the court while strengthening that of France.[83] During the autumn of 1892 Smith continued to send alarming reports of French activity, trying to convince Rosebery that they were attempting to dominate the country. The French, he said, were demanding a land concession in Figuig for a railway to connect with Algeria, the creation of a Franco-Moroccan bank, and, most alarming, the construction, under French supervision, of batteries at Tangier.[84] Rosebery replied to these warnings by dismissing Smith from the diplomatic service, the first indication that he was not prepared to risk a quarrel with the French in Morocco. Smith's replacement reported that the rumours could be traced to the head of the Italian military mission at Fez, the first indication received by Rosebery that the members of the Triple Alliance would attempt to set Britain at odds with France in Morocco.[85]

Even to Charles Eliot, Smith's less ambitious and more trustworthy replacement, it seemed clear that the French intended to dominate Morocco. Where he differed from Smith was in his assessment of French strategy. The French, he argued, were prepared to move slowly, gaining as many commercial advantages as they could in the form most acceptable to His Shereefian Majesty. They deliberately avoided "showy" concessions in order that they might "pose as the Friends and protectors of this Kingdom, who desire to maintain the status quo, which other Powers are represented as wishing to alter."[86] Eliot's assessment therefore lent substance to the German and Italian argument that the French were aiming to dominate Morocco to the detriment of British interests.

But what were British interests in Morocco? Rosebery never said. The British were certainly involved in a number of commercial ventures, but none of any great significance: the Germans dominated Moroccan trade, and the French ranked second.[87] British interests were strategic, revolving around the future of Tangier and the safety of Gibraltar. While some naval planners would have liked to obtain Tangier as a base for Britain, Rosebery never gave a hint that he intended to try, and throughout his time at the Foreign Office he appeared content with the way things stood in Morocco. As long as the French did not actually possess and fortify Tangier, the situation was not dangerous to the British. Gibraltar, which was more complicated, fortunately led to the same conclusion.

Rosebery regarded the goodwill of the Spanish as essential to the safety of Gibraltar because, either alone or in combination with the French, they could pose a direct threat to Britain's position there. But the Spanish were sensitive on the question of Gibraltar, which they regarded as rightfully theirs. The Republican party in Spain was particularly eager to recover Gibraltar and was prepared to ally with the French in order to get it. Nor were Spanish sensitivities limited to this question; they also felt that they had a stake at the fortress of Melilla.[88] Therefore, if Rosebery were to succeed in maintaining the goodwill of the Spanish, he would have to consider their interests in Morocco.

All questions of foreign policy interact; no action on the part of a great power occurs in a vacuum; every move causes repercussions.

When Rosebery decided to strengthen the Egyptian garrison in January he did so for Egyptian reasons, partly connected with Germany's policy during the Kaulla affair. The Spanish, however, feared that his decision indicated a policy of strengthening the position of Britain throughout the Mediterranean and that the occupation of Tangier might be the next step in this program. Newspaper articles advocating the neutralization of the Straits of Gibraltar began to appear. The Spanish minister for foreign affairs, the Marquis de la Vega de Armigo, declared that he would not repeat the error of the French in Egypt. Whatever course England pursued, he promised, "Spain would be found at her side ship for ship."[89] Thus Rosebery might reasonably worry that strengthening Egypt would have the result of pushing the Spaniards onto the side of the French.

Rosebery began a campaign to convince the Spanish of his intention to uphold the current state of affairs in the western Mediterranean. Convincing the Spanish was not easy. Until something happened that would offer a concrete opportunity to demonstrate this intention, Rosebery could provide only intangible evidence. Consequently, he ordered the Channel squadron, which would normally have touched at Gibraltar, to proceed directly to Madeira, thereby entirely avoiding Moroccan waters. He was anxious, he said, "to pay every possible consideration to the susceptibilities of the Spanish Government."[90] When he sent Sir West Ridgeway on a special mission to Morocco in an attempt to undo the damage done by Smith, he ordered him to proceed first to Madrid. Again, Rosebery was trying to make it clear that Britain would not undertake any activities in Morocco without first arranging matters with Spain. Ridgeway assured the queen regent that the policy of Britain was to uphold the status quo in Morocco.[91]

In Morocco, therefore, as in Persia and the Pamirs, a situation appeared to be developing that would compel Britain to rely increasingly on the assistance of the Triple Alliance. The French appeared determined to dominate Morocco, possibly in conjunction with republicans in Spain. But, as in Persia, Rosebery refused to do anything that might make a clash more likely. He abandoned Smith's ambitious designs, refused to be alarmed by reports of French intrigue, and attempted to reassure the Spanish that he had no intention of upsetting the current state of affairs in Morocco. As long as Gibraltar was safe, as long as there appeared to be no immediate likelihood of France capturing Tangier, then Rosebery was prepared to allow French intrigues at Fez to continue.

Rosebery's policy on the questions that arose in the aftermath of the

Kaulla affair was consistent. In Egypt, he told Cromer, "we must go on as we were." In Persia, he told Lascelles, "we must do our best to keep the rickety concern going." In the Pamirs, he tried to arrange for a negotiated settlement, while in Morocco he deliberately avoided change in the hope that the country would remain quiet. All of these plans, none of them in the least dramatic (which probably explains why so little attention has been given to them), were designed to confute the argument of the Triple Alliance that French and Russian policy must eventually compel the British to become a member of it. Rosebery aimed to use the balance of power in Europe to safeguard the imperial interests of Britain, but he wished to avoid a situation in which those interests might force Britain into fighting a war in Europe.

Given Rosebery's reputation as a Liberal imperialist, his diplomacy has an ironic aspect: surely imperial considerations should have come before continental ones? But Rosebery, widely regarded as one of the outspoken advocates of expansion in the age of the "new Imperialism," always considered himself to be a consolidationist, and saw no contradiction between this view of himself and his enthusiasm for empire. His diplomacy supports the claim of consolidation. British interests, he argued, were too numerous, too varied, too widespread to extend them any further; it would require all the strength Britain could muster to keep what she already had; further extensions of territory would reduce her freedom of action by making her more dependent on the alliance politics of the continent.

Historians of diplomacy are misled when they are attracted to the dramatic. Evidence to support the argument that Rosebery was an expansionist is more striking, and more readily accessible, than evidence to the contrary, because most of it is rhetorical. The phrase "pegging out claims for the future" has cleaved to Rosebery (to use the words of George Eliot in another connection) like a hereditary odour. It was a phrase he almost immediately regretted; it did not represent his real views: in fact, even in Uganda, he simply wanted to keep and consolidate what Britain already had, and encouraging the vague hope that Uganda might some day pay for itself was clear evidence that it was going to be expensive for a long time to come. Rosebery's real purpose for wishing to remain in Uganda was strategic and diplomatic: to consolidate Britain's position in Egypt, and thereby strengthen her relations with the great powers of Europe.

Rosebery's real views become evident only through the close study of the day-to-day tedium of diplomacy. His private correspondence and the diplomatic documents show few signs of any desire to go forward, but they do show a determination that Britain should hold on to what she already had. He was certainly an imperialist: Britain, without her empire, would be reduced to the ranks of the second-rate. But the empire was already big enough; his job was not to see that it got bigger, but to ensure that it did not get smaller. The best guarantee of achieving this goal was the balance of power in Europe, but, paradoxically, the greater single threat to the empire was the danger that it might be dragged into a great war in Europe. Rosebery never departed from his explanation to Gladstone of July 1891. "I am," he said, "entirely in agreement with you as to the paramount necessity of our holding aloof from the Triple Alliance or any other such engagement for the same reason for which I am hostile to the Channel Tunnel: that I am anxious to obtain the full advantage of the insular position with which Providence has endowed us."[92] Rosebery never had the slightest intention of joining the Triple Alliance. When he told the Germans, Austrians, and Italians that the cabinet would not allow any closer arrangement than the one that already existed, he was telling the truth, but hiding the fact that he agreed with them. Moreover, his decision to throw the weight of Britain, informally, onto the side of the alliance did not arise from a careful, mechanical assessment of the relative power of the two sides in Europe. The aim of the Triple Alliance was to maintain the current state of affairs in Europe; the policy of its members was peaceful and conservative (although Italy had to be restrained), while the policy of France and Russia, and France in particular, was dissatisfied and revisionist. Britain's role therefore was not to "balance" the two sides, but to give the conservative side such power as to make it the dominant factor in European diplomacy.

The Kaulla affair gave Rosebery trouble because it provided a hint that his assessment of German policy might be wrong. His actions during the affair showed that he had no objection to the extension of German commerce and finance into the Near East; but he refused to allow this action to be turned into a general principle whereby Britain would automatically assist Germany's transformation into a world power. If the Germans were too ambitious, they, and not the French, might prove the greater threat to European peace, and thereby to imperial security. This explains why the Germans always had to work hard for colonial concessions: the British were usually prepared to concede them something – and there was little of value left – but the concession had to arise from the particular features of the situation. Every alteration in colonial arrangements had to be negotiated; there was to be no general principle of assisting German ambitions.

In the early months of 1893 Rosebery did what he could to avoid becoming entangled in new difficulties in Persia and Morocco, because avoiding them meant relying less on the Triple Alliance. He remained convinced that France, not Germany, was the more aggressive power. The French penchant for intrigue, he told his ambassador to Germany, might finally seal an Anglo-German understanding by creating in Britain a body of sentiment favourable to that alliance. He knew that the next crisis with France would renew the efforts of Germany to push Britain into the alliance. Earlier, he had sensed that the diplomatic scene was changing, when he wished it to stay the same. He sensed, instinctively, that this change was somehow due to the departure of Bismarck. "I feel the alteration," he wrote, "though I could not well explain to myself how it shows itself. It is perhaps like shooting at a place where the head gamekeeper has been changed. The pheasants are as numerous, the woods are the same, one sees no difference in the beaters: and yet one feels that the scene is different."[93]

CHAPTER FOUR

The Far East in World Policy: The Crisis of Consolidation

It cannot be doubted that Pitt would learn from his father that a foreign policy required firmness and purpose; that in that, as in other things, vacillation was the one unpardonable sin; but that the arm of this country should never be put further forward than it could be maintained.

Pitt (1891)

In the years 1893-5 all questions in diplomacy centred on the future intentions of France and Russia. In 1893, although it was not yet clear what the rumoured arrangement between them might entail, two simple interpretations were offered. The Germans argued that the arrangement was aimed at Britain, and that it was designed to coordinate the activities of France and Russia in the Mediterranean, Egypt, and Asia. The British replied that the arrangement was continental, aimed at the Triple Alliance in Europe. Obviously, the future pattern of European diplomacy depended a great deal on which of these two interpretations was correct. If the arrangement were imperial, then it would make Britain more dependent on the support of the Triple Alliance; if it were continental, then the Triple Alliance would depend more on Britain. The big question in these years then, was "who faces the greater danger?"

Most of Rosebery's diplomacy was calculated to avoid danger, and thus avoid being drawn into the Triple Alliance. Because attention has for so long been focused on Uganda and Egypt, it has been widely assumed that Rosebery was inclined to follow an aggressive policy of expansion. This is not so. In Persia, he refused to go forward and seemed prepared to acquiesce in the eventual domination of that country by Russia. In the Pamirs his talk about a British expedition to counter the Russian was merely a diplomatic manoeuvre designed to induce the Russians to negotiate a settlement; he was equally willing to uphold Chinese claims in the area if doing so would keep the strategic passes free from Russian control. In Morocco, he was doing his best to quiet things down, and refused to be caught up in a contest for predominance with the French. Even in Egypt, Rosebery had refused to assist Cromer's efforts to assert more direct authority over the government of Egypt. Finally, in Uganda, two features are often overlooked. First, Rosebery was working to keep, and consolidate, what had already been "pegged out" by the Imperial British East Africa Company, and second, this policy could really give very little offence to foreign powers, who had no territorial claims of their own.

Although Rosebery's diplomacy as a whole was defensive and consolidationist, one distinction must be made: he was more willing to antagonize the French than he was the Russians. Britain, he believed, was in a position to defend herself against France, as any attack on her or her possessions must come by sea, and her navy was vastly superior to that of France. Russia was in a stronger position than France, as she could threaten Britain in several areas where sea power was of little value, especially in central Asia. But there was a diplomatic element as well as a strategic one in Rosebery's thinking. Germany could hardly threaten to reach an understanding with France without preparing to overturn the settlement of 1871. Thus Germany had no choice, so far as France was concerned, but to assist Britain, indirectly at least, by maintaining a large military force on her western frontier. In the east, however, it was reasonable that Rosebery should fear an understanding between Germany and Russia, for, if the new course in her policy failed, Germany might return to the old Bismarckian strategy of the *Dreikaiserbund*. Russia might be persuaded to reject this possibility if it could be shown that Britain posed no danger to her. For these reasons, Rosebery was more anxious to accommodate the Russians than he was the French.

Nevertheless, Rosebery's diplomacy was generally defensive, since he aimed to avoid new obligations and complications, which, he believed, would certainly lead to both strategic and diplomatic weakness. Historians who assume that Rosebery was determined to expand, to peg out claims, to thwart French ambitions at every opportunity, judge him accordingly: if he failed to expand, if he failed to thwart the French, then his policy failed generally. Arguing thus, they account for his failure in one of two ways. First, they look at his personality. His nervous temperament, they say, led to a collapse of will in times of crisis. Second, they look at the politics of the government. The cabinet, they say, was too divisive to agree on any foreign or imperial policy and was therefore bound to be ineffectual in times of crisis. This argument and the proof offered to substantiate it have dominated interpretations of the first foreign crisis faced by Rosebery after returning to office.

As with most crises, it is difficult to say when the Siam crisis of 1893 began. Tension between Britain and France in Southeast Asia had been building up over the last decade as their spheres of influence moved closer to one another – the French through Indo-China, the British through Burma. During Salisbury's last government the French had proposed that the Mekong be used to limit the French and British spheres, but the government of India had objected and thereby managed to forestall a settlement. The complicating factor was the province of Kyaing Chiang, which straddled the Mekong in that part of the river to the immediate south of China.

When the government of India annexed Burma in 1886, it inherited Burmese feudatory rights in Kyaington, and Kyaington, in turn, claimed rights in Kyaing Chiang. Siam contested these rights, claiming the province for herself. Lord Kimberley's predecessor at the India Office, Viscount Cross, had handed over the government of Kyaing Chiang to Siam, but insisted on retaining for the government of India the right to resume possession of the province at any future time "should circumstances demand it."[1] Kimberley, who thought this came too close to being a "forward" doctrine, altered the situation slightly in favour of Siam when he proposed that Siam should simply undertake not to cede Kyaing Chiang to a foreign power without first consulting Britain.

Kyaing Chiang became the focal point of the crisis of 1893 because France also claimed a right to it as the successor to the empire of Annam.[2] The French asserted their claim to that part of the province's territory on the left bank of the Mekong and refused to recognize the right of the British even to discuss the future of the territory. When public meetings were held in France to discuss the situation in Indo-China, the permanent under-secretary for foreign affairs, Sir Philip Currie, noted that the French appeared "to be working themselves up into a state of excitement against Siam with the view of plundering them."[3] In order to show that they were serious, the French sent a gunboat to Bangkok and the crisis appeared to be under way.

Rosebery's response to the moves of the French is illuminating because it was the first instance in which he was forced to respond to a forward movement on their part. When the British minister at Bangkok, Captain Jones, requested that a gunboat be sent to match the French one, Rosebery refused. Such a step, he said, might be misconstrued.[4] He hesitated to undertake any action that might encourage the Siamese to resist. He was prepared, if Kimberley agreed, to declare that British dominions and protectorates would nowhere extend to the east of the Mekong, thereby giving up Britain's claim to the eastern part of Kyaing Chiang.[5] "The quarrel," the British ambassador at Paris was told, "is not one in which Lord Rosebery desires to be mixed up."[6] In this, the first opportunity to forestall French imperial ambitions, Rosebery took a conciliatory line and prepared to give up a British territorial claim.

The crisis that followed these initial moves is difficult to comprehend if it is not recognized that Rosebery was willing to concede, without fuss, most of what the French were demanding. He never saw any danger in the French extending their territory up to the Mekong to the south of Kyaing Chiang. He did, however, foresee other dangers. If Siam resisted, war might break out, with France gaining the whole of Siam and establishing a frontier with British India. Avoiding this possibility was Rosebery's primary aim during the crisis.

It is easy to see why a frontier with France in Southeast Asia was to be avoided. More troops would be needed, more forts would have to be built to accommodate them, more railways constructed to transport them. The added expense would be enormous, and Rosebery wished to avoid it if possible. But the real danger, although less obvious, was diplomatic. Thus far, France and Russia had had little opportunity of working together; the French had talked of an alliance in Morocco, but it is difficult to see what part the Russians would play; and, more significantly, the Russians had refused to act with the French in Egypt. The French, of course, could do little to help the Russians in central Asia; but, with a frontier on the southeastern flank of British India, their capacity for cooperation would increase significantly. The real danger then was that Britain might be forced into the Triple Alliance by events in Asia, because she could not afford to stand alone against the combined efforts of France and Russia.

Thus, from the very beginning of the crisis, it was the survival of Siam as a buffer between the empires of France and Britain in Asia that concerned Rosebery. He saw no reason why this buffer could not begin at the Mekong. His first concern was to restrain the Siamese from doing anything that might lead to war with France, and thereby to the loss of the whole buffer. The Siamese were reported to be purchasing gunpowder and preparing to sink ships in the entrance of the river; Rosebery cautioned them to be prudent and do nothing that might precipitate a rupture with France. He went further. Siam, he told the minister in London, should endeavour to settle the affair by direct negotiation with France. Britain, in other words, had no interest in the territory being discussed. Siam, he continued, would probably find it necessary to surrender something of what she considered herself entitled to. Britain, in other words, would not even recognize the validity of Siam's international claims. "An attitude of defiance and of unyielding opposition," he concluded, was "only too likely to lead to an increase" in French demands.[7]

What Rosebery wished to avoid, however, the Siamese determined to make unavoidable. The only way they could retain their territory was to pretend that their very existence was at stake, and the only way to do this was to make a crisis of the situation. Although they realized that their forces were no match for the French, they decided nevertheless to resist the French. They played the crisis with their customary skill, the skill that enabled them to remain the only independent state in Southeast Asia. They prepared to go to war with France neither because they wanted to fight, nor because they thought they could win, but because they calculated that the British could not permit them to lose.

From the beginning of the crisis, Rosebery regarded Siamese resistance as a complicating feature in the situation; the British minister at Bangkok quickly proved to be another. The best course for the Siamese to follow, Captain Jones told Rosebery, was to resist. The French, he said, believed that the Siamese would submit without a struggle – exactly what Rosebery wished them to do – while "the mere prospect of a struggle would I believe modify considerably the preposterous pretensions of France."[8] Rosebery, who had no intention of testing his assumption, ordered Jones to impress upon the Siamese the extreme importance of avoiding a rupture with the French. He continued counselling caution and moderation even when it was announced that a French admiral, commanding five gunboats, had sailed from Hong Kong for Siamese waters.[9] Jones replied that the Siamese had, by agreeing to release a Frenchman taken prisoner in a frontier skirmish, already demonstrated their inclination to avoid a rupture. The French colonials, he argued, desired to provoke a war that would entail the annexation of the entire Siamese kingdom.[10] The Siamese had obviously succeeded in convincing Jones that their existence was at stake.

Rosebery was more difficult to convince. Develle, the French foreign secretary, had promised to notify the British government before he activated the French fleet poised at Saigon. Consequently, Rosebery was sceptical of the French intention, reported by Jones, of ascending the Menam to Bangkok. In London, the Siamese began to cite Jones as approving their resolution to resist the passage of the French gunboats, and Rosebery again instructed him to be careful in his communications with them.[11] In Paris, Edmund Phipps, acting head of the British legation in the absence of Lord Dufferin, was assured by Develle that the government had abandoned its intention of sending ships to Bangkok.[12] Unfortunately, half an hour before this message was communicated to London, Jones had cabled that the gunboats, having stormed the defences of the harbour, were now anchored opposite the French legation.[13] It began to look as if Jones might be right: perhaps Siam's existence was at stake; perhaps Develle had deliberately deceived Rosebery. However, in spite of the reports from Siam and in spite of the apparent deception practised on him by Develle, Rosebery persisted in following a moderate policy. "I may be wrong," he declared, "but I still believe in M. Develle's loyalty." The secret, he explained, was that Develle had to deal with "uncontrollable and hotheaded agents."[14] It was a favourite explanation. Men at the metropolis, whether Paris, Berlin, Rome, St Petersburg, or London, removed from the action, often felt a greater sympathy for one another than they did for their own agents. Blaming the men on the spot was convenient and often satisfied both parties to a dispute: if the activities of agents threatened no vital interest, the rift between promises and actions could be patched over. French gunboats in Bangkok were unwelcome to Rosebery, but they were truly alarming only if they presaged war and the eventual annexation of Siam.

Rosebery did not welcome gunboats in Bangkok because they aroused the anger of British merchants. The Chambers of Commerce of Manchester, Sheffield, and Liverpool protested the French action. The Bombay-Burmah Trading Company, Clark and Company, the Scottish Oriental Steamship Company, and others urged Rosebery to protect their interests. In fact, Rosebery complained to Jones, he depended for information mainly on naval officers and the Borneo Company.[15] To prove his desire to protect British property and subjects in Bangkok, and thereby forestall commercial and Conservative critics, Rosebery had asked the Admiralty to dispatch to Bangkok HMS *Pallas* and *Pigmy*, which were lying at Singapore.[16] His action was misleading. The Siamese imagined it was to protect Bangkok; they thought they had succeeded in convincing him that the French threatened their existence. Jones likely stimulated their imagination. The Siamese minister for foreign affairs cabled his minister in London that, in the opinion of the British captain, the two warships, together with the Siamese, could defend the capital against the French, but that the British minister would not act without further instructions, instructions that might arrive too late. The Siamese, therefore, would be forced to choose between accepting the French demands and seeing Bangkok burn – alternatives equally unwelcome to the Siamese, and, so they hoped, to the British.

Rosebery was incensed when the Siamese interpreted the arrival of the British gunboats as a demonstration of support, since "there has never been any intention that the gunboats should take any action except for protection of foreign life and property against popular outbreak."[17] While he demanded to know exactly what advice Jones and the naval officers had given the Siamese, he also made his own intentions explicit. Jones was commanded to "dispel any idea that we are contemplating joint action with Siam to defend Bangkok." Siam's attitude, Rosebery declared, was ill-judged, futile, and "has been maintained in direct opposition to our advice." The Siamese had posed the question of whether Britain would countenance the burning of Bangkok, and Rosebery had answered it. He would, apparently, allow it to burn before he risked war with the French. In vain, Jones raised another spectre: if Siam found herself without help or sympathy, she might, in despair, throw herself unreservedly into the arms of France.[18] Though the form was somewhat altered, this was no more than the old suicide threat, and Rosebery, who disbelieved the original threat, was no more inclined to believe the new one. Develle had promised to respect the integrity and independence of Siam; and, until the French formulated their demands, no British action was necessary. If the French demands threatened a vital British interest, Rosebery would have no difficulty in discovering a reason for fighting. In the meantime, nothing was to be gained by precipitating a war.

When it finally came, the French ultimatum was ambiguous. It demanded financial compensation and the punishment of Siamese officers who had clashed with the French in the territory under dispute and apparently killed a French officer, but neither of these demands concerned Rosebery, as the ultimatum did not make clear how much of the left bank was being claimed by the French.[19] Although he had earlier prepared, in conjunction with Kimberley, to abandon Britain's pretension to dominion over the eastern half of Kyaing Chiang, he had also asserted Britain's right to the territory should Siam abandon it. In other words, in spite of his efforts to conciliate the French, he had no intention of allowing them to establish themselves in territory bordering on British India. His policy during the crisis was consistent from start to finish: Siam had to be preserved as an independent buffer between the British and French empires in Asia, but in order to fulfil this aim the Siamese had to be restrained from giving the French unnecessary offence. In other

words, while Siam should concede any territory not essential to her
future as an independent state, she should not concede territory that
would bring French Indo-China next to British India.

Rosebery's actions thus far in the crisis had demonstrated his
adherence to these aims. He undertook no action that the French
might regard as hostile and he consistently urged the Siamese to take
a moderate line and not to be drawn into a war. When it seemed that
the French might be prepared to take advantage of his restraint, by
claiming the eastern half of Kyaing Chiang for themselves, Rosebery's
mood began to change. He refused to recognize that France had any
right to Kyaing Chiang and instructed Lord Dufferin that a considerable belt of territory under the control of an independent kingdom
must be preserved between the French and British frontiers.[20]

As the danger of the French establishing themselves in Kyaing
Chiang drew nearer, Rosebery moved closer to the Siamese. While he
continued his efforts to keep them from fighting, he now promised,
for the first time, to reward restraint. From the beginning of the crisis,
the Siamese had been searching for a way of inducing the British to
act for them, but as long as the French seemed prepared to satisfy
themselves with concessions along the lower Mekong, Rosebery had
refused to be drawn in. On 19 July he told the French ambassador
that he hoped his recent remarks in the House of Lords "showed the
friendly disposition I desired to evince, for H.M.G. hoped not to be
drawn into the question at all."[21] Later that day, the French demands
on Siam, with their threat to Kyaing Chiang, arrived from Paris. The
next day, following Rosebery's attempts to clarify what the demands
entailed, Develle said he did not know how far up the Mekong the
French intended to go. On 21 July Rosebery cabled Bangkok that he
would negotiate with the French government in order to settle satis-
factorily the limits of their territorial demands; for the first time he
appeared ready to act on behalf of Siam.[22]

Good relations with the Siamese were one of the advantages Rosebery enjoyed during the crisis. Although they had not been as yielding to the French as he would have liked, the Siamese had nevertheless remained reasonably moderate. Britain's advantage here is
easily explained. She appeared to have no territorial designs on Siam.
At the very moment when it was most essential that the Siamese
allow themselves to be guided by Britain, however, the unexpected
action of a British official abruptly threatened to place in jeopardy
the good relations that existed.

Without notifying London beforehand, the governor of the Straits
Settlement, Sir Cecil Smith, left Singapore on 18 July to visit the provinces of Pahang, Kelantin, and Tringam on the Malay Peninsula, all of

which bordered on Siam.[23] British officials had publicly mooted in the past the possible necessity of taking possession of the whole peninsula, so it was not unreasonable that the Siamese should worry that Britain might now decide, in the midst of the crisis with France, to abandon the policy of upholding Siam's independence and seize the territory she regarded as vital to her security. If the Siamese accepted this interpretation of Smith's visit, Rosebery might lose all control over them; they might even, as Jones had suggested, throw in their lot with the French.

Rosebery's reaction to this unexpected event showed that he was sincere in his desire to uphold Siam's independence. He disavowed the governor's action, which was, he said, unauthorized, unexplained, and ill-advised. "Our policy is unaltered," he announced.[24] The problem he faced in dealing with the Siamese was that, in order to control them, he must appear to be friendly and to desire their independence, but he must not appear so friendly as to encourage their resistance. In the India Office Lord Kimberley continued to fear that they would "play the French game by prolonging the affair in the vain hope of being able to resist," and that if this resulted in war, "the French might then attempt to seize the whole country." Any interpretation of the Siam crisis that suggests Rosebery opposed all concessions to France, and therefore that any concession represented a defeat for his policy, is obviously mistaken.

Rosebery had established his aims in Southeast Asia early on in the crisis, and he had not wavered from them; they included neither the expansion of British territory nor the confinement of French Indo-China within her present boundaries. Now, when France and Siam appeared to be on the brink of war, he continued to seek only that "considerable belt of territory under an independent kingdom between the British and French frontiers" that he had outlined to Dufferin. The government of India warned that any other solution would be expensive; a frontier with France would require a garrison of three regiments, the construction of a railway, and £200,000 a year.[25] But how was the principle of the buffer state to be achieved if, as historians have consistently argued, Rosebery was hampered by the weakness of Britain's position throughout the crisis?

When the crisis reached its highest point at the end of July, Rosebery's actions show that, rather than being hampered by weakness, he was bargaining from a position of strength. On the night of 24 July he was roused from his bed to be told that the French had announced the blockade of Bangkok. His policy of moderation having failed, he immediately decided to act, proposing to Gladstone that the government declare that the dispute now involved Britain. "We have always advised Siam to make her peace with France and that quickly. We have accepted all the French pledges and promises, all of which have been violated." But, he continued, "the time seems to me to have come when we are bound to abandon this attitude and do what we can to prevent this great and increasing burden on India." Finally, he assured the prime minister, "I do not doubt that if we are firm the French will give way."

During the crisis, the Germans assumed that Gladstone was preventing Rosebery from executing a more vigorous policy, and historians have accepted this explanation. It is not true. Although Rosebery believed he would not get much backing for a resolute policy from the cabinet, he did not need it; he undertook strong measures, or at least threatened the French with them, and simply informed the cabinet of what he had done. He did not find it necessary to threaten resignation, but most of the cabinet must have realized that, as he told Dufferin, "we *must* get a buffer state or I will go."[26] Friends and enemies alike were watching Rosebery carefully to see how he responded to the first real crisis in foreign affairs; "I am quite glad he has this chance of showing what he really is," Eddie Hamilton noted in his diary, "for my belief is that the real powers of the man will never properly be displayed, until he is in some tight place. The tighter the place: the greater his opportunities."[27]

The situation in Siam by 25 July was certainly tight enough to offer the opportunity Hamilton desired. To back up their ultimatum, the French had gunboats at Bangkok that far outnumbered the British naval force, while their troops had crossed the border and moved into the southern provinces of Battambang and Angkor. Rosebery, faced with this difficult situation, according to A.J.P. Taylor, "lost his nerve."[28]

On the morning of 25 July, d'Estournelles, the French ambassador, was summoned to the Foreign Office for an interview. Rosebery, after denying the suggestion that he had in any way encouraged the Siamese to resist, began to outline the consequences of the French action. When the French next referred to British promises about Egypt, he said, "We should reply that they were in the same boat as the French promises respecting the independence and integrity of Siam." Moreover, if the Siamese affair ended as the French appeared to desire, he warned, "there would be no negotiations about Egypt."[29] If the French intended to use Siam as a lever to pry the British out of Egypt, therefore, they were mistaken, as Rosebery promised to become even more obdurate there.

It has been argued that Rosebery reluctantly resigned himself to French expansion into Siam because he regarded Egypt as more important than Laos, and because he wanted to avoid a crisis with France in Europe.[30] This is not so. Rosebery not only threatened the French with consequences in Egypt, but declared that "we were moving fast to a word I shuddered to pronounce, which was 'war'." Even if actual war did not result from the policy France was pursuing, he declared, "we should carry on a silent war – 'une guerre sourde' – all over the world."[31] The British interest in Siam, he pointed out once more, was clear and definite: they could not allow the French to establish a frontier coterminous with Burma. Quite clearly, Rosebery was not frightened by the prospect of French retaliation in Europe, but instead expected to frighten them with British retaliation.

Rosebery had changed only his tactics, not his aims: when moderation failed, he did not hesitate to adopt vigorous measures. Throughout the long process of negotiations over Siam, which had now been going on for more than four months, the ambassador at Paris, Lord Dufferin, had consistently maintained that Develle himself was moderate, but that behind him there lay "a little knot of fanatics who are pushing him to extremities."[32] Perhaps Rosebery's patience had succeeded only in encouraging the hotheads at the French Colonial Office. Dufferin noted that, far from becoming angry with Rosebery for the language he had used, Develle actually seemed pleased by it. The ambassador thought he knew why: the harsh words were the ammunition Develle needed to win the battle with his opponents in the cabinet.[33] The threat of war, he said, combined with Rosebery's success in encouraging the Siamese to submit to most of the French demands, deprived the French colonial party of its best arguments, that the British were not prepared to fight and that the Siamese were unreasonable.[34]

The effect of Rosebery's harsh words exceeded his expectation. Part of the escalating demands of France had included the cession of Siam's two richest provinces, Battambang and Angkor, which French military forces had just entered. Rosebery doubted whether even a complete Siamese surrender would dislodge the French from the two provinces. The threat of war moved them. Three days after the interview with d'Estournelles he was congratulating Dufferin: "They had certainly gorged the two provinces already, and the disgorging is a noble operation."[35] Develle, on 31 July, committed himself to the buffer principle, and negotiations almost immediately passed into the endless tedium of territorial arrangements. Rosebery, his purpose accomplished, the crisis ended, prepared for a vacation in Hamburg.[36]

Three reasons have been advanced in support of the contention that Rosebery, the imperialist, was forced to back down in the face of French expansion in southeast Asia: Gladstone and the cabinet were not willing to support a vigorous policy; Germany was not prepared to assist in restraining France; the Dual Alliance was too strong for Britain in Asia. These arguments betray a fundamental misunderstanding of the condition of political and diplomatic affairs at the time of the crisis. They also demonstrate how easily historians are misled when they begin with a false assumption, in this case that Rosebery would have prevented any French forward movement had he been able to do so.

In the first place, neither Gladstone nor the cabinet held Rosebery back at any time during the crisis. In the months preceding the French blockade and their ultimatum to Siam, Rosebery did not find it necessary to seek the support of the cabinet. As he had never intended to take anything but a moderate line, support for a vigorous policy was unnecessary. In the week before the crisis, Harcourt had tried to be disagreeable, "but Rosebery stood up against him and he shut up instantly."[37] Even though Rosebery told Dufferin, at the height of the crisis, that he was unlikely to get much backing for a resolute policy, he certainly got as much as he needed. The threat of a "silent war" was embodied in a printed dispatch available for all the cabinet to see, although the references to Egypt were removed. No one objected to the threat and Rosebery did not even have to hint at resignation. When Develle signed the protocol accepting the principle of the buffer state, Harcourt wrote to congratulate Rosebery "on your brilliant success in the settlement of Siam." Gladstone described himself as being "in full sympathy" with the way in which Rosebery had taken up his "position on this Siamese business," even though the aggressive policy of France had given him extreme pain as "I retain from my youth a feeling for the old idea of a French alliance."[38]

Cabinet politics gave Rosebery no trouble during the crisis and neither did the Germans, but a myth has somehow been established that, at the height of the crisis, Rosebery appealed to William II for backing.[39] It is difficult to understand how the notion of Rosebery turning to Germany for help fits into the available evidence. The queen, on 26 July, did suggest to Rosebery that Germany, Austria, and above all Italy should be urged to support Britain, but Rosebery immediately replied that it was becoming to Her Majesty's dignity to settle the matter without appealing to the Triple Alliance. There is no evidence to indicate that he changed his mind. In fact, it was essential to Rosebery's whole diplomatic design that the Triple Alliance should not be permitted to think that Britain depended on its support in affairs outside of Europe.

The Austrians had recently renewed the efforts of the alliance to draw Britain into a closer arrangement, but their efforts had failed, as would all such efforts while Rosebery was at the Foreign Office. The Austrian foreign minister concluded his effort by saying that he understood the reasons for Rosebery's reserve, "but that he did not doubt from my general character and policy that I should generally be ready to act with him in European affairs."[40] This was precisely the kind of arrangement Rosebery wished to have with the alliance; but, to maintain it, he could not create the impression of relying on them when crises arose outside Europe, or they would be in a position to demand that Britain join the alliance. Therefore, he made no appeal to them for assistance. The Siam crisis, in one sense, was strictly an Anglo-French affair.

A third reason has been advanced to support the argument that Rosebery backed down in Siam. The Franco-Russian alliance, it is said, was too strong for the British in Asia. Rosebery, in contrast, always maintained that the alliance did not operate outside Europe, and he had evidence to support this argument. After almost a year in office, he had not witnessed a single situation in which the two had combined against Britain. But perhaps the crisis in Siam would draw France and Russia closer, because here was a situation where they faced Britain alone, without Germany, Austria, or Italy to intervene. The situation was, in fact, ideal for Franco-Russian cooperation. Russia had a grievance on the northern frontier of British India, France on the southern. Europe was quiet. On 21 July Rosebery cabled St Petersburg to ask if there were any truth in newspaper reports published in Britain that the Russian government had promised full support to the French in Siam and that they were sending ships.[41]

Even as he asked, Rosebery thought the reports, "very improbable." The colonial party in France was certainly making a parade of the alliance, and the Paris *Journal* proclaimed that a Russian squadron was being dispatched to the Gulf of Siam. The rumour, the British minister reported from St Petersburg, "is entirely disbelieved in diplomatic circles." The Russians denied that they had any such intention, and, in fact, never uttered a single word about Siam to the British. Russia's government-inspired press, notably the *Journal de St Petersburg* and the *Novoe Vremya*, which failed to respond to the proclamations of the Paris *Journal*, confined itself to reporting the events of the crisis and failed even to show a bias in favour of the French.[42]

Perhaps more important to Rosebery than these opinions in the press, Russia did not attempt to take advantage of the situation in Siam by launching a new movement in the Pamirs. In fact, at the height of the crisis, Russian officials continued to assure the British of their good intentions.[43] Sir Robert Morier had anticipated that this would be the case. "They haven't the slightest idea of fighting about this Pamir business, because just now they will do anything rather than fight."[44] The impression that prevailed in Russia, he reported, was that Britain was infinitely stronger in Asia. The Franco-Russian alliance, it seemed, did not operate outside Europe, or, if it did, it certainly did nothing to restrain Rosebery from taking a firmer line with the French in Siam.

The absence of Russian support was, perhaps, as important as Rosebery's threat of silent war in convincing the French to limit their demands in Siam. In any case, when the French accepted the principle of the buffer, the crisis began to pass away and the blockade was lifted. The affair was destined to drag on for some time, however, because the details of the territorial settlement had to be worked out and this was never easy. Rosebery was under no illusion so far as the future of Siam was concerned. "The serpent is scotched but not killed," he told Gladstone. "We shall have more trouble there yet: but not till after the French elections."[45]

One of the difficulties of assessing the role of the Franco-Russian alliance in British foreign policy is the use made of it by Rosebery and Kimberley, for, although the events of the crisis in Siam had shown that the alliance did not operate in Asia, they sometimes claimed that it did. The occasion for making this claim was quite specific. The government of India, throughout the spring and summer of 1893, had continued to be troublesome about the Pamirs. In London, Rosebery and Kimberley decided to use the threat of the alliance as a stick with which to beat the viceroy and his council into submitting to the policy of conciliation with Russia. "A combination between Russia and France is perhaps the most formidable of all possible combinations against us," Kimberley warned Lansdowne, so "what is now happening about Siam emphasizes the importance of not getting into a quarrel with Russia."[46] This argument was used a number of times during the next two years, whenever the tall talk of Indian jingoes endangered relations with Russia.

Using the Franco-Russian alliance in this way was a tactical device, but one that demonstrated an important change in policy, for Rosebery was, in fact, the leading advocate of what might be termed the "neo-Punjab school" of Indian defence. Like the advocates of the original school, Rosebery believed that the best way to defend India was by diplomacy, not by the extension of frontiers as proposed by the Bombay school. Diplomacy, in this case, meant two distinct, though connected, things. It meant moderation and conciliation in relations with Russia in central Asia; but it also meant threatening them with war outside Asia. Until the 1880s the second part of this program, expressed most clearly by Sir Garnet Wolseley, meant attacking Russia in the Black Sea, through the Straits. By 1893 such an attack was out of the question. Because the British had occupied Egypt, the Turks had begun to fortify the Straits, but with the guns pointing to the Mediterranean; or, in other words, at the British instead of the Russians. The Admiralty did not believe it would be possible to force the Straits unless Britain enjoyed a safe position in the Mediterranean.

During the war in the Crimea, the British enjoyed free passage through the Straits and an alliance with the Turks, and they had still found immense difficulties in fighting the Russians. They had, moreover, enjoyed free movement in the Mediterranean as a result of their alliance with France. By 1893 this second advantage had also disappeared. Now, instead of considering the possibility of forcing the Straits, the Admiralty was preoccupied with the question of whether or not the Mediterranean would have to be abandoned altogether in the event of war. The situation in the Mediterranean had clearly changed as a result of the occupation of Egypt and the formation of the Franco-Russian alliance. It had changed in favour of the Bombay school, for how was Britain to defend India by diplomacy, by threatening Russia with war outside Asia, when she no longer enjoyed the means of giving substance to such a threat?

Rosebery's neo-Punjab answer to this question was to substitute the Triple Alliance for an attack at the Straits. As he saw it, the Russians, while they faced the menace of combined German and Austrian military might, would not undertake an aggressive policy of expansion in central Asia. As long as Britain remained moderate along the northern frontier, as long as the Indian jingoes could be controlled, then Russia would subordinate her interests there to those in Europe. It was also essential to this solution that the Triple Alliance remain intact, and that the old Bismarckian policy of the *Dreikaiserbund* not be renewed. Thus two quite different kinds of rumours bothered Rosebery: those suggesting that British agents in Asia were planning aggressive actions; and those suggesting that the Germans were contemplating an understanding with the Russians.

Rosebery tried to avoid the dangers involved in rumours about aggressive agents by seeing that men who embodied the proper view of Indian defence were appointed to positions of importance. The good relations that he enjoyed with Kimberley stemmed from their agreement on policy; they had little enough in common in the way of personality. In 1892 Kimberley had refused Lansdowne's request that he renew Roberts's term in India, describing Roberts as "the powerful representative of a forward policy which had gone very far already and if it goes on, may involve us in serious dangers."[47] In 1893 the Liberal government, after much searching, finally found a replacement for Lansdowne. "I do not suppose that anyone came to India more inclined to follow the doctrines of the Lawrence school, than I," the earl of Elgin, who was persuaded by Rosebery to go out as viceroy, later declared.[48] But of course the dangers persisted: Elgin was eventually converted to a forward policy, while men like Sir Mortimer Durand, commander of the Simla Volunteers, continued to complain that the government of India seemed inclined to throw everything away on the frontier. Rosebery and Kimberley were never able to relax their control of Indian officials.

As long as Rosebery was able to control these forward tendencies, he lessened the danger that Russia would come to terms with Germany; and yet, ironically, it seemed that he might increase the possibility that Germany would come to terms with Russia. The Germans always expected that they would one day benefit from an Asian war between Britain and Russia. The new course, the policy of abandoning Bismarck's ties with Russia, assumed that Russian designs in central Asia would eventually force the British into the Triple Alliance. With Austria-Hungary, Italy, and Britain firmly in her camp, Germany could proceed with her plans of expansion in southern Europe and the Near East. This calculation would naturally be upset if Britain and Russia were to come to terms in Asia, and it is for this reason that the Germans put their own gloss on every Asian problem that arose. The Russians, they repeatedly warned the British, would never abandon their designs on India.

Rosebery's neo-Punjab doctrine was based on the assumption that, while Russia might not finally abandon her designs on India, she would hold them in abeyance as long as Britain did not provoke her and as long as she faced the Triple Alliance in Europe. This was one assumption that threatened to upset the calculations that lay behind the new course in German foreign policy. The Kaulla incident had suggested another. The Germans had shown in January that the British must allow them a privileged position in Turkish affairs or they would create repercussions in Egypt. The expansion of German interests in Turkey was one of the aims implicit in the new course, and if it appeared that this aim was not likely to be fulfilled, the Germans might decide, once more, to abandon the new course and return to the policy of cooperating with Russia.

The events of the spring and summer of 1893 suggested that Germany's position at Constantinople was weakening. An outstanding feature of the years between 1888 and 1893 had been the ascendancy of German influence at Constantinople, an influence closely connected with the personal position of Kaiser Wilhelm II, and symbolized by his choice of the sultan as the first head of state whom he visited in his official capacity as emperor of Germany.[49] The Germans, of course, offered other advantages besides William II's taste for Turkish coffee: they had loans to offer, money to invest, technicians and military men to provide advice. But their real advantage, in Turkish eyes, was their distance and their power. Unlike the British, their previous protector, the Germans had no territorial stake in the Near East and therefore posed no apparent threat, yet the power of their army might be used to restrain the Russians.[50] If the Turks were lucky, the next war for the Near East might be fought along the Oder, possibly along the Rhine.

When the new German army bill was presented to the Bundestag it caused the Turks to reconsider their assessment of the situation. Like most governments placed in a similar situation, the German government was forced to complain of its weakness in order to justify an increase in expenditure. Therefore, when Caprivi announced that the Reich faced imminent danger because of its weakness, he seemed to confirm what Russia and France had been arguing at Constantinople: that their alliance made them the stronger combination in Europe. Moreover, the German parliament rejected the bill, one to which the kaiser had given his personal approval, thereby casting doubt on the value of good relations with him. A Turkish tack over to the Neva was noted at Constantinople, and the sultan was rumoured to be considering some kind of agreement with the Russians.[51]

The repercussions of the German army debate did not, apparently, end at Constantinople. Tsar Alexander III, himself facing enormous expenses in maintaining the military, had adopted the cause of universal disarmament. No one took the cause seriously, but the manner in which statesmen replied to his call became a touchstone for judging their intentions. Thus, when the Austrian foreign secretary, Count Kálnoky, publicly declared the cause of disarmament as desirable, even feasible, he gave the Germans some cause for alarm.[52] The Bismarckian press in Germany relished this opportunity of pointing out the consequences of the new course: Austria, moving to the side of Russia, would isolate Germany; the Kaunitz coalition of the previous century might be revived by the ineptitude of Germany's new masters.[53] Instead of going forward, as the new course promised, Germany might lose what she already had.

The reconsideration of Austria's position that was apparently under way in Vienna was probably not to be accounted for by the failure of the German army bill alone. At the time, it was believed that they were also responding to Italian fears. Everyone assumed that the Italians, given their indefensible coastline, would join whoever controlled the Mediterranean. The Mediterranean agreements had thus contributed to a steady deterioration in Franco-Italian relations between 1888 and 1892.[54] This, of course, was the reason why Britain was important to Germany and Austria: by safeguarding Italy from France, she made it possible for Italy to join them, thus relieving the pressure on Austria's southern frontier and allowing her to concentrate her forces on the frontier with Russia. But, in June 1893, rumours had started to circulate concerning the visit of a Russian naval squadron to Toulon. Then, in July, the semi-official *Novoe Vremya* declared that Russia's peaceful defensive alliance with France "would become converted into a mere lifeless diplomatic combination, would remain a mere theoretical scheme, if both powers did not afford one another real support in cases where their political or economic interests require it."[55] The newspaper proposed a joint, Russo-French fleet for the Mediterranean.

Such a proposal was alarming to the Italians. If France and Russia combined to overpower Britain in the Mediterranean, Italy would be vulnerable to attack, and the Triple Alliance would do her little good. What alarmed the Italians alarmed the Germans and the Austrians. The Germans, who had hoped, and expected, that the Franco-Russian alliance would materialize in Asia, where it would imperil the British alone, saw it materializing in the Mediterranean instead, where it imperilled Italy and thereby the Triple Alliance.

Given this state of affairs, it was to be expected that the Triple Alliance would try to manoeuvre Britain into a closer understanding. The occasion that provided the setting for this particular manoeuvre was the retirement of Britain's ambassador at Vienna, Sir Augustus Paget, who, preparing to take his leave, uttered some commonplace remarks concerning the "natural" alliance between Austria and Brittain.[56] The Austrians assumed, or hoped, that he had been inspired by Rosebery. Kálnoky, taking the role Pillersdorf had played almost half a century earlier, tried to transform these sentiments into something useful. What he wanted was an assurance that neither the changing balance in the Mediterranean nor the flagging German influence at Constantinople would induce Britain to abandon her position in the Mediterranean or at the Straits. Count Deym, the Austrian ambassador at London, who was to play the part of Hümmelauer in 1848, returned to London to talk to Rosebery.

At the height of the crisis in Siam – on the day following the announcement of the French blockade – and at the moment when the Triple Alliance might reasonably expect the British to be most vulnerable, Deym called on Rosebery, who said that he agreed with everything Paget had said. But the Austrians wanted more than vague talk about natural allies. If Russia threatened Constantinople they wanted Britain to support Turkey in order to ward off the Russian attack. Rosebery refused to undertake any such obligations, and reverted to the arguments he had used since returning to the Foreign Office. If the Russians attacked the Turks at the Straits, he said, it would raise a war cry among the British that would drown and overwhelm those who favoured peace at any price. The Austrians would also see that the prime minister and his colleagues had given him quite a free hand in foreign policy, and they would know what that policy was. Finally, the French, he said, were doing their best to drive Britain into the arms of the Triple Alliance.[57]

Rosebery could not agree to undertake the kind of commitment the Austrians sought, and therefore he argued that the nature of the situation really gave them what they needed. The three parts of this argument never changed: the opinion of the British people, Rosebery's personal policy and power in the government, and the aggressive tactics of the French all combined to provide the Austrians with an informal guarantee at the Straits and in the Mediterranean. Rosebery could offer no more than this; nor did he want to. As long as Britain's association with the Triple Alliance remained informal, he could decide when, and under what conditions, it operated, and this was essential as far as he was concerned, for it meant that Britain would not be drawn into a continental war against her will.

The members of the Triple Alliance were visibly worried by the prospect of changes in the Mediterranean and the Near East. The Italians were asking for a visit by Britain's Mediterranean squadron in order to counteract the effects of the Russian visit to Toulon. The Germans were warning that a new crisis might develop in the Balkans, where, Marschall said, the Bulgarian fire was banked up but not extinguished.[58] In the meantime, the Austrians were pursuing a British alliance along the lines of Salisbury's Mediterranean agreements, but Rosebery refused to give them any hope that this would succeed. As far as Salisbury's agreements were concerned, "I was not sure if I even knew of them," he told Count Deym, "but I at any rate avoided inspecting them, as not wishing to know in case of enquiry what was the nature of those notes." When Deym suggested they go over the points of the agreement in order that Rosebery might indicate his opinions, this too was refused. "It would be better," Rosebery replied, "to leave the great European questions as regards Great Britain, free of engagements, and rather to reckon on the forces of sympathy and interest when the crisis should arise."[59]

This conclusion was the one sought by Rosebery throughout his time at the Foreign Office, but it was difficult to achieve. Informal understandings, even more than formal ones, are open to continual revaluation, misunderstanding, and negotiation. As long as interests remain unclear and reactions to specific events unplanned, both parties to an understanding will attempt to shape that understanding according to their own interests. Rosebery believed that this uncertainty suited Britain's interests. As far as he was concerned, it was enough that the European alliance system created an approximate balance of power whereby both France and Russia were strained to the point where they could not really afford the men or the money to undertake a truly aggressive program against Britain outside of Europe. Moreover, the Triple Alliance, especially Italy and Austria, might be inclined to undertake some unnecessarily aggressive program against France or Russia if they were certain of the assistance of Britain in advance. In midsummer 1893 it suited Rosebery to keep the general European situation just as it stood.

To keep thing as they stand can be, as all conservatives know, as difficult as to change things. In this particular instance, Rosebery's refusal to contemplate a closer understanding with the Triple Alliance, or even to admit that Salisbury's Mediterranean agreements existed, threatened to upset the current state of affairs. If France and Russia were to strengthen their connection in the Mediterranean, the Triple Alliance might reasonably ask, what would Britain do? If she gave signs of withdrawing her interest from Constantinople, if she appeared ready to evacuate Egypt, surely these would be indications that she considered it necessary to withdraw from the Mediterranean in the face of the superior strength of France and Russia. If she did withdraw, then she would be of little use to the Triple Alliance, which might, as a result, collapse.[60]

The idea of the Triple Alliance collapsing was no more pleasant to Rosebery than the idea that he might be forced to join it. His task in midsummer 1893, then, was to keep the Triple Alliance in being by showing that the old formula still held good, that Britain still considered herself the superior naval power in the Mediterranean, and as such would not abandon her role at Constantinople and the Straits or in Egypt. To achieve this he decided to do three things: strengthen British forces in the Mediterranean and indicate that he intended to continue to strengthen them; clarify Britain's position in Egypt and show that she intended to stay; and demonstrate continued British interest in Turkey by taking up the cause of the Armenian Christians.

The Armenian Christians, like the Latin and Greek ones of forty years before, were employed as a pretext for exercising power and demonstrating influence at Constantinople. In March 1893 rumours had started to circulate concerning a massacre in an Armenian village, but nothing much was heard about the situation during the next few months. Rosebery showed little interest in the affair. In the middle of June, however, two Armenian professors were tried and found guilty of inciting their people to rebellion. The British vice-consul in the area reported that this was a scandalous decision, as no evidence of their guilt had been produced by the government. While details of the affair were of little significance in European diplomacy, the timing was fortuitous; it occurred just when it suited Rosebery to show that he had no intention of abandoning his interest in Turkish affairs.

Rosebery sent his first strong words to Constantinople four days after Deym inquired whether Britain would assist Turkey in the event of a Russian attack. The British minister at Constantinople was instructed to warn the Porte that Britain might demand the release of Armenian prisoners. In order to demonstrate his continuing interest in the affairs of Turkey, Rosebery chose to intimidate, rather than befriend, the sultan. If the British chose to encourage the Armenians, he warned the British ambassador, they could transform a partial conspiracy into a serious revolution, and he refused to promise that he would not give such encouragement in the future.

Obviously Rosebery wished to avoid allowing the situation in Armenia to develop to the point where it might become a crisis involving Russia, in which Britain might be forced to compete with her in claiming to act as the guardian of the Armenian Christians. One way to avoid such a crisis was to compel the Turks to behave well. Nevertheless, shadowy claims to the guardianship of the sultan's Christian subjects had regularly preceded the successive eastern crises of the nineteenth century. Compelling the Turks to behave well demonstrated that Rosebery was going to continue exerting British interests at Constantinople. He had little interest in the merits of the situation; when his strong words succeeded in winning the release of the two Armenian professors, Gladstone was encouraged to ask him to go further, but Rosebery refused. "I do not see why we should bear the whole burden of this astute if pious race," he sarcastically replied. "Unless Armenian crime is to be protected by a halo of hereditary holiness I do not see how they can be exempted in Turkey from the punishment they would have met with here."[61] He was satisfied that he had demonstrated an interest in Turkish affairs, and an ability to influence Turkish policies; he cared nothing for the Armenians themselves.

One probable reason why the sultan proved susceptible to British pressure, in what would prove to be but an early stage in the Armenian affair, was that Rosebery had agreed to reopen the negotiations on the evacuation of Egypt that had resulted in the abortive Drummond-Wolff Convention. Immediately after the January crisis, when the khedive had attempted to replace anglophile ministers with anglophobe ones, Rosebery had decided to use the sultan as a device in his Egyptian policy.[62] This plan worked initially because the sultan, foreseeing the possibility of a British withdrawal and the return of Turkish suzerainty, urged the khedive to adopt a policy of moderation and said he would negotiate on his behalf. Rosebery was aware that this was working, just as he was aware of most facets of Turkish diplomacy, because the British were intercepting most Turkish messages. The device worked because the khedive, especially after the failure of isolated action in January, looked to the sultan to assist him.

The young khedive's grandfather, the deposed Ismail, had been urging him to rely on the sultan.[63] The French had also been encouraging this idea and suggested that he should go to Constantinople and discuss matters with the sultan himself.[64] Neither Rosebery nor Cromer opposed the idea, as they calculated that talks of this kind were more likely to drive the Turks and Egyptians apart than to bring them together. The khedive, accompanied by a deputation of Egyptian notables, arrived in Constantinople in early July. The deputation prepared an address to the sultan, lamenting the hardships entailed for Egypt by the British occupation, and appealing to the sultan as caliph to free them from it. The sultan refused to receive the address and suggested they leave the matter in the hands of the Sovereign Power, which was negotiating the subject of withdrawal with Britain. The khedive appealed for Turkish troops, but the sultan refused to give any. Instead, "as a father would," he counselled the khedive to bear with his lot, keep well with the English, and trust to time.

The impatient young khedive was understandably disheartened by the sultan's advice, and the deputation was indignant.[65] Tigrane Pasha, the Egyptian prime minister, assured Nicolson that the khedive and the Egyptian government now desired to work well with Britain, and begged that Britain indicate any complaints so that they could prove their sincerity.[66] Emphasizing this new attitude, the khedive protested that he had never intended to ask for Turkish troops, that he had nothing to do with the Egyptian deputation, and that he was anxious to go to London and exchange views frankly.[67] The khedive's illusions had been dispelled: he no longer trusted to the sultan to relieve him of the British yoke. Rosebery, suspectig the new mood to be humbug or spite against the sultan, distrusted it. Possibly, however, the khedive now thought it wise to be agreeable to the British. "Milk and honey are in his mouth, and his lips drop fatness. I would have you cordially reciprocate this," Rosebery told Hardinge.[68] The events at Constantinople had worked to Rosebery's advantage: not only had the French attempt to coordinate action with the Turks and the Egyptians failed, but Rosebery had shown that he was far from agreeing to an evacuation of Egypt. The khedive, or his advisers, had miscalculated, and had had his hopes dashed. But so had the sultan for, in alienating the khedive, he had induced him to act with moderation, with the paradoxical result that the British could dispense with the sultan's assistance. If the khedive behaved himself, for whatever reason, then the renewal of the Drummond-Wolff Convention was unnecessary. Rosebery had reopened the negotiations partly to please Gladstone, but when the rift between the khedive and the sultan became apparent, he began to display his true feelings.[69] The sultan's draft convention, he told Gladstone, was illusory; after the khedive promised to behave himself, he told Gladstone that the whole convention was "a futile proposal." Rosebery had no intention of evacuating Egypt.[70]

Rosebery's determination to stay in Egypt suited the Germans. The Kaulla affair, earlier in the year, had shown how useful the *báton* was in bringing the British to support German commercial interests. As long as the British remained in Egypt, at the behest of the European powers, then the Germans could exercise an influence on their policy. But the situation was more complicated than that. In the summer of 1893, when the French and the Russians appeared to be attempting to overpower the British in the Mediterranean, the Germans needed the British to remain in Egypt for the sake of Austria and Italy, not for the sake of railway concessions in Asia Minor. If the British showed that they considered themselves too weak to remain in Egypt and abandoned it, perhaps to the French, and if they abandoned their position at Constantinople, perhaps to the Russians, they would imperil the Triple Alliance by inclining the Italians and the Austrians to detach themselves from it.

In this situation, Rosebery used the Armenian troubles and the visit of the khedive to demonstrate his intention that Britain should remain in power in the Mediterranean. The Armenians were useful in showing that the British could still influence policy at Constantinople, while the journey of the khedive was equally useful in showing that even an attempt at Turco-Egyptian cooperation could not pry the British loose from Egypt. "Since the Khedive's visit, the fuss about Thoumian and especially since the unkind language that has been

held to Rustem [the Turkish ambassador] in London," wrote one of
the British secretaries at the embassy in Constantinople, "*we* are on
the top of the wave."[71]

Diplomatists who look for ways to display their intentions never have
far to seek: the number and variety of international questions that
exist at any moment invariably provide the opportunity they need.
The historian's task is more difficult. It is possible, perhaps desirable,
to follow the story of particular diplomatic negotiations or international problems, and certainly histories of the Armenian problem and
the Egyptian question have been, and will continue to be, written.
This particular perspective, however, while highlighting the importance of local detail and illuminating the continuity of problems, also
distorts, in the way any perspective is bound to. It is easy to lose sight
of the fact that initiatives taken on any particular issue may be the
result of considerations having little or nothing to do with the matter
at hand. The Armenians, for example, simply provided Rosebery with
a suitable occasion for producing an effect at Berlin, Vienna, and
Constantinople; what happened in Asia Minor was of secondary
importance.

The effect Rosebery was trying to produce centred, as it always did
in these years, in Berlin, but it was to be accomplished indirectly,
through Vienna and Rome. Britain was never able to influence Germany directly. The Armenian affair and the khedive's visit were especially useful so far as Vienna was concerned, for it was Britain's
interest in, and influence at, the Straits and Constantinople that concerned the Austrians.[72] The Italians were more concerned with the
general situation in the Mediterranean, and the influence of foreign
affairs on domestic politics. Rosebery had to give them some sign of
his desire to assist them against the French, and this had to be overt,
something that the Italian people could see, because the French had
launched a tariff war that had made the Triple Alliance increasingly
unpopular in Italy.

Rosebery decided to do two things to reassure the Italians. Earlier
in the year, they had requested that the British join them in some
sort of naval demonstration, but Rosebery, following his policy of
quiet conciliation in Morocco, Egypt, and the Mediterranean generally, had refused the request. The fears produced by the coming
Russian naval demonstration at Toulon induced him to change his
mind, and he arranged with the Admiralty that a portion of the
Mediterranean fleet should visit Italy in the autumn.[73] This, he calculated, would provide the public symbol in their negotiations at the
Porte concerning the delimitation of their frontiers in Tripoli and

Eritrea. Rosebery was prepared to show the Italians that their informal arrangement with the British guaranteed them from attack by sea, and at the same time provided them with the means of realizing some of their imperial ambitions in Africa.

Rosebery knew that these displays of good intentions did not go far enough, that Vienna and Rome required evidence not only of his desire to remain a Mediterranean power, but of his ability to do so. In the summer of 1893 this requirement could mean only one thing: he would have to strengthen British forces in the Mediterranean to the point of matching the combined forces of France and Russia. Given the time it required to build a battleship, this goal was going to take some time to achieve, and given the expense involved in naval construction, it was going to be difficult to convince the cabinet of the necessity. Therefore, while this was his long-term aim, he hit upon two devices as temporary measures. He asked the earl of Spencer, first lord of the admiralty, to increase the navy's Mediterranean strength, even if this meant weakening the Channel and Pacific squadrons.[74] He also asked Campbell-Bannerman, the secretary for war, to have the garrison at Malta reinforced.[75]

Rosebery's thinking on this matter provides one of the clearest indications of how he viewed the connection between Britain's imperial and continental interests. The empire's first line of defence was in Europe. He was prepared to weaken British naval forces outside the Mediterranean, even in the midst of the crisis in Siam, for the sake of bolstering the Triple Alliance, and he admitted as much to Campbell-Bannerman. The Russian fleet in the Mediterranean, he said, "is intended as a menace to us, and through Italy to the Triple Alliance."[76] If Britain was to fulfil her role as an informal member of the Triple Alliance, she had to provide Austria with some security at the Straits and Italy with security in the Mediterranean; if she failed to provide this, and Austria accommodated herself to Russia and Italy to France, the position of Britain's imperial competitors would be strengthened enormously.

Thus Rosebery sought to increase British strength in the Mediterranean for diplomatic reasons. In order to continue to work with the Triple Alliance, he had to show that Britain was the equal of France and Russia, or at least that she would be. But the British cabinet, made up of insular politicians who were usually prepared to accept imperial reasons for committing themselves to increased expense, were either not interested in, or not capable of understanding, the subtleties of continental diplomacy. For this reason, students of British foreign policy are often misled by the evidence. Rosebery quickly recognized that the cabinet were not going to accept arguments

concerning continental diplomacy as sufficient reasons for undertaking the expense of increased naval armaments in the Mediterranean. Therefore, during the cabinet debate on naval spending that
began in the summer of 1893, few documents were produced that
considered the question as part of European diplomacy.

Faced with a cabinet that preferred retrenchment if possible and
accepted new spending only if there seemed no other choice, Rosebery tried to show that Britain faced immediate danger from France
and Russia. The presence of the Russian fleet in the Mediterranean
would, he said, "intoxicate the French." He made a point of circulating
to the cabinet the *Novoe Vremya* article that proposed a joint Franco-
Russian Mediterranean fleet be created to overawe the British. This
became Rosebery's argument for the next six months: the French
were a rash, truculent people who, excited by the Russian alliance
and the appearance of British weakness, might do something silly,
like attacking the British in the Mediterranean. "I do not say they
want to go to war with us in cold blood," he assured Campbell-
Bannerman. "What I fear is lest they slide involuntarily into war and
find they have gone too far to recede."[77] Rosebery used the prospect
of a sudden, unmeditated attack – as the fear of Mussolini's mad dog
act was used in a Mediterranean crisis forty years later – to induce
the cabinet to spend when they would have preferred to retrench.

The question of a large-scale increase in naval spending was a
long-term problem that was not going to be resolved for months to
come. In the meantime, Rosebery had to satisfy himself with immediate measures on a much smaller scale, though even small measures
proved difficult. He had an easy time arranging a shift in Mediterranean forces with Spencer at the Admiralty, but arranging with Campbell-Bannerman to increase the garrison at Malta proved a tedious
process. It proved tedious partly because the secretary for war was
irritated by Rosebery's methods, and herein lies a small story that
says much about the relations between the Foreign Office and the
two ministries of defence, and much about Rosebery's way of doing
business.

The proposal to reinforce the garrison at Malta had originated not
with Rosebery but with General Chapman, the director of military
intelligence at the War Office. Chapman had, at the end of July,
started to communicate secretly with Rosebery's private secretary at
the Foreign Office, Frank Villiers, whom he warned that it would be
difficult to convoy men to Malta once war broke out.[78] He proposed,
therefore, that Malta should be garrisoned at war strength as long as
the Russian squadron remained in the Mediterranean.[79] He also proposed this through regular channels, via the adjutant general, Sir

Redvers Buller. Because he did not rely on Buller, however, he made sure that Rosebery received, through Villiers, copies of the memoranda he was writing on the question. Rosebery did nothing to stop the subordinate of one of his colleagues from communicating privately with him.[80]

Rosebery undoubtedly allowed this procedure to continue because Chapman's aims were similar to his own. Not only did Chapman concur in the necessity of strengthening Britain's position in the Mediterranean, but he also advocated using the Triple Alliance as Britain's first line of defence against France and Russia. Moreover, he clearly regarded France as Britain's most likely enemy, and he proposed accordingly an aggressive campaign to seize the French overseas possessions of most strategic value: Dakar, Diego Suarez, and Martinique. If war broke out, Germany would occupy the French army while Britain dismantled the French empire.

Campbell-Bannerman distrusted Chapman, and was entirely averse to the suggestion that Malta be reinforced.[81] His distrust arose partly from his irritation with the methods being employed. The proposed reinforcement, he complained to Rosebery, apparently originated in a conference held at the Foreign Office and attended by Chapman, but of which neither he nor the adjutant-general had been aware.[82] The idea of reinforcing Malta came to him "like a bolt from the blue," and he complained that he could discover no cause for alarm. "I am most sceptical about the whole thing," he told Spencer.[83] Consequently, he tried to avoid acting by turning the question over to the joint Naval and Military Committee, which would "at its leisure" consider what steps should be taken. He saw no need for haste: "Buller is grouse-shooting."[84]

Campbell-Bannerman would have been justified in having more general reasons for distrusting the manoeuvres of his director of military intelligence. Campbell-Bannerman was not an ambitious man; he had no great plans for reforming the army or redirecting strategic planning.[85] In 1894 he would put himself forward for the speakership of the House when it became vacant, a move that would have removed him from the real battleground of politics. Home Rule for Ireland was not a matter of principle for him, but was justified by sheer necessity. He preferred to act only when forced to do so, and later became leader of the Liberal party because he was regarded as a moderate in practically everything. Chapman was a different sort of man; he was ambitious, an intriguer, and he saw in the Mediterranean crisis of 1893 the possibility of redefining the role of the British army.

Redirecting policy in a period of calm is a slow and tedious business, but crises provide opportunities for change. Consequently, those who want change exaggerate the critical nature of events, while those who want things to stay the same minimize them. "I cannot help thinking that we have now an opportunity of urging the necessity of an increase to the strength of the Navy and the Army," confided Chapman to his naval counterpart, Admiral Bridge.[86] The Mediterranean fleet, he said, should be increased in numbers equal to the Russian ships at present locked up in the Black Sea. To accomplish this goal meant redefining the Mediterranean to include the Black Sea, which meant confessing that Britain would not be able to prevent Russian ships from forcing the Straits and entering the Mediterranean. This signified some change in strategic thinking, but it was less controversial than the rest of Chapman's program, for he also wanted a more important and more active role for the British army.

Chapman's proposal for an aggressive campaign against France overseas was closely connected to his future plans for the British army. If Britain had to call up reserves in order to dispatch the expeditions to Dakar and Martinique that he envisioned, he said, "we shall never send them." The army, he told Bridge, would require an extra thirty thousand men if it were to assist the navy in the active policy they both favoured. He asked Bridge to stress the importance of the army assisting the navy in this policy; the Malta plan was part of this more general program.[87] But, as Campbell-Bannerman refused to participate, Chapman attempted to use his Foreign Office connection to overcome the opposition of his superior. "Unless Lord Rosebery can make this a Cabinet question," he told Villiers, "I do not see how it may be dealt with."[88]

Rosebery not only listened to Chapman's advice, but acted on it, insisting that the question be placed before the joint committee.[89] Campbell-Bannerman reluctantly agreed, probably hoping that, committees being what they are, this one would deliberate at length and arrive at a compromise. Here, however, Chapman saw another opportunity by which defence policy might be transformed: "I consider it indispensable that the general principles, which should direct our naval and military policy in such a case as war with France, should be clearly laid down, in an authoritative manner, by the highest naval and military authorities, and that these principles should be thoroughly understood in India, and the Colonies, in order that there should be continuity of effort in all our possessions abroad."[90]

Rosebery stood firmly at Chapman's side while the issue of strategic planning was being considered. He did so because of his belief in the necessity of the connection between imperial and continental policies, between naval and military planning. One of the difficulties he faced as foreign secretary was that of making the various parts of the government, and the various parts of the empire, see how their interests were connected, and why they should therefore be considered jointly. Perhaps this joint committee, as envisioned by Chapman, would allow the various branches of government to see why continental diplomacy was critical to their plans of defence; as affairs stood at present, Rosebery, or any foreign secretary, was obligated to argue every case strictly on its own merits. Campbell-Bannerman, for example, proved entirely unmoved by Rosebery's argument that reinforcements in the Mediterranean were necessary for the sake of relations with the Triple Alliance. Moreover, the actual experience of the joint committee in the autumn of 1893, limited as it was to considering relatively minor and actual questions of mutual interest to the army and navy, confirmed Rosebery in the belief that something on a bigger scale was necessary.

It took time to bring the committee together. Rosebery, on 1 September, urged them to make their decision, but they had not yet met.[91] The adjutant-general and the first sea lord, it was explained, were on manoeuvres. It took a month before the committee could meet, and then, Spencer reported, "I expect they did no more than set things in train for future decision."[92] The Russian fleet arrived at Toulon while the committee was deliberating. Rosebery was still asking Campbell-Bannerman for the decision of the committee on 29 November.[93] Finally, four months after Rosebery had asked for a quick, decisive display of British intentions in the Mediterranean, the committee decided to act: a battalion that was about to be withdrawn from Egypt would be sent to Malta instead of returning to Britain.[94] This was hardly the striking demonstration that Rosebery had hoped for.

Rosebery's attempts to enlist the support of the defence departments in his Mediterranean policy convinced him that some new administrative procedures were called for. He first proposed that a representative of the Foreign Office be appointed to the joint committee, but, upon learning that it considered mainly technical questions, proposed to alter the committee fundamentally.[95] He recommended that he, the first lord of the admiralty, and the secretary of state for war should meet from time to time with the committee, and their discussions should be enlarged to encompass more than technical questions. It was obvious to Rosebery that the arrangements currently available for coordinating foreign and defence policies were insufficient for his purpose.[96]

Some of Rosebery's ideas on the problem of administrative arrangements were the result of his experience in 1893, but his efforts in this direction also arose from fundamental ideas that preceded

events in the Mediterranean. Rosebery believed that a successful foreign policy necessitated a coordinated effort among government
departments; he also believed, however, that it should be placed
above the vicissitudes of party politics. The most obvious indication
of this belief is found in his advocacy of continuity in foreign policy,
but he also contemplated the possibility of constitutional changes
that would make this goal attainable. In 1887, it will be recalled, he
had told Edward Hamilton that he favoured the appointment of the
foreign secretary and the heads of the military and naval departments
for terms of years, rather than subjecting them to the whims of the
electorate. "Rosebery is all for as little Parliamentary interference as
possible with the Executive Government."[97]

Ideas like the one outlined to Hamilton were probably no more
than daydreams, but they did show the direction in which Rosebery
was moving. He had launched his political career by attacking the
secrecy and parliamentary irresponsibility of Disraeli's government
during the Great Eastern Crisis; within a decade he was contemplating measures to remove foreign affairs from parliamentary politics. During his time at the Foreign Office in 1892–4, Rosebery did
what he could to avoid making foreign policy a political issue. Historians, who have concentrated their attention on the Uganda debate,
have failed to notice that there was no cabinet interference in foreign
affairs in 1893. After the Siam crisis, Rosebery noted his surprise that
no issue of foreign policy had come up in cabinet since the Egyptian
situation in January. His colleagues, it seemed, were prepared to
allow him to go his own way.

The larger measure that Rosebery thought he needed in the Mediterranean, the permanent reinforcement of the fleet there, was, however, certain to become an issue in the cabinet, and one that Rosebery
could see no way of avoiding. Harsh words to the sultan of Turkey
about the Armenians, clever manipulations of the khedive of Egypt,
even naval visits to Italy and army reinforcements to Malta, were no
substitute for battleships in the Mediterranean. If Rosebery were going
to keep working with the Triple Alliance, he had to demonstrate his
determination that Britain should remain supreme, or at least the
equal of the combined fleets of France and Russia, in the Mediterranean. Spencer and the Admiralty would, naturally, be keen on the
idea of building more ships, but the experience of dealing with
Campbell-Bannerman during the autumn was not likely to make
Rosebery optimistic. The secretary for war was not impressed with
the urgency of the matter; he could see no immediate threat to the
security of British interests.

Rosebery believed that he must have the ships; to have the ships he must have the money; to have the money he had to have the approval of cabinet; to have the approval of cabinet he had to show that Britain faced immediate danger. Showing that Britain was in danger was not difficult – empires are always in danger – but showing it meant taking foreign policy to the cabinet, where arguments were certain to develop. The issue that really interested the cabinet in the debate on naval construction was the expense of the undertaking. The same had been true of Uganda the year before. Practically the only restraint Rosebery faced in his management of foreign policy was the money it cost the British taxpayer, and the political consequences that, the politicians of the cabinet guessed, would arise from spending. Once these debates were started, they were expanded to include all facets of foreign policy, and of course Rosebery wished to avoid such a situation; but as long as there was no expense, there was no debate. The temptation facing British foreign secretaries to follow the cheapest policy was almost overpowering.

The trouble began with the first sign that money would be asked for, when Spencer presented the preliminary naval budget in December. Harcourt, the chancellor of the exchequer, could see no need for an increase. Britain, he said, could easily double the number of French ships in the Mediterranean by redistributing her own. If Rosebery was disposed "to doubt our power to blow the French fleet to the bottom in the Mediterranean," Harcourt invited him to examine the Admiralty's own lists.[98] If the Admiralty chose to keep ships in the Channel instead of the Mediterranean, then that was their affair. Although Harcourt was destined to fail in the end, his initial response set the tone, and established the ground of the debate: how much danger was Britain facing in the Mediterranean?

The question posed by Harcourt made things difficult for Rosebery because Britain faced no immediate danger of attack and he knew it. The French had, following their agreement to the buffer principle in Siam on 31 August, attempted to destroy the agreement by advancing their claims, possibly as a result of the encouragement they received from the Toulon demonstration. Rosebery staunchly held out for the buffer, however, and after a few trivial concessions, the French backed down. The Russians had also, around the time of the Toulon demonstration, extended their claim in the Pamirs; but Rosebery dismissed the claim as wholly inadmissible and threatened to break off negotiations. The Russians, too, backed down and submitted what Rosebery believed a reasonable basis for a settlement. Military intelligence reports indicated that neither Russia nor France appeared to be planning any dramatic act in the near future.

Rosebery wanted to reinforce the Mediterranean for political reasons that the cabinet would have found difficult to understand, and which they would have disliked had they understood them. He could not accept Harcourt's argument on behalf of redistribution, even though he had persuaded Spencer to move extra ships into the Mediterranean as a temporary measure. If Britain could not meet the combined sea power of France and Russia in the Mediterranean without permanently weakening herself elsewhere, then she would lend weight to Germany's argument that she could not match Franco-Russian power without the assistance of the Triple Alliance. If Rosebery were to accept the German argument, it would mean abandoning the principal point in his diplomatic program: working with the Triple Alliance without becoming a part of it. This program made possible the neo-Punjab school of Indian defence, which was, in fact, extended to apply to the rest of the empire as well.

Rosebery was an imperialist throughout his political career. He believed that Britain would be reduced to the status of a second-rate power if she lost the empire. He believed in this so deeply that he spent little time in analysing how the empire worked, or how it should be organized in the future. As chairman of the Imperial Federation League he commissioned a prize competition for the best constitutional scheme; as a politican he drew upon trade and investment figures to show how important the empire was. These efforts were fragmentary and superficial because Rosebery thought the significance of the empire to Britain was self-evident, and his thinking was historical: Britain was the greatest power since Rome, and Rome had started to crumble when she lost the will to maintain her empire. This was the profound difference separating him from Gladstone, who, he said after the Siam crisis, "would have made an admirable Minister of the Lower Empire." "When the barbarians swarmed into an outlying province he would have discovered there were no Treaty Rights over it; when they took another he would have made a neat little speech in Council to prove the advantage of its loss."[99]

Rosebery's public duty was to prevent the empire from shrinking by defending it from the barbarians on the outside and from the heretics on the inside. His rhetorical defence of the imperial idea has, therefore, sometimes misled observers into thinking that he wished the empire to expand and grow. This is not true, at least as far as territorial expansion is concerned. He believed the empire was already large enough, and that new responsibilities would drain the strength necessary to maintain it. "Imperialism," he later wrote, "should have for its main object the maintenance and consolidation of the Empire: extension should be avoided if possible." How was the empire to be maintained and consolidated? Through the diplomacy of imperialism. Although Britain must undertake to defend the empire to the best of her ability, her greatest advantage was the division of the European powers into hostile, armed camps.

As long as a balance of power existed in Europe, the situation worked to the advantage of Britain; but Rosebery's calculation was more complicated. In his opinion, France and Russia were great imperial powers with a direct interest in the decay and destruction of the British Empire, from which they were certain to benefit, should it occur. Moreover, they were the powers who stood to gain the most from an upheaval in Europe, whereas the powers of the Triple Alliance were reasonably satisfied with the way things stood. Although Germany was obviously interested in commercial expansion, and Italy had territorial interests in North Africa, neither of these interests seemed to pose any real threat to the British Empire. Therefore, by working with the Triple Alliance, Rosebery was doing more than throwing the weight of Britain on the side of a weaker combination in order to create a balance and maintain peace in Europe. As he saw it, he was throwing the weight of Britain on the side of the combination whose interests were primarily European, in order to restrain the combination which combined European with imperial interests.

In one sense this was the simplest of policies and an easy one to follow. All Rosebery needed was that the Triple Alliance continue to exist, because its existence would automatically compel France and Russia to devote most of their military resources to defending themselves on the continent, thereby relieving Britain of much strain on her arrangements for defence of the empire. But one might assume, under those circumstances, that Rosebery would think it possible to take up an aggressive policy toward France and Russia. He did not, and the Siam crisis of 1893 provides a convincing demonstration of how his diplomacy actually worked. Rosebery quickly defined the limits of British interests and never moved from them, threatening war when the French appeared ready to trespass upon them. Beyond this, however, Rosebery was quite prepared to be conciliatory, repeatedly urging the Siamese to give in to French demands as long as doing so did not entail the destruction of their independence or of the buffer area between Burma and French Indo-China.

The policy followed in Siam was repeated elsewhere, in Russia, the Pamirs, and Morocco, because Rosebery wanted to avoid upsetting the situation in Europe. If he had taken advantage of the continental alliance system and attempted to expand the limits of the empire or to oppose France and Russia on every issue that arose outside Europe, he might have provoked them into reversing their policy in

Europe, into giving up their designs in Alsace-Lorraine and the Balkans in favour of their interests in Africa and Asia. This policy of conciliation, always more notable with France than with Russia, was the first complication in what appears at first glance to have been simple and straightforward. It complicated matters further because it gave the Triple Alliance cause for concern.

If Rosebery succeeded in conciliating France and Russia in some way that created an impression of permanence, for instance, through "ententes" settling all their outstanding differences beyond Europe, then of what use would Britain be to the Triple Alliance? If Britain could not be of use to the Triple Alliance, then she would not be able to influence their policy. This version of the complication would see Germany, Austria-Hungary, and Italy giving in to the pressure of France and Russia in Europe. The consequences for Britain would be disastrous: France and Russia would be stronger and more secure in Europe, and ready to turn their attention outside Europe once more.

Rosebery tried to avoid this version of the complication in two ways. First, he always painted as black a picture of the French as he could manage, suggesting that their ungovernable, unstable, and truculent nature would make them enemies of Britain under any circumstances. If Britain gave them what they wanted in Egypt, Morocco, Nigeria, and Siam, they would not be satisfied, but would go on demanding more concessions. In this way, he suggested to the Germans that they had a permanent interest in opposing the French, regardless of treaty stipulations or alliance commitments. Painting the French black came easily to Rosebery, since black was how he saw them. If Germany accepted this portrait as accurate, then Britain would continue to be of some use to her in restraining France.

The second way in which Rosebery tried to overcome the possibility of the Triple Alliance submitting to France and Russia, and the way that led to the cabinet debate on naval estimates, was to demonstrate that Britain was prepared to oppose the Franco-Russian attempt to combine their forces in the Mediterranean. The real purpose of building up Britain's strength in the Mediterranean was, as he tried to tell Gladstone, moral, not physical. But the moral purpose was twofold – to show France and Russia that Britain would not stand idly by while they tried to gain control of the Mediterranean, and to demonstrate her determination to assist the Triple Alliance. Rosebery calculated that he had to do more than demonstrate an intention to oppose France and Russia. He had also to show that Britain had the power to oppose them; otherwise Italy, fearing for her security, might abandon the Triple Alliance in favour of the irridentist program against Austria.

There was a final complication in Rosebery's policy of relying on the Triple Alliance as Britain's first line of imperial defence. If he appeared to depend too much on the alliance, then they could reasonably demand that Britain join as a full-fledged member. Rosebery steadfastly denied that Britain depended on the alliance, attempting to show instead that Britain was able to match any of the efforts of France and Russia in areas of concern to Britain – in other words, that he did not require anything more of the Triple Alliance than its existence. Thus, both in the Pamirs and in Siam, Rosebery tried to show that Britain was strong enough to bargain with Russia and France without the diplomatic intervention of Germany. In the Mediterranean he tried to show that Italy and Austria depended on Britain, and that they could trust her to assist them.

Remaining outside the alliance, however, gave Rosebery the advantage of deciding when and how Britain would assist its members. He was resolved to maintain this advantage because without it Britain would almost certainly be drawn into war in Europe for the sake of interests that did not really concern her. Working informally with the alliance enabled him to restrain the ambitions of its members, as they could not be certain of the timeliness, or extent, of the assistance they might receive. Therefore, the policy of being with the Triple Alliance but not of it, which appeared simple and straightforward, was full of complications. Every question that arose, whether in Europe or beyond, was examined for its repercussions on the European alliance system, for its display of intentions and abilities.

Rosebery had come unscathed through the trials of the crisis in Siam. During the spring and summer of 1893 his temperament remained calm and steady, and there does not exist a single shred of evidence to suggest that events were unnerving him. Although he was prepared to resign if the cabinet did not support his buffer policy, it proved unnecessary to threaten them. In fact, his colleagues had practically ignored him and his foreign policy since January.[100] They only became interested when Rosebery once more started to insist on an increase in naval expenditure, and here it was Spencer who took the brunt of their attack. Rosebery was following the policy he had decided on; he was not opposed and thus far he had succeeded. Nevertheless, the complications of his policy imposed a severe strain, and it was questionable whether he would be able to stand up to it in the months that followed.

CHAPTER FIVE

Alignment without Alliance, Connection without Commitment

It would be well enough if we could lie on a bank of asphodel, basking in our history, our glory, and our past. That, however, is not possible. Never was it less possible than now. Fifty years ago we had to face a world that was comparatively inert. Europe was concerned with Europe and little more. The armies of Europe were relatively small and not wholly disproportionate to ours ... Twenty years later a national war arose between France and Germany, which produced a potent German Empire, and converted all the nations of Europe into passive armies. We remained complacent in the confidence that these storms could not pass the Channel. The Channel has indeed done much for us. It has often protected us from the broils of the Continent. It has been our bulwark, though heedless speculators have sought to undermine it. But it cannot guard us from the peaceful attacks of trained and scientific rivalry in the arts of peace. It cannot protect us against the increasing subtlety and development of the arts of war.

Rectorial Address, University of Glasgow (1900)

The most remarkable feature of Rosebery's term of office between 1892 and 1895 was the persistence with which tension developed in relations with Germany. This feature is also the most ironic, because the informal diplomatic connection with Germany constituted the foundation upon which Rosebery constructed his foreign policy. The historian of diplomacy, in attempting to explain this irony, is attracted to the possibility of an easy explanation, one that makes the British or German officials responsible for the deterioration in relations, either through their incompetence or their malevolence. Besides, the bad feelings that existed in diplomatic circles are easily documented, as officials on one side complained repeatedly of the treatment they received from the other, and diplomatic historians are especially fond of documentary evidence.

The temptation, then, is to write the diplomatic history of these years as if it were mainly the conjunction of the personalities and temperaments of the individuals involved. The temptation is even greater in the case of Rosebery, whose personality has long seemed the most interesting aspect of his political career, because he was a man who was widely expected to accomplish much but who, in fact, accomplished practically nothing. This failure certainly appears evident in his foreign relations where, according to a historian of Liberal imperialism, the conclusion of his ministry found Britain isolated. "Negotiations with France had broken down over the Nile valley question, and attempts to co-operate with the Triple Alliance had collapsed through the German attitude to the Anglo-Congolese treaty and through German failure to support Britain at the Straits."[1] The explanations offered for this failure usually centre on personality: German methods enraged Rosebery, he hated the French, his troubles with the cabinet made a coherent policy impossible.

It is more difficult, when attempting to explain Rosebery's place in Anglo-German relations, to see the wider context that defined the limits within which diplomacy operated. At bottom, Anglo-German relations arose from a dilemma that transcended personality, a dilemma that was never resolved. How does an insular power act in conjunction with a continental one? How does one assist the other when they have no areas of mutual interest? How does one bring pressure to bear on the other when one is a naval power and the other a military? The dilemma gives a heightened, but false, sense of importance to negotiations concerning those places where one does touch the other. Thus, in the eighties and nineties, Samoa, Togoland, South-West Africa, and the Cameroons appeared to be real issues that divided the two powers, when in fact their interests in these regions were of minor significance. The negotiations over boundary settlements and commercial arrangements were important primarily as indications of wider policy, of an intention to be friendly and helpful when possible, or to cause trouble when suitable.

The Germans, therefore, always took British colonial policy seriously, far more seriously than local interests warranted. Throughout these years, negotiations repeatedly led the Germans to the same conclusion, that the British were not prepared to concede anything of real value. It would have been absurd for the Germans to have expected to accomplish much empire-building by means of British concessions, but the difficulties raised by the British on every colonial question showed that they did not consider themselves dependent on German support, and the question of who was the more dependent on the other was at the bottom of every argument.

The mutual interest that most often brings about a partnership between an insular and a continental power is the existence of a third power, or combination of powers, that threatens them both, and leads them to act in conjunction by applying their power against the common threat. This was the way in which the informal understanding between Britain and Germany operated while Rosebery was in office: Germany, along with Austria and Italy, applied, or threatened to apply, military power against France and Russia, while Britain applied, or threatened to apply, naval power against them. There were no commitments to act under a certain set of circumstances, no promises, no guarantees, and thus insignificant questions gained added weight as each side tried to gauge the intentions of the other. The problem here was that, while both powers felt threatened by the Franco-Russian alliance, neither felt the threat to be so direct or overwhelming as to compel them to submit to the leadership of the other. The Germans believed that the British, who faced so many dangers in so many places, must eventually become their clients, while the British believed that the Franco-Russian threat on the continent was such that the Germans had little choice but to submit to the British definition of their understanding.

Rosebery, for all his talk about the dangers of expansion and the need for consolidation, was convinced that Britain was more secure than Germany, and it was this conviction that made his relations with Germany so tense. Rosebery believed that the European balance of power was Britain's best guarantee of imperial security, because neither Russia nor France could afford a war with Britain while they faced the Triple Alliance in Europe. At the same time, he was determined that his country should resist being drawn into the alliance as a full member, with clear obligations and commitments, because, as far as he was concerned, joining the alliance would destroy the advantage that had made the empire possible, for Britain would inevitably be drawn into war in Europe. Committing himself to the Triple Alliance would have proved that Britain was no longer able to act as an imperial power.

Because Rosebery refused to be drawn into an alliance, he has acquired a reputation as an isolationist, but this is either meaningless or misleading. He realized that it was not possible for Britain to isolate herself from European affairs; even the most cursory glance at the diplomatic record will show the extent to which Britain as a great power was bound up in European diplomacy. But perhaps historians have used isolation to mean something narrower than the word immediately suggests; perhaps they have meant it to refer only to relying on European allies. Here the term is misleading, at least in the case of Rosebery, because he certainly relied on the Triple Alliance. The error that is made in analysing this connection with Europe is the failure to understand that maintaining an informal understanding with the alliance represented a British victory in defining its terms.

"Splendid isolation" was a phrase coined for use as political currency and as such should be of interest to the historian of politics rather than diplomacy; the task of the diplomatic historian is to explain the subtleties of the connections that did exist between Britain and Europe, not to dismiss them as nonexistent because they were not cast into concrete forms. The informal nature of the Anglo-German connection was bound to create tension for which Rosebery was, in a sense, responsible, because he was resolved that the connection should remain informal. He could have removed much of the tension by giving the Germans what they wanted, by joining the Triple Alliance, or at least by adhering to Salisbury's Mediterranean agreements. But he believed these alternatives to be undesirable and unnecessary, as the European situation committed the Triple Alliance to acting on behalf of Britain in Europe.

The Germans continued to hope that the situation outside Europe would eventually commit the British to act on their behalf inside it. Rosebery had, therefore, to demonstrate that they hoped in vain, that Britain was capable of meeting the challenge of France and Russia without submitting to a German-dominated alliance. This demonstration took two forms: first, Rosebery, though cooperating with Germany, never asked for her assistance, except in Egypt; second, he sought to limit the frequency and the variety of the challenges that Britain faced. Both forms of this demonstration would deny the logic of the German argument that Britain's imperial commitments made her dependent upon Germany's military power on the continent. Thus, even though each question that arose in the diplomacy of these years had its own peculiar characteristics, it also conformed to a coherent pattern of relationships. Such was the case in Morocco during the Melilla crisis of 1893.

The crisis arose from factors having little to do with either British or German interests in the area. The treaty of 1861, which had closed the Spanish-Moroccan War, had secured for Spain additional territory surrounding her fortress at Melilla. The Spanish, who had left the area alone until the Carlist wars ended, began in 1884 to construct a series of detached forts throughout the valley of the Rio Oro, and by 1893 only the fort at Sidi Anariach remained to be built. The local Riff tribe, the Kabyles, objected to the construction of this last fort, as it seemed destined to give the Spanish control over their village of

Fajana. The Kabyles harassed the builders of the fort and on 2 October killed several of the Spanish garrison. The Spanish replied by reinforcing the garrison and seeking the opinion of the great powers.

Rosebery urged the Spanish to avoid any action that might upset the delicate state of affairs in Morocco. He had, over the past year, received alarming reports on the Moroccan situation from four different representatives. Sir Charles Euan Smith, Charles Eliot, Sir West Ridgeway, and, most recently, Ernest Satow had, despite differences of temperament and training, reached the same conclusion: the French were trying, through a variety of measures, to establish themselves as the dominant power in Morocco. One of the ways they were attempting to achieve this domination was by working in conjunction with the Spanish, apparently by encouraging them to demand the return of Gibraltar. The situation in Morocco, then, appeared to be one in which Rosebery would increasingly be forced to rely upon the assistance of the Triple Alliance.

As we have seen, Rosebery tried to avoid relying on the Triple Alliance any more than was absolutely necessary, and Morocco provides a good example of how the understanding with the alliance worked in the Mediterranean. British representatives in Morocco cooperated as closely as they could with the representatives of the Triple Alliance – in all minor affairs. Municipal reforms, commercial concessions, even sewage removal, were usually discussed among the British, German, Italian, and Austrian ministers. Ernest Satow, a bright young diplomat sent to Morocco by Rosebery, kept a diary that attests to the nature of the understanding among the four powers: there was no doubt that they were on one side in Morocco, France on the other. Nevertheless, Satow guarded against giving the impression that Britain was in any way dependent on the Triple Alliance. In fact, he was instructed before going to Morocco that the real key was to remain on good terms not with the Triple Alliance, but with the Spanish.[2]

If the Spanish were to combine forces with the French, then the British position at Gibraltar would be endangered, and, as a consequence, Britain would become more dependent on the assistance of the Triple Alliance in the Mediterranean. During the Melilla crisis, therefore, Rosebery aimed to act as closely as he could with the Spanish, without encouraging them to the point where the active intervention of other powers might be called for. He promised to assist the Spanish in their negotiations with the sultan, but suggested that any action hostile to Morocco would simply provide other powers with the excuse to intervene. "Her Majesty's Government," he declared, "do not wish to see the question of Morocco suddenly and forcibly raised. Should this be done they would know how to secure what British interests might be affected." British interests meant Tangier, and Rosebery, in effect, was warning the Spanish that if they went to war with "the object of dismembering the Shereefian Empire," they would cause the British to seize Tangier.[3] However, if they localized the dispute and upheld the principle of Moroccan independence, Rosebery would give them his support.

Morocco therefore fixed the pattern already established by Rosebery elsewhere: he would try to avoid becoming entangled in a competition for concessions and to avoid acting altogether unless interests clearly vital to imperial security were threatened. Morocco demonstrated the limits to which he was prepared to go in applying this program. "England," Satow concluded, having been schooled by Rosebery and Currie before leaving London, "did not desire Tangier for herself, but would strongly oppose its being possessed by any Power whose policy was not friendly."[4] Therefore, when the Spanish minister in Morocco asked if Britain would countenance a Spanish occupation of Tangier, Satow, in an effort to reassure the Spanish that Britain had no aggressive designs in Morocco, replied that she would, as long as there were a preliminary agreement that the occupation was to be temporary.

The parallels between Rosebery's policy in the Moroccan and the Siamese crises are striking. He avoided every possible appearance of undertaking an aggressive policy of expansion; he defined certain British interests early on in the crises and never departed from them; although he worked with the Triple Alliance and kept its members informed, he never relied on their assistance. He urged the Moroccans, as he had the Siamese, to resign themselves to the demands being made upon them, however immoderate these might be, while he simultaneously encouraged the Spanish to be as moderate as possible.[5] These diplomatic manoeuvres were not contradictory. Rosebery believed the Moroccan situation to be very dangerous and had confided earlier in the year that he would not be surprised if it became the cause of a European war.[6]

Morocco was unlikely to become the cause of war as long as Britain was able to control the local factors that had caused the crisis. But Rosebery recognized the limits within which a great power had to operate in a local crisis: he could urge moderation on the contestants, promise not to put British claims forward, even threaten to take decisive action in certain circumstances. None of these moves, however, could guarantee that local factors beyond his control would not come to dominate. The sultan of Morocco, for example, tried to avoid acknowledging that a crisis existed, because such an acknowledgment might result in his being forced to exert authority over the Riff tribes, and if he exerted himself the tribes might attack him instead of the Spanish. Similarly, the Spanish government feared that if they did not take a firm line in Morocco, they would be attacked by their political opponents: "Better war than a revolution in Spain," their minister told Satow.[7] Over these factors Rosebery could exert little control.

Early in November 1893 another tribe, thirty thousand strong, joined the insurgents at Melilla. On 5 November the Spanish called up their active reserves and began to prepare schemes for arming the Spanish citizens of Morocco and landing ships at Algeciras.[8] The issue seemed about to be decided by force of arms when the sultan apparently decided that the danger of war with Spain was greater than that of revolution on the Riff, and agreed to send troops to restrain the tribesmen. In London, Currie rejoiced.[9] "The Sultan," he wrote, "ought to march with all the force he can collect against the tribes."[10] But this temporary resolution of the crisis showed how little Britain was able to influence the situation, because the local factors were really beyond her control, and consequently the dangers there were bound to persist.

The immediate danger was that the Spanish government, for the sake of domestic politics, would insist on some striking demonstration that the affair had ended in their favour. Rosebery feared that if they demanded too much a war might still erupt, and he calculated that any real change in Morocco was likely to work to the advantage of France. It certainly appeared that France was hoping to keep the crisis going. Reports from Spain indicated that the French ambassador was offering to support a Spanish demand for the cession of Tetuan.[11] Rosebery, although he wished to act with Spain, was not prepared to offer similar assistance, and had offered to assist her only in securing a small piece of territory that would make Melilla secure. He refused to become engaged in a competition for the friendship of Spain if that friendship could be purchased only at the price of Moroccan independence.

Fortunately for Rosebery, the queen regent of Spain declined to take up the French suggestion that she demand Tetuan as compensation for the expenses involved in protecting Melilla, and the danger of an immediate partition of Morocco passed.[12] Still, Rosebery and his advisers at the Foreign Office recognized that the queen regent and the constitutionalist party faced considerable political danger if the republicans could attack them for failing to uphold the dignity of Spain in Morocco. The question, therefore, began to turn on the size of the financial indemnity that Spain would receive. Rosebery did what he could to limit the size of the indemnity, arguing that the demand, if it exceeded what the Moors were able to pay, would lead to foreign intervention. This argument placed Rosebery in an awkward position, since he had, throughout the crisis, attempted to act in cooperation with Spain; he had to argue, therefore, that the real friends of Spain wished to see her act with moderation. He had to argue in this way because the French, it appeared, were encouraging the Spanish to demand the maximum indemnity.

Rosebery and his advisers believed they understood what the French were up to, because reports from Morocco indicated that the French were encouraging the sultan not to yield to the Spanish demand.[13] Thus, the British concluded, the Moroccans would be faced with an indemnity that they could not pay; the French would then step in and provide them with a loan; if the Moors later found themselves unable to meet the payments, then the French would have a useful pretext for intervening in Morocco. Therefore, even though the immediate crisis appeared to have passed when the sultan undertook to restrain the tribesmen of the Riff, the diplomatic situation remained a dangerous one as far as Rosebery was concerned.

Following a conservative policy in a crisis is often more hazardous than following an aggressive one. Rosebery's diplomacy during the Melilla crisis would have been much simpler had he chosen to align himself with either Spain or Morocco. But the situation that Rosebery was seeking to conserve was the general one in the western Mediterranean, not simply in Morocco. He wanted to preserve good relations with Spain, if only for the sake of Gibraltar, while simultaneously upholding the principle of Moroccan independence, if only for the sake of Tangier. Posing as the friend of Spain and the protector of Morocco was not easy when the two states appeared to be on the brink of war with one another. At Madrid Rosebery urged the Spanish to be moderate in their demands, while at Fez he urged the Moroccans to accept whatever the Spanish asked for. The danger of this policy, obviously, was that he would succeed in offending one, or both, of the parties whom he was trying to befriend.

Throughout the Moroccan crisis, Rosebery worked closely with the Italians. Satow, the minister in Morocco, met daily with his Italian and Austrian counterparts (although the Austrians took less interest and exercised less influence than the Italians), and they had no difficulty agreeing on policy. The German minister, however, did not conform to this pattern: he often remained aloof when the other three agreed, or declined to act until he had received further instructions from Berlin. Satow and Rosebery believed they understood the reasoning behind German policy, and their explanation had little to do with local factors. "The real reason" for the German decision not to work with the British in Morocco, Satow confided to his diary, "was that Germany in order to force us to join the triple alliance is resolved to 'bounder' England everywhere."[14] The future of Britain's connection with the Triple Alliance was in the background of every diplomatic question that arose while Rosebery was in office.

It turned out that, in spite of the difficulties involved, the amount of the Moroccan indemnity to Spain was fixed before long, and without causing either side any real distress. This resolution of the crisis, while it certainly left the future of Morocco unresolved, was due in large part to Rosebery's policy of upholding the current state of affairs in the western Mediterranean, although he had been able, in fact, to exercise only limited control over local factors. Because no dramatic changes occurred, the Melilla crisis has attracted little attention; no historian writing about Rosebery's foreign policy has even mentioned it, although it clearly fits into his general diplomatic design. Once again he had refused to undertake any new commitments on behalf of Britain; he had successfully tried to uphold the independence of a non-European state, when France seemed determined to establish her sway; and he had left no doubt that he would, if he were forced, seize what he considered to be a vital interest, in this case Tangier.

Even when it appeared that the sultan would agree to pay the indemnity demanded by Spain (after this had been reduced from five million to three million dollars), the Germans refused to assist Rosebery in his attempt to bring about a quick settlement of the affair. Rosebery had suggested that, rather than permit France to control the Moroccan customs as security for a loan, or allow Spain to control them as security for the indemnity, the representatives of Britain, Germany, France, Austria, Italy, and Spain should be given the right, if Morocco defaulted in payment of a loan or the indemnity, to examine the customs accounts.[15] The Germans refused to take part in this, "as the Government desired to hold aloof from future responsibilities in a matter which was outside their political activity."[16] The Germans, in other words, were not going to assist the British in the Mediterranean. "The motive," Rosebery noted, "is obvious enough."[17]

The Germans never passed up an opportunity of turning a local diplomatic question into a wider one that might strengthen their connection with Britain. Satow, who had arrived in Morocco prepared to work closely with the Germans, was at first puzzled by their attitude. "Is it that Germany does not really wish for the success of our policy, or wishes to play an isolated game?"[18] He was soon convinced that Germany was using Morocco to push Britain into the Triple Alliance.

During the course of the crisis in Morocco, the British ambassador at Madrid, Sir Henry Drummond Wolff, had discussed with his German and Austrian colleagues the general changes that were occurring in the Mediterranean. "They seem to think that the civilities between France and Russia portend the transfer of political danger from Europe to Asia and that England if she does not join the triple alliance will be isolated." This was the customary argument: Britain, threatened by the Franco-Russian alliance outside Europe, must come to recognize that she depended on the Triple Alliance. The Franco-Russian alliance did not, according to the Germans, threaten them, because the transfer from Europe to Asia "relieved Germany from the danger of war either from France or Russia," and, the German ambassador argued, "as soon as the works at Biserta are complete the forces of the two countries will be directed against Turkey and England."[19] Drummond Wolff, not the most astute of diplomats, swallowed the argument whole; but had the Germans and Austrians seen his response to their warning they might have been less eager to push their argument any further.

Drummond Wolff concluded that, rather than join the Triple Alliance, Britain should, in order to safeguard the passage to India and the Pacific, align herself with France, Italy, and Turkey as Mediterranean powers, and with Russia as an Asiatic and, possibly, a Mediterranean one. This was not the conclusion that the Germans hoped to force on the British; nor was it the conclusion reached by Rosebery in 1893. Rosebery continued to believe that he could avoid joining either alliance by playing the one off against the other. The alliance between France and Russia was the more aggressive of the two, and the one in the best position to threaten the imperial interests of Britain. Therefore, he favoured working with the Triple Alliance as the best means of restraining the imperial ambitions of France and Russia, but he did not feel that Britain was sufficiently endangered to warrant her submitting to Germany's demand that she become a full member of the alliance.

In an important meeting on 5 December 1893 the German ambassador warned Rosebery that the present attitude of Britain was causing disquietude everywhere. Count Hatzfeldt pointed especially to the situation in Italy and Austria. In Rome, he said, Premier Crispi "was supposed to be shaky with regard to the Triple Alliance, and the main cause of his hesitation was said to be doubt as to the present policy of Great Britain."[20] In Vienna, the Austrians were reported to be considering whether they might come to some arrangement with Russia, and concluding that they could not by themselves resist the entrance of Russia into Constantinople. According to Hatzfeldt, then, the Triple Alliance appeared to be rapidly arriving at the point of dissolution, and only Rosebery could save the situation, as "in the present strain and nearly balanced condition of Europe the position of England was supremely important." He hoped Rosebery would act quickly in order "to prevent any disposition on the part of other Governments to enter into new arrangements."

In reply to these German worries, Rosebery offered soothing words, referring to his personal position and British naval power in the Mediterranean, but he offered no hope that the changing situation in the Mediterranean might eventually induce Britain to join the Triple Alliance. After the crisis in Siam, and while a new one developed in Morocco, Rosebery still felt certain that the policy he had endorsed on his return to office was the correct one. He assured Hatzfeldt of his certainty that "a material and adequate" increase was still being debated by the cabinet.[21] There was no doubt what the increase of the fleet was intended to achieve; no commitment to the Triple Alliance was necessary because Britain would act on its behalf in the Mediterranean simply as a result of the situation that existed there. If France were to attack Italy in the Mediterranean, Rosebery said, Britain could do only one of two things: she could retire altogether from the Mediterranean or come to the assistance of Italy. "In my personal opinion, should Great Britain retire from the Mediterranean and leave the field clear to France and Russia, she would only encourage those powers to persevere in aggression, and force England into a war under the most unfavourable circumstances."[22]

Rosebery undoubtedly believed every word of this argument because every diplomatic action he undertook supported it. Nevertheless, although he could sincerely maintain that "an increase of our fleet would tend more to the preservation of peace than any other measure that could be adopted," his real reason for wishing to increase the fleet was that he believed Britain to be strong enough to resist the temptation of joining the Triple Alliance. He would offer the alliance no promises beyond himself, and then only to assist Italy if she were attacked by France. Britain was in a position to decide how, when, and where she would aid her informal allies. Whenever the Germans asked for some concrete assurance of British intentions, Rosebery fell back on his sympathies. "I had occasion during this interview," he recorded, "to allude more than was agreeable to my personal position and to the fact that while I was here, it was a symptom and a pledge of the policy of the country."[23]

The real cause of Anglo-German tension in these years is not to be found in their differences outside Europe, but in their debate over who was the dominant power in their relationship and who, therefore, was to define the nature of their understanding. Germany was the one dissatisfied with the way things stood, and consequently it was Germany who kept raising difficulties, who kept warning Britain that things could not long remain as they were. One day near the end of 1893, Sir Edward Malet, the British ambassador at Berlin, met the chief of the German diplomatic department, Baron von Holstein, in the street. Although Holstein used often to meet with Malet during Bismarck's day, he had ceased to receive visits from the heads of missions after Marschall took office. The two men immediately began to discuss the Italian situation, perhaps because it had just been announced that a bright young diplomat, Bernhard von Bülow, had been appointed ambassador at Rome, over the heads of many senior men in the diplomatic corps.[24]

Affairs in Italy, Holstein rmarked, were becoming very critical. Although Crispi, upon assuming office, had assured Italy's allies of his intention to continue the policy of his predecessors, "it was difficult to have complete confidence in the continuity of Italian policy, while it was under his control." Everything, Holstein told Malet, depended on the attitude of Britain. Italy always had the alternative of the irridentist program, with the alluring prospects held out to her by France and Russia, should she decide to abandon the Triple Alliance. Italy's decision would depend on whether or not Britain gave her confidence in the safety of her coasts from attack. Holstein predicted that Crispi would soon begin to sound the British on whether or not he could rely on their assistance if attacked. Holstein hoped that Britain would not be altogether discouraging, "for he could not help fearing that the day that Signor Crispi was convinced that he had nothing to hope for in that quarter, he would turn his face towards France and Russia."[25]

Informal understandings between great powers are always being tested in order to enable diplomatists to gauge the conditions under which they apply and to judge the limits of their effectiveness. Observers are often misled into thinking that this is not true of formal understandings, but in fact the same principle applies; the difference is only one of degree. Although formal understandings are likely to stipulate conditions and limits, allies are nevertheless forced to recognize that obligations might not be met, particularly if the conditions on which they were undertaken have changed. When Malet, replying to the misgivings of Holstein regarding the future course of Italian diplomacy, suggested that Italy could not escape from the obligations imposed on her by the treaties with Germany and Austria, Holstein was not convinced.

The head of the German diplomatic department declared that he had not much faith in the efficacy of treaties of the kind existing between Italy and her allies if a country did not wish to be bound by them. Besides, "if a treaty is to die, it is very useless during the time that precedes its decease."[26] This was one of the clearest statements of the paradox that bedevilled German policy throughout the nineties: her concrete and visible alliance with Italy hinged on her amorphous and invisible understanding with Britain. As a consequence, the Germans had little choice but to persist in their attempts to draw Britain into the alliance whenever Italy seemed to be reconsidering her position.

One of the ways by which the Germans tried to induce the British to join them was to raise the spectre of French ambitions. Although they had been using this argument for some time, it seemed more believable, and more urgent, following the Toulon demonstration. Marschall declared that, as a consequence of the excitement, the French would be more difficult to manage: "their heads have been turned by all the speeches, toasting and enthusiasm." Anyone who had negotiations pending would soon feel the effects of the demonstration, but fortunately for the Germans, Marschall said, they had no question under discussion, except that of the Cameroons hinterland. "I venture to predict, however, that the solution of the Siamese and African negotiations will not be facilitated to Her Majesty's Government by the recent events of Toulon and Paris."[27]

The threat posed by France in Africa and Asia constituted only one part of the German argument; according to the Germans, she also threatened Britain in the Mediterranean. In the midst of the crisis in Morocco the kaiser had warned the British ambassador that the French were working for a triple maritime alliance in the Mediterranean, "and that as the inducement to the Spaniards to come into it, they have offered their assistance towards the recovery of Gibraltar."[28] Unfortunately for the Germans, there seemed to be little evidence to prove that the Russians were as anxious to cause trouble as the French, and it was difficult to see how the British were threatened unless the Russians were prepared to come to the assistance of the French. Marschall had the solution. Russia, he argued, might have her hand forced by France: "when a runaway horse is harnessed with a quiet horse he often drags his companion with him."

Rosebery, though he was inclined to believe the worst of the French, found the German argument less than convincing. As long as he succeeded in conciliating the Russians, he had little to fear from the French, and the Russians had given no signs in Morocco, Siam, or Egypt of coordinating their policy with the French. But, although Rosebery was prepared to dismiss the logic of the German argument, its presentation nevertheless troubled him because it signified a dangerous state of affairs within the Triple Alliance itself. The prospect of the alliance breaking up, of Italy accommodating herself to France, and Austria to Russia, was more worrying than the possibility of any immediate danger from France. If France and Russia did not have to face the prospect of fighting the combined forces of the Triple Alliance, then they really would be in a position to threaten Britain outside Europe. On the day following his important conversation with Hatzfeldt, when he had refused to hold out any hope that Britain might join the alliance, Rosebery wrote privately to Malet, asking to be kept very fully informed of the situation in Germany. "The German Government," he explained, "is evidently uncomfortable and one of their methods of easing their discomfort is to complain of our fleet and our government and everything about us."[29]

Rosebery believed that he understood the reasons for Germany's discomfort: she distrusted Italy and was doubtful even about Austria. Mutual distrust was threatening to destroy the alliance. "Germany thinks Austria a bit of a flirt," he told his ambassador at Paris, "both of them think Italy no better than she should be. On the other hand Austria knows that the two others will not help her in the East; and the German ladies both fear that Italy will slip away from them unless fortified by some strong naval power."[30] Calculations of this kind troubled Rosebery, because the continued existence of the Triple Alliance was the main stratagem of his foreign policy. The predicament he had to face, then, was how to keep the Triple Alliance going without actually becoming a part of it and thereby abandoning Britain's most valuable advantage, her ability to act independently.

In spite of the changes that had taken place since August 1892, and in spite of the diplomatic tangles that had arisen over the last year and a half, Rosebery continued to believe that Britain held the key to the situation. "She alone can help Austria at Constantinople, or prevent Italy walking the streets." The Germans insisted that the understanding between France and Russia was aimed at Britain in order to induce Rosebery to give Austria and Italy the reassurance they needed. Rosebery agreed with the conclusion of the German argument, but not the premise. He doubted that Britain was the real objective of France and Russia, for, were this the case, it would seem so much the better for the Germans "that one can hardly understand their disinterested uneasiness." "The tender disquietudes of the Triple Alliance," he concluded, "are for themselves and not for us."[31] Therefore, while Rosebery wished to reassure the members of the Triple Alliance, he did not feel compelled to do so in consequence of an immediate Franco-Russian threat.

Because Britain was in no immediate danger, Rosebery calculated that she could safely remain outside the alliance. But Britain had a role to perform nevertheless: she was to "give Italy sufficient confidence, so that she may repair from dalliance with France," and to "give Austria sufficient confidence (as to Constantinople) – to prevent her dallying with Russia."[32] He had already decided that this role could be performed if Britain strengthened her position in the Mediterranean. Gibraltar and Malta were to be reinforced; ships would be added to the Mediterranean fleet. As far as Rosebery was concerned, these moves would provide assurance sufficient to keep the Triple Alliance together, enabling it to fulfil its appointed function as the guardian of British interests.

Perhaps the Germans would have found Rosebery's promise to reinforce the Mediterranean sufficiently reassuring had their worries been exclusively international. If, after all, Rosebery succeeded in quieting the fears of Italy and Austria, then the Triple Alliance was likely to remain intact. But the worries of the German government arose partly from domestic politics, where Britain's reinforcement of her fleet in the Mediterranean was unlikely to do the government much good. The problem was that the new course in German foreign policy, to which the kaiser had committed himself almost as soon as he ascended the throne, was beginning to look like a failure and was coming under attack from several directions within Germany. The new course was premised upon the assumption that Germany was strong enough to abandon Bismarck's policy of conciliating Russia in the Near East, to dominate the foreign policy of Austria, and to compel Britain eventually to enter into the orbit of her diplomacy. Events over the past two years caused these assumptions to be questioned.

The enthusiastic demonstration of Franco-Russian solidarity during the autumn of 1893 was obviously a blow to the kaiser, who had believed that tsarist Russia and republican France could never sufficiently overcome their political differences to form an alliance. The Bismarckian press in Germany especially delighted in pointing out the risks entailed in abandoning the policy of the "honest broker" in the Near East. Moreover, the Austrian government, under the leadership of the Hungarian Count Taafe, was actively soliciting the support of the anti-German element within the Dual Monarchy. Finally, Rosebery had given the Germans no tangible signs of support since he came into office, leading the radical right in particular to attack the idea that Germany's imperial future lay in a policy of cooperation with Britain.

These were the circumstances that led the kaiser to ask the British for a new set of clothes. On 12 January 1894, the British military attaché at Berlin, Colonel Swaine, wrote to Queen Victoria's private secretary to suggest that the kaiser be given the honorary colonelcy in a British cavalry regiment.[33] The kaiser, on the same day, wrote to the queen to request her permission to place "Uncle Bertie," the prince of Wales, à la suite of the German Dragoon Guards.[34] The kaiser needed some evidence, however trifling, of the fact that Britain and Germany were working together in a friendly spirit. The military uniforms would, no doubt, have suited the kaiser's taste in clothes, but this particular outfit was also tailored to suit his political requirements. With the kaiser and the prince of Wales parading through the streets of Berlin in the uniforms of one another's armies, perhaps the German public would be convinced that an alliance with the British really did exist.

Colonel Swaine warned the kaiser that there might be some difficulty in fulfilling the request, as no foreign prince had ever held such an office in the British army. But it was probably for precisely this reason that William had chosen to ask for this honour. "All rules," he told the colonel, "are broken sooner or later"; perhaps an exception could be made for him "both on family and political grounds."[35] Rosebery, who advised the queen against granting the honour, dismissed the whole idea as bizarre and impolitic. The colonelcy sought by William was that of a highland regiment, which "sufficiently comic in itself is rendered inexpressibly so by the fact that he has forbidden the kilt to appear at his Court balls as being an indecent costume."[36] The honour, he told the queen's secretary, would be considered a declaration of policy, "which, just now, is neither desirable nor desired."[37] Rosebery was unwilling to offer the kaiser even the token demonstration of a new set of clothes in exchange for German cooperation.

This apparently trivial affair of the German emperor's new clothes symbolized, as well as anything could, the condition of Anglo-German relations at the beginning of 1894. According to Bismarck's appropriately metaphoric aphorism, every alliance has a horse and rider; any time the Germans succeeded in drawing the British closer to the Triple Alliance, or in forcing a colonial concession out of them, they contributed to the impression that they were in the saddle. For this reason Rosebery was reluctant to give them anything more than was absolutely necessary, and at the beginning of 1894 there seemed to him no good reason why Britain should not continue to remain outside the alliance. This affair, like every question that arose between Britain and Germany, was a competition for control of their understanding. Ironically, while the competition continued, both sides seemed determined to win the other's friendship by making themselves as disagreeable as possible.

The thinking behind this competition was, on Rosebery's side at least, perfectly clear. While he sincerely deplored the fact that the Triple Alliance was rife with mutual suspicion, he had already ruled out the possibility of either joining it or entering into a secret treaty with Italy. "Our only sure policy," he wrote privately to the ambassador at Berlin, "is to strengthen our fleet, and that will be done."[38] Any reassurance that might be given to the Triple Alliance must be founded explicitly on the principle of British independence. Reinforcing the Mediterranean fleet, therefore, suited his requirements exactly. He had instructed Sir Philip Currie, about to proceed to Constantinople as the new British ambassador, to act cordially toward Austria, but there too the principle of independent action was not to be compromised. "Though our interests are clear, our hands must be free: we must co-operate but not be handcuffed to anyone." As long as Rosebery maintained this attitude, relations with the Triple Alliance were bound to remain tense.

Count Hatzfeldt, one of the leading exponents of an Anglo-German alliance, hoped that French ambitions would force the British to abandon their independence and join the Triple Alliance. "I would give much if I were quite certain that the French would become downright impertinent as a result of Russia's embraces and tread heavily on the arms of the English everywhere – Egypt, Madagascar, Tuat, etc., etc." "What makes Rosebery gloomy," he wrote to Holstein, "makes me pleased as Punch."[39] Unfortunately, by mid-January of 1894, following the decision of Spain to propose the reduced demands on Morocco that had been suggested by Rosebery, France was not causing Britain any real difficulty. In fact, the solution of the crisis in Morocco, achieved without the assistance of Germany, seemed to suggest that Britain was stronger in the Mediterranean than most observers had been inclined to believe. Rosebery's policy of adhering informally to the Triple Alliance was a declaration of British strength, not a confession of weakness.

The attempts of the Triple Alliance to demonstrate that the Franco-Russian alliance meant imminent danger for Britain had been frustrated. There was no sign of a *coup de main* on Constantinople, no sign of a forceful movement through the Balkans, and the Pamirs negotiation was nearing an amicable settlement. The Austrian ambassador, Count Deym, admitted all this in an illuminating conversation with Rosebery at the end of January. He raised, instead, another possibility. "The object of Russia was not so much to advance through the Balkan states or to seize Constantinople by a *coup de main*, but their object was rather to obtain the passage of the Straits."[40] This was a more reasonable possibility, because more vague. The

Austrians and Germans could argue, and indeed the kaiser had already hinted, that while the Russians were not apparently threatening British interests, they were intending to do so by more subtle methods. If the British were inclined to adhere to the lines of the Derby dispatch of 1877, Deym assured him that Austria could give her support. But he warned Rosebery that if Austria were left to face Russia on her own, then she would have to come to terms with her.

The Austrian initiative on the Straits question confirmed Rosebery in his belief that Britain held the key to the situation in the Mediterranean, that she alone could provide the support the Austrians needed in the Near East. The Austrian initiative was a confession of weakness, showing the British to be in the stronger position. The Austrians, however, were attempting to turn their weakness to their advantage: if they could convince Rosebery that their weakness was making them desperate, he might then decide that the risk of an Austro-Russian understanding in the Near East was more dangerous to Britain than a commitment to the Triple Alliance. Rosebery's reply to the Austrian manoeuvre was, therefore, a clear indication of his assessment of the situation in the Near East.

Rosebery refused to go any farther in assuaging the fears of the Austrians than he had in the past. He told Deym that he had not submitted the question of the Straits to the cabinet, nor did he intend to do so "until it arose in a concrete form."[41] He would not commit Britain to any particular action in anticipation of the event. It would not even be possible, he said, for Britain to declare that she would, in any event, oppose the passage of the Straits by Russia. Rosebery refused to commit himself to abstract principles: under his guidance, Britain would respond only to events, only as the situation demanded. He explained to the Austrians that there was a simple reason why he could not commit himself in advance: "If France and Russia were allied on this question, England could not single-handed fight at Constantinople, because her bases would be menaced by the French fleet."[42]

Rosebery refused to adhere to the traditional policy of denying Russia the passage of the Straits, and he did so for the practical reason that Britain would be unable to enforce it should she be faced with a simultaneous threat from France. In taking this position, his real purpose was to commit the Triple Alliance to the role he wished them to play. If Britain were not menaced by the French fleet in the Mediterranean, if "she had only to deal with Russia single-handed," he assured the Austrian ambassador, "it would not be so difficult for her to resist Russian aggression in this form." In other words, Rosebery was prepared to stop Russia at the Straits only if the Triple Alliance were prepared, in return, to neutralize France. He would wait upon events to see if Austria, Italy, and Germany accomplished the task he had assigned them; no declaration in advance, no abstract principle was possible in this matter, because "we should require to know whether we had to deal with Russia alone, or with France and Russia."[43]

Because nothing of substance ever arose from such conversations as the one between Rosebery and Deym it is easy to overlook their importance. But the absence of substantial change represented, in fact, a victory for Rosebery's interpretation of the understanding. Although he refused to commit himself to act, he made it clear that he considered the interests of Britain and Austria at the Straits to be the same. "It was clear that to allow Russia the passage of the Straits would be to place Constantinople absolutely in her power, and therefore I believed that this country would not tolerate it." Interests, not treaties, would cause Britain to act. Almost casually, however, Rosebery held out an alternative solution to the Straits question: "I remarked that the only condition under which the passage of the Straits could be safely allowed, would be that the Straits should be open to the ships of all nations, and that Constantinople should be neutralized or placed under the guarantee of Europe."[44]

This last remark was not taken up by the Austrian ambassador because it lay outside the scope of his instructions. Instead, he tried to force Rosebery into committing himself by arguing that, if Britain abandoned her traditional policy at the Straits, Austria would be compelled to confine her activities to "the maintenance and safeguarding of Austro-Hungarian interests in the Balkans and to leave the Straits to their fate, i.e., to Russia."[45] According to Deym, Rosebery expressed his astonishment that Austria might rest content with this policy, but repeatedly declared, nevertheless, that he was unable to give any guarantees beyond his personal policy of acting in accord with the Triple Alliance. He declined, when Deym persisted, to take the matter to the cabinet.

The accounts of these discussions differ in one important respect. According to Rosebery, when Deym called on him again on 1 February, he came to explain what he had meant when he had spoken of the possibility of Austria coming to an arrangement with Russia. The Austrian ambassador, Rosebery said, feared that he might have been misunderstood, for "It would of course be impossible for Austria to come to any compromise with Russia as regards the passage of the Straits, because in her opinion the concession of the passage of the Straits would imply the termination of the Eastern Question and the predominance of Russia."[46] If Deym did offer this explanation, then it removed some of the force behind his argument. It suggested, in fact, that the bogeyman the Austrians had constructed to frighten the British was actually more frightening to themselves. Perhaps, if Rosebery took their threat too seriously, he might decide to compete with them in seeking an arrangement with Russia in the Near East; he already appeared to be close to an arrangement with them in central Asia.

Although Deym's account of these conversations is the more detailed, Rosebery's seems the more believable. Deym had been instructed to persuade the British government to define their attitude to the Straits question, and his dispatch to Count Kálnoky is a record of his failure. It would not be surprising, therefore, if he painted as bright a picture as he could, and this appears to have been the case. Even if Rosebery had not bound himself to a protocol, he reported, "he has committed himself personally, and, at least as long as he is in charge of English policy, we know how far we can rely on England."[47] Deym appears to have fitted into the mould of his German colleague, Count Hatzfeldt, in actively working for a British alliance, and perhaps, like Hatzfeldt, he coloured his accounts accordingly. Rosebery, in contrast, had little to gain from colouring his accounts, as he showed them to no one. The possibility always exists, however, that he hoped to mislead posterity.

One point on which the two men had no difficulty in agreeing was the role that Germany should play in the Near East. In their first conversation, Rosebery had noted that Germany professed to have no interest in this question, but told Deym that he considered this profession spurious. "The interest of Germany was not so close or direct as that of Austria, or even of England, but if England abandoned the contest and the policy of keeping the Russians out of Constantinople, it was clear that Italy would be lost to the Triple Alliance, and that Austria might make her own terms with Russia, leaving Germany isolated." Therefore, he concluded, he "never attached any importance to these professions of German policy." Deym agreed with these views and thought that Germany used this language in order to please Russia. Moreover, the Austrian said that he shared Rosebery's opinion that it was incumbent on the Triple Alliance to check France if Russia attempted to force the passage of the Straits: "it must necessarily be the case."[48]

Diplomatists, when they compete for control of an alliance, try to prove they do not need that which they seek. Kálnoky pretended to contemplate abandoning Constantinople and the Straits to Russia if Britain failed to guarantee that she would come to Austria's assistance; Rosebery pretended he could leave Constantinople and the

Straits to Russia if the Triple Alliance did not neutralize France. In fact, the possibility of Russia controlling the Straits was equally frightening to them both, which explains why they found it easy to agree on the role Germany should play. Neutralizing France could be accomplished only by the threat of German arms, so the British and Austrians agreed that it was a good idea that Germany should risk a war with France for the sake of British and Austrian interests in the Near East. The Germans did not find the prospect so agreeable.

On 14 February the German ambassador called on Rosebery in order to discover what impression he had received as a result of Sir Philip Currie's visit to Count Kálnoky on his way to the embassy at Constantinople. Rosebery painted a gloomy picture: "Austria was likely to come to terms with Russia, that Germany was not unlikely, and that Italy was equally so disposed."[49] He went on to outline his recent conversations with Deym, implying that whether or not Germany would keep France in check in the event that Russia attempted to seize control of the Straits was crucial to the outcome of their discussions. Rosebery was trying to extract a promise from Germany without making one on behalf of Britain.

Hatzfeldt countered Rosebery's move by arguing that Britain must first offer something to Austria. Kálnoky, he indicated, "would require some definite assurance on the part of Her Majesty's Government, in order to enable him to give a counter assurance that the Triple Alliance would keep France in check." Hatzfeldt did not bother to point out that such an assurance was not Kálnoky's to give, that it could only come from Germany. Britain, in other words, had to guarantee to act against Russia on behalf of Austria before Germany would promise to check France. Germany, Hatzfeldt suggested, had less need of this arrangement than did Britain because, as "Prince Bismarck had told him more than once ... he did not fear an alliance between France and Russia against Germany, for at the last moment he could always play a trump card, which would prevent Russia from attacking Germany." He could, Bismarck said, "abandon the East to Russia."[50]

Hatzfeldt was determined to do everything he could to transform the understanding between Britain and Germany into an alliance. Therefore, while he was prepared to use Bismarck's argument concerning the Eastern Question, and to suggest that "there was a strong school that held it in Germany," he was careful to dissociate himself from it. The possession of Constantinople, he said, would give Russia the supremacy of the world. According to this view, it was in the mutual interest of Britain, Austria, and Germany to prevent Russia from controlling the Straits.

Rosebery agreed that the outcome of the Eastern Question was of interest to all three powers, although he was not prepared to concede that an unfavourable outcome would give Russia the supremacy of the world. Germany, he argued, could not afford to ignore the Eastern Question because of the effect this would have on her diplomatic position in Europe: "it would deprive Germany of the alliance to Italy, and possibly Austria." These speculations in the void about an unknown future were really a part of the competition for control of the Anglo-German understanding. Who needed the other more? Hatzfeldt, by arguing that it was Britain, hoped for a definite commitment from her. Rosebery, by arguing that it was Germany, continued to offer sentiment: anyone who knew Britain, he said, "would rather rely on the interests and passions of the people than on any Governmental declaration."[51]

That Rosebery never managed to satisfy the Germans with these professions of sentiment is hardly surprising, given that this informal arrangement clearly left him in a position to decide when, or if, the understanding was to operate. As a result of his persistent refusal to commit himself in advance, his relations with Germany were certain to remain tense in the months that followed. The possible consequences of his refusal were revealed almost immediately. In the middle of February, two weeks after the discussion of the Straits question had begun, rumours reached London that the Germans were contemplating the cession to France of a port on the Benue River in West Africa. The Benue flowed into the Niger, a particularly delicate connection at this moment, as Britain and France were entangled in a dispute over the boundaries of Nigeria. Rosebery immediately telegraphed to Malet in Berlin, instructing him to raise the matter without delay. Britain, he said, would deplore any such cession, "which we could not regard as a friendly act in view of the assistance we have recently given to German enterprise in that region." France could use the port only "as a means of annoyance to us."[52]

Rosebery had been careful in recent months to avoid giving the Germans any cause for complaint in Africa, and had in fact met their wishes on a number of small matters. He had, for example, abandoned a British claim to territory east of the neutral zone in the rear of the Gold Coast Colony, and ceded it to Germany, explaining that he was "anxious to act in a friendly spirit and to meet the wishes of the German Government so far as possible," even though he refused to accept their argument that these territories fell into the German sphere of influence.[53] The position Rosebery adopted on relations with Germany outside Europe was really twofold: he tried to cooperate with her, in a vague and general way, whenever it seemed possible to do so, but this cooperation was to be negotiated as the occasion for it arose and on the basis of the character of the local situation. It was not a mechanical arrangement that operated automatically. Rosebery would never agree to such an operation, as he regarded many of Britain's imperial interests to be primary, while Germany's were obviously secondary. Nevertheless, he had been careful, especially since the Kaulla affair of January 1893, to avoid wounding German sensibilities. When he heard that an Austro-German consortium was about to take over the Smyrna-Cassaba railway line in Asia Minor, for example, with the sultan's proviso that British capital and British employees be excluded from the concession, he did not object. "You know what happened last year," he told Currie; "I am not much inclined to take any active part."[54]

When Rosebery took this line in his relations with Germany outside Europe, he was tacitly accepting the argument of those German imperialists, like Albert Ballin, Karl Supf, and Alfred von Kiderlen-Wächter, who believed that cooperation and market allocation between the two countries were both possible and to their mutual advantage. But these men also believed that Britain would not consent to such an arrangement unless she were convinced that she had no choice, that she would suffer undesirable consequences should she resist an arrangement. These men also supported the building of the risk fleet. Rosebery's method of working out cooperation with the Germans certainly fell far short of what they had in mind, suggesting that threats might be necessary in order to induce him to broaden the definition of Anglo-German cooperation. Before the risk fleet was built, the simplest way for Germany to threaten Britain was to assist, or suggest that she might assist, France and Russia in making themselves more dangerous to Britain.

As far as Nigeria was concerned, Marschall denied having ceded a port on the Benue to France, and assured Malet that he would not do so.[55] Malet worried that the French might have "jockeyed both him and us by their more accurate knowledge of the geography of those regions."[56] He explained to Marschall that the French would use this continuous water communication to the Niger to harass and annoy the British. If Marschall needed proof that colonial manoeuvres could be useful in influencing British policy, then Malet provided it. British fears were renewed on 3 March when secret reports received from Paris warned that the Germans had in fact given the village of Bifara to the French.[57] It soon became apparent that the Germans had indeed given the French access to the Niger although, strictly speaking, Marschall had not lied in the first instance, as Bifara was not on the Benue, but on the Kebbi, a navigable effluent of the former.

Rosebery had already instructed his ambassador to urge on Marschall that the agreement should stipulate that no port be assigned to France, either on the Benue or on a navigable effluent.[58] But he was too late: the Franco-German protocol had been signed on 4 February, almost two weeks before the first alarms reached London. The inescapable conclusion arising from these events was that Germany had deliberately, and secretly, wished to injure Britain in Africa. Two days after Rosebery learned that Germany had enabled France to pose this new threat to Nigeria, he initiated secret discussions with King Leopold of Belgium for the purpose of safeguarding the British position in Africa, discussions that eventually resulted in the Anglo-Congolese Agreement of 12 April.[59]

Germany's African initiative did not end with the Franco-German protocol; in the weeks after it was signed the Germans made themselves troublesome elsewhere. The question of the Gold Coast–Togo hinterland, which the British had assumed to be near settlement, was suddenly raised again, with the Germans declaring the British offers to be unacceptable. The Germans then objected to the manner in which licences for the sale of wine and spirits were to be issued by the British in Zanzibar, even though the French had raised no objection. Lord Kimberley, who succeeded Rosebery at the Foreign Office while these moves were being made, concluded that Britain and Germany had reached "a temporary cessation in that policy of cordial cooperation between the two countries in all matters relating to Africa."[60] After another month in office and more discussions on African affairs, Kimberley concluded that the situation had grown worse. The general impression he received, he told Malet, was that "we must not count on support from Germany and that the present disposition of the German Government is rather to seek the cooperation of the French in Africa than to act with us."[61]

Historians who focus their attention on Africa rightly stress the importance of local factors in the diplomacy of the African partition. But the moves made by Germany in the first months of 1894 were too general and too well coordinated to be regarded simply in the light of local factors. The future course of Anglo-German relations was at stake, and the Germans conducted their policy accordingly. Along with their moves in Africa, they had initiated a policy of conciliation with Russia. The first signs of a possible change came in January when the kaiser had a public reconciliation with Bismarck. One of the criticisms levelled by the Bismarckian press against the kaiser's new course had been the rapid deterioration in relations with Russia. The kaiser, they said, had adroitly manoeuvred Germany into a position of having to fight a war on two fronts, possibly for the sake of

Anglo-Austrian interests in the Near East. Partly to allay this criticism, and partly to satisfy the demands of German industrialists, the German government concluded a commercial treaty with Russia in March, ending the tariff war they had been fighting for several years. The political effect of this arrangement had been felt in France even before the official conclusion of the treaty, as French newspapers anticipated that the improvement in Russo-German relations would prejudice the good understanding between Russia and France.[62]

The kaiser's *coup de théatre* in becoming formally reconciled with Bismarck seemed to symbolize a decision to return to Bismarckian diplomacy as well; perhaps Germany was, as Hatzfeldt had earlier hinted, preparing to abandon the east to Russia. Kálnoky certainly appeared to worry that this might be the case. He foresaw that the conclusion of the commercial treaty with Russia was going to make "the attempt to bring Germany into line over the Straits question very difficult." The Austrian foreign minister could not believe that Russia would abandon her aims in the east, which, he said, "will always remain the same, however amiable and conciliatory her present demeanour may be."[63] Germany was successfully demonstrating to Austria and Britain that she had an alternative to supporting them at the Straits, that she was not committed by the situation in Europe to supporting them against Russia regardless of what the circumstances happened to be.

Rosebery took the occasion of Currie's visit to Vienna in mid-February to refer again to the possible solution of the Straits question that he had only hinted at in his discussions with the Austrian ambassador at the end of January. If Russia succeeded in manoeuvring the powers into a position where they had to admit the right of passage through the Straits, "guarantees would have to be required, and among them I had suggested that of the placing of Constantinople under the guarantees of the Great Powers."[64] Kálnoky said he appreciated the suggestion, but that it would require careful consideration.

Although it came to nothing, Rosebery's idea of a guarantee again revealed the essence of his policy in the Near East. A joint guarantee such as the one he hinted at would have created a lasting connection between Germany and the Eastern Question. Like Sir William White, Rosebery thought that drawing Germany into the affairs of the Near East, whether through political or commercial means, would work to the benefit of Britain. The Russian right to passage of the Straits would mean little if the armies of the Triple Alliance neutralized France and pinned down the Russian armies along the eastern frontier – Austria's performance during the Crimean War had demonstrated how useful a role this could be. If Britain faced Russia alone, and at sea, the conditions of war would favour Britain, especially as Russia's Black Sea fleet amounted to very little in 1894. Nor would Russia, while facing the possibility of attack from the Triple Alliance, be able to transfer her European armies to central Asia where they might endanger the British in India.

Rosebery therefore affirmed, in the clearest way that he could without actually committing the government to signing a treaty, that if Britain were placed in the position of facing Russia alone, she could "prevent Russia from obtaining her object."[65] He assured the Austrians that he did not propose that the Triple Alliance should go to war in the event of the Russians attempting to use force in the question of the Straits, but rather that they should "keep France in check." He was anxious to avoid, he said, "that great European conflict" into which they would all be plunged if the Triple Alliance went to war on this question. He did not even require that the Italian fleet should act with the British in resisting Russia. "Italy," Rosebery said, "was in such a condition that no friend of hers could wish to impose fresh burdens and responsibilities upon her." While Italy should come to Britain's assistance if necessary, "it would not be necessary," in Rosebery's judgment.

This conversation was the closest Rosebery ever came to complying with the wishes of the Triple Alliance, and he appears to have gone very far indeed. He did not ask the alliance for any direct support, and certainly he did not ask for a commitment that they should go to war. In return for the indirect support of the alliance in checking France, Rosebery appeared to promise to stop Russia at the Straits. But what he offered the Triple Alliance was, in fact, an illusion. It is difficult to see how it was possible to "check France" without at least threatening her with war, which, of course, entailed the risk of actually having to fight. Moreover, Rosebery was careful to limit his forecast concerning Britain's ability to prevent Russia from obtaining her object: "so far as sea forces were concerned," was what he contemplated. This implied that the Triple Alliance would be responsible for pinning down Russia's land forces, which, in turn, implied the risk of war, if not the actuality. Finally, Rosebery knew that the Admiralty did not believe that the Levant squadron was capable of preventing a Russian *coup de main* at the Straits, that is, he knew that Britain was not in a position to do what he appeared to promise.

The object that Rosebery aimed for in these discussions explains his diplomacy. He was satisfied that the existence of the Triple Alliance offered Britain sufficient safeguards against attack from France and Russia. It was not necessary that they should promise, in advance, to go to war for the sake of British interests in the Eastern Question. But the Triple Alliance during recent months had appeared to be on the verge of breaking up, mainly as the result of Austrian fears concerning the lack of support against Russia in the Near East. Therefore, in these conversations about a hypothetical future – a future in which he did not much believe – Rosebery tried to go as far as he could in assuaging Austrian fears.

The apparent promise to stop Russia from seizing control of Constantinople and the Straits satisfied Austria for a time. Rosebery held out other hopes: of bringing the Germans into a joint guarantee, and of "uniting all possible Mediterranean Powers in a common understanding on the subject."[66] It did not matter much that these hopes were unlikely to be realized; what did matter was that the Austrians should be made to believe in Rosebery's determination to uphold Britain's position as a Mediterranean power and to fulfil her traditional policy of preventing Russian domination of the Straits. His soothing words, along with the increase in the Mediterranean fleet, satisfied the Austrians, who now turned to Berlin in their search for support. The Austrian ambassador told Rosebery "that my assigning to the Triple Alliance the function of keeping France in check would facilitate the task at Berlin, where there was all the difference in the world between the peaceful sphere I suggested, and an act which would bring about a terrible war." The contest for control of the understanding between Britain and the Triple Alliance was far from over. Rosebery had succeeded only in shifting the scene of the contest from London to Berlin.

A peculiar kind of difficulty exists in the relations between states whose power, while hypothetically equal, differs fundamentally in kind. The hypothesis of equality is itself difficult to test. When Britain, a great naval power, had confronted Napoleonic France, a great military power, she relied for her success on allied military powers. Opposing forces, if they are to be measured accurately, must be similar in kind. Many observers have noted that in the generation preceding World War I the industrial capacity of Imperial Germany drew close to, or even surpassed, that of Great Britain. Industrial capacity is easier to measure: coal extraction, iron production, manufacturing capacity, lend themselves to comparison. As the industrial strength of the two states grew roughly equal, the question of who would be the dominant power in international politics arose as a logical consequence. Had this industrial strength manifested itself in like terms, in mechanized armies or iron ships, the question would have been easier to answer. Because their strength was different, because the question was difficult to answer, tension dominated the relations between Britain and Germany.

While the power of the Triple Alliance appeared to be only marginally greater than that of the Dual Alliance, most Englishmen assumed that the increase of German industrial and military might did not endanger them. The tension that existed in these years did not arise from a direct confrontation, from a German threat to the British Empire. Most Englishmen continued to assume that the threats to the empire would continue to come from the traditional enemies, France and Russia. The tension in Anglo-German relations arose from the assumption on both sides that they had a common interest in resisting France and Russia, which combined with a disagreement concerning when, where, and under what circumstances they would join forces to meet this threat. The tension developed throughout the 1890s as first one side, then the other, worried, not that they would one day fight each other, but that it might be manoeuvred into the position of being forced to fight the Dual Alliance in the interests of the other.

This tension in the relations between the two states was bound to persist as long as one side was not clearly stronger than the other, and the difference in the nature of the power they were able to exercise continued to fog the attempts at comparison. Each question that arose in those years became a test case, and, because the situation in Europe was relatively stable, most of the questions arose outside Europe. Although the nature of the test varied with the local circumstances, the Moroccan crisis showed one of the patterns that dominated these affairs. The Germans tried to show that Britain was being threatened by France, and that German interest in the affair was such that they were able to remain aloof. In this way they hoped that Britain would be persuaded that she could win the contest with France only if she could count on the assistance of the Triple Alliance; this assistance was to be purchased at the price of committing herself to assist the Triple Alliance in the European interests of its members.

Rosebery tried to resist this conclusion in two ways: by trying to avoid confrontation with France, and by trying to demonstrate that Britain could defend her interests without depending on the assistance of the Triple Alliance. As far as the contest in Morocco was concerned, Rosebery won. But he could continue to win only as long as Britain was strong enough to meet the threat of France – that is, only as long as Britain, as an imperial power, was able to meet imperial threats.

G.N. Sanderson, who has argued convincingly on behalf of the importance of local factors in the partition of Africa, has pointed to the Franco-German protocol of 1894 as evidence supporting his argument. That protocol, according to Sanderson, was a German retaliation for Rosebery's "Zubair letter," wherein he encouraged Rabih Zubair, a wayward military ruler in the region east of Lake Chad, to cooperate with Britain in resisting French penetration of the area. But Zubair's dominions were mostly incorporated into the German sphere in the Cameroons in a protocol with Britain, signed on 15 November 1893. By continuing to encourage Zubair, therefore, Rosebery created the impression in Germany that he was trying "to insinuate British influence into territory which he had just recognised as German a bare five weeks earlier."[67] The Germans, offended by this apparent disregard of their local interests in Africa, retaliated by giving the French the village of Bifara, and thus the possibility of direct water communication with the Niger. The British were, in turn, offended by this manoeuvre and undertook to retaliate by negotiating a settlement with King Leopold wherein they disregarded German interests. Thus, Sanderson argues, local factors gradually gave rise to the bitterness that came to dominate Anglo-German relations for the next two decades.

But the German campaign of retaliation, if this is what it was, went beyond the protocol with France in the Cameroons. The Germans had already made it clear that they would not go out of their way to assist the British in Morocco. More strikingly, in the months that followed the Zubair letter, it appeared as if the Germans might reverse the eastern policy of the new course, and return to the old Bismarckian policy of accommodating Russia. The commercial treaty with Russia and the kaiser's public reconciliation with Bismarck appeared to presage a revival of the role of honest broker in the Near East. Surely these changes in the grand strategy of Germany were caused by events more fundamental than Rosebery's Zubair letter? Sanderson offers no evidence, other than timing, as proof that the protocol was in retaliation for the letter. If timing was important, then it is more striking that the Germans offered Bifara to the French only two weeks after Hatzfeldt's interview with Rosebery, in which the ambassador had complained generally that "the present attitude of England was causing some disquietude everywhere," and specifically of Rosebery's failure to provide Italy and Austria with guarantees in the Mediterranean sufficient to prevent them from contemplating a settlement of their differences with France and Russia.

Were local manoeuvres in the partition of Africa then the result of local factors or grand strategy? In the case of Anglo-German relations the answer is both: policy in Africa was simultaneously the cause and effect of policy in Europe and elsewhere. The manner in which

Rosebery conducted his African policy was the clearest demonstration of what he conceived to be the fundamental nature of Anglo-German relations. Britain's imperial interests were essential; Germany's were a luxury. Although he was quite prepared to allow Germany her place in the sun, the property she occupied was certain to be in the poor districts and not of much value to anyone. The Germans should recognize, therefore, that it was improper for them to place their imperial interests at the same level as those of the British. Moreover, Germany was not capable of defending the property she occupied, whereas Britain was. Germany had become an imperial power by virtue of her status as a great military power on the continent of Europe; as long as she was prepared to perform the historical role assigned to her by Britain, that of counterbalancing the power of France and Russia, then Rosebery was prepared to meet her wishes outside Europe – as long as these did not damage any important interest of Britain.

As the Germans gradually realized, Rosebery was never prepared to anticipate their wishes, to offer them cooperation in advance of the event. Every concession the Germans received had to be carefully negotiated, and Hatzfeldt was not far from the truth when he complained to Kimberley that France was easier to deal with than Britain. But Rosebery's refusal to cooperate in advance served to symbolize how he saw the connection between the naval power of imperial Britain and the military power of continental Germany. Of the two, Britain was in the stronger position, and she could dominate their understanding accordingly. Rosebery's conclusion that he could disregard German colonial sensibilities was drawn from the same set of facts that led him to conclude that Britain could remain an informal partner in the Triple Alliance. Colonial policy and grand strategy, in the era of global politics, were the same thing.

Rosebery's ability to conduct his diplomacy depended largely on the personal position he occupied in the cabinet and in politics generally. In spite of the myth to the contrary, Rosebery had encountered few limitations on his control of foreign policy. Nor had he threatened to resign: although he had considered the possibility several times in the first year and a half of the government, it had never proved necessary to apply more than an urgent hint. The only occasions on which cabinet politics had intruded into the realm of diplomacy had been those affairs – Uganda, the reinforcement of Egypt – that appeared to contain the possibility of political repercussions within Britain. Rosebery had, nevertheless, used the excuse of politics to restrain the Germans in their effort to push the British into the Triple Alliance. The cabinet, he warned, would never contemplate such a possibility; he was the best friend Germany had. If they persisted in their efforts they might succeed in driving Rosebery out of the Foreign Office, and would they really prefer a Morley, or even a Labouchere, to himself? Surely they must prefer to go on as before, relying on Rosebery's goodwill and known preference for an informal partnership with them rather than risk everything for the sake of guarantees that no English politician would ever give? But quite suddenly, in March 1894, the questions posed seemed less straightforward; Gladstone resigned as prime minister and Rosebery succeeded him. He was now in a position to do what the Germans wished.

CHAPTER SIX

Unmasterly Activity:
The Congolese Agreement
and Its Repercussions

A very great change has come over our foreign policy in the last twenty years, and I think you will see a much greater change in it in the next twenty years. Our foreign policy has become more of a colonial policy, and is becoming every day more entwined with our colonial interests than has ever been the case before.

Speech at Leeds (1888)

The story of the succession has often been told. Simply put, the contest to succeed Gladstone was fought between Rosebery and Harcourt, but it was a curious contest because Rosebery refused to fight. Few events offer more convincing proof of the position that Rosebery had attained in politics than the fact that he was able to form a government despite the opposition of Harcourt and Morley, and despite his repeated announcements that he had no desire, and little ability, to be prime minister. But Rosebery's friends and admirers had heard this refrain many times before, and they disregarded it now as they had disregarded it then – after all, what man in politics does not want to be at the top?[1]

Rosebery did not. Over the course of a political life, politicians often contradict themselves, and in this respect Rosebery was no different from the rest, but on one subject the record is free of contradiction. The Foreign Office, he always maintained, was the height of his ambition; the office of prime minister was something to which he had never aspired. During the discussions about who would succeed Gladstone, Rosebery declared that he was prepared to serve under anyone satisfactory to the party. He was even prepared to serve under Harcourt, who, he thought, would become more conciliatory, more anxious to patch up differences in order to make a success of the job and to stay in power. But the party, or rather the cabinet, would not have Harcourt, and Rosebery could not bring himself to admit that the party was unable to survive the retirement of an 84-year-old man who was almost deaf and blind. "It would be a disgrace if it were to break up simply because of Mr. Gladstone's retirement ... any defeat would be better than a confession of futility and helplessness which would imply – and be – the suicide of the Liberal party."[2]

Rosebery sacrificed his personal inclinations for the sake of the party – and almost destroyed it as a result. His devotion to the party arose from his sense of history and from his championship of Liberal imperialism. He had learned his history from Macaulay: he believed that civil upheaval had been avoided by timely compromise, and that the Whig principle of admitting responsible elements into the political life of the nation had been instrumental in Britain's rise to unparalleled greatness. The Tories were still the party of obstruction and obscurantism; they were the party of the minority, trying to get into power through the back door by pretending to be democrats – as in 1867 – or imperialists – as in 1874.

Rosebery had faith that the domestic politics of reformist liberalism would ensure continued progress – but politics of that nature bored him. When, in his early days, he had transformed himself into an expert on the affairs of Scotland and put himself forward as her advocate, he quickly lost interest when actually given responsibility at the Home Office. His other great cause, technical education, bored him so much that he could barely bring himself to speak on it. (Fortunately he was not forced to speak often, as it bored almost everyone else as well.) This is not to suggest that Rosebery was disingenuous, for he no doubt sincerely believed in the necessity of safeguarding the individuality of the nations that constituted the empire, and he never ceased to advocate the continued advance of technical education. But his attraction to such causes arose from conviction, not devotion; he was prepared to make speeches, not to work out the details.

Perhaps Rosebery avoided responsibility because he recognized that it would damage his reputation. At the Foreign Office it was easy to shelter behind the cloak of secrecy; and sincere, statesmanlike speeches on the necessity of upholding imperial interests could take the place of the heated debate that normally arose over domestic issues. Only occasionally, when a crisis erupted, was the public gaze turned to foreign affairs. So far, his conduct of foreign policy had done little to excite the public imagination, though his reputation had certainly not suffered as a result of the debates on Uganda and Egypt. The queen continued to admire him for his handling of foreign affairs, while the commercial classes were relieved that he, and not Morley or Labouchere, controlled Liberal foreign policy.

In fact, when 1894 began, Rosebery was still all things to all people. Would-be social reformers such as R.B. Haldane regarded him as sympathetic to the cause of "national efficiency." Lib-Labs such as Henry Broadhurst asked for, and received, Rosebery money in order to remain in politics. Many of the leading journalists of the day regarded Rosebery as the best hope for the Liberal party – perhaps even for the nation. George Buckle of the *Times*, W.S. Stead of the *Review of Reviews* and the *Pall Mall Gazette*, and Wemyss Reid of the *Leeds Mercury* – an eclectic group – all regarded Rosebery as a friend and supported him in their publications. The young generally admired him: "To us, the young men of that day who had aspirations towards Parliament and ambition for public service, Lord Rosebery was the *beau ideal* whether we were Liberals or Conservatives."[3] This widespread admiration, these vague hopes for a new leader who would reunite the country and overcome the petty factional squabbles that had come to dominate politics, could be maintained only as long as Rosebery was not at the centre of affairs and forced to take responsibility for their direction.

Rosebery was an avid reader of the newspapers; for all his apparent indifference and aristocratic hauteur, he cared deeply for the opinions of others, and it is this characteristic which helps to explain one of the contradictions of his career that has struck many observers. By 1894 Rosebery was known to have a prickly temper and a thin skin, and yet his subordinates at the Foreign Office uniformly regarded him as good-natured and conciliatory – a good master – and his fellow members of cabinet found him amiable and inclined not to interfere in their affairs – a good colleague. What brought out the black side of Rosebery's nature was anything which would tarnish his reputation in the eyes of the public: the appearance of having been tried and found wanting would send Rosebery into a deep depression. As long as things went smoothly he was a kind and effective master and colleague.

Rosebery's need for public adulation explains his performances on the platform. A lonely man, with few close friends and a huge circle of acquaintances, he was brilliant in front of large audiences, appearing bright, witty, and high-spirited. But few realized the price he paid for these performances. He had to work himself into a fever pitch in order to rise to the occasion. Both before and after a performance he needed repeated assurances that he would do, or had done brilliantly. The slightest hint that he had not done well would lead him to despair of his future in politics. In private, his humour was sardonic, easily giving way to melancholia, and it now seems clear that he could not keep up this pace for long: if things started to go wrong there would be real trouble.

The problem with Rosebery was that – apart from the defence of the empire – he had no cause. There was nothing in politics that he wished to achieve so much that he was prepared on its behalf to suffer the attacks of journalists or colleagues. He craved popularity and respect, and he was not prepared to risk them for the sake of pushing some measure through Parliament. He was no Gladstone.

But Harcourt was no Gladstone either – he had no great moral causes, no principles that he wished to turn into effective legislation – and yet the politics of 1894–5 did not turn him into a dyspeptic as they did Rosebery. Harcourt's temperament, which ensured that no significant number of colleagues would ever support him for the prime ministership, also gave him a distinct advantage over Rosebery when the battle lines began to be drawn after March 1894. Harcourt exasperated his colleagues: he constantly meddled in the affairs of their departments, complained of their stupidity and ignorance, and fought with them whenever possible, but unlike Rosebery he enjoyed every moment of these battles. He could rage at a colleague in cabinet in the morning, and treat him as a bosom friend by nightfall. As home secretary, his blood had boiled at the miserliness of the Exchequer, but as chancellor of the exchequer his blood boiled at the extravagance of other departments. "His time-serving, his sudden changes of opinion, and his cantankerous temper put him quite out of the running" in the contest to succeed Gladstone.[4] But he had no problem with his digestion, and he was able to sleep at night.

Harcourt, pushed forward by his ambitious son, saw himself as the legitimate and logical successor to Gladstone and he was deeply wounded when his colleagues saw it differently. As a consequence, he had little devotion to the new government. If it failed under Rosebery's leadership, he would, in part at least, be vindicated. He was especially determined to show that a peer, as the Malwood Compact with Morley had supposedly guaranteed, could no longer lead the party. Thus, whenever an opportunity arose of highlighting the problems of having the prime minister in the House of Lords, Harcourt grabbed at it with zeal.

Rosebery, by contrast, felt that he had been impelled against his will into undertaking a task for which he was not suited and for which he had little taste. He felt that he had been forced out of a job he liked, and for which he was widely respected, into one that was almost impossible, given the divisions in the party both at the top and at the bottom. One of the most remarkable features of his tenure at the Foreign Office was the admiration he aroused in his subordinates, and years later men like Viscount Hardinge and Sir James Rennell Rodd recalled the care and patience that he had taken in bringing along the younger men in the diplomatic service. But the point was that Rosebery was clearly in charge; he was a kind master, but his decision was final. As prime minister, he would suddenly be responsible for the actions of his colleagues and he would have to defend their politics in the House and in the country. He would no longer be able to avoid taking a clear stand on the leading issues of the day, like Home Rule. Yet, as he would soon discover, neither could he make policies himself in the way he had done at the Foreign Office, and he was almost powerless to control the behaviour of his cabinet colleagues.

Rosebery undoubtedly sensed that in becoming prime minister he would have to alienate some of those who supported him, because they supported him for such different reasons. Many hoped that he would give the Liberals a new direction. Buckle, who was instrumental in persuading Rosebery to take on the leadership, told him, even before he moved into Downing Street, that "my most ardent political wish and hope is that you may be able to modify the domestic policy of your party, as you have beyond all expectation been successful in modifying their foreign policy."[5] The editor of the *Times* promised to do his best to achieve this wish by actively assisting in having Rosebery's new government defeated. A defeat, he said, would enable Rosebery to formulate his own policy. This kind of help bedevilled Rosebery from the start.

During the discussions of whether or not he ought to succeed Gladstone, Rosebery suggested to the queen that he was hesitant because he thought it might lead to conflicts with her, as he was bound to advocate policies that had already been laid down.[6] He did not have to wait for long to see his prediction realized. Within a week of his taking over, the queen declared that she was "horrified" that her speech was to include bills for the abolition of the Ecclesiastical Establishments of Wales and Scotland.[7] Rosebery patiently replied that the government had come in on Welsh and Scottish disestablishment, that notice had been given in the queen's last speech, and that, in any case, "we could not exist for a moment without dealing with these questions."[8] Like many of his admirers on the right, the queen and Buckle assumed Rosebery to be, at heart, a lukearm Liberal who, free of the reforming fever of Gladstone, would reduce the temperature of British politics.

Admirers on the left judged Rosebery differently. Many believed him to be more modern than Gladstone, less concerned with the great moral problems of the day and more eager to tackle the questions posed by the rise of the new unionism, to face the challenge created by the burgeoning economies of Germany and the United States. Rosebery's success in chairing the new London County Council and his triumph in ending the miners' strike of 1893 contributed to their belief that he was more closely attuned to contemporary social and political problems. Richard Haldane, connected with Sidney and Beatrice Webb, and one of those behind the establishment of the London School of Economics and Political Science as a centre for imperial training in the new disciplines that would lead to greater efficiency in handling social problems, expected a great deal from Rosebery. He wanted the new prime minister to make a great speech on "the social side of politics," to "give a form to the inarticulate ideals of which I have spoken."[9] Rosebery was to discuss the "classes and the masses," "the relations of labour and capital," and do so "by a method which will arouse the imagination of the people." The naive hope that Rosebery could overnight push the party in a new direction testifies to the expectations that his appointment aroused.

While the Left and the Right hoped that Rosebery would lead the Liberals in a new direction, the Irish feared such a turn of events. They had been concerned, since the Newcastle Programme in 1891, that new politics might mean the abandonment of Home Rule, and they now anxiously awaited a declaration of intentions from Rosebery. He did not keep them waiting for long. He took the opportunity of his first meeting with the party – at the Foreign Office on 12 March – to assure them that he was a convinced Home Ruler, in spite of assertions to the contrary. But, he added characteristically, there were many roads to Rome.[10]

When the opportunity came, Rosebery proved unable to resist the temptation of trying to lead the party in some new direction. Ironically, in view of what was to be the result of his leadership, he hoped to reunite the party, to smooth over the ruptures and ripples that had appeared in its fabric since 1885. Although he refused to commit himself to the "programme" approach adopted at Newcastle, he agreed with those in the party who argued that the concentration on Home Rule was gradually eroding their support in England, Scotland, and Wales. Therefore, without dropping the aim of Home Rule, he sought some new formula that would enable him to put it into the background of affairs and concentrate, in the meantime, on less ambitious projects.

The formula he thought he had discovered was that of the "predominant partner." On the evening of the day on which he had assured the party gathering at the Foreign Office of his devotion to

Home Rule, he expanded on his views in the House of Lords. He first argued that the recent quiet in Ireland was due, not to light railways or other such remedies, "but to the hope held out by the Liberal party that the great boon of local self-government for purely local affairs, so far as it is consonant with the supremacy of the Imperial Parliament, would not be long delayed." This was, quite clearly, a narrow definition of Home Rule: it was to be limited to "purely local affairs," and it would have to be consonant with the principle of the supremacy of the imperial Parliament. Not content with a narrow definition, Rosebery went on to qualify the procedure by which Home Rule was to be achieved. Before it was conceded in Ireland, he said, "England, as the predominant member of the partnership of the three kingdoms, will have to be convinced of its justice."[11] He suggested that convincing England would not be difficult if Irish conduct continued to improve.

In other words, it was unreasonable of the Irish to expect Home Rule immediately, and they must be made to realize that the burden of proof was on them, that they must, by virtue of their good behaviour, prove to the English that they were sufficiently responsible to warrant this measure of independence. And, when Home Rule was finally granted, it would be limited strictly to local affairs. If the Irish were to accept this formula, they would have to allow their affairs to recede quietly into the background of the political scene, leaving Rosebery in a position to draw back into the party some of those elements that had withdrawn during the crisis of 1885-6.

Morley had forewarned Rosebery that his speech ought to contain "nothing halting," but he chose to ignore the warning – or convinced himself that his proposal was not "halting."[12] The Irish responded by giving him a quick lesson in the realities of parliamentary politics when, on the day after his speech, they joined with the Labouchere wing to defeat the government in the Commons by two votes on an amendment on the powers of the House of Lords. "The Irish rose in a body," the chief whip explained, "and went into the Lobby against us, as did about an equal number of our own men."[13]

Writing in the *Times*, Buckle declared that Rosebery's speech had shattered the Liberal party. A section of Irish MPs, reported Morley, were considering overthrowing the government, and although they were at present a minority, they would, he predicted, become a majority if Rosebery's next speech were chilly or ambiguous.[14] The chief whip, Tom Ellis, echoed Morley's warnings, explaining that the sentence concerning the "predominant partner" was the cause of the concern. "The sentence is being read as if great questions affecting Ireland, Scotland and Wales could not be legislatively solved in accordance with the wishes of the electorate of the respective nationalities without the assent of a majority from England."[15]

A turning-point had already been reached in Rosebery's leadership of the party, because practically his sole ambition as leader was to revive party unity by ending the domination of Irish business. He believed he had found a way to do this in his formula for narrow Home Rule achieved by wider means, as it did not abandon the goal, but made it less frightening and less immediate. His reaction to the Irish manoeuvre in the House of Commons was therefore going to be decisive: it would show the degree of determination he was going to bring to the task he had set himself.

Rosebery had given the "predominant partner" speech in London and he chose Edinburgh to be the scene of the encore, perhaps for symbolic reasons. He began by recalling the glorious days of the Midlothian campaign, the campaign that had, after all, linked his destiny to Gladstone's star. "If he is not here to-night," he declared, "his inspiration is with us ... and it is in the inspiration that we derive from him ... that the Government proposes to proceed."[16] Rosebery's leadership, in other words, would continue to guide the party along the Gladstonian path. Those in the House of Commons who thought otherwise did not appreciate the difficulties that Rosebery faced in being secluded in the Lords: "it is a little difficult to explain yourself to an assembly of which you are not a member." Besides, people were trying to read too much into his speeches, and his words had been misinterpreted. He certainly had not meant that great measures affecting the partnership of the United Kingdom must await the predominant vote of England. His purpose had been simply to bring conviction, "to the mind of the partner in our partnership that has the greatest population and the most votes," and that purpose had been deliberately misconstrued by the Unionists, led by their fountainhead, the *Times*, who were trying to shatter the Liberal party.

Rosebery's Edinburgh speech succeeded in closing the wound that his own words had opened. "The tension is off and Edinburgh has cleared the air," Ellis reported. "Irish and British members instead of being nervous and suspicious are hopeful and buoyant."[17] But the change marked Rosebery's defeat: his first attempt to sketch the outlines of a new policy had ended in a retreat to the shelter of the old Gladstonian umbrella. The Edinburgh speech showed that he depended too much on the support of the Irish to abandon them. He resented the suggestion that abandoning the Irish had been the real aim behind the "predominant partner" statement. "Those papers who thought they would do us a service by indicating that we were prepared at a moment's notice to leave every sentiment of honour and policy in abeyance, and to march over to the other camp, must have misconstrued either our sense or our conscience."

This passage, with its reference to "at a moment's notice," suggested that Rosebery still had some hope of redirecting the party, but there was no doubt, after Edinburgh, that he would have to proceed slowly and cautiously. In fact, after having once had his fingers burned, Rosebery was reluctant to put his hands anywhere near the fire, and in the time that remained to him as prime minister he never attempted anything so dramatic as the design suggested in the "predominant partner" speech. Gradually, he lost hope. Instead of throwing all his energies into a great campaign, as Gladstone might have done, or beginning a complicated series of manoeuvres behind the scenes, as Disraeli might have done, Rosebery came to be convinced that the party would have to undergo some great defeat before it would see the error of its ways.

The refusal to fight was an easy answer, and one suited to Rosebery's character. Never in his career did he devote his energies to a campaign that had to be prosecuted slowly and for which he would have to face great abuse. His political life consisted of two quite distinct parts: one consisted of those great bursts of energy and initiative associated with the Midlothian campaign or his "rallying round the government" at the time of Khartoum, but these were always sporadic and short-lived; the other was his day-to-day administration of affairs at the Foreign Office, where he was removed from the glare of the limelight, and where he could perform the noble duty of conducting the empire's business almost without interference. Rosebery's career as prime minister was, through the combination of political circumstances and the pattern of his personality, probably doomed from the start. After the fiasco of the predominant partner speech he occasionally returned to the dream of rebuilding the party, but he never did more than wish for its fulfilment; he was never again prepared to do the work and face the abuse.

The easiest mistake to make about Rosebery, however, is to assume that these same conclusions can be applied to his management of foreign affairs, and those who have made such a mistake betray a fundamental misunderstanding of the nature and purpose of his political life. Although he lacked the conviction necessary to the waging of great political campaigns within the party and out in the country, he never doubted himself where foreign policy was concerned. He was attracted to the Foreign Office largely because it seemed to him that there should be no argument about the purpose of policy; everyone, of whatever political stripe, should be able to agree that the empire must be secure. Moreover, only those who had been initiated into the intricacies of diplomacy were in a position to determine what means ought to be employed to guarantee this security. This view of things gave Rosebery a formula whereby he could dispense with criticism: those who attacked his management were either so wicked that they did not share his purpose of safeguarding the empire, or so ignorant of affairs that they were not in a position to understand his methods.

Therefore, although Rosebery tended to be accommodating on domestic matters, and although he left their management to the ministers responsible, he was absolutely determined that his views on foreign policy should continue to prevail. He never had the slightest difficulty in justifying deception where the interests of the empire were at stake. He had already cheated on Uganda and Egypt, in issuing secret instructions to Portal, mobilizing Lugard to campaign against the government, and telling Cromer to conjure up threats where they did not exist. There was no reason for him not to go on playing these tricks when they had succeeded so well, and when he still faced the ignorant opposition of men like Harcourt and Morley. Rosebery's failure in domestic politics merely increased his determination to keep the strings of foreign policy in his hands.

But Harcourt was equally determined to demonstrate both the general principle that a Liberal government could no longer be run from the Lords, and the particular application of this principle, that Rosebery's government could not operate without Harcourt sharing the leadership. He therefore insisted that he be empowered to take decisions in the Commons without reference to the prime minister, that he should have a fair share of patronage, and that he should see all important Foreign Office dispatches. Rosebery was inclined to refuse all concessions. "I don't want to be Prime Minister at all," he said, "but if I am to be I must be a real one."[18]

Harcourt's insistence that he should have some control over foreign policy was partly genuine, but it was also a tactical manoeuvre in politics, designed by his son. Loulou's idea was that his father and Morley would refuse to serve in a government with a peer as both prime minister and foreign secretary. The queen would then be forced to call on Harcourt to form a government, and Rosebery would take the Foreign Office. This strategy showed that the Harcourts were not deeply interested in the actual control of foreign policy; the question was "who's to be master, that's all." But Loulou saw that he would have to abandon the manoeuvre once Rosebery had actually been called upon, because "there would be an outcry if Rosebery were displaced and W.V.H. substituted and the public would never understand the importance of the point on which it was done."[19]

Harcourt's manoeuvres did have one important result: they strengthened Rosebery's determination to frustrate the attempt to interfere with foreign policy. He had developed, he told Hamilton, "the profoundest distrust of Harcourt, and they had absolutely nothing in common with one another."[20] Therefore, even against the advice of Edward Marjoribanks, a friend and Liberal whip who considered it to be essential that the new foreign secretary come from the Commons, especially when only one of the five offices concerned with national security, the War Office, was headed by a commoner, Rosebery chose to appoint a peer to replace him at the Foreign Office. His friends might have anticipated the decision; after all, he had told Morley in 1892 that "if the House of Lords didn't exist it ought to be created for the Foreign Secretary."[21]

The appointment of Lord Kimberley, which was controversial at the time, has aroused little controversy since, the assumption appearing to be that he was chosen because he was unknown in the country and inconsequential in the cabinet, and that Rosebery could, therefore, expect to control him. However, this was not the case. As far back as 1885, in his first cabinet, Rosebery had been impressed by Kimberley, "a stronger man than he ever imagined."[22] In the summer of 1892, when so many were insisting that Rosebery was the only one capable of taking the Foreign Office, he had consistently recommended Kimberley who, he said, would make an excellent foreign secretary.[23]

Rosebery's experience in the government of 1892–4 added to his enthusiasm for Kimberley, and their relations throughout that period were cordial. They worked well together because Kimberley's policies at the India Office were practically identical with Rosebery's at the Foreign: they opposed the forward school on the Indian frontier; they agreed, during the Siam crisis, that the essential point was to create a buffer between Britain and France; they were prepared to abandon Persia if the "rickety concern" could no longer be kept going. Given these facts it is not surprising that Rosebery believed Kimberley would continue to follow the lines of policy he had laid down for him, and he was, he told the queen, prepared to refuse office, "rather than yield the right of submitting to your Majesty the person he deems best qualified for this important office."[24]

Under these circumstances it is not surprising that Harcourt was forced to abandon his strategy of refusing to serve under a peer who was both prime minister and foreign secretary. "I doubt if we shall succeed on the question of personnel," he told Morley. "It would be a mistake to make a demand on which we cannot insist," and he admitted to Rosebery that, his peerage aside, Kimberley was the fittest person for the office and that Harcourt could not designate any special person in the Commons to occupy the post.[25] Harcourt lowered his aim considerably. "What we can and ought to obtain is an arrangement which shall secure a *sufficient* communication between the F.O. and the H. of C.."[26] By this time Harcourt was in no position to bargain. The other members of the cabinet were, on the same day, calling on Rosebery to signify their willingness to remain at their posts, and Morley refused to cooperate with Harcourt in the affair of the Foreign Office, or indeed regarding any of the new arrangements.

Nonetheless, a legend has grown up around this issue. Rosebery, it has been argued, "saddled himself with a contract with Harcourt which amounted to an extraordinary and essentially impractical supervision of his action in foreign affairs."[27] The legend is based on a single piece of documentary evidence, a diary entry in Loulou Harcourt's journal. Two statements in the journal are important: first, that Rosebery agreed with Harcourt's opinion that "the Foreign Secretary should communicate as fully and freely with the Leader of the House of Commons as he did with the Prime Minister"; and second, that it was understood that the object of this was that "the Leader of the House of Commons should have notice not only when foreign affairs reached a crisis but *ab initio* when affairs were beginning at all to "creak."[28] None of this suggests that Harcourt was given the right to supervise Rosebery's policy; it provides only for Kimberley communicating with Harcourt, or giving him notice that affairs were beginning to creak. This really does not appear to be extraordinary or particularly impractical.

Moreover, to accept the legend is to accept Harcourt's account of what transpired, or, more correctly, the account that he appears to have given his son. On this point it is worth noting that Loulou's journal reflects a rather odd relationship, in which Loulou was the real schemer of the two and undoubtedly the more ambitious. It seems that Harcourt frequently deceived his son into believing that he had taken a stronger line than he had and took credit for things when he was not really responsible for them, rather than admit that he was not the strong man Loulou wished him to be.

Finally, there was no practical reason for Rosebery to give way to Harcourt on any essential point, as Harcourt could find no one to support him, and if he had left the government, he would have left alone. On 4 March, the day of the interview recorded by Loulou, Rosebery had made his position abundantly clear, writing to Harcourt that "I cannot have any conditions imposed on me which have not been accepted by previous Ministers. I must either be a real Prime Minister or I will not be Prime Minister at all."[29] So what did the "contract" amount to? Harcourt dropped his objection to Kimberley, and in return Rosebery must have agreed, in some vague way, that Kimberley would keep Harcourt informed. This really amounted to very little. Gladstone had certainly been in a much stronger position from which to supervise Rosebery, and he had failed to control him. The negotiations over the control of policy reflect the tension and the suspicion that existed among the leaders of the party; they created nothing new. No contract, foolishly agreed to, can be held responsible for the events that followed.

The intrigues of domestic politics have exercised such a hold on the imaginations of the historians of this period that the realities of international politics have been almost forgotten. The importance of the clash between the Little Englanders and the imperialists in the new government has been exaggerated, partly because the arguments that ensued were really between Harcourt on the one side and Rosebery and Kimberley on the other, with few others in the cabinet really concerning themselves about foreign affairs. The issues that arose from the time the Rosebery government was formed until its fall were seldom of the kind that lent themselves to a simple division along pro- and anti-imperialist lines. More often, the issues were complicated manoeuvres in tactics rather than clear confrontations between competing ideologies. The importance of ideas should not be underestimated, because their ideas accounted for the way in which men viewed the events that were occurring around them; but the policies of Germany, France, and Russia were usually of more decisive and immediate importance to the formation of British policy.

The general aim of British policy in the nineties was to maintain the security of the empire, and most of the threats to this security seemed to originate far beyond the shores of the British Isles. Invasion by a foreign power seemed about as realistic in the nineties as the threat of attack from Mars conjured up by H.G. Wells near the end of the decade in his *War of the Worlds*. The most striking feature of British policy was the extent of agreement on the aim to be pursued, for, while Gladstone might occasionally mumble that taking India had been a mistake, no one who mattered ever proposed to abandon it, and while a few railway men and intelligence officers might dream of taking Turkey, or China, no one bothered to work out such a takeover and how this might be accomplished. Comparisons with France, Russia, and Germany, where different factions or parties had fundamentally different aims, and sometimes alternative plans by which these might be achieved, serve to show how united the British really were.

William II's apparent decision to return German policy to its Bismarckian course, when combined with the activities of the French colonial party, was far more important to Rosebery's policy than the cabinet arrangements with Harcourt. In the two months that followed the kaiser's meeting with his former chancellor in January 1894, the Germans proceeded to give a port on the Benue to the French, thereby giving them access to the Niger; to raise difficulties in Cairo, and to block an agreement over Zanzibar. Kimberley, in office less than two weeks, interpreted these manoeuvres as a "cessation in that policy of cordial co-operation between the two countries in all matters relating to Africa which it has been the earnest desire of H.M. Government to create and maintain."[30]

The German moves in Africa made the British more vulnerable in Egypt, but the German rapprochement with Russia, marked by their commercial treaty, simultaneously increased Egypt's strategic significance. By 1894 the British were dependent on the support of the Triple Alliance for their position at the Straits, a position which could be sustained only by the latent hostility that existed between the alliance and Russia. Even if Britain's Mediterranean squadron had still been in a position to force its way through the Straits, and it was not, it would have been madness to enter the Black Sea or to try to dominate Turkey in the face of the united opposition of Russia, France, and Germany. If the new German moves represented a real change in direction, therefore, Britain's status as a Mediterranean power was going to be more dependent than ever on her position in Egypt.

The only immediate threat to Egypt was a French one, but it could be launched from two different directions. The less likely possibility was that it would come from the south, with the French advancing from Ethiopia, should the Italians permit it. Negotiations were therefore initiated that eventually resulted in the secret Anglo-Italian agreement of May 1894, which placed Harrar in the Italian sphere, but which authorized Britain to occupy and administer it until Italy was prepared to take over.[31] It was more likely that an advance would come from the west, through the Bahr Al-Ghazal, should the Belgians permit it. Negotiations were initiated to prevent this possibility.

The negotiations were conducted with some sense of urgency because the British believed that a military force, under the leadership of the ambitious Monteil, was preparing to advance to the headwaters of the Nile.[32] Either Fashoda, on the White Nile, or Lado, on the Bar El Jebel, were assumed to be the object of the French force, and both these villages were located in territory still dominated by the Mahdi.[33] Although the British considered the territory to be theirs in a technical sense, maintaining that it was part of the Sudan and therefore belonged to Egypt, of which Britain was the occupying power, they were far from exercising effective control. Equally important, the Germans were the only Europeans to have recognized the territory as belonging to the British sphere of influence; both the Belgians and the French claimed the territory for themselves and they were in a better position to enforce their claims than were the British. Moreover, the French and the Belgians were known to be negotiating a settlement of their conflicting claims. Especially worrying was the possibility that, because they possessed reversionary rights to King Leopold's territories in the Congo, the French might retract some of their claims in order to establish Leopold on the Nile, on the assumption that these too would revert to France.

Rosebery, for his part, had no intention of forestalling the French by attempting to reconquer the Sudan. He consistently rejected any suggestion of this kind as precipitate, expensive, and likely to split the Liberal party in half.[34] As always, he preferred a diplomatic solution. He decided to lease the disputed territory along the Nile headwaters to King Leopold for the duration of his reign, and to lease the territory to the east to the king and his successors; in return the king would recognize the British sphere as defined by the Anglo-German agreement and abandon any claims to the Nile Basin.[35]

No single act demonstrates as accurately as the ill-fated Congolese agreement Rosebery's management of imperial affairs. He abandoned, with equanimity, claims to a large tract of territory that might have been pegged out "for the future," showing once again that he was never interested in territorial expansion for its own sake. His motive was strategic: he bartered away possible claims in order to protect Britain's position on the Nile; and his thinking was traditional: unable to match the military strength of another great power, he preferred to use a small state to build a buffer between Britain and her powerful competitor. It was the Germans who had precipitated his negotiations with Leopold by their recent unfriendly moves in Africa and their attempt to restore good relations with Russia. By showing them how easy it was for him to manipulate the situation without their assistance, Rosebery thought he could demonstrate again that Britain was in the stronger position and therefore able to define the terms of their relationship.

The Congolese agreement, as Rosebery and Kimberley saw it, would forestall the French, make the Germans more pliable, and cost the British very little. The cost was important. The enormous expense of sending an expedition to reconquer the Sudan would have aroused heated opposition in Parliament, and especially within the Liberal party. Here, then, was one instance in which "anti-imperialism" succeeded in delineating the limits within which those responsible for the management of affairs were forced to work; but everyone recognized that it was the expense that would antagonize people, not the idea of subjugating non-Europeans to British rule. For this reason Kimberley assumed that Harcourt would not object to the proposed arrangements. "He ought not to kick at it," he told Rosebery, "as it really tends to narrow our responsibilities," and besides, "if we leave him in ignorance, we shall have trouble I fear worse than by letting him know early."[36]

Rosebery concurred in Kimberley's assessment of how to proceed with Harcourt, and rejected the possibility of keeping him in the dark. On 28 March, in a straightforward and concise letter, Kimberley informed Harcourt that they were engaged in secret negotiations with Leopold, with a view to transferring to him a long lease on the British sphere of influence on the Upper Nile. The object, he stated candidly, was to prevent the French from establishing themselves there and to settle with the Belgians, who were already there. He tried to hide nothing from the chancellor, outlining the advantages that would accrue to Britain: "We shall have a friendly neighbour; we shall not be under pressure to extend our operations to that district; we shall prevent the French from interfering." He made no pretence of negotiating with Leopold for any reason other than that of protecting the British position in Egypt: "The presence of the French there would be a serious danger to Egypt, and might easily involve us in complications with them."[37]

Kimberley hid nothing from Harcourt, nor did he try to avoid future consultation on the subject of the negotiations. The matter, he said, was "*very* secret," but he promised to give "verbally, at any time," any further explanations that Harcourt might desire. The chancellor quickly replied on the same day, thanking Kimberley for the note and saying that he would speak to him about it; but he was not heard from again until after the agreement had been made.[38]

On 21 April Kimberley circulated to cabinet a memorandum outlining the agreement that had been reached with King Leopold. Harcourt exploded. "The whole agreement," he announced, was "extremely unwise and unpolitic, inspired apparently by a constant jealousy of France."[39] What Harcourt decided to attack, however, was not so much the substance of the agreement, but the procedure by which it had been arrived at. Although he admitted that he had had a "slight hint that something of this kind was in the wind," he had given it no encouragement, and he had every right to expect that nothing would be concluded without his knowledge. But, as no information had been supplied to him, "I can accept no responsibility for such a transaction nor do I see how the Government is to be carried on if things of this importance are to be completed in secret without the knowledge of those who will have to answer for them in the House of Commons." He set out to mobilize support on this issue by focusing the debate on the question of the rights of those in the Commons, i.e., of himself, as leader of the House. He told Campbell-Bannerman, one of those who had earlier objected to having a peer as foreign secretary, that the Foreign Office practice of suppressing their proceedings, "in spite of the pledge given to me when I undertook the leadership of the House of Commons that I should be fully informed as to all that was going on," was a serious business, and that he would bring the matter before the next meeting of the cabinet. "On their decision my future will depend."[40]

When the cabinet met on 23 April Harcourt's position collapsed. He had chosen to make his attack on the point of his not having been consulted, but Kimberley had only to repeat that he had been informed and that he had neither objected nor asked for further explanation.[41] Harcourt had never responded to Kimberley's invitation to speak to him on the subject, and, as Kimberley actually had a copy of the letter that he had sent to Harcourt, "there was nothing for it but for him to cave in."[42] It was precisely this way of doing business that offended Harcourt's colleagues and had put him out of the running in the leadership race.

Nevertheless, a curious legend has arisen from the cabinet meeting of 23 April. A majority of ministers is supposed to have supported Harcourt, and insisted that Rosebery and Kimberley send Percy Anderson to Brussels to discover whether or not Leopold might be induced to abandon the agreement of 12 April. The legend, the source of which is an entry in the journal of Loulou Harcourt written a fortnight after the event, is preposterous.[43] Not a word has been recorded elsewhere that might sustain the incredible proposition that Rosebery and Kimberley had suddenly acquiesced in Harcourt's demand that the agreement be dropped, and Hamilton's note on the cabinet meeting, made on the day of the meeting, contradicts the legend.[44] But common sense contradicts it as well. Is it likely that, if the cabinet had insisted on the agreement being dropped, Harcourt would have let Rosebery and Kimberley forget it? Is it likely that Kimberley, having agreed to send Anderson to Brussels to back out of the agreement, would, the very next day, threaten King Leopold with immediate publication of the agreement should *he* attempt to back out? Would he have done so in official correspondence? Would Rosebery and Kimberley, having agreed to send Anderson to Brussels, proceed to keep him in London?

What happened then? It seems likely that Harcourt, who always wanted to appear to his son as the big man who was able to bring the cabinet to its knees, tried to save face when relating the incident to him. The son duly recorded the father's version of the meeting, the official biographer of Harcourt repeated the error, and it has since passed from historian to historian, treated as gospel, and sometimes embellished.[45]

But something did happen at that meeting of the 23rd, although it was much less dramatic than the legendary version. Kimberley had explained in the memorandum on the agreement, circulated to the cabinet on the 21st, that the Belgians had been working their way toward the Nile for some time, and that under this agreement they would hold their position subject to British rights, while barring the way to the French. "The Agreement," he concluded "involves us in no responsibility, and will prevent the serious complications which would have been inevitable if the French had occupied this region."[46] What the cabinet objected to was the provision, insisted on by Leopold, that the agreement be kept secret for three months; and what Rosebery and Kimberley agreed to at the cabinet meeting was to reopen discussions with the king on the provision for secrecy – not to drop the substance of the agreement. On the 23rd no one, including Harcourt, appears to have objected to the substance: after all, no new obligations had been undertaken, no new expenses would be incurred. Moreover, no one appears to have supported Harcourt's claim to some sort of special status as leader of the House of Commons.

This explanation of the meeting of the 23rd explains why, when Kimberley five days later circulated a memorandum announcing that "the King is willing that the Agreement should be presented to Parliament, and I propose to present it shortly,"[47] no one in the cabinet objected. It is ludicrous to suppose that Kimberley would have dared to make such an announcement if the cabinet had instructed him to drop the agreement altogether. But now that the agreement was to be published, another consideration began to colour the cabinet's view. The Foreign Office anticipated that the French would be furious when they learned of the agreement, and the dispatches coming in from Brussels outlined what their objections would be. Rosebery would have preferred to keep the cabinet in the dark, but Kimberley succeeded in convincing him that "if anything serious were to happen, we should be in a very awkward position if we keep them in ignorance, and I do not think we could justify ourselves."[48]

It was at this point, and not before, that things began to go seriously wrong. Kimberley, who had anticipated that "we shall have a very unpleasant 'quart d'heure'" when they laid the dispatches from

Brussels before the cabinet, ended up facing a storm for two months. Harcourt was furious. The correspondence, he declared, "reveals a situation so dangerous as regards France and I must add so discreditable alike to the Belgian and British Governments that it is one which I think is absolutely necessary that the Cabinet should carefully consider."[49] Kimberley asserted that he could not understand the cause of Harcourt's fury, as "nothing has been done except to induce the King to agree that the secrecy which you and others objected to should be put an end to."[50] The cabinet, he concluded, would now have the opportunity to reconsider the agreement and advise as they thought best.

If Kimberley thought the cabinet would support him he was sadly mistaken. As long as the discussions had turned on the question of Harcourt's right to information, or on that of the secrecy of the agreement, there had been no real problem, since the cabinet had failed to back Harcourt, and Rosebery and Kimberley had agreed to renegotiate the provision for secrecy. But the question now began to turn on a much more substantial point, and one that frightened a majority of the cabinet: the possibility of European complications arising with France. Harcourt's reaction that "the whole thing is a wanton provocation of France" was predictable, and it was not surprising when Morley looked upon the transaction "with the very deepest misgivings" and refused "to defend our share in it."[51] The trouble came when cabinet members like Asquith concluded that Leopold was attempting to jockey France and the Belgian cabinet and that "he wishes to make us an active partner in his transaction," and when Ripon joined him in thinking that the cabinet should discuss and reconsider the whole matter, even though he was "most anxious to support Kimberley and Rosebery."[52]

The reactions of the cabinet are interesting partly because they revealed that no one supported Harcourt's claim to oversee the Foreign Office. They are more interesting, however, in revealing the cabinet's insularity. There were only two cogent objections to imperialism in the nineties: first, that it cost too much; second, that it would draw Britain in to war in Europe. The second accounted for Harcourt's principal objection to the occupation of Egypt – that it turned Britain in to a continental power. And it was the second objection that now concerned the cabinet. Ripon, for example, who dismissed Harcourt's point that the Congolese Agreement would worsen relations with France, as "they are already too bad for that," feared the possibility of a quarrel between France and Belgium because, if the French tried to stir up trouble, it would be impossible to say where it might lead. "If I were sure that it would lead to

European complications I should say that we ought to give it up."[53] What Ripon and the rest of the cabinet really feared was that complications arising from the protection of imperial interests would embroil them in a war in Europe.

When the cabinet met on 4 May, a compromise arrangement was arrived at whereby the original agreement was dropped in favour of a more general solution in which Leopold recognized that he occupied a position in the British sphere under the authority of the British government, and that he must evacuate it on due notice.[54] They believed this solution would lighten the wrath of the French, while Kimberley maintained that it would "practically come to the same thing."[55] Only one additional change was made, this time at the request of Leopold, who wished to deny the contention of the French that he had ignored their right of preference to the disposal of his Congo territories when he ceded to Britain rights that he had acquired in the Nile Basin. To do this he wished to disavow any claims arising from the Mackinnon Treaty or from prior occupation by Belgian forces. This disavowal was so much to the advantage of Britain that the cabinet had no difficulty in sanctioning the new agreement in their meeting of 8 May. Harcourt was alone in objecting to it. The agreement was signed on 12 May and published ten days later. "As to its contents," Kimberley concluded, "there is practically no difference from the old one."[56]

If the Congolese agreement had offended the French alone the controversy surrounding it would almost certainly have ended here, as it was the French against whom it was directed, and their objections came as no surprise to Rosebery and Kimberley. The controversy persisted, however, when the Germans joined the French in opposing the agreement. Harcourt's official biographer maintained that Harcourt had clearly foreseen, from the beginning, the united antagonism that the agreement would create in France and Germany.[57] But this is nonsense. Harcourt did not mention the possibility of German opposition until 6 June, six weeks after he launched his attack on the agreement and more than a month after the Germans began to voice their opposition.[58] In fact it seems that no one, including Rosebery and Kimberley, anticipated that the Germans would object.

The trouble arose from an arrangement proposed by Sir Percy Anderson, former head of the African department at the Foreign Office and, in 1894, assistant under-secretary, to allow for a road and telegraph right-of-way through Congo territory that would effectively link the British spheres in the north and south of Africa – the "Cape to Cairo corridor" that Mackinnon had hoped for, but failed to establish, in 1890. Anderson, to whom Rosebery had given the responsibility for the negotiations with King Leopold, had proposed, in the midst of the discussions, that the king should lease to Britain a port on Lake Tanganyika, with a road from Lake Albert Edward, as an equivalent to the port on Lake Albert that the British had agreed to lease to the king.[59] It appears from the evidence available that Anderson made the proposal spontaneously, as part of the bargaining process; no evidence can be found to indicate that either Rosebery or Kimberley had any interest in the project. The real purpose of the Congolese agreement, in their minds, was to forestall a French drive to the Nile through central Africa, not to erect a Cape to Cairo empire.

When the Germans learned of the first, abortive agreement of 12 April, they immediately began to complain that it would disturb the frontier arrangement between themselves and the Belgians. They proposed that the road should be moved back from the frontier a minimum of twenty kilometres, and Kimberley immediately agreed to this modification, which seemed to satisfy the German concern, as they remained silent for the month that the cabinet spent wrangling over the provisions for secrecy and renegotiating the agreement.[60] Almost a week after the publication of the agreement, however, the German minister at Brussels informed Leopold that, if he did not receive written assurance that the British strip would be placed at least twenty kilometres from the German frontier, "Germany will openly take part with France in [the] forthcoming discussion."[61] The assurance was required by 6 P.M. the following day, and Kimberley gave it at once. He had never contemplated disturbing the frontier arrangements with Germany, he said, and therefore he was able to give them a complete and unqualified assurance on this point.[62]

The Germans, however, were not satisfied, and they suddenly began to elevate the level at which the discussions took place. During the interval in a court concert at Berlin, William II told the British ambassador that the leasing of this little strip of land was fatal to the future of German East Africa because it would give the whole of the trade of the interior to British outlets. "Believe me," he said, "it would be best to allow the Agreement to drop."[63] Before this conversation, the Germans had raised only the question of technical difficulties arising from the British replacing the Belgians along the frontier; now they objected that the agreement represented a serious violation of German interests and they were prepared to use threats accordingly. "It is above all things your interest to avoid a Conference," the kaiser declared.

The British knew what the kaiser's declaration meant: if they failed to comply with the German demand, they would have to face the reopening of the Egyptian question, likely with France and Germany united against them. This was an ironic turn of events because one of Rosebery's aims in initiating the Congolese discussions had been to reduce Britain's dependence on the Germans for her security in Egypt. One of the attractions of an arrangement with Leopold was that it would show the Germans that the British could find ways of forestalling the French threat without going through Berlin; but now, through Anderson's blunder, they were reduced to dependence on Germany once again. Anderson suggested that they could calm the Germans about the threat to their trade by making a secret arrangement that promised not to build the road if the Germans made no difficulty about the telegraph.[64] This showed that Anderson himself did not place great value on the road, but it came too late – the damage had been done and Kimberley concluded that this new proposal would fail to satisfy the Germans.[65]

No evidence exists to support the contention that Rosebery had "gone out of his way to offend Germany" by including the corridor clause in the agreement.[66] He and Kimberley alike appear to have assumed that the clause was harmless enough, and Rosebery later claimed to have been assured by Anderson that German rights were in no way affected by the arrangement. In the correspondence that passed between Rosebery and Kimberley on the subject of the agreement – and it is bulky – there is no mention of taking revenge on Germany or of preparing for her reaction when it came. In fact the corridor clause was considered to be so minor that Kimberley agreed to the twenty-kilometre revision without so much as a word to Rosebery.

Nevertheless, in a deeper and more important sense, the whole Congolese agreement, and not merely the corridor clause, was a kind of revenge taken against Germany because of the Franco-German protocol. Rosebery had initiated the discussions with the Belgians when the Germans appeared to be returning to their strategy of using France and Russia outside Europe in order to force Britain into the Triple Alliance. Kimberley took the same view. He told the German ambassador on 17 April that the Franco-German protocol had made a "disagreeable impression" on him but that he was prepared, nevertheless, to let bygones be bygones, and he stressed his desire to cooperate with Germany on questions that remained to be settled.[67] A week later Hatzfeldt replied that German cooperation would depend on what the British gave in return. "The general impression which I derived from this conversation was that we must not count on support from Germany, and that the present disposition of the German Government is rather to seek the co-operation of the French in Africa than to act with us."[68] The general impression that Rosebery and Kimberley had of Germany's African policy does not explain the introduction of the corridor clause, but it does provide one reason why they wished to strike a bargain with Leopold, and it also explains why they failed to consult the Germans during the course of negotiations: the Germans would probably have demanded compensation or, more likely, have informed the French and thereby wrecked the proposed agreement altogether.

What was really at stake in the discussions with Germany, which now determined the fate of the whole agreement, was the old question of who was to dominate the other: if the Germans, without a navy and without any substantial power in central Africa, could, through their diplomacy in Europe, destroy an arrangement so useful to the defence of British interests in Africa, then they would win a substantial victory in the contest for control. And win they did. But they won partly through a legal technicality, as the British were forced to agree that documentary evidence of the discussions surrounding the Mackinnon agreement of 1890 showed that they had agreed that taking territory in the area of the corridor would violate German interests.[69] The lease of territory, the Germans argued, was tantamount to cession of it, and the British could not really argue the point.

In private, Rosebery admitted that there had been some *maladresse* in the later stages of negotiating the agreement. The Foreign Office, he claimed, had misled him when they failed to inform him of the earlier German objections to something analogous in the corridor clause.[70] Rosebery concluded that they had "blundered in not communicating the Treaty to the German Government before it was laid before Parliament," and for this Kimberley, and not Anderson, was responsible.[71] Rosebery's criticism draws attention to the important point, usually overlooked, that in his early months as prime minister he exercised little control over Kimberley at the Foreign Office; he saw only the most important dispatches, made only the occasional minute on them, and gave few suggestions to Kimberley. The mess created by the Congolese agreement contributed to Rosebery's reluctant conclusion that Kimberley had come to the Foreign Office "too late"; and not the least important effect of the affair was to increase Rosebery's supervision of foreign policy.[72]

The Congolese agreement was, nevertheless, a typical piece of Roseberian diplomacy, and its flaws reflected his personality and way of doing business. He loved secrecy to the point where he was easily drawn into schemes where it seemed essential; so it never really occurred to him that Leopold might be using secrecy in order to manipulate the British. When he directly supervised affairs, his secret manoeuvres – with Portal in Uganda, Cromer in Egypt, the discussions with the Triple Alliance – had always succeeded, but the Congolese negotiations retained their aura of secrecy without his supervision. He had, moreover, great faith in the ability of experts and always preferred to let them handle the details while he carried out the grand strategy. This is one of the points at which he parted company with Salisbury, who never trusted experts. When Rosebery saw that Anderson's mastery of the intricacies of the African situation was unparalleled, he came to rely on his judgment. He was as surprised by Anderson's mistake as was Sir John Kirk, the former consul-general in Zanzibar, who wondered, "As Percy Anderson was the negotiator of that agreement in Berlin how is it that he never realised what the effect of the agreement with the Congo State must be?"[73] Salisbury would not have been surprised.

The reliance upon experts who proved defective, combined with the secrecy that surrounded the Congolese negotiation, produced a situation in which Germany threatened to engage in united action with France. If Leopold persisted in the agreement, the Germans warned, they might declare that the Congo State had violated its obligations as a neutral power and withdraw Germany's guarantee of its neutrality. Harcourt's worst predictions seemed about to be realized: "No settlement of the question can be arrived at without the intervention of Germany, so that as the German Emperor says, unless the Treaty is abandoned there must be a Conference, and at that Conference (which must involve a new partition of Africa) we shall be in a minority of one."[74] This would prove Harcourt's point that the agreement had been a disaster from the start, because no concession would now satisfy the Germans: "they are determined to tear up the Treaty and make the King eat it."[75] The blunders of Rosebery and Kimberley, he argued, had succeeded in uniting the French and Germans against the British, and reaffirmed his contention that he must be given the authority to oversee the administration of foreign policy.

The German foreign minister, Marschall, told the British ambassador on 15 June that Germany would not be satisfied with compensation, and the point was underscored when the German minister at Brussels declared that nothing would satisfy his government except the king's withdrawal of his signature from the agreement.[76] But the Germans had not restricted themselves to threats against the Congo State. The real point that they wished to make was that Britain could not act in Africa without going through Berlin, and they had already started to make this point by bringing pressure to bear on London, as well as on Brussels. Rumours soon started to reach Kimberley that the Germans were contemplating making mischief in Morocco. More worrying still, the Germans joined the French at Cairo when they advised the khedive, who was about to undertake a trip to Britain, to stay in Egypt.[77]

The German move in Egypt was decisive. Rosebery, who had remained in the background, decided to act, and took over the controls from Kimberley. On 13 June he sent for the Austrian ambassador. If Germany were going to side with France or even *appear* to side with her, in this and other African questions, he bluntly declared, "we must reconsider our position as regards our general attitude in Europe, more particularly in the Mediterranean and the East." This language, he assured the queen, "will ricochet through Vienna to Berlin."[78] He knew the Austrians were already worried about their position as a result of the Russo-German commerical treaty, which Kálnoky feared would make the attempt to bring Germany into line over the Straits question very difficult, and so Rosebery could be quite certain that the threat of withdrawing British support would have a decisive effect on the Austrians.[79]

Rosebery's move, striking in its simplicity, had the desired effect. On 16 June, the day after Germany had insisted that the agreement be dropped altogether, Marschall declared that he would be satisfied if Britain gave up article III, which provided for the corridor. The source of the trouble, he said, was the feeling that Germany had been "jockeyed," but he was prepared, if the British dropped article III, to recognize that this had not been their intention.[80] "The change of tone," Kimberley told Rosebery, "is remarkable."[81] "My general impression," the British ambassador in Berlin reported, "is that we shall now go on smoothly."[82]

It is easy to see that the Germans had succeeded in making their point. The value to Britain of the proposed corridor through the Congo was small when compared with the results of forfeiting German cooperation on Africa, so the Germans could insist on being consulted when any African arrangements were being considered that touched on their interests. To conclude that this was the only lesson learned from the Congolese affair would be a mistake, however, for Rosebery had also succeeded in making Britain's point: if Germany went too far in working with France, then Britain could abandon Germany's allies in the Mediterranean. It is naive to imagine that the controversy over the Congolese agreement led to bad feelings and mutual distrust and thereby contributed to the growing separation between Britain and Germany. Both sides were engaged in a struggle to dominate the other by insisting on their own definition of the terms upon which their understanding operated. Until one side or the other won there was bound to be bad feeling and mutual distrust; the Congolese imbroglio was not a cause, but an effect.

The continuing struggle with Germany partly explains Britain's treatment of France in what remained of the Congolese imbroglio, because, whenever the Germans raised the spectre of common action with France, Rosebery would attempt to reply by showing that he could, if pushed too far, appease the French himself, and thereby render useless the German threat.

Rosebery and Kimberley regarded the French attack on the Congolese convention as flimsy.[83] The French argued that they knew nothing of the 1890 agreement – but it had been published and made available to the world; they argued that the convention violated Turkish or Egyptian rights in the region – but these had been expressly reserved; and they argued that the territory of the Congo State could not go north of the fourth parallel – but the Franco-Congolese agreement of 1887 had permitted this. Nevertheless, although they regarded the French legal argument as weak, and although they had managed to remove the possibility of German cooperation with France, Rosebery and Kimberley did not reject the French arguments out of hand, but chose instead to negotiate.

Dufferin, the British ambassador in Paris, was instructed to hold out no hopes that Britain might revise the convention, yet to declare his willingness "to enter into a general review and adjustment of all our pending African questions."[84] Egypt was to be specifically excluded from such a review. Dufferin's instructions revealed again the essential purpose of the Congolese convention in barring the way to the Nile, and showed that, if the French were finally prepared to accept the British regime in Egypt, then the British were willing to be conciliatory elsewhere, particularly since improved relations with France would reduce British dependence on Germany. Rosebery never believed that the French would give up their pretensions in Egypt, but he was prepared to use the opportunity to test their policy.

Once Rosebery had succeeded in dividing Germany from France, he realized that he had little to lose in agreeing to the proposed general conference on Africa that had originally been brandished as a threat to force the British into submission. He saw that the French ground of protesting the convention as violating Ottoman rights was not unsatisfactory. "The Nile is Egypt, and Egypt is the Nile. And it should be our first interest, as the occupying Power, to obtain a recognition of this principle by the Great Powers."[85] He suggested a conference in which Britain would renew the declaration made to Germany regarding the road and Germany would support the establishment of the British sphere of influence as settled by the 1890 agreement. "We might further add a protocol to the effect that in the opinion of the Powers the Nile should be considered as belonging to Egypt and the Ottoman Empire, and that when Egypt is in a position to re-occupy it, we shall with pleasure hand over to her that part which is at present under our control."

Without Germany's support for one side or the other, neither Britain nor France was likely to win the general settlement they sought, and negotiations settled into a long process of fruitless discussions in which neither had much faith. But the temporary illusion that they might settle their differences without Germany's participation, or without pushing the situation in Africa to the brink of war, did help to avoid what might have been a crisis in Morocco. When the sultan died unexpectedly, rumours reached London that the French were mobilizing their forces in Algeria.[86] The Germans, who anticipated that they might create another Egypt, with the British and French vying for control of Morocco, refused to join the other powers in recognizing the most obvious successor to the throne, the sultan's eldest son.[87] But while there seemed to be a possibility of a general African settlement, and while it was clear that Germany would not throw her weight fully behind one side, both Britain and France were reluctant to quarrel, and thus they easily agreed on a successor to the throne and avoided a crisis.[88]

One of the most interesting features of the diplomatic tangle that arose from the Congolese negotiation was the confirmation that it gave to Rosebery's appraisal of the Franco-Russian alliance. He had always maintained that this alliance was aimed at Germany and the Triple Alliance, not at the British Empire. When the French asked for Russian support in opposing the Congolese agreement they were rewarded with a terse sentence; the Russians failed to utter a single harsh word in London. The Siam crisis of 1893 had previously convinced Rosebery that the Franco-Russian alliance did not apply in Asia, and now the Russian failure to march in step with the French over the Congo and Egypt convinced him that it did not apply in Africa either. Rosebery's foreign policy was built on the assumption that the alliance between France and Russia could succeed only as a European arrangement, that the alliance made Germany more vulnerable than Britain, and that Britain could accordingly control the vague Anglo-German understanding.

Rosebery never assumed, however, that the Franco-Russian alliance could not be transformed into an anti-British coalition that worked against Britain's imperial interests, so he attempted to improve Anglo-Russian relations and thereby split the alliance. In this decision his timing was fortunate, because it coincided with a Russian decision to subordinate her interests in central Asia and the Near East to her emerging interests in the Far East, a decision symbolized by the enormously ambitious undertaking of the trans-Siberian railway. Thus Rosebery's moves to conciliate Russia in the Pamirs, Persia, and even Turkey matched Russian ambitions exactly. But the fundamental question here, and one that did not arise during the first two years of the Liberal government, was how this new era of Anglo-Russian friendship would work in the Far East if a question arose that involved a conflict in the interests of the two powers.

The Anglo-Russian understanding for which Rosebery had been working since 1892 began to come apart as the result of a native uprising in Korea. The British knew practically nothing about the rebels, the Tonghaks, beyond the fact that they were a nationalist group attempting to kill off the old feudatory-tributary relationship between Korea and the Manchu dynasty. This was knowledge enough. Revolts created the opportunity of intervention by ambitious powers, and Rosebery, who regarded China as Britain's natural ally in Asia – after Britain had captured the bulk of her trade and control of the customs – was anxious to avoid a Russian intervention.[89] For a moment, therefore, it seemed as if Britain and Russia might clash over Korea, because the Russians would find it difficult to pass up such an opportunity for intervention in Chinese affairs while the British would support the principle of Chinese territorial integrity.

Fortunately for Rosebery, the Russians were not yet prepared to intervene because their Far Eastern strategy was a long-term design, closely connected to the building of the trans-Siberian railway, which was still far from complete. The trouble came not from the Russians, but from the Japanese, who, in June, landed troops for the declared purpose of quelling the uprising. The question the British now faced was how far they were prepared to go in preventing war between China and Japan.

Rosebery and Kimberley recognized that the Japanese were the aggressors and they made no effort to pretend otherwise. They used only one argument in their attempt to restrain them: that a war with China would invite the intervention of Russia.[90] The Japanese replied that China had become too weak to prevent the expansion of Russia in the Far East and that they had, therefore, no choice but to go into Korea themselves before it was too late. It soon became clear that the only way to restrain the Japanese was through the armed mediation of Britain and Russia, but Rosebery and Kimberley had no difficulty in agreeing to reject this course of action. If the European powers succeeded, Kimberley said, it would make them jointly responsible for affairs in Korea, "a very disagreeable prospect."[91] Rosebery concurred: a joint occupation of Korea "would as a matter of certainty only rebound to the advantage of Russia, while it might engage us in great complications."[92]

The British knew, from their Egyptian experience, that a condominium was not the easiest system to manage successfully and they resolved to avoid a repetition of it in Korea. But Rosebery had another reason for permitting the Japanese to proceed unhindered by European intervention. It would be impolitic to act against the Japanese, he concluded, because "we should weaken and alienate a Power of great magnitude in those seas and which is a bulwark against Russia."[93] Although he aimed to improve British relations with Russia, Rosebery assumed that their interests would continue to conflict, and that a third power, particularly a local one with territorial interests to defend, would be useful to Britain in limiting Russian expansion.

It is tempting to credit Rosebery with a prescience that was not in fact his. Although he obviously looked forward to the possibility of an arrangement with Japan, he never outlined how this might come about, nor did he predict anything like the eventual alliance that emerged. More important, he never foresaw the rise of Japan to the status of world power. When he spoke of Japan as a power of "great magnitude," he was not thinking of her on a European scale, but rather on an Asiatic. He looked forward to no more than Japan's being a state strong enough to resist Russian expansion. He did not consider Japan as an alternative to China, preferring to think that she might one day unite with China in a common defence against Russia. The world would continue to arrange its affairs in a way that would suit British interests.

The size and speed of the Japanese victory in Korea came as a shock to the European powers. When Asiatics fought one another, their wars were supposed to be slow affairs that did little to alter the actual situation – a supposition that helps to explain why Rosebery was prepared to countenance the Japanese attack when they finally declared war on 1 August. Rosebery expected a Japanese victory, but not an overwhelming one. Chinese methods, he declared, "are too languid to admit of their being rapidly or sensibly weakened."[94] At first this expectation seemed justified, as battles were conducted on a small scale and preparations seemed to be proceeding at a leisurely pace. Kimberley asked for, and received, the assurance of the Japanese that they would not interfere with the approaches to Shanghai.[95] When the Japanese sank a ship that flew the British flag, but which was carrying Chinese troops, the British refused to be provoked or to use the occasion as an excuse to interfere.

The situation suddenly changed when, in mid-September, the Japanese scored a great victory at Pingyang. The British Foreign Office immediately regretted that the victory was so pronounced, and feared the effect it would have on China.[96] The ambassador in Peking reported that there was considerable restlessness in Manchuria – perhaps the revolt would spread – and that further Japanese victories would render insecure the position of foreign residents in Peking.[97] It now appeared that an overwhelming victory by Japan might stir up a revolt against European influence, or even against the dynasty itself, a situation that would make European intervention a practical certainty, with Britain being drawn into Chinese affairs more closely than she wished. The Japanese, Kimberley feared, "will be very cock-a-whoop with their victories."[98]

Besides rebellion or a xenophobic insurrection, the British had to concern themselves with a third possibility. The Englishman who knew China best, Sir Robert Hart, who for the last forty years had directed the Chinese Imperial Maritime Customs, began to warn Rosebery privately, through a confidant in London, that, if Japanese troops were allowed to march on Peking, "China may have to throw herself into Russian arms. I think England should intervene and forcibly." "The opportunity," he argued, "will never recur and all the future will take new colour."[99] But Rosebery declined to act. "All that we could do," he told Kimberley, "would be to declare to Japan that we could cut off the troops that she has landed. This would be an unprovoked declaration of war of the most unjustifiable kind."[100]

Rosebery's refusal to act on behalf of China, even when it became apparent that Japan had far surpassed her in military strength, represented a considerable risk, and shows the lengths to which he was now prepared to go rather than alienate Japan. He was not willing to forgo the possibility of erecting a stronger barrier to Russian expansion in the Far East; and, if the Japanese could beat the Chinese so easily, they were obviously the ones to count on in the future. Nevertheless, Rosebery still hoped to avoid choosing between the two and, therefore, while conscientiously refraining from any moves that might alienate Japan, he tried not to give the appearance of partiality, as China was still "almost our only natural ally."[101] Thus, when a minister of the Tsungli Yamen informed Hart that "without stooping to sue for peace the Chinese Government consent to terminate the tributary relation if the Powers concerned mutually guarantee Corean independence and neutrality," Rosebery actively took up the proposal.[102]

Rosebery was in charge of the Foreign Office once again because Kimberley, who had gone home to Norfolk for the holidays, refused to bestir himself, forcing Rosebery to come up from Scotland to initiate the fruitless attempt to arrange for a six-power mediation of the war and guarantee of Korean independence.[103] In this attempt he was acting largely on the private information and advice of Sir Robert Hart, rather than on that provided by the ambassador. When Kimberley complained that they ought to be using the regular channels of diplomacy, Rosebery dismissed the complaint: "we have no wish to embarrass ourselves with punctilio in this matter."[104] The secrecy suited Rosebery's tastes, but it also suited his purpose. He had little faith in the possible success of a joint mediation, but he wished, privately, to do what he could to appear to be working on behalf of the Chinese. When Germany and the United States refused to join any mediation effort, and Russia used their refusal as an excuse to reject the proposal, Rosebery was not surprised, nor was he particularly worried.

Following the failure of the proposed mediation, the Japanese attitude began to stiffen. Their ambassador in London suggested privately that nothing less than Korean independence, with Japan as the predominant power, would satisfy them. He proposed to recognize the Korean army, create a new administration, and demand from China an indemnity and some territorial compensation such as Formosa.[105] China was reported to be prepared to accept any reasonable terms, but Japan refused to give any. "Thus far Japan's arms have been attended with complete success; nevertheless the Japanese Government are inclined to think that in the present stage of the war affairs have not made sufficient progress to ensure a satisfactory result of negotiations."[106] The Chinese, at last, decided that they must make a real effort: "every nerve will now be strained to resist Japanese aggression."[107]

The actions of China, however, served only to confirm Rosebery's growing belief that Japan was replacing her as Britain's natural ally in the Far East. Each morning, Hart reported, the Chinese ministers were eager to fight, but by evening they were prepared to give away anything.[108] The Chinese officially requested the intervention of the six powers, who would set an indemnity and create an independent Korea; but Germany and the United States again refused to act.[109] When Kimberley then suggested that the Chinese request an armistice, and that Britain and Russia convey the request to the Japanese, he demonstrated that Britain was not prepared to act in any way that might appear unfriendly to the Japanese. When the Japanese landed a force on the Liaotung Peninsula and captured Port Arthur on 21 November, the Chinese decided that they had no alternative to suing for peace, and when Japan insisted that the Chinese must send to them a plenipotentiary to whom they would communicate their peace terms, Kimberley urged the Chinese to accept.[110] Although sporadic fighting continued over the next four months, Rosebery and Kimberley had made their choice: Japan now came first, and the two men were prepared to run the risk of upheaval in China, or a Sino-Russian partnership, rather than alienate her. It was a fateful choice.

Historians of diplomacy sometimes display the occupational hazard of taking diplomacy too seriously. They sometimes proceed as if every course of action is open to the diplomatist, as if great cleverness or goodwill could overcome the difficulties to be found in any situation, as if conflicts in the affairs of states arise merely from the temperament of those in charge. But the diplomatist, more often than not, faces a situation where the choices of policy are rather limited, where the exercise of goodwill will be interpreted as simple weakness, and where conflicts of interest appear to supersede those of personality. The diplomatist operates within a restricted, and restrictive, environment wherein he can do very little to alter the power of his own state or of other states; nor can he do much to change the way of thinking of those around him, those upon whom he must depend for his political position and whom he must trust to apply his policies. It is the task of the historian of diplomacy to understand the restrictions under which diplomatists have worked, to distinguish between conflicts of interest and conflicts of personality, to clarify the responsibility for changes in the direction of diplomatic history.

Rosebery is always assumed to have faced severe restrictions on his diplomacy because of the opposition of the Little Englanders in the cabinet – Gladstone, Harcourt, Morley – to his imperial designs. These three men did consistently oppose the expansion of Britain during Rosebery's time in office, but the significance of their opposition has been exaggerated. They were the ones who faced the restrictions, not Rosebery. They vaguely thought of abandoning the empire from time to time, but this course was so far removed from the realm of practical possibility that it must be seen as idle day-dreaming. Even in Egypt, where the situation appeared fluid, or unstable enough to allow for discussion about leaving, the Little Englanders saw that they had little hope for success and they turned their attention instead to those places where it seemed possible that the empire might continue to go forward. Any restrictions that they succeeded in placing on Rosebery, therefore, came when he wished to go forward.

Rosebery faced no restrictions that meant anything because, with one notable exception, he never wished to advance. The British

Empire, he believed, was already big enough, and the task of defending it was already too difficult. He was, as we have seen, a consolidationist. The purpose of diplomacy was to safeguard the empire while it developed internal cohesion, while the colonies gained strength; this is what he meant when he declared that foreign policy was really colonial policy. Whenever the occasion for expansion arose, in Morocco, the Congo, Persia, Afghanistan, Siam, the Far East, Rosebery rejected it in favour of limiting British interests. Uganda was the only exception to this policy, albeit a glaring one, and here Rosebery felt that there was no alternative, that to abandon Uganda would be to imperil Egypt, upon which Britain had come to depend for her position in the Mediterranean and thus, perhaps, in India.

After Gladstone retired, the opposition of the remaining Little Englanders counted for little. Neither Harcourt nor Morley had anything like the respect or support that Gladstone had carried in the cabinet and the country, while the wounded vanity and bad feelings caused by the failure of the Malwood Compact during the contest for the leadership meant that the two men no longer maintained a united front in cabinet. Morley practically withdrew from all discussions that did not pertain to Ireland, leaving Harcourt virtually isolated. Harcourt claimed to have demanded, and received, a special position in connection with foreign affairs in virtue of his being leader in the House of Commons while both the prime minister and foreign secretary were in the House of Lords. The only evidence in support of this claim comes from Harcourt, and no other minister appears to have supported it during the cabinet's discussion of the Congolese agreement. Harcourt was usually informed of foreign affairs in the same manner as the rest of the cabinet, through the circulation of printed dispatches in the cabinet box.

To the Germans and the French, and not to Harcourt, must go the credit for wrecking the Congolese agreement. Concentrating on Harcourt's vituperative attacks has diverted students of this period from a proper understanding of the real restrictions that accounted for the direction of Rosebery's policy.

The Congolese affair and the Sino-Japanese War showed how limited were the possibilities open to Britain in the nineties. In both cases Britain was incapable of exerting local power sufficient to manipulate the policies of a small European state and a middling Asiatic one. The sense of weakness that was beginning to run through British official circles was reflected in their willingness to believe the fictional tales told by Leopold about the strength of his forces in the area of the Nile. But the British continued to trust that destiny could be turned to their advantage as it had been in the past: Rosebery tried to manoeuvre the Congo State and Japan into a position where they would act on behalf of the British, the Congo interposing a barrier between the French and the Nile, and Japan replacing China as the nucleus of Oriental resistance to the expansion of the Russian empire. The alternative to this strategy appeared to be to admit defeat, to recognize equality of status with the French in Africa, to recognize the superiority of Russia to Asia.

Britain was on the defensive in the nineties, and Rosebery's diplomacy was a reaction to initiatives undertaken by others. Britain had devoted a century to the task of making the empire defensible, of rendering it immune to the inevitable challenges posed to the balance of power in Europe; but by the nineties the empire was dependent upon, not immune to, the European balance. If those millions of men under arms in France and Russia could ever be turned against Britain outside Europe, then the British Empire would be indefensible. The Triple Alliance was the first line of imperial defence, but if the Germans succeeded in forcing the British into it as a full partner, they would have succeeded in demonstrating that Britain was a European power after all, and a second-rate one at that. The alternative at which Rosebery hinted when the Germans became too demanding, that he might settle Britain's colonial differences with Russia and France, would have been a confession of the same thing in different words, that Russia and France had become too powerful for the British to resist.

This was the real dilemma that Rosebery faced, and compared with it the attacks of Harcourt were a minor irritant. Being a great imperial power meant not having to choose between the Triple and Dual alliances, and to avoid choosing, Rosebery came up with a patchwork quilt of a policy, using the Congo State here, the Japanese there, the Siamese somewhere else. He felt the empire could not go forward, but it must not go backward. He convinced himself that he was playing for time, that the colonies of white settlers would grow big and strong, that the Asian and African possessions of the empire would be gradually modernized, that all would be a glorious, coherent whole. The British Empire, he believed, was only just beginning. Statesmen live by these illusions.

CHAPTER SEVEN

Declarations, Threats, and Refusals: The Program Falls Apart

Men who pine for unofficial repose dread the painful process of quitting office – the triumph of enemies and the discomfiture of friends and the wrench of habit – as men weary of life fear the actual process of death ... [a minister] has to deal not with angels but with men; with passions, prejudices and interests, often sordid or misguided. He must, therefore, compromise the ideal, and do, not the best, but the nearest practicable to the best.

Pitt (1891)

Relations among the great powers of Europe were remarkably unstable towards the end of 1894 and at the beginning of 1895, largely because of the uncertainty generated by British policy. Rosebery was convinced that Britain's position as an imperial power could be maintained only through the balance of power in Europe, and his informal understanding with the Triple Alliance was an effort to see that the balance continued to operate. This meant walking on eggs. He was prepared to work with the Triple Alliance because it restrained the imperial ambitions of France and Russia by tying up their money and manpower in Europe, but he refused to join the alliance because to do so might tip the balance so far in its favour that it would embolden its members to undertake an aggressive policy in Europe. Germany's imperial ambitions outside Europe never worried Rosebery; what did worry him was the prospect of being drawn into Europe to the point where Britain would be compelled to fight in the interest of others.

Rosebery's method of avoiding the commitment that the Germans were trying to force on him was to improve relations with Russia to the point where it was demonstrable that Britain needed the Triple Alliance less than it needed her. Being with the alliance but not of it gave Rosebery a degree of control, as he could decide when, where, and how it operated; he would not be drawn into a war for the sake of the ambitions of Italy in the Mediterranean, of Austria-Hungary in the Balkans, or of Germany in eastern Europe. From the time that he returned to the Foreign Office in 1892, therefore, Rosebery had applied himself to the task of improving relations with Russia. The most important symbol of this policy was to be found in the ongoing Pamirs negotiation, but the policy was pursued just as steadily in the Near and Far East. As long as Rosebery stuck to this strategy, there was bound to be widespread uncertainty in Europe.

German irritation with Rosebery's policy was a sign of its success. The Germans expected that the British and the Russians would quarrel in central Asia, but by late 1894 it was apparent to all of Europe that the Pamirs question was practically settled. Both sides had agreed not to advance until a convention was signed, and the signing was delayed only because of the long illness, and finally the death, of the tsar. The Germans hoped, and tried to arrange, for an Anglo-Russian confrontation over the future of Korea, but both Britain and Russia refused to participate actively in the dispute. When Rosebery eulogized the tsar in glowing phrases, he gave more public evidence of his intentions, and these were reciprocated by the Russians. The *Novoe Vremya*, the usually anglophobe newspaper, contemplated the possibility of an Anglo-Russian understanding in the Far East arising out of the Pamirs settlement.[1] Moscow society, the British ambassador reported, had "developed a very friendly feeling for everything English."[2]

Rosebery had no difficulty in arranging for Kimberley to continue the pursuit of the Russian understanding, because the foreign secretary disbelieved the rumours that Russia was planning a conquest of India. Kimberley distrusted the Russians because he thought they were not above turning the spontaneous activities of their agents to their advantage, but he believed they were sincere in not wishing to disrupt the current state of affairs in the Far East.[3] Kimberley's attitude to Russian policy was one of the crucial factors in recommending him to Rosebery as a worthy successor at the Foreign Office.

Where Rosebery and Kimberley began to reach a parting of the ways was on the question of German colonial policy. The difference was signalled first by a typically inconsequential event: a German protest lodged against the British capture of a slaver flying German colours in Zanzibar waters. Kimberley concluded from this incident that "we must expect their ill-will in all African affairs."[4] German moves since March 1894 had convinced Kimberley that the Germans were unfriendly and that they would improve their behaviour only if

Britain threatened them with unhappy consequences. Henceforth, he had little patience with them, and he resorted more frequently to the tactic of laying "stress on the consequences which will follow German action."[5] Kimberley wished to apply the lesson Rosebery had taught him when, in the midst of the Congolese imbroglio, he had quieted the Germans by sending them a message through Vienna.

Kimberley, however, had misconstrued the lesson – perhaps he was not capable of understanding it. Rosebery resorted to this tactic only when the Germans threatened to cooperate with France. Rosebery never brought any pressure to bear on the whole structure of the Triple Alliance as long as Germany saw to it that her colonial disputes with Britain remained bilateral. Therefore, on this minor affair of the Zanzibar seizure, Rosebery proposed the conciliatory course of approaching the Germans privately to see where they stood: did the Germans deny them ordinary police rights, or the right to search for slaves under the Brussels Act, or both? He proposed to make little of the affair and suggested that they ought not to remonstrate with the Germans. As to the offensive manner of the note, to which Kimberley took exception, Rosebery found "the style ... neither worse nor better than the ordinary run of the German note."[6]

Although Rosebery was never willing to concede the second principle the Germans were trying to establish as part of the understanding – that the British must automatically defer to them where their colonial interests were concerned, unless these conflicted with an interest vital to Britain – neither was he prepared to provoke them. He never considered Germany to be a threat to the colonial interests of Britain. Kimberley saw things differently. He believed that the understanding with Germany ought to make her willing to subordinate her colonial interests, which were trivial, to those of Britain, which were essential. When a Lisbon mob rioted in October 1894, giving rise to speculation that Portugal might abandon her possessions in East Africa, an article in the *Kölnische Zeitung*, said to be inspired by the government, declared that Germany would say "hands off" to Britain as regards Delagoa Bay. The article, Kimberley said, was insolent.[7]

What sort of an understanding did the Germans think they had with Britain when they were prepared to cause her trouble in areas vital to the empire? "If the Germans attempt to interfere," Kimberley declared, "I should (if I can have my own way) make them clearly understand that we are determined and able to maintain our supremacy in that quarter of the world."[8] Britain, he proposed, ought to send a large ship to the bay, because "a demonstration of force is necessary in face of the arrogant attitude of Germany." Kimberley did not see that Germany's power in Europe gave her the right, or the strength, to demand concessions in Africa: "We are too strong to be meddled with by any other Power especially one whose naval force is so palpably inferior to ours. The Germans must learn that though they have a huge army, we are supreme at sea."[9] The change in British thinking was about to begin.

Curiously, the first to change were not the "new" imperialists, but the old, those who remembered the happy days of the liberal alliance with France, who believed that British sea power still gave her sufficient strength to ignore the balance of power in Europe. Ripon, who, like Kimberley, was serving his last term in office, also regretted that Harcourt's dread of a strong word, combined with Rosebery's hatred of the French, "throws us inevitably on German support."[10] Both men wished to return to the old days when they imagined that Britain could stand aloof from the balance and rely upon the navy. The trouble, as they saw it, was not that Britain was "isolated" from other European powers, but that she had grown too dependent upon them. Both men had joined Spencer – equally ancient – in insisting upon the massive new naval building program of the 1894 budget.

Kimberley was shocked when Germany raised the question of Delagoa Bay because he assumed that no friend of Britain's would seek to make trouble for her in that area; everyone knew that Britain's "safe route to India is round the cape."[11] Rosebery, sensing that Kimberley was beginning to think of a settlement of differences with France as easier to arrange than a truly amicable relationship with Germany, tried to set him back on the proper course. He reminded him that an agreement on the British sphere on the Nile was the pivot to any general African settlement and that the French were not likely to consent to it. "In fact we do not want to press negotiations."[12] He reminded him that the French, not the Germans, were causing trouble on the Indian frontier, that Britain must find a way to put some backbone into Siam, "otherwise she will be eaten like an artichoke, leaf by leaf."[13]

Kimberley was not the man to change his views overnight. His growing disenchantment with German policy did not move him straight into the arms of the French, and he accepted Rosebery's pessimistic view of French intentions. But neither did he abandon his position on the Germans: "They thwart us wherever they can all over the world," he told Ripon.[14] And matters promised to get worse. When Caprivi suddenly resigned at the end of October, the Foreign Office feared that "under any new Chancellor the forward Colonial Party will make themselves *more* disagreeable to us."[15] If this were the case, Rosebery was going to have a difficult time controlling Kimberley and the others who were beginning to despair of the understanding with Germany. He wrote, privately, and rather desperately, to the ambassador in Berlin, to try to discover whether the Germans were motivated by any particular ill-will towards him or his government.

Malet cautiously replied that he could discern nothing personal in German animosity for Britain, although the German government did dislike Home Rule, fearing that it would weaken Britain.[16] The kaiser was less delicate in revealing what was really at issue. Britain and Russia were becoming so cordial in their relations, he told the British military attaché, that he expected they would soon arrive at a mutual settlement of their differences. The price Britain would have to pay for this settlement would be the free passage of Russian warships through the Straits. Germany had no intention of acting on Britain's behalf: she would simply declare that she had no interest in the matter beyond securing a similar right of passage for the other powers. In other words, the real price of an Anglo-Russian entente would be the termination of the understanding between Britain and the Triple Alliance.

Hatzfeldt, the German ambassador in London, and a sincere exponent of an Anglo-German alliance, explained more clearly still the cause of Germany's distress. It could not be in the interests of Britain to see a junction of the French and Russian fleets in the Mediterranean because, he said, such a junction would probably result in Britain losing her position in that sea. A close understanding with Germany, however, would place the British in a position of almost absolute safety because Germany could always prevent France from attacking. In other words, the British ought not to be misled into believing that colonial agreements with Russia and France would afford them any real security; in the final analysis, the Dual Alliance was restrained only by the Triple. "However he was bound to say that after eight years' strenuous efforts to induce the Government of this country to come to a close understanding with the Triple Alliance, he found that his efforts in that direction were fruitless, and that Germany must not look for any effective co-operation from us."[17]

How did Hatzfeldt propose that Britain give proof of her good intentions? In the past she had shown a want of goodwill towards Germany in colonial matters, making it clear that Germany had nothing to expect from their friendship. "Why could not England let Germany have Samoa?" He confessed that Samoa was really of little value to Germany, but such an act, he argued, would show that Britain was inclined to consult her wishes. Colonial policy, as always, would effectively dramatize the nature of relationships in Europe.

The same principle applied to the future of southeast Africa, where "Germany could not, in the event of the Portuguese colonies being broken up, permit them to become a British territory."[18]

Kimberley resisted this last link in the chain of the argument because he perceived a substantial difference so far as Delagoa Bay was concerned. Giving Germany control of a point of such strategic significance would do more than symbolize an understanding in Europe: it would provide the Germans with a most valuable lever in future efforts to direct British policy. Conceding Delagoa Bay would not bring stability to the Anglo-German understanding; it would merely increase the ability of the Germans to control it. Kimberley officially recorded one of these considerations, noting only that Britain, like Germany, wished to maintain the current state of affairs in the Portuguese colonies, and that if doing so became impracticable, he was certain they would be able to arrange matters in a way conducive to the interests of both parties.

Kimberley's private rendering of the discussion was quite different from the official one. He bluntly told Hatzfeldt that "if the questions of the disposal of those colonies should ever require to be considered, this country with its great sea power would be able to speak the strongest word." What he obviously resented was Germany's ability, or attempt, to use her power in Europe to control British policy outside. When Hatzfeldt began to reply that Britain "could easily crush Germany at sea but," and paused, searching for an inoffensive phrase, Kimberley finished the sentence for him: "you would be able to do us much mischief elsewhere." Kimberley recognized the force of this argument, but he wished it to be clearly understood that, if German power was far greater than British by land, Britain's was "much greater by sea and that such language as 'permit' [was] altogether out of place."[19]

Language like Kimberley's would before long convince the Germans of the necessity of developing their power at sea. For almost a decade they had been attempting to manoeuvre the British into an European alliance; now, with what appeared to be a growing Anglo-Russian entente and with Anglo-French discussions of a general African settlement under way, that goal appeared farther away than ever. When reports of an Armenian massacre by the Turks reached the capitals of Europe, Germany might reasonably have expected that this event would reopen the Eastern Question and thereby force the British back into dependence upon the Triple Alliance. Instead, Britain and Russia immediately agreed that a full inquiry would be necessary in order to satisfy Christian opinion in Europe, and that France ought to be made a party to the inquiry. Equally important, they agreed that the enquiry was to be "non-political," that there must be no question of arousing Armenian hopes of independence. The three powers were resolved that the Eastern Question would not be reopened.[20]

The trend of European diplomacy seemed about to shift, and diplomats began to contemplate the possibility of some sort of general rearrangement. When the French ambassador in St Petersburg asked Lascelles for his opinion of the new Anglo-Russian friendship and the dissatisfaction it had aroused in Germany, the British ambassador replied that he had recently begun to hope that an understanding might be brought about. "A clear and frank understanding between England and Russia upon Asiatic questions would in my opinion go far to guarantee the Peace of the World." Moreover, "if France would also join in such an understanding it appeared to me that Peace would be secured for a very long period."[21] The British military attaché reported that Staal, the Russian ambassador to Britain, temporarily at home in St Petersburg, "was most anxious to get matters on a permanently friendly footing between England and Russia, in which case no other Power could cause them any uneasiness." The ambassador had concluded that the time had now arrived when something "solid" might be done.[22]

Although the possibility of a general settlement appeared to be a long way off, even the hint of it worried the lesser members of the Triple Alliance. Anglo-French discussions of an African settlement were proceeding slowly, partly because Hanotaux was ill, but the new French ambassador in London thought that their cooperation in the Armenian inquiry and the Sino-Japanese War was "an excellent beginning and a good augury for the future."[23] The Italians tacitly affirmed this forecast when they began to worry about the growing Anglo-French cordiality in Morocco, which was, they said, encouraging Spain to persevere in her francophile policy. They wished to know what course they ought to pursue in order "to avoid our common interests turning toward France instead of toward the Triple Alliance."[24] Kimberley merely assured them that there was nothing in Britain's Moroccan policy that could be turned to the detriment of Italy.[25]

The Italians were not alone in their fear that British diplomacy might be taking a new direction. When the Austrians heard that Kimberley was incensed by the provocative *Kölnische Zeitung* article on Delagoa Bay, they tried to warn the Germans of the possible consequences. Kálnoky told the German ambassador in Vienna that if they had ground for complaint against the British they ought to address themselves frankly to London, "instead of authorizing the appearance of mischievous articles in newspapers reputed semi-official."[26] A week later he told the Germans that if anything occurred to induce them to change their policy, he must be informed frankly of the causes of irritation against England.[27] Kimberley thought he knew what this meant: "What he fears is that Germany by her conduct will weaken the Triple Alliance and drive us into the arms of Russia and France."[28]

The mutual fears of Austria and Italy succeeded in moderating the tone of German discussions with Britain. The German foreign minister assured the British ambassador that he regarded the better feeling between Britain and Russia only as a further guarantee of European peace. Marschall, Malet reported, did not wish to carry the African affair any further, and he had "quite climbed down from any aggressive attitude towards us."[29] At the German Foreign Office, Holstein repeated to Malet the conclusion that an understanding between Britain and Russia was all right – if the Triple Alliance participated, and "if England was careful by flattery and sympathy to maintain Italy in its wake in all things which regarded the Mediterranean."[30]

Rosebery was convinced, in spite of all the turmoil surrounding the Congolese agreement, that the formula that had guided his policy since 1892 was still effective. He believed that Britain continued to hold the key to the situation, that the Triple Alliance, which depended on British cooperation for its existence, worked to check the imperial aspirations of France and Russia in Africa and Asia. Hence, in the midst of the Congolese imbroglio, "when Germany began to talk of being able to pursue a French policy in Africa, while maintaining the Triple Alliance in Europe, it was time to speak out, for this ignored the central keystone of the situation – through Italy, England."[31] It seemed to Rosebery that whenever the Germans threatened to cause any real trouble, as they had most recently done in the discussions on Delagoa Bay, he had only to tug on the Italian or Austrian strings in order to bring the alliance instrument back into tune.

Rosebery's explanation of the repeated displays of German animosity toward Britain demonstrated his limitations as foreign secretary and prime minister. He failed to see that Germany might not appreciate the fact that her historic mission was to safeguard the British Empire by remaining in a state of perpetual tension and balance with France and Russia. He failed to see that Germany might feel she commanded sufficient power to have real imperial aspirations of her own, and that she might be prepared to continue the British connection only if it assisted her in realizing these aspirations. He instead preferred to interpret German animosity as arising from the personal and political inclinations of the kaiser. In the midst of the

Congo affair he had drafted a letter to the queen explaining that his difficulties with Germany arose "from the German Emperor's hatred of the Bismarcks and His Majesty's belief that Lord Rosebery is closely allied with them."[32] He never sent the letter but he remained of that opinion. After the Delagoa Bay discussions he told Malet that "what I have always believed is also now avowed – that Berlin, or he who guides Berlin, has been actuated by hostility to the Liberal Government in England."[33]

This explanation displayed that propensity for taking any criticism of his policies as an attack upon himself which was a persistent feature of Rosebery's character; it also showed that he was now beginning to lose his grip. The bitterness stirred up by his accession to the leadership of the party was proving to be too much for him. Everyone seemed to be joining in the attack, from the Laboucheres to the Tories, from the Irish to the *Times*. His closest friends thought that he paid too much attention to opinion, that he should not bother himself about the newspapers. But they also realized that he lacked the moral stamina, the commitment to a cause, that would allow him to disregard criticism. Edward Hamilton predicted that, after the government fell, Rosebery would try to "cut the whole thing"; his excuse would be "that neither the party nor country have appreciated his policy."[34]

Rosebery's sensitivity to criticism further divided him from his cabinet. James Bryce, who had served Rosebery faithfully as his under-secretary in 1886, and who had combined with him in the Uganda debate, began working against him, encouraging Gladstone to speak out on the massacre of the Armenians. When the retired statesman did speak out, Bryce congratulated him for his "immense service in rousing the country to realize the horrors that have been committed and the duty that lies on us to make their recurrence impossible."[35] He was attempting to manipulate Gladstone in order to redirect the policy of the government of which Bryce was a part, because he believed that Rosebery was failing to take a firm enough line with the Turks.

Few movements could have hurt Rosebery more than a repeat performance of the old Bulgarian atrocities campaign conducted by the Grand Old Man; the moral of the tale was almost certain to be that Rosebery's authority as leader was no greater than Granville's had been in 1874.[36] The blow was even more personal because it appeared that Rosebery's abandonment of traditional liberal principles had necessitated Gladstone's intervention. Moreover, Rosebery's coolness to the campaign was part of his foreign policy: he was doing his best to continue to cooperate with Russia on this question as on others. He suggested to Kimberley, therefore, that they should try to counteract the influence of Gladstone's speeches by doing something to soothe the feelings of the sultan.

Kimberley refused. It would be more appropriate, he said, if the sultan "were to do something to soothe the feelings of those who are indignant at his proceedings."[37] Kimberley, convinced that the sultan himself was the author of the "merciless massacres," proposed that, rather than accept Rosebery's suggestion, they point out to the sultan that the only way he could meet the attacks on himself was to take every measure to ensure that the inquiry was thorough and impartial. "It is not our business as a Government to explain or defend Mr Gladstone's speeches, if they need any defence."[38] Kimberley did not feel threatened by the apparent revival of Gladstonian morality in the way that Rosebery did, and thus another rift was opened between the two men.

The difference between Rosebery and Kimberley over Armenia was not substantial, and it came to little because they were agreed that the essential element in their policy was cooperation with Russia. But their agreement hid the fact that they had reached this conclusion through quite different processes of logical thought. In essence, Kimberley looked forward to cooperating with Russia because it was Russia who had given the British Empire most of its difficulties since 1815. He attributed these difficulties largely to the complexities arising from local situations, especially to the ambitions of the men on the spot from both sides. If Russia were now prepared to assert some real control over her agents, and if she were prepared to abandon the dream of establishing control over the Ottoman and Chinese empires, and to engage in peaceful commercial competition with Britain instead, then a general policy of cooperation with her was both possible and desirable.

At bottom, Kimberley believed that colonial disputes could be resolved by goodwill and competent management. Rosebery, in contrast, believed that they would never be resolved, that they arose naturally from the logic of competition among great powers, that the best a British statesman could do was use, or manipulate, the balance of power in such a way as to restrain Britain's most powerful antagonists from pushing the competition too far. Kimberley's way of thinking led straight to Lansdowne and the Entente Cordiale; Rosebery's led nowhere, certainly not to the military conversations with France. His diplomacy, like Salisbury's, was a last futile effort to demonstrate that the British Empire could be defended in Europe without cost to Britain. The Crimean War, which Rosebery always regarded as a great mistake, had proved that British India could not be defended by military means. The understanding that he sought to establish with Russia was not an effort to permanently remove the possibility of conflict, but an attempt to show Germany that the British could always find room for colonial compromises, whereas Germany would always have to face the fundamental reality of her European geography: because she was caught in the middle her only compromise was to cease being a great power.

Roseberian diplomacy was designed to show the Germans that they had no choice but to play the role that had been scripted for them by the British. The talks with France in Africa were to be a minor scene in the drama. The Germans had threatened to cooperate with the French over the Congo, but the British, as Rosebery could show, would always be in a position to offer the French more. He had no intention of reaching a settlement with France because, in the long run, it would do nothing to resolve their conflict – frontiers were never permanent – while it might destroy the partnership with the Triple Alliance. He worried that Kimberley might not see this point, that the older man might be deceived into thinking that a general settlement with France, which temporarily reduced costs and tensions, might be of some permanent value. He warned Kimberley not to trust in any arrangements that rested on "Gallic good faith."[39]

It seemed to Rosebery that Kimberley was too much inclined to dismiss the troubles with France as arising from the hotheadedness of her agents outside Europe and to take French susceptibilities into account in his relations with other powers. When the Italians tried to arrange a deal with the British in Somaliland, whereby they would exchange Cape Guardafui for Zeyla, the strategically valuable port near the Straits of Bab-el-Mandeb, Kimberley turned them down because it "could not fail to have a most prejudicial effect on our negotiations with France on other African questions."[40] When the French tried to abandon the principle of a buffer state in their continuing discussions with the British on the fate of Siam, Kimberley argued that a common frontier would lead to complications because "there was always a danger that agents on the spot might stir up trouble."[41] Nor did the trouble always come from the French. "If your colonial officials are like our Consuls," he told Ripon, "I have no doubt our interests suffer from undue suspicion and jealousy of the French."[42]

Kimberley appeared to be working towards a redefinition of Britain's imperial policy whereby whoever promoted trouble was to be regarded as an enemy of Britain, while whoever promoted conciliation was to be regarded as a friend. Rosebery defined things differently, considering that the troubles caused by the Germans and Italians were trifling in comparison with the long-term threat posed by the French and Russians, no matter how cordial they might appear at any given moment. Rosebery, however, was in no position to exert his authority: he had temporarily lost control of Kimberley and the cabinet.

It was in this setting that, when Dilke and Labouchere on 18 February used an Egyptian incident to attack Rosebery in the Commons, and no minister rose to defend him, he immediately informed the cabinet of his intention to resign. "No man with a vestige of self respect could under the circumstances continue to hold the place I occupy."[43] No satisfactory explanation has been given for this sudden outburst. It appears, of course, to fit neatly into Rosebery's character. He could not resist the opportunity of reminding his colleagues that they had sought him, not the reverse. "All the prophecies with which I combated those who wished me to take the government have been fulfilled to the letter, and I rightly pay the price of having allowed myself to be overruled on that question."[44] Because the threat of resignation seems to be yet another manifestation of Rosebery's temperament, the tactical significance of the outburst has been overlooked. Rosebery later explained that it would, in fact, have been impossible for him to resign, "but it was the only way in which I could restore any discipline."[45]

Despite the general impression that Rosebery was forever threatening to resign, this occasion was in fact the first time he had actually gone farther than hint at the possibility. Kimberley, who recorded that the announcement came "like a thunderbolt," persuaded Rosebery to give up the idea. The remonstrance, he said, would clear the air and improve Rosebery's position by strengthening his authority. Privately, he recorded that his confidence in Rosebery's judgment had been seriously shaken: "His extreme sensitiveness to personal attacks indicates a certain weakness in his character."[46] Kimberley did not appreciate that Rosebery's manoeuvre was also directed at him, that he too would have to be more cautious in departing from Rosebery's policy if he wished to remain in office – the highest office he had achieved in a long public life.

It is impossible to tell how effective, or important, Rosebery's threat of resignation was in bringing Kimberley back onto the path of Roseberian diplomacy, because external events combined with the threat to dispel the idea of a general settlement with France. German intransigence had been one of the basic elements in moving Kimberley in the direction of France, but now the Germans became quiet. Malet reported from Berlin that the kaiser was taking particular pains to appear friendly, and this change in behaviour was soon reflected in renewed discussion of the future of Portuguese Africa.[47] Hatzfeldt suggested that Britain and Germany should have some understanding on the fate of the Portuguese colonies – should the Portuguese decide to relinquish them. Rosebery anxiously approved of the suggestions, and the first of several conversations between Kimberley and Hatzfeldt took place on 7 February 1895.

The conversations were never officially recorded and, because they never amounted to anything, they remained secret. Kimberley began by explaining, quite simply, that, if the Portuguese territories were to be divided between Britain and Germany, Britain would claim all territory south of the Zambezi River. A slight addition would be necessary to the north of the Zambezi, west of the Shire River, but Germany would receive all the land north of the Zambezi, bounded on the west by the Nyasa lake and river. The navigation of the Zambezi would be free to both powers. Hatzfeldt promised to consider these propositions and respond to them in due course.[48]

Hatzfeldt responded to Kimberley's opening position on 9 March, a week after the Austrian foreign minister reported his impression to the British ambassador that the kaiser was now showing moderation and good sense in foreign affairs, "especially on the value of thorough friendship with England."[49] Hatzfeldt proposed two alterations to Kimberley's position. First, Germany would expect to receive the territory to the north of the Zambezi and east of the Shire, which would give her a small piece of the British Nyassa Protectorate, including Blantyre and other places occupied by the Scottish Missions.[50] Second, Germany proposed that Delagoa Bay be neutralized. The first alteration was minor; the two men had no difficulty agreeing on the more basic proposition that the Zambezi be taken as the line of demarcation. The second alteration was more significant: it was Germany's pretensions there that had caused Kimberley to begin reassessing his colonial policy.

The Hatzfeldt-Kimberley talks never resulted in any agreement, partly because the British government fell before they could get much farther. Their significance was in giving some important reassurance to Kimberley at a critical juncture. He made no effort to hide from the Germans the fact that he considered Delagoa Bay to be important because of future British relations with the Transvaal. The majority of the population in the Boer republic, he pointed out to Hatzfeldt, were not of British origin and it was manifest "that the time might come when the Transvaal would practically cease to be a Dutch State." He did not mean to suggest that Britain would disturb the existing state of affairs, "but it might be looked upon as certain that the Transvaal would ultimately become closely connected with the British colonies, and possibly might some day become a portion of a South African Confederation."[51]

Kimberley had laid out Britain's design for the future of South Africa as clearly, and as candidly, as possible. He told Hatzfeldt that the proposed neutrality of Delagoa Bay was vague, and the German ambassador agreed, promising to respond with something more precise. He never did. Before the talks ended, however, the two sides did informally agree that they would do nothing to disturb the current state of affairs in the Portuguese colonies. Moreover, Kimberley declared that the Transvaal was within the British sphere of influence, and that this fact was shown unmistakably by Britain's treaty with the republic, which contained a condition that it could not conclude a treaty with a foreign power without the consent of the queen. "Count Hatzfeldt," Kimberley recorded, "took no objection to my statement."[52]

The talks with Hatzfeldt appear to have eased Kimberley's suspicion of an imminent German move in the direction of South Africa and, combined with French moves and Rosebery's threat of resignation, led him to reconsider his colonial policy. Because Kimberley thought in colonial terms, he considered the policy of others at the Cape, on the Nile, along the Indian frontier, to constitute the essence of their policy. This explains why, in the aftermath of the Congolese affair, when the French seemed ready to consider a general African settlement and when the Germans began to make difficulties about Delagoa Bay, Kimberley anticipated the possibility of a new course in British policy. By early 1895, however, the French had come nowhere close to accepting British predominance on the Nile, and such acceptance was essential if Kimberley was to agree to any general settlement. By early March, when Hatzfeldt urged the British to make a proposal respecting the territory to the north of the German Protectorate in Togoland, Kimberley despaired of a settlement with France; he had, he said, made an offer to the French respecting this territory, but it was contingent upon a settlement of the question of the Nile Basin. "As no such settlement had been arrived at, I considered that our offer had fallen to the ground, and I was quite willing to endeavour to come to an arrangement with Germany."[53]

The refusal of the French to recognize the British position on the Nile began to dishearten Kimberley, but their actions in Siam caused him to give up hope in them altogether. Reports began to come in that made it clear that the French were preparing to abandon the principle of a buffer state agreed to during the crisis of 1893, a principle that Kimberley considered essential. The British minister in Siam reported the French to be fortifying a post at Chieng Kong on the left bank of the Mekong, and urged that Britain ought to respond by occupying Kengtung.[54] Kimberley replied by asking the India Office to dispatch a political officer, escorted by a military force, to Kyaing Chiang, "to leave no doubt whatever as to the British supremacy over that state"; this force, he said, "should remain there permanently."[55]

Rosebery seized the opportunity to convince Kimberley that the French attitude on the Nile and in Siam was not mere coincidence, but an accurate representation of enduring French policy. The opportunity became still more attractive when news reached London that a French force had "deliberately marched into the heart of our Niger sphere." Kimberley was persuaded to act. "We must demand their withdrawal," he told Rosebery, adding, however, that "I think the consequences if they do not comply, may be so grave that it ought to be referred to the Cabinet."[56] Rosebery wished to avoid a cabinet meeting; it would be better to present his colleagues with an accomplished fact. He suggested, therefore, that Kimberley give the French the opportunity of contradicting the news, and "I should be inclined to add that this intelligence coupled with that from Siam has caused a painful impression on yourself and will when known make an impression on the public which you can scarcely bring yourself to measure."[57]

The manoeuvre succeeded. "Kimberley," reported Rosebery's private secretary, "has wound himself up to use the most vigorous language in his vocabulary."[58] The official record of the conversation, Kimberley explained to Rosebery, would not contain all of the strong language that he had used, because what he had said was not to be regarded as a formal communication, but he had referred to the Niger, the Nile, and Siam.[59] The connections between Africa and Asia had been made; Kimberley had committed himself to a strong policy and thus a debate in cabinet had been avoided. Rosebery, doing his best to guide affairs from his sick-bed, could feel reasonably satisfied that he had succeeded in moving Kimberley back onto the proper course.

Events assisted Rosebery in reestablishing control. In addition to the reports of a French expedition to the Niger, rumours now reached London of a similar expedition to the Nile, and Percy Anderson, who thought it was "pretty plain sailing" for the British on the Niger, was much less at ease concerning the Nile, where he thought "we may expect to hear of their appearance any day."[60] On 28 March Kimberley warned the French ambassador that the rumour was very disquieting and that it would probably be referred to in the House of Commons that evening. It was. Kimberley had already instructed Edward Grey, the parliamentary under-secretary for foreign affairs, to be prepared to use firm language if he were questioned about French encroachments in West Africa; but he was questioned, instead, about the Nile. Grey afterwards explained that he decided, on the spot, to transfer to the Nile the firm language he had intended to use regarding the Niger. "The advance of a French Expedition under secret instructions right from the other side of Africa into a territory over which our claims have been known for so long," he declared, would be "an inconsistent and unexpected act."[61]

The importance of the Grey declaration, and much of the controversy that surrounded it, hinged on an additional clause. Not only would an expedition be inconsistent and unexpected, "but it must be perfectly well known to the French Government that it would be an unfriendly act and would be so viewed by England."[62] Did Grey thereby threaten the French with war? Ronald Robinson and John Gallagher have argued that he did; "unfriendly act," they said, "was a strident declaration that the ownership of a desert might be worth a war."[63] Contemporaries were less certain. Harcourt denounced Grey, but said only that the speech was "menacing," "a deliberate tirade."[64] Kimberley doubted that an "unfriendly act" would necessarily be treated as an hostile one: "I should have thought that its meaning must be construed by the context, like that of ordinary words."[65] In Kimberley's opinion, the declaration was sufficiently vague to accomplish its real purpose: to warn off the French without committing the British to any definite course of action.

Rosebery and Kimberley entirely approved of the declaration, although there is no reason to doubt Grey's explanation that he made his decision on the spot. He did not have to be given explicit instructions beforehand because he knew what was expected of him. When Rosebery congratulated him on the speech, he replied, "I did not doubt that you would approve of the line which I took, but I had to choose the occasion and I am delighted to know that you approve that too."[66] Kimberley, the day after the speech, told Rosebery that he thought the speech excellent, "combining prudence with firmness of language in a remarkable degree." He regretted that strong words were likely to excite angry passions, "but I am not sure that the time had not come for a little plain speaking."[67]

In the controversy that has surrounded the Grey declaration, the most interesting aspect of the incident has been overlooked: it was a typical piece of Roseberian diplomacy in the way that it attempted to compensate for local weakness by applying the grand strategy of world politics. The Congolese agreement was one attempt to overcome British weakness in the Nile Basin, the Grey declaration another.

The only barriers standing in the way of a French advance on the Nile were the tribes of the Bahr Al-Ghazal and the Dervishes. The tribes were small and hostile to one another and therefore could not be combined effectively against the French; a small Belgian force had already pushed its way up through them almost to Darfur. The Dervishes had never effectively occupied the country and they were fully occupied in dealing with their own rebellious tribes. Two weeks after the Grey declaration, a report concluded that "the French could, with ease, occupy the Bahr Al-Ghazal," and, this accomplished, "they would have little or no difficulty" in reaching the Nile.[68]

The failure of the Congolese agreement had already shown the futility of conjuring up a Belgian buffer – but what other possibilities were there? Rosebery consistently ruled out the reconquering of the Sudan as beyond the realm of practical politics: the government lacked the requisite forces and the cabinet would balk at both the cost and the possible complications.[69] Faced with this situation, the British had to rely upon the dark threats conjured up in the vague phrase "unfriendly act." Rosebery had already successfully used a variation of this tactic during the Siam crisis, when he had threatened to conduct a "silent war" against the French all over the world. In other words, British weakness on the spot, whether it be in Siam or in the Nile Basin, must not be misconstrued by the French as adding up to weakness generally, because British naval power would, if the question were put to the test, be sufficient to overcome any temporary military advantages that the French might enjoy.

This was the lesson of an elaborate memorandum drawn up in the Intelligence Division of the War Office in April 1894, and which had been secretly sent to Rosebery eighteen days before the Grey declaration. The author, Hubert Foster, whose conclusions were supported by the head of his division, Colonel Chapman, argued that the new naval act would enable the British to take the offensive against the French in the Mediterranean in the event of war, refuting the claim of those who continued to argue that the British would have to evacuate that sea. "Our command of the Mediterranean in war," he argued, "will cause considerable injury to France. It will cut off her communications with her African possessions and will threaten those with Corsica."[70] It would also do great injury to French trade: in 1891 that passing through Gibraltar amounted to £25 million, through Suez to £26 million, with £34 million in local Mediterranean trade, chiefly with Africa. This memorandum, sent on to Kimberley, and almost certainly seen by Grey before his declaration, gave the British the confidence they needed in taking a firm line with the French.

The missing factor in this equation was Russia, and Rosebery intended that it should remain missing. If France ever succeeded in transforming the alliance into one that worked outside of Europe, the consequences to Britain could only be guessed at. Achieving good relations with Russia was an essential component of Rosebery's diplomacy, and, by the time of the Grey declaration, he had apparently succeeded in his aim. "Our relations with Russia," he had told a British ambassador in January, "are, I honestly believe, more cordial than at any period since the German war."[71] On 11 March, after more than two years of negotiations, the Pamirs agreement was finally signed, delimiting the British and Russian frontiers in the Hindu Kush.[72] Throughout the Sino-Japanese War, Rosebery and Kimberley had consistently aimed at acting in conjunction with Russia, and so far they had succeeded. When, a fortnight before the Grey declaration, the government decided to send a relief expedition to Chitral, near the new frontier, where a small British party was besieged by a local military adventurer, Kimberley was careful to assure the Russians in advance that the expedition was intended only to relieve the besieged party, and not to remain there permanently.

The moment was, therefore, a propitious one for the British to threaten the French with global consequences. The premise behind the Grey declaration was that the French colonial party could be restrained only by the application of world policy, an essential component of which was good relations with Russia. "Were a French expedition to appear now upon the Nile," Rosebery told Dufferin a few days after the declaration, "I could not answer for the consequences."[73] But the French, in the immediate aftermath of the event, reacted moderately. Hanotaux, Dufferin reported, gave a "temperate and carefully worded reply" to a question asked in the French senate on the subject of the declaration.[74] Rosebery's strategy seemed to have succeeded.

It is usually assumed that by this time, a year after the formation of the Rosebery government, and following the disasters associated with the Congolese agreement, Harcourt had established his ascendancy in the cabinet to the point where he was able to obstruct the diplomacy of Rosebery and Kimberley. This is not true. The responsibility for their failures, and successes, must go to the two men who were conducting British foreign policy. When Harcourt attempted to mobilize the cabinet against the Grey declaration, which, having been absent from the House, he had read "with infinite suspicion and regret," he failed.[75] Only one resignation was threatened at the cabinet meeting, and that came from Morley, not Harcourt. Morley backed down when he was assured that the sphere Grey had claimed to protect was Egyptian, and not British.[76] Rosebery, during the evening after the cabinet on 30 March, "was wonderfully cheerful and indeed quite like himself at dinner."[77]

Harcourt had seen in the Grey declaration another opportunity to try to establish some control over foreign policy, indicating that he had not yet succeeded in this aim. He told Kimberley that he wished to see, in advance, all answers to important questions of foreign policy before they were given in the House of Commons. He would also undertake, on behalf of the cabinet, to make all the important statements in debates on foreign affairs.[78] Kimberley was generally prepared to assent to these propositions, but Rosebery was not. The prime minister was prepared to allow Harcourt to read statements directly drawn up or resolved upon in cabinet, no more. Harcourt could not be given authority to speak on behalf of the government where foreign policy was concerned, because "there is a deep-seated and radical difference between Harcourt and myself on questions of foreign policy."[79] If Harcourt spoke without prior consultation and approval, he could express nothing more than his personal opinions; "It is true that Edward Grey made his statement without consulting me; but that was unnecessary as he knows the views I hold and the policy I maintain ... Harcourt knows them too, but the difference between them is that Grey shares them and Harcourt does not."[80]

Rosebery's control of foreign policy did not weaken during the last few months of life remaining to his government; in fact, it grew stronger. Harcourt failed once again to establish any real authority. With the Grey affair practically at an end, Harcourt had launched into the affairs of China and Japan, writing a letter to Kimberley, "which displays in its worst form his combined ignorance and arrogance in relation to foreign affairs."[81] Kimberley complained that Harcourt was persisting in his efforts to play the part of joint prime minister and he worried that the continued bickering this created would lead to drifting in foreign policy. Rosebery commiserated with Kimberley and assured him that "we are approaching the parting of the ways because I cannot compromise on these vital matters." He reminded his foreign secretary, however, that "our policy has prevailed, and has been satisfactory and efficient." Someone who was determined to cling to office might have allowed Harcourt the authority he sought, but Rosebery was not so determined, in fact he viewed "the approach of the critical moment with a certain sense of relief."[82]

Harcourt succeeded in making the business of government a less than pleasurable experience for Rosebery and Kimberley, but this was his only success. He never succeeded in moving Rosebery from the course he had set for Britain in foreign affairs. In the immediate aftermath of the government's collapse, and in the years that followed, it became convenient for Rosebery and his supporters to blame the failures of the government on Harcourt, but historians need not accept the verdict of a self-interested party.

Because historians have regarded the confrontation between Rosebery and Harcourt as the most prominent feature of the Liberal governments of 1892–5, they have overlooked the fact that Rosebery's foreign policy was in the process of falling apart in the last two months of the government's life. It fell apart because Rosebery, who had staked almost everything on his policy of cooperating with Russia, backed away when the Russians attempted to push the policy to what they regarded as its logical conclusion in the Far East.

After months of fitful negotiations, the Japanese finally presented, on 4 April, their conditions of peace to the Chinese. The conditions were not light. Korea was to be made independent, with Japan as the predominant power; the Liaotung Peninsula, Formosa, and the Pescadores were all to be ceded to Japan; there was to be a new commercial treaty in which Japan would receive most-favoured nation treatment; and there was to be an indemnity of £40 million.[83] Russia regarded the terms as too harsh and immediately asked Britain whether she would cooperate in moderating them.[84]

The Russian question posed a real dilemma for Rosebery and Kimberley. Throughout the Sino-Japanese War they had been extremely careful to work in the closest cooperation with Russia, but the situation had now been changed dramatically as a result of the Japanese victory and the proposed conditions of peace. If the British did as the Russians wished, and advised the Japanese to moderate the terms, they might have to act; "I do not think we could accept a rebuff from Japan by a refusal to listen to it," Kimberley argued.[85] Great powers cease to be great when lesser powers stop listening to them; the British could not afford such a blow in the Far East, where so much of their power rested on their prestige. The advice the British government was receiving from Japan suggested that the Japanese would not listen; the military party was reported to regard the terms as too moderate already. It seemed to Rosebery and Kimberley that to do as the Russians wished would end in some kind of armed confrontation with the Japanese.

"On the whole my mind *inclines* to non-interference," Kimberley concluded, but he preferred to leave the final decision to Rosebery.[86] Rosebery had no difficulty with the principle involved: "We cannot go to war with Japan unless she directly and immediately threatens British interests." But he failed to appreciate what the application of this principle would do to his understanding with Russia, and he deceived himself into believing that soothing words could be used as an effective substitute for action. Rosebery's decision not to act was eagerly approved by the cabinet, so he was not restricted by any political opposition.[87] He proposed that they communicate the decision to Russia with boundless expressions of regret that Britain did not feel justified in resorting to force of arms, without which intervention would be futile. "This is the language I should use at St Petersburg. Moreover I should not shut the door with a clang, or indeed shut it at all."[88] On Kimberley's behalf he drafted a letter that emphasized their desire to continue the policy of close cooperation with Russia in the Far East.[89]

Kimberley, who by this time was becoming a cipher, read Rosebery's letter to the Russian ambassador. Staal was not persuaded by the soothing words, and warned Kimberley that the British attitude must have a most unfavourable effect on the understanding with Russia. The anglophobe party would now exclaim, "just what we always told you, that England would leave us in the lurch whenever a pinch came."[90] The Russians had proved receptive to Rosebery's policy of cooperation in the Near East and central Asia because they had shifted the focus of their ambitions to the Far East. Their great fear now was that the Japanese would manage to establish themselves in a position that would enable them to dominate China before the Russians were in a position to stop them. Quite abruptly, then, an understanding with the British, which rested upon Russia limiting her activities in the Near East and central Asia but which did not provide for any positive, coordinated action in the Far East, appeared to be a very bad bargain for the Russians indeed.

The Russians had only twenty thousand men at Vladivostock and could transport only another nine thousand by September. They were not in a position to fight the Japanese on land; nor was their naval force believed capable of dealing a crushing blow. If the British joined the Russians, however, the Japanese would find it difficult to resist the demand for more moderate terms.[91] If there was any substance to the Anglo-Russian understanding, this was the moment for it; when it failed to materialize, the Russians were greatly annoyed. Rosebery looked hard to find some way of satisfying them: "We must remember Armenia and Central Asia even in the far East." He suggested, therefore, that they join the Russians in taking up a Chinese proposal to prolong the armistice, but only "on the footing that it is a concession made to regain the confidence and cordiality of Russia."[92] This suggestion was as far as he was prepared to go; he refused to act on behalf of the Russians if doing so involved even the slightest risk to Britain.

When Rosebery saw the Russian understanding begin to dissolve before his eyes, he imagined that he could restore it through personal diplomacy. Kimberley had again retreated to the country at a critical moment, and Rosebery complained that, excellent as Kimberley was, "he is apt to take things too easily and he lacks initiative power."[93] The next day, on 13 April, Rosebery met with Staal to deny that he had dropped the Russians or left them in the lurch. "We most earnestly longed to continue the harmonious understanding between the two Powers," he assured the ambassador, and he was prepared to act with the Russians "if a practicable opportunity offered."[94] But he offered nothing tangible. The best he could do, a few days later, was suggest that the powers request an authentic copy of the draft treaty, a rather feeble effort at cooperation. His personal intervention accomplished nothing; it was policy, not management, that was creating the difficulty.[95]

It is tempting to see in Rosebery's Far Eastern policy a fundamental change in direction, one that anticipated the Anglo-Japanese Alliance of 1904, but to do so would be to credit Rosebery with a prescience that was not his. Rosebery and Kimberley – especially Kimberley – had been impressed by the demonstration of Japanese power, but they never came close to suggesting that they should henceforth rely upon her in the Far East and in doing so abandon China or the understanding with Russia. No one, or at least no one who counted, promoted anything like a Japanese alliance. Harcourt, who regarded Japan as the "rising power in the east," was concerned only that Britain not intervene against her and thereby enable Russia to pose as her friend.[96] British thinking was defensive and cautious.

The reason that Rosebery refused to cooperate as fully with Russia as was necessary to save the understanding had less to do with guesses concerning the future of Japan than with assumptions about the ambitions of Russia. The advice of the ambassador in St Petersburg, Sir Frank Lascelles, was pertinent in forming these assumptions. He advised that it would be a mistake to adopt a policy that had the effect of turning Japan into an enemy, and yet he did not believe that Japan was a match for Russia, nor did he forecast that she would be in the future. He assumed that Russian opposition to the cession of the Liaotung Peninsula arose from "the hope that she may some day get possession of the territory in question herself."[97] If the British acted as the Russians wished, they would, in effect, be undertaking the risk of alienating the Japanese for the sake of Russian territorial ambitions in China.

Rosebery's aversion to assisting Russian designs actively in China explains why he was prepared to risk the understanding he had worked so long to achieve. The understanding was designed to fulfil two closely related purposes: first, to divide the Franco-Russian alliance and thereby deprive France of Russian assistance in Africa and Asia; second, to demonstrate to Germany and the Triple Alliance that Britain could secure her imperial interests without relying upon them. If the Russians were able to use the understanding to assist them in furthering their imperial ambitions in the Far East, then Rosebery would be risking failure in both his purposes, because the Russians would have demonstrated that Britain lacked the power to resist becoming the cat's-paw of Russia in Asia.

Rosebery was not prepared, however, to abandon Russia in favour of Japan because he was uncertain about the balance of power in Asia, and because he feared that Japanese ambitions might be as damaging as Russian ones. For a moment, when a report of a secret Sino-Japanese alliance was received in London, it appeared that the Japanese were establishing a virtual protectorate on the mainland.[98] The report proved false and the immediate worry passed, but Rosebery concluded that it was practically impossible to assess accurately the new situation as "we have not really sufficient data for the purpose." It was clear only that the settlement of the Sino-Japanese War had opened a new Eastern Question, "pregnant with possibilities of a disastrous kind, and it might indeed result in an Armageddon between the European Powers struggling for the ruins of the Chinese Empire."[99]

These fears moved Rosebery, paradoxically perhaps, back in the direction of Russia. He continued to act, in central Asia and the Near East, as if the understanding had not been shaken to its foundations. There was no shift in British policy so far as the Armenian question was concerned. More strikingly, the difficulties with Russia made him more conciliatory on the Indian frontier rather than less. When the government of India proposed to establish a permanent garrison in Chitral following the relief of the besieged party there, he warned that this might not be possible and that it would be necessary to give assurances to the Russians even if the troops remained for only a few months.[100] When Lascelles proposed, in a private letter to Rosebery (another indication of the decline of Kimberley), that they might approach Japan "as a friend" and point out to her that the Russian objections to her possession of the Liaotung Peninsula were "serious and reasonable," Rosebery at once took up the suggestion, hoping, as Lascelles had suggested, that "it might do something towards soothing the ruffled feelings of the Russians.[101]

Thus, when Russia, France, and Germany combined to insist that Japan give up the claim to the Liaotung Peninsula, and Japan turned to Britain for assistance, she received none. The principle, Rosebery repeated in a memorandum to Kimberley, remained the same: "We cannot embroil ourselves in the quarrels of others unless our interests imperatively demand it." The practical question was how to apply this principle without alienating either Russia or Japan, or both. "Japan," he concluded, "cannot receive our support and cannot need our advice. She can judge quite as acutely as we can what is the course for her to adopt, and has I doubt not long ago decided it, for this war is directed against Russia more than against China." But Rosebery did instruct Kimberley to emphasize the advice he had given along the lines suggested by Lascelles, that Japan could moderate her conditions after such a successful war without sacrificing her honour, "and that we are convinced that Russia at any rate is in earnest."[102] In other words, if Japan did not back down over the peninsula, Russia, possibly joined by France and Germany, would fight and Britain would do nothing to aid Japan.

Two days after Kimberley had assured the Japanese ambassador that Britain would not assist Japan in her argument with the three powers, the Japanese offered to give up most of the Liaotung Peninsula, keeping only Port Arthur and the immediate vicinity.[103] The three powers refused to accept this compromise, however, and Japan was forced to give in altogether – although she did increase the indemnity somewhat in lieu of the peninsula.[104] Rosebery had successfully avoided a situation in which Britain would be drawn into acting on behalf of either Russia or Japan in a partition of the Chinese Empire. But at what cost? The understanding with Russia, so important to his world policy, had fallen apart in the Far East. Could it continue to work elsewhere?

The events of the crisis in the Far East emboldened the French. In January their representative on the Siamese Buffer Commission had claimed a tract of territory on the left bank of the Mekong that the British regarded as their own by virtue of its being a part of Kyaing Tong. Immediately following the successful Franco-Russian representations at Tokyo, the French ambassador in Britain took up the claim, declaring that "he could not admit that England had any right to interfere with it."[105] He then asked Kimberley if it were true that a British force was being sent to occupy Mong Singh; when Kimberley replied that it was, Courcel insisted that the British were disturbing the state of affairs that they had agreed to maintain until the commission reported. Clearly, the first repercussion of the rupture in the Anglo-Russian understanding was to put in jeopardy the creation of a buffer between British India and French Indo-China.

Two weeks after the conversation with Courcel, the French

government gave official notice that they considered the occupation of Mong Singh to violate the conditions that had been a prerequisite to the establishment of the buffer commission. The British action, they declared, "compromised the principle of the formation of a neutral territory or buffer state between the British and French possessions, and rendered it almost impossible to resume the consideration of such an arrangement."[106] They proposed instead to adopt the Mekong as the line dividing British and French possessions in Siam. They felt they were now in a position to kill the buffer idea, which they had never liked and which they had consented to only when Rosebery threatened them with war. Perhaps a coterminous frontier with both the Russians and the French in Asia would be the unforeseen result of Rosebery's policy in the Sino-Japanese War.

Rosebery became almost desperate in his attempt to repair the damage to the understanding with Russia that had resulted from his refusal to assist her in the Far East. He became more conscious than ever in trying to keep in step with Russia in Armenia. When the Gladstone-Bryce wing of the Liberal party began to insist on stronger reforms than those being proposed by the British, Russian, and French ambassadors, Kimberley feared that adopting this line might risk the achievement of any reform.[107] Rosebery cared nothing for the reforms; his only concern was to avoid another rupture with Russia. "We must not merely run any risk of the rupture of concerted action," he told Kimberley, "but, under present circumstances, not give an opening for either of the other Powers to back out."[108]

Acting with Russia in the Armenian inquiry meant going against the wishes of an important section of the Liberal party. When Kimberley unofficially put the Bryce scheme forward to test the Russian reaction, the reply came back that it would mean too much interference in the internal affairs of the Ottoman Empire.[109] By the end of May Lascelles was warning that, were a general insurrection to break out in Armenia, the Russians might intervene on behalf of the Turks.[110] If Rosebery were determined to persist in his efforts to act with Russia in the Near East – and he was – he would have to do so against the opposition of an important wing of his party.

The other arena of cooperation with Russia, central Asia, proved even more troublesome, although for different reasons. The trouble here came from the government of India, which resolved to stay in Chitral, even after the besieged British force there had been relieved. Their determination to stay arose from two separate, although related, considerations. One argument maintained that as any Anglo-Russian understanding was bound to be short-lived, the British must not pass up any opportunity of improving their position on the frontier. This argument was expressed most stridently by Roberts's successor as commander-in-chief of the Indian army, Sir George White, who looked to events in the Far East to support his position. Because of Britain's refusal to cooperate with the Russians there, the Russian press had started to talk about making a move on the Indian frontier. White argued that the Russians, who realized how weak Britain was on the frontier, could use this weakness to cajole Britain into supporting them in the Far East.

White, in other words, was clever enough to turn Rosebery's own arguments against him: Russia would use the frontier to compel Britain to act as her pawn in her version of world policy. The only way for Britain to avoid this subordinate role was to make the frontier sufficiently strong that Russia could not threaten it. "We shall never," White declared, "be at rest after the Russian frontier has been advanced to a line within 50 miles of Chitral as long as that state is in the keeping of others or is open to Russian aggression without involving an unmistakeable casus belli with England."[111] According to White, as long as Chitral – or an entity like Chitral – was permitted to retain some sort of fuzzy, independent existence, Russia could continue to brandish the frontier as a weapon in order to compel Britain to submit to her policy elsewhere.

White's arguments were the traditional stuff of the forward school, and as such were easily pigeon-holed by the men at the Indian and Foreign offices in London. Putting arguments in an old pigeon-hole has the great virtue of making it possible to avoid thinking about the issues anew. Rosebery, Kimberley, and Fowler knew a "forward" argument when they saw it, and were thereby able to dispose of it in a single sentence. More troublesome was the position taken by the viceroy, the earl of Elgin, who insisted that the issues be reconsidered. "Where general lines of policy such as is represented by 'Forward' are concerned," he wrote to complain, "there is a tendency of Anglo Indians at home to deal with them from the standpoint where they knew them and not always give full weight to the intervening events which we who are responsible for the present cannot ignore."[112]

Elgin could cause Rosebery to think, because, after all, he was Rosebery's creature. Elgin had not wished to go to India; Rosebery had talked him into it. Rosebery had looked for a Liberal with whom he could work, one who was known to dislike the pretensions of the forward school, one who was capable of reversing the Lansdowne-Roberts policy of recent years. What, then, had happened?

Elgin insisted that he was as opposed to the frontier policy of Roberts as he had ever been. What he claimed to fear, what, he argued, had changed his mind once he was actually in India, was the threat from below. The entire British position in India, he now saw, rested on Britain's reputation for honesty and fearlessness. She had guaranteed to Kashmir the rights to Chitral: if she were incapable of, or unwilling to, enforce such a guarantee she would suffer a heavy blow to the prestige upon which her rule rested. Men in London, he insisted, were incapable of appreciating the weight of this argument.

Rosebery and Kimberley persisted in their policy nevertheless, concluding that Elgin had proved to be too weak to resist the domination of his military advisers. In the long run the argument counted for little, because Salisbury reversed Rosebery's decision on Chitral after the government fell in June.[113] But the arguments that Rosebery privately offered to Elgin, even after the government's fall, testify to the sincerity of his views. "While you are guarding against Russia on every peak of the Hindu Kush, a great military &. in these matters most unveracious and unscrupulous Government is about to establish a coterminous frontier with you – I mean France. While France is menacing you and menacing you in strict alliance with Russia it would take much to make me agree to any such dispersal of force as is involved in the occupation of Chitral."[114]

Either Rosebery was overstating his case for dramatic effect, or he had come to recognize that his policy had failed. Throughout his term in office, he had steadfastly refused to accept the idea that the Franco-Russian alliance was aimed at Britain; now, in the final days of his government, he was prepared to argue that the alliance was "strict" and "menacing" – in order to defend his policy in India. But Rosebery, like all diplomats, used any arguments that seemed suited to his purpose. He had used this particular argument before, once to persuade the government of India to follow his lead in Siam, and once again to convince the government of Britain of the necessity of an increased ship-building program. In neither instance did he truly believe that the British Empire was immediately endangered by the Franco-Russian alliance. The danger he was concerned with was at once more subtle and more frightening: a working arrangement between France and Russia outside Europe would almost certainly compel Britain to join the Triple Alliance, wherein she would become a subordinate partner in a continental arrangement.

It is doubtful that Rosebery believed the Franco-Russian alliance had been transformed into a strict one that menaced Britain, but his foreign policy was falling to pieces nevertheless. The next round of the crisis in the Far East, the negotiations for a loan to China with which she would pay the indemnity to Japan, provided the final link in the chain of events that precipitated the resignation of Rosebery's government.

After the failure to cooperate with Russia against Japan over the terms of the peace with China, Rosebery was anxious to avoid any move that might further antagonize Russia, as he had earlier shown himself to be in Armenia and over Chitral. Therefore, when discussions of a loan began, he and Kimberley tried to avoid taking a leading role, fearing that such participation would convince Russia that they were trying for a diplomatic victory in China. They were also concerned, however, that Russia and France should not become responsible for the entire amount of the loan, as this responsibility would supply them with a diplomatic pretext for joint intervention should the Chinese fail to keep up the payments – a distinct possibility. The British ambassador at Peking assured them that the latter concern was unwarranted; the Tsungli Yamen, he said, had promised him that they had no intention of excluding Britain.[115] This assurance appeared to satisfy Rosebery, who, for the sake of relations with Russia, preferred to leave the negotiations in the hands of private interests. "We do not wish to interfere for or against," he concluded when an English financier sought government support for bringing out the entire loan in England.[116]

A century of commercial supremacy misled Rosebery into believing that Britain would participate in the loan, regardless of the politics involved. Kimberley, too, assured his ambassadors that it was inconceivable that a loan of sufficient size to pay the indemnity could be raised without British participation.[117] Both thought it was possible to assuage Russian feelings by removing the British government from the loan competition, but they never imagined that this would mean the exclusion of Britain. "We cannot with our enormously preponderant commercial interests in China," Kimberley told Rosebery, "afford to be left out in the cold."[118] But left out in the cold they were. Russia, France, and Germany negotiated a loan of £16 million for the Chinese. The three powers, and especially Russia, it was reported from Peking, had rendered China such a service by their diplomatic intervention over the terms of peace "that Chinese eyes blinded by glare see nothing else."[119]

Now Kimberley began to reverse his ground. He appealed to the Japanese to accept the opening of more ports and rivers in exchange for some of the indemnity. Otherwise, he argued, China would be thrown "into great difficulties and a position of subservience to the three Powers."[120] The revolution in Britain's Far Eastern policy had begun at last. It was clear that if Britain wished to act with Russia in the Far East she must do so as a subordinate – a formula that no responsible Englishman was prepared to accept. The balance of power had long worked to Britain's advantage in Europe, so perhaps it could be made to work in Asia as well. Kimberley now began to refer to Japan as Britain's "natural ally" against Russia.[121] When the Japanese minister in London informed him that his government hesitated to withdraw its troops before effecting the necessary reforms, Kimberley spontaneously suggested that before withdrawing the government might ask for an engagement on the part of Russia, "not to interfere with the independence and integrity of that country."[122]

Kimberley seemed prepared to undertake the new course necessary in the Far East. Rosebery was not. He recognized that such a dramatic shift in policy would have repercussions throughout the world, that the management of these repercussions would require great patience and energy. He did not have much of either left. When the government was defeated on a minor issue in the House of Commons, he seized the opportunity to resign. His political career – although not his political life – was over.

"Genius," Rosebery had written as a young man, "appears to me to be a divine impulse compelling a person to labour in a particular manner for which he is preeminently adapted."[123] His time in office proved that, by his own definition, he was no genius. He had laboured mightily in the service of the one cause to which he could truly devote his energies – the British Empire. Nor had he laboured in vain: the position of the empire was no weaker than it had been when he took office. But neither was it any stronger: his policy was falling to pieces in the spring of 1895. His great idea, a friendly understanding with Russia that would simultaneously reduce the threat from France and bring the Germans to order, had proved unworkable. It took a decade and an engagement in the Tsushima Strait to make it workable – and then it became twisted beyond recognition.

Rosebery left office a tired, dispirited man. The aura of failure surrounded him ever after. From time to time he would scale new rhetorical heights and the aura would temporarily dissipate; but whenever the talk became serious, whenever a return to power seemed a practical possibility, he would draw back instinctively, as from a flame. He knew how lofty had been his ambitions. "Life," he had written, "is a toiling up a ladder."[124] He knew how far he had failed to climb. He went back to his horses, his books, and his solitude. Perhaps these were what he had really wanted.

CHAPTER EIGHT

Rosebery and the Primacy of Diplomatic History

If I regarded the Empire simply as a means of painting so much of the world red, or as an emporium for trade, I should not ask you to work for it. The land hunger is apt to become land fever, and land fever is apt to breed indigestion, while trade, however important and desirable in itself, can never be the sole foundation of an empire. Empires founded on trade alone must irresistibly crumble. But the Empire that is sacred to me is sacred for this reason, that I believe it to be the noblest example yet known to mankind of free, adaptable, just government ... I ask you, then, to keep this motive before you of public duty and public service, for the sake of the Empire, and also on your own account. You will find it, I believe, the most ennobling human motive that can guide your actions.

Presidential Address, Associated Society of University of Edinburgh (1898)

Historians today are widely agreed that "pure" diplomatic history, history "from the documents," should be permitted to die a natural death. The assumption underlying this agreement is that diplomatic documents, and probably diplomacy itself, are superficial: if we are to understand historical relations among states, or even the foreign policy of a single state, we must go deeper. We must, according to the modern view, analyse at least the social structure, political arrangements, and economy of the state under examination if we are to make sense of its diplomacy. It was with these modern views in mind that this study was undertaken.

I was convinced that my pursuit of Rosebery would lead me far beyond the man himself, to financiers and merchants, to admirals and generals, to politicians and academics. They are certainly there. The Rosebery Papers clearly reveal a man who corresponded, talked, walked, dined, and even bet with men from all these sections of society. And yet, try as desperately to resist as I could, I gradually realized that to shift my attention to them was to miss the point. The point, I finally concluded, was that in late nineteenth-century Britain the foreign secretary made foreign policy.

This is a simple conclusion to a complicated subject and therefore requires some elaboration. To argue that Rosebery made his foreign policy is not to argue that he controlled events, or that he stood outside his society. Like all diplomatists, he spent most of his time responding to events, and, like all men, he was a creature of his time and place. Like most men born to his station in life, he believed in social inequality, especially in the duty of the governing class to govern. Like most Liberals of his age, he believed in the future, in the ability of men to take charge of their own destiny; he believed in progress, in the capacity of mankind to improve its material circumstances, its knowledge of the world, and its moral behaviour. Most deeply he believed in the British Empire as the most progressive of politcal institutions.

The manner in which Rosebery pieced together these beliefs would certainly fail to satisfy the philosopher's requirement for systematic rigour, but taken as a whole, they served as sufficient foundation for his foreign policy. Most significant to the historian of diplomacy is Rosebery's understanding of the place occupied by the foreign secretary, who was to stand above sectional interests and temporary enthusiasms, whose duty it was to safegard the enduring interests of the empire as a whole. Chambers of commerce, missionary organizations, and public-spirited associations had the right to make their views known, and indeed it was the duty of the foreign secretary to consider these views in conducting his diplomacy. But the foreign secretary alone was in a position to see the whole picture, and therefore able to take a balanced view.

This attitude, which was fundamental to Rosebery's diplomacy, accounts for the old-fashioned perspective of this book. No religious group, no political association, had any important influence on Rosebery's foreign policy. The historian who searches the record of these years for evidence of direct influence searches in vain. Histories of missionary societies or chambers of commerce are interesting and useful, but they are more properly viewed as studies in social and economic history rather than diplomatic. The history of the British Empire would certainly have been different had such organizations not existed, had they not developed interests abroad. But the foreign secretary, in conjunction with the cabinet, decided when, where, and how the interests of such organizations would be protected. If Rosebery ever worried that his policies might hurt him or his party at the polls, he kept his fears to himself.

Rosebery could not have put his beliefs into practice had there not been widespread agreement that he was right. Particular groups or interests might disagree with the direction of his policy, and attempt to redirect it, but most agreed with the argument that what was needed at the Foreign Office was strong leadership. Rosebery was popular with the public because of the apparent strength of his leadership: his most popular rallying cries were "continuity in foreign policy" and "peace through firmness." Both of these slogans were vague, but they satisfied the public. Foreign policy under Rosebery would not be a matter of political debate, nor would it be weak or vacillating. The public generally accepted this, and so did the houses of Parliament.

The outstanding exception to the rule of exempting issues of foreign policy from political debate came early in Rosebery's career, when he attacked Disraeli. The attack was particularly interesting not only because it thrust Rosebery forward into the political limelight, but because it was founded upon the assumption that certain traditional rules had been violated by Disraeli, rules that had been responsible for Britain's rise to preeminence among nations. The most important rule, according to Rosebery, was the one stipulating that Britain's foreign policy must not be erected on a false foundation, that policy must be consistent with the power to put it into effect. Disraeli had also violated the rule that the government must have the people of the country behind it in its execution of policy, and had reversed the tradition whereby nations "struggling to be free" could count on the assistance of Britain. Because of these various sins, Rosebery was able to justify his attack on Disraeli's foreign policy – but it was the only attack of this kind that he ever made. Although he differed with some of the details of Salisbury's policy, and with the general direction of Grey's, he restrained himself from attacking their policies in public.

Rosebery believed that the British people would support his non-partisan approach to foreign policy, and there is little evidence to show that he was wrong. Apart from a few extreme anti-imperialists like Labouchere, Rosebery faced little opposition to his foreign policy, either in Parliament or in the country. The parliamentary debates for these years are notable mainly for the restraint shown by the participants, even over such a controversial issue as Uganda; Rosebery enjoyed the support of such dissident, and disparate, groups as the Irish MPs and the Lib-Labs. Nor did the newspapers mount any sort of consistent attack on his policies; indeed, Rosebery was supported by a number of influential editors and writers whose political views varied widely: men like Buckle, Spender, and Reid.

This situation began to change, of course, when Rosebery became prime minister. By this time accustomed to popular acclaim, he grew increasingly distressed by the attacks he faced in his new office.

The point to remember here is that this general support for Rosebery's foreign (as distinct from his domestic) policy confirmed him in the belief that he need not pay particular attention to those sectional interests whose special concerns were being pressed by a number of organizations and associations. So, in this area at least, the making of British foreign policy was quite distinct from that of German, French, and Italian. The shifts in thinking from Salisbury to Rosebery to Kimberley to Balfour to Lansdowne to Grey were gradual and unspectacular, and one has to look very hard at these men to see such differences in their political views as might explain the changing direction of British foreign policy.

In other words, Rosebery's foreign policy, like that of his predecessors and his successors, was not seriously limited by a consideration of the consequences in domestic politics. There was, however, one limitation on his policy that overshadowed all others.

Historians have long assumed that Rosebery was severely limited by the opposition he faced from his own cabinet. More specifically, the hostility of Harcourt and Morley, following Gladstone's retirement, is supposed to have proved too much for Rosebery to bear. In one sense this is true: in the spring of 1895 Rosebery decided that the constant quarrelling in the cabinet had become too high a price to pay for the privilege of forming the government. Consequently, he decided to submit his government's resignation when it was defeated on the minor question of whether or not enough cordite had been provided for in the army estimates. But, so far as Rosebery's foreign policy is concerned, the opposition of Harcourt and Morley proved merely an irritation – a constant, nagging irritation, but nothing more.

Historians who subscribe to the idea that Harcourt and Morley severely limited Rosebery's diplomacy are fond of quoting Harcourt's remarks on a variety of subjects. It is an easy exercise to perform, because Harcourt wrote long and bitter denunciations of almost every significant diplomatic manoeuvre undertaken by Rosebery. It is more difficult to perform this exercise with Morley, because his complaints were, it turns out, quite rare. But the Harcourt-Rosebery and Harcourt-Kimberley correspondence forms a curiosity in the history of nineteenth-century British politics, and historians will long cite it as evidence of how bitter relations were inside this government. No other correspondence can match its venom.

The question that the historian of diplomacy must ask, however, is: how effective was Harcourt? The answer is: not effective at all. He never succeeded in changing the direction of Rosebery's policy by even a fraction. The Anglo-Congolese agreement, usually regarded as Harcourt's ultimate triumph over Rosebery, failed because of the opposition of Germany and France, because of the deviousness of King Leopold and his associates, and, finally, because of blunders within the British Foreign Office – blunders for which Rosebery must take the ultimate responsibility. When Harcourt ranted and raved over the Grey declaration, he got nowhere; no-one supported his pretensions to some special place within the foreign policy-making process. Rosebery dismissed the claims as bizarre and impractical. Finally, the records clearly show that the Rosebery-Kimberley policy during the Sino-Japanese War – such as it was – was of their own making, the fact that Harcourt for once agreed with it having resulted only in a saving of expensive stationery.

Perhaps historians would not have been so quick to conclude that Harcourt was an effective critic were it not for Rosebery's own reputation for being thin-skinned and temperamental. Here again, the conclusion is well grounded in fact, but misleading nevertheless. Rosebery certainly was temperamental, owing mainly to the fact that, in spite of his arrogance, he lacked confidence. Whenever he felt slighted, whenever he felt that people thought he had failed, he had an attack of nerves, the result of which was sometimes blustering talk about resigning from government or retiring from politics altogether. But once again the truth has been reshaped into legend. Rosebery never once actually threatened to resign while he was foreign secretary; he did once threaten to resign when he was prime minister, but even this was a calculated political move – in private he admitted that he could not have resigned. Perhaps the legend grew because his colleagues, knowing that his commitment to political life was not wholehearted, feared that he would abandon them at a crucial moment. Each time a difficult question arose, therefore, whether over Uganda, Egypt, the naval estimates, or the Congo, his colleagues naturally thought he might resign, or at least threaten to, and so the rumours abounded.

More than anything, however, Rosebery was able to use his reputed temperament as a tool. Politicians who have been out of office for some length of time, as the Liberals had in 1892, are not keen on the idea of a quick return to the wilderness of opposition. Rosebery was, next to Gladstone, the best-known and most popular member of the government. His colleagues did not regard lightly the idea of his abandoning them. Thus, when rumours of a possible resignation circulated, Rosebery did little to stop them. It suited his purpose that his colleagues should be wary of opposing him too forcefully.

As a limitation on Rosebery's foreign policy, therefore, the opposition of some cabinet ministers counted for little. He sometimes complained to the Germans that it was the opposition of the cabinet that prevented him from agreeing to the closer alignment that they desired, but this was disingenuous; he had no intention of agreeing to a more formal arrangement, and the cabinet's views on the subject, similar to his own, merely served as a convenient excuse.

The real limitation on Rosebery's foreign policy had little to do with cabinet opposition or domestic politics. It had to do, instead, with Britain's position in the real world of international politics.

In spite of the complexities that always confuse the international scene, Rosebery's view of Britain's position in the international setting was surprisingly simple. The security of the empire was challenged first by the French and second by the Russians. The French threat was mainly naval and located primarily in the Mediterranean; the Russian threat was mainly military, and located primarily in central Asia. The great danger, however, was that, instead of presenting two quite distinct threats, these two antagonists might combine to pose a challenge to Britain unparalleled since Napoleon and Alexander met at Tilsit. The Toulon naval demonstration suggested that the growing Russian fleet might combine with the French in the Mediterranean, while the Siamese crisis suggested that a coterminous frontier between the British and the French in Asia might enable the French to combine forces with the Russians against British India.

Beside these dangers, all others seemed but minor annoyances. The Americans, whose strength was obviously increasing, were occasionally irritating in the Caribbean; the Japanese, also growing stronger, were causing some uncertainty about the future of China; the Spanish were sometimes rude about Gibraltar. In this category must be placed the noisy movements of the restless Germans. Rosebery tried to be patient with the Germans in Africa, Asia, and the Pacific, but he never regarded them as any kind of threat to the real security of the empire. His tone, and Kimberley's, always seemed condescending to the Germans, who did not appreciate being ranked alongside the Americans, the Japanese, and the Spanish.

The crucial point is that, in the 1890s, only the French and the Russians were in a position to endanger the British Empire. The question Rosebery asked was, "how is this danger to be met?" His diplomacy revealed a twofold answer. First, he attempted to keep the French and the Russians from combining against the British. This he attempted to do by demonstrating to the Russians that most of their differences with the British could be resolved. Resolving differences with Russia formed the foundation of his policy in the Near East, in central Asia, and, up to a point, in the Far East. At the same time he took a strong position in his relations with the French: he moved to increase Britain's naval strength in the Mediterranean, he undertook his most aggressive and daring – perhaps foolhardy – diplomatic manoeuvres in Uganda and the Congo, both in order to forestall a French threat to the British position in Egypt. He even talked of war, either real or silent, breaking out if the French refused to accept the principle of a buffer state between the two empires in Asia. In short, the first part of Rosebery's answer to the question was designed to show the Russians that the British would be fair and reasonable in resolving the differences between them, but that they were likely to come to blows if they worked too closely in harness with the French.

But it is the second part of Rosebery's answer that is the more exciting to the diplomatic historian. It derived from the belief that the greatest advantage that the British enjoyed in their relations with France and Russia – greater than either British sea power or the English Channel – was the existence of the German Empire. The Germans, in combination with the Austrians and the Italians in the Triple Alliance, compelled France and Russia to maintain such massive military establishments in Europe that the two powers could utilize only a fraction of their resources against the British in the Mediterranean, in Africa, and in Asia. Thus the second part of his answer was to have Britain act as an informal member of the Triple Alliance, in order to keep it in being as a singularly fortunate stroke of fate.

It should be pointed out that this scheme was not original: it was designed, and first managed, by the more brilliant diplomatic mind of Salisbury. But with all the talk of Rosebery's aggressive imperialism, his francophobia, and his political difficulties, it has often been forgotten that in this scheme of relations is to be found the essence of his diplomacy.

What made this scheme so attractive to Rosebery was that the Germans, by logic of geography and recent history, were going to act on behalf of Britain, whether they wished to or not. So he was not surprised when the Germans blustered about coolies and liquor licensing in the tropics: they were naturally annoyed at having to work in the service of Britain without receiving anything of substance in return. Their tone annoyed the equable Kimberley, whereas the temperamental Rosebery took it in stride; he knew what it meant. He did his best to assuage the German passions stirred up by annoyances abroad, although, as he showed in the Kaulla affair, he was not sufficiently aware of all the nuances to play this game as masterfully as one might have hoped.

Rosebery continued to believe, despite the bluster, that the Germans would play the role he and Salisbury had assigned to them. He was convinced that the Franco-Russian alliance was aimed at Germany, and that it increased her dependence upon Austria-Hungary and Italy through the Triple Alliance. But he was equally convinced that the Triple Alliance was tottering on its foundations, and that a vibration sent out from London might shake it to pieces. Without the continued support of Britain, Italy would almost certainly detach herself from the alliance. With Italy gone, Austria-Hungary might decide that the risk of a two-front war was too great and, therefore, that a negotiated settlement of her differences with Russia was to be preferred. Nothing that occurred during his tenure of office induced Rosebery to consider that he might be wrong. All three members of the alliance made repeated efforts to draw Britain into a formal arrangement, and, whenever the Germans went too far in expressing their dislike of some British move, he had only to send them a few sharp words through Rome or Vienna to cause an improvement in their behaviour. Thus, while the Triple Alliance acted as a gigantic magnet that drew French and Russian strength into the centre of the European continent, it might shatter if it were not bolstered by the strength of Great Britain.

Given this outlook, it is hardly surprising that Rosebery believed the best guarantee of British security was to be with the Triple Alliance, but not of it.

Rosebery's greatest worry during these years was that his refusal to join the alliance might induce the Germans to revive the Bismarckian policy of an arrangement with Russia. If Russia were relieved of the massive drain on her men and money in Europe, she might then be prepared to contemplate transforming the alliance with France into the anti-British arrangement that the French appeared to desire. This consideration meant that Rosebery had a twofold reason for improving relations with Russia: to avoid driving her into the arms of Germany, and to ensure that her arrangement with France operated in Europe, but not beyond.

In view of these considerations, it is ironic that Rosebery has been portrayed consistently as an aggressive imperialist, hungry for new territory and prepared to risk trouble with the great powers for the sake of unprofitable places in remote lands. It is ironic because Rosebery was as much a "consolidationist" as was Salisbury. And the origins of his plan to consolidate are clearly located in his general diplomatic calculations. If the British acted aggressively in those territories that bordered on Russia, then they might succeed in driving Russia to seek an accommodation with Germany and Austria-Hungary. Rosebery was fully alive to the presence of the "Asiatic" school in Russia, which argued that the costs of acting as a European power were not worth the benefits, that Russia's future lay in Asia, and that the power blocking the road to the future was Britain. Rosebery sought to deprive this school of one of its strongest arguments by making it appear that Britain was content with what she already possessed, that she was anxious to cooperate with Russia whenever there arose an opportunity to do so. Thus did Rosebery, in combination with Kimberley, seek to keep the "forward" elements in British India in check. In the Pamirs and in Persia, during the Armenian massacres and the Sino-Japanese War, he tried to show the Russians that he desired their friendship. But the war in the Far East demonstrated the limits to which he was prepared to go: he was not willing to run the risk of antagonizing a third power for the sake of Russian interests. The Chitral affair showed, however, that his policy in the Far East was not to be regarded as a sign that his desire for Russian friendship had flagged. Consolidation, not expansion, remained the cornerstone of his foreign policy.

The great exception to this rule was Uganda, and it is from the Uganda debate that most of the evidence supporting the picture of Rosebery as expansionist is drawn. The phrase "pegging out claims for the future" will probably cling to him forever, because it seems to sum up the scramble for territory that typified the "new imperialism." But Rosebery was rather desperately attempting to drum up support for what was an unpopular and expensive move, and he soon regretted using the phrase.

The fact remains, however, that along the Nile he was prepared to go forward, and this stance needs to be accounted for. Perhaps it can be accounted for by his views of the French. It would be easy to compile a list of remarks to demonstrate his contemptuous mistrust of both the French people and their government. Unfortunately, it would be almost as easy to compile a similar list for the Germans and the Russians. Rosebery was as xenophobic as most of the English governing class of the nineteenth century.

Moreover, while Rosebery was willing to run the risk of further antagonizing the French by expanding British responsibilities in the general vicinity of the Nile, he was not willing to run similar risks in Morocco or Siam. On the contrary, in Southeast Asia he was prepared to countenance French expansion – on the condition that the French limit their pretensions short of a coterminous frontier with the British Empire. Rosebery enjoyed, had he wished to take advantage of the situation, numerous opportunities to expand British claims during the Siamese affair. Equally striking is his determination to keep affairs in Morocco as quiet as he could. Here again, had he been bent upon forestalling the French at every opportunity, he could have taken a very different position than the one he adopted.

It was not a peculiar hatred for the French that moved Rosebery to break from his policy of consolidation, but a keen sense that international politics in general hinged upon the situation in the eastern Mediterranean. This area was, after all, the one place in the world where the interests and ambitions of all the European powers met. Britain, France, and Russia had fought over it in mid-century; the interests of Austria-Hungary there were immediate and undeniable; Italy had, since her unification, been attempting to find a foothold there, and, finally, it was one of the aims of the *neue Kurs* to establish Germany as a leading power there. It was the one area where naval power and strategy were inextricably bound up with military considerations. If only for these reasons, Rosebery was more likely to press forward with a determined policy in the eastern Mediterranean than he was elsewhere.

But there was a further, and finally conclusive, reason why Rosebery was prepared to act differently in this general area. Throughout his career he stressed, both publicy and privately, the absolute necessity of matching diplomatic policies to the power available for putting the into effect. No area was more important to British diplomacy than the eastern Mediterranean because it was here that the politics of Europe joined with the politics of empire. The British Empire rested, ultimately, upon the stroke of fate that had allowed Britain to remain relatively aloof from the complications, the expense, and the carnage of European power politics. But this aloofness had never been absolute. In the 1890s, perhaps as never before, Britain's ability to profit from this aloofness appeared to depend, paradoxically, on her ability to influence European relations without herself becoming a European power. Therefore, given the Roseberian formula, this was the one area where Britain must be absolutely certain that her policies rested upon a firm foundation of actual power. Consequently, he was prepared to risk his own career, drive Gladstone from office, and jeopardize the unity of the Liberal party for the sake of maintaining an overwhelming preponderance of naval power in the Mediterranean, and for the sake of establishing a firm territorial foothold in Eygpt.

Rosebery's strategy was not so much based upon the "route to India" school of thought, although this certainly entered into it, as upon his conception of European politics. Britain's relationship with Germany, so beneficial and so cheap, depended on Italy and Austria-Hungary. If either of the lesser powers in the Triple Alliance came to believe that Britain could not be relied upon to counter France and

Russia in the Mediterranean and at the Straits, then Britain would be deprived of the opportunity to influence their policies and, consequently, that of Germany. Rosebery understood that this was not an easy policy to pursue, that the Germans, Austrians, and Italians would always be complaining and attempting to manoeuvre Britain into taking out full membership in the alliance. He believed, however, that once a formal continental commitment was made, Britain would lose control of her own destiny. The way to avoid being compelled to undertake a formal commitment was to maintain naval supremacy in the Mediterranean, and to guarantee that the British position in Egypt was impregnable from a military point of view.

Rosebery's speeches show that he anticipated a final, more pervasive, difficulty in defending the empire. For all his talk of the glory of empire, the duties of an imperial race, and the necessity of developing the estates already owned by the British, it seems clear that he was moved to affirm such doctrines because he felt that the people of Britain were losing their sense of mission, that the empire was ceasing to appear to be part of divine providence. The empire, for all the blessings that it brought, was costly and difficult to manage, and it was easier for people to see the costs than the benefits. If the British people refused to pay the costs of defending the empire they would ineluctably be drawn into some political commitment in Europe. The cost of refusing to shoulder the burden of empire, he believed, would ultimately be the empire itself, and with it the peace and the prosperity of the British Isles.

Was he wrong?

Notes

INTRODUCTION

1 On Rosebery's background and early career see Robert Rhodes James, *Rosebery: A Biography of Archibald Philip, Fifth Earl of Rosebery*, which is by far the best account.

2 "The True Leverage of Empire" (30 September 1874), *Speeches of Lord Rosebery, 1874 to 1896* (London 1896), 23–4.

3 Rosebery Journal, 10 April 1873, Rosebery Papers, 10191, f.15.

4 Rosebery Journal, n.d. (c. May 1872), Rosebery Papers, 10189, f.38.

5 Rosebery Journal, 8 November 1872, Rosebery Papers, 10189, f.88.

6 Ibid.

7 Rosebery Journal, n.d. (c. February 1872), Rosebery Papers, 10189, f.14.

8 Ibid.

9 Ibid.

10 Rosebery Journal, 8 November 1872, Rosebery Papers, 10189, f.89.

11 Rosebery Journal, 24 December 1874, Rosebery Papers, 10192, f.4.

12 Hamilton Diary, 1 January 1888, Hamilton Papers, Add.Mss. 48647, f.105.

13 Rosebery Journal, 24 December 1874, Rosebery Papers, 10192, f.4.

14 Rosebery Journal, 8 November 1872, Rosebery Papers, 10189, f.86.

15 Rosebery Journal, n.d. (November 1872), Rosebery Papers, 10189, f.94.

16 Rosebery Journal, 25 April 1873, Rosebery Papers, 10191, f.49.

17 Hamilton Diary, 21 April 1889, Hamilton Papers, 48650, f.107.

18 For an explanation of the Oxford episode see Rhodes James, *Rosebery*, 51–3; on educational reform see A.R.C. Grant, ed., *Lord Rosebery's North American Journal, 1873* (London 1967), 121, and Rosebery Journal, 1 February 1872, Rosebery Papers, 10191, f.49.

19 "True Leverage of Empire," 13.

20 Ibid., 6.

21 See Charles Cooper (editor of the *Scotsman*) to Rosebery, 7 July 1880,

Rosebery Papers, 10010, ff.5–6; J.S. Blackie (professor of philosophy, University of Edinburgh) to Rosebery, 6 March 1884, Rosebery Papers, 10081, ff.9–10; and James Donaldson (rector, University of St Andrews) to Rosebery, 6 October 1880, Rosebery Papers, 10013, ff.19–22.

22 Address to the Edinburgh Philosophical Society, *Times*, 4 November 1872.

23 Hamilton Diary, 19 September 1891, Hamilton Papers, 48656, f.85.

24 *Times*, 4 April 1876.

25 Ibid.

26 Speech to the East and North of Scotland Liberal Association, ibid., 17 November 1879.

27 Speech to the National Reform Union, Manchester, ibid., 2 April 1885.

28 Ibid., 20 April 1877.

29 Ibid., 27 July 1878.

30 Ibid., 19 October 1878.

31 Ibid.

32 Ibid., 17 November 1879.

33 Ibid., 4 November 1881.

34 Ibid., 31 March 1880.

35 Ibid., 16 October 1885.

36 Ibid., 21 October 1885.

37 Agatha Ramm, ed., *The Political Correspondence of Mr Gladstone and Lord Granville, 1876–86* (Oxford 1962), 105.

38 Ibid., 116.

39 See Rhodes James, *Rosebery*, 115–51; Rosebery to Sir William Harcourt (copy), 13 January 1881, Rosebery Papers, 10034, ff.44–59; Hamilton Diary, 7 December 1882, Hamilton Papers, 48633, f.31; Cooper to Rosebery, 7 August 1881, Rosebery Papers, 10010, ff.40–1.

40 Ronald Munro-Ferguson to Lord Crewe (Rosebery's biographer and son-in-law), 26 March 1930, Crewe Papers, 10195, ff.324–5; Hamilton Diary, 6 April 1883, Hamilton Papers, 48633, f.81; Rosebery to Harcourt, n.d. (December 1880), Rosebery Papers (copy), confidential, 10034, ff.19–28.

41 Rosebery to Gladstone, 11 November 1884, Gladstone Papers, 44288, f.214.

42 Rosebery to Gladstone, 12 November 1884, Gladstone Papers, 44288, f.215.

43 He told Granville as much and pointed out that he could hardly use the weapon of resignation once in office, after having already resigned last year. Rosebery to Granville (copy), 12 November 1884, Rosebery Papers, 10081, ff.301–2. This letter is quoted in its entirety in Marquess of Crewe, *Lord Rosebery* (London 1931), 1: 212.

44 Hamilton Diary, 11 November 1884, Hamilton Papers, 48638, f.45.

45 *Times*, 4 December 1884.

46 Rosebery to Brett, most secret, 7 February 1885, Esher Papers, 10/9.

47 Ibid.; see also Rosebery to Hamilton, secret, 31 December 1884, Hamilton Papers, 48612A, f.67.

48 Rosebery to Esher, most secret, 7 February 1885, Esher Papers, 10/9.

49 Brett to Rosebery, 7 February 1885, Rosebery Papers, 10006, f.15; Hamilton Diary, 8 February 1885, Hamilton Papers, 48639, ff.42–3; Lord Reay (governor of Bombay) to Rosebery, 12 February 1885, Rosebery Papers, 10044, ff.7–8; and see Crewe, *Rosebery* 1: 219.

50 *Times*, 10 February 1885.

51 Ibid.

52 Ibid.

53 Ibid.

54 See especially A.B. Cooke and J.R. Vincent, eds., *Lord Carlingford's Journal* (Oxford 1971).

55 Memorandum by Rosebery, n.d. (between 11 and 14 April 1885), Rosebery Papers, 10132, f.44.

56 *Times*, 2 April 1885.

57 Memorandum by Rosebery, "The Situation with Russia," 26 April 1885, Rosebery Papers, 10132, f.40.

58 Ibid.

59 Ibid.

60 Kimberley Journal, 810; from an extract by Rosebery, Rosebery Papers, 10186, f.272.

61 Hamilton Diary, 4 February 1886, Hamilton Papers, 48642, f.132.

CHAPTER ONE

1 W.N. Medlicott, "The Powers and the Unification of the Two Bulgarias, 1885," *English Historical Review* 54 (1939): 268; Colin L. Smith, *The Embassy of Sir William White at Constantinople, 1886–1891*, 41–2; M.S. Anderson, *The Eastern Question* (New York 1964), 230; A.J.P. Taylor, *The Struggle for Mastery in Europe*, 305; but especially Agatha Ramm, *Sir Robert Morier: Envoy and Ambassador in the Age of Imperialism, 1876–93*, chap. 8.

2 Colin L. Smith, *Sir William White*, 21–2.

3 Rosebery to Sir Augustus Paget (ambassador at Vienna), no. 44A, 10 February 1886, FO7/1091.

4 Colin L. Smith, *Sir William White*, 41–2; A.P. Thornton, *The Habit of Authority: Paternalism in British History* (Toronto 1966), 238, 301.

5 Rosebery to Paget, private and confidential, 10 February 1886, Paget Papers, Add.Mss. 51230 (emphasis added).

6 Speech to the London and Counties Liberal Union at Reigate, *Times*, 29 September 1885.

7 W.N. Medlicott, *The Congress of Berlin and After* (London 1963), 208.

8 See Colin L. Smith, *Sir William White*, 21–2.

9 Speech at Leeds, 11 October 1888, *Lord Rosebery's Speeches* (London 1896), 42.

10 Gladstone to Rosebery, secret, 28 April 1886, Rosebery Papers, 10023, f.177.
11 Lewis Harcourt Journal, 14 February 1886, Harcourt Papers.
12 Rosebery to Baring, most private, 19 February 1886, Cromer Papers, FO633/7.
13 Hamilton Diary, 22 January 1885, Hamilton Papers, 48639, f.15.
14 The *Novoe Vremya*, for example, stated in January that "Lord Salisbury and his friends, like the majority of Englishmen are deeply convinced that Russia intends sooner or later to strike a blow at India and consequently every step we take in Central Asia produces in them irritation, under the influence of which, they turn all their efforts towards checking us in every possible way. Mister Gladstone is moved by no such considerations. He knows and understands Russia better than anyone else, and does not doubt our sincere desire to solve, in a peaceable manner, the question of the delimitation of the spheres of influence of England and Russia in Asia." Morier to Salisbury, no.46, 5 February 1886, FO65/1256.
15 See W.E. Gladstone, "The Hellenic Factor in the Eastern Question," *Contemporary Review*, December 1876; *Times*, 2 December 1880, Rosebery's speech to the Greek Committee; and Esher Journal, 3 February 1886, Esher Papers, 2/7.
16 Rosebery to Rumbold, no.25A 8 February 1886, FO32/571; Rosebery to Malet, private, 10 March 1886, Malet Papers, FO343/2.
17 Hamilton Diary, 5 September 1883, Hamilton Papers, 48634, f.66.
18 Gladstone to Bryce, 2 December 1885, Bryce Papers, 10.
19 Rosebery to Gladstone, 11 May 1886, Gladstone Papers, 44289, f.39.
20 Hamilton Diary, 5 September 1883, Hamilton Papers, 48634, f.66.
21 Bryce to E.A. Freeman, 25 July 1886, Bryce Papers, 9, f.25.
22 Rumbold to Salisbury, no.5, 9 January 1886, FO32/572; Memorandum on Bulgaria and Greece, very confidential, 10 February 1886, Rosebery Papers, box 90.
23 Rumbold to Salisbury, no.8, confidential, 10 January 1886, FO32/572.
24 Rumbold to Rosebery, no.59, confidential, 26 February 1886, FO32/572; Lascelles to Paget (private), 7 January 1886, Lascelles Papers, FO800/7; Lascelles to Rosebery, no.80, 15 March 1886. FO78/3892; White to Rosebery, telegram, n.d., White Papers, FO364/3.
25 Rosebery to Rumbold, no.25A, 8 February 1886, FO32/571; Rosebery to Paget, no.44A, 10 February 1886, FO7/1091; Rosebery to Gladstone, 10 February 1886, Gladstone Papers, 44289, f.14.
26 Rosebery to Paget, private and confidential, 10 February 1886, Paget Papers, 51230; Rosebery to Gladstone, 10 February 1886, Gladstone Papers, 44289, f.14; Rosebery to Paget, February 1886, FO7/1091; Rosebery to Malet, private, 24 February 1886, Malet Papers, FO343/2.
27 Paget to Rosebery, no.73, 15 February 1886, FO7/1094; Malet to Rosebery,

telegram 31, confidential, 15 February 1886, FO64/1120.

28 Paget to Rosebery, private, 14 February 1886, Paget Papers, 51230; Colin L. Smith, *Sir William White*, 32–4; Paget to White, private, 19 February 1886, White Papers, FO364/9.

29 Paget to Rosebery, no.64, 11 February 1886, FO7/1094; Paget to Rosebery, no.116, 12 March 1886, FO7/1094.

30 Scott to Salisbury, telegram 19, 6 February 1886, FO64/1120; Lumley to Rosebery, no.53, 18 February 1886, FO45/546; Rosebery to Lumley, no.57, 22 February 1886, FO45/544; Lyons to Rosebery, no.81, 17 February 1886, FO27/2794.

31 White to Paget, private, 9 February 1886, Paget Papers, 51231.

32 White to Rosebery, telegram 32, 11 February 1886, FO78/3879.

33 White to Rosebery, telegram 38, 15 February 1886, FO78/3879.

34 See Colin L. Smith, *Sir William White*, 26–9; and H.S. Edwards, *The Career and Correspondence of Sir William White* (London 1902), 231–4.

35 See Colin L. Smith, *Sir William White*, 3–5, for an explanation of the obstacles White faced.

36 Morier to Rosebery, telegram 22, secret, 18 February 1886. FO65/1264.

37 Morier to Rosebery, private and confidential, 19 February 1886, Morier Papers.

38 See Cedric J. Lowe, *The Reluctant Imperialists*, 73–8.

39 Morier to Rosebery, private and confidential, 19 February 1886, Morier Papers; Roberts to Ridgeway, Private, 27 March 1886, Ridgeway Papers.

40 Morier to Rosebery, private and confidential, 19 February 1886, Morier Papers; Morier to Rosebery, no.56, 13 February 1886, FO65/1256; Lascelles himself never regarded the prince as a puppet, but certainly did everything he could to establish himself as his principal foreign adviser. See Lascelles to Paget, private, 7 January 1886, Lascelles Papers, FO800/7.

41 Morier's memorandum, "For August Critics," n.d. 1886; Morier Papers; Morier to Sanderson, most secret, 14 March 1886, Morier Papers.

42 Morier to Rosebery, private and confidential, 19 February 1886, Morier Papers.

43 Morier to Sanderson, most secret, 14 March 1886, Morier Papers.

44 Rosebery to White, no.54, 11 February 1886, FO78/3865.

45 *Times*, leading article of 22 February 1886. In spite of Rosebery's declared intention of removing foreign affairs from public controversy, he had no hesitation in using organs like the *Times*, and his personal associations with journalists, to support his policies. Reginald Brett, later Lord Esher, was often the go-between. See, for example, Brett's letter to Buckle, editor of the *Times*, which followed a long conversation with Rosebery. Memorandum by Brett, 24 February 1886, Esher Papers, 2/7; Brett to Buckle, private and confidential, 25 February 1886, Esher Papers, 2/7; Brett to Rosebery, private, 19 February 1886, Rosebery Papers, 10006, f.46; and

Henry Lucy to Rosebery, 7 January 1886, Rosebery Papers, 10085, f.12.

46 Sanderson to Morier, private and confidential, 17 March 1886, Morier Papers; White to Rosebery, telegram 38, 15 February 1886, FO78/3879; White to Rosebery, private and confidential, 15 February 1886, White Papers, FO364/1; Rosebery to Malet, telegram 69, 12 February 1886, FO64/1120.

47 Rosebery to White, confidential, 10 February 1886, White Papers, FO364/1.

48 Rosebery to Paget, private and confidential, 10 February 1886, Paget Papers, 51230.

49 Rosebery to White, no.56, 15 February 1886, FO78/3865.

50 Sanderson to Morier, private and confidential, 17 March 1886, Morier Papers.

51 Colin L. Smith, *Sir William White*, 81.

52 Rosebery to White, no.51A and no.58A, 10 and 16 February 1886, FO78/3865.

53 White to Rosebery, telegram 40, 16 February 1886, FO78/3879; White to Rosebery, telegram 41, 16 February 1886, FO78/3879; White to Rosebery, telegram 45, 18 February 1886, FO78/3879; Rosebery to White, no.60, 19 February 1886, FO78/3865.

54 White to Rosebery, telegram 36, 15 February 1886, FO78/3879.

55 Rosebery to Malet, Private, 17 February 1886, Malet Papers, FO343/2.

56 Speech to the Greek Committee, *Times*, 2 December 1880.

57 Rosebery to Lascelles, telegram 61, 14 March 1886, FO78/3898; Lascelles to Rosebery, no.89, secret, 21 March 1886, FO78/3892.

58 Thornton to Rosebery, no.140, 22 March 1886, FO78/3869.

59 Rosebery to Lascelles, private, 24 March 1886, Lascelles Papers, FO800/7.

60 Rosebery to Malet, private, 17 March 1886, Malet Papers, FO343/7.

61 Rumbold to Rosebery, no,49, confidential, 18 February 1886, FO32/572.

62 Rosebery to Malet, private, 7 April 1886, Malet Papers, FO343/7.

63 Gladstone to Rosebery, secret, 28 September 1886, Rosebery Papers, 10023, ff.176–7.

64 Paget to Rosebery, private, 22 April 1886, Paget Papers, 51230.

65 Morier to Rosebery, private, 3 June 1886, Morier Papers.

66 Morier to Rosebery, telegram 82, 27 May 1886, FO65/1264.

67 Paget to Rosebery, private, 3 June 1886, Malet Papers, FO343/8.

68 Morier to Rosebery, no.185, most secret, 29 May 1886, FO65/1258.

69 Morier to Rosebery, private, 17 July 1886, Morier Papers.

70 Rosebery to Morier, private, 7 July 1886, Morier Papers.

71 Morier to Rosebery, telegram 89, 3 July 1886, FO65/1264.

72 Rosebery to Morier, no.153, confidential, 3 July 1886, FO65/1255.

73 Paget to Rosebery, no.233, confidential, 14 July 1886, FO7/1095; Scott to Rosebery, no.284, 10 July 1886, FO64/1116; Scott to Rosebery, no.304, very confidential, 31 July 1886, FO64/1116; Rosebery to Lumley, no.188, confi-

dential, 6 July 1886, FO45/544; Lumley to Rosebery, no.204, most confidential, 27 July 1886, FO45/548.

74 Bryce to Rosebery, private, 9 July 1886, Rosebery Papers, 10086, ff.9–14.

75 Rosebery to Morier, private, 13 July 1886, Morier Papers.

76 Secret memorandum (on Rosebery's conversation with Staal), 20 July 1886, Rosebery Papers, 10132, ff.79–82.

77 Rosebery to Morier, private, 13 July 1886, Morier Papers.

78 Rosebery to Gladstone, 3 July 1886, Gladstone Papers, 44289, f.4.

79 Rosebery's memorandum on Batoum, 14 July 1886, Rosebery Papers, 10132, ff.79–82; Rosebery to Gladstone, 12 July 1886, Gladstone Papers, 44289, f.55.

80 Morier to Rosebery, telegram, private, 12 July 1886, Morier Papers.

81 Morier to Rosebery, private, 3 June 1886, Morier Papers.

82 Morier to Rosebery, private, 17 July 1886, Morier Papers.

83 The dispatch is reprinted in H.W.V. Temperley and L.M. Penson, *Foundations of British Foreign Policy* (London 1938), 437–41.

84 Morier to Rosebery, telegram 106, secret, 18 July 1886, FO65/1264.

85 Rosebery to Morier, private, 21 July 1886, Morier Papers.

86 Morier to Rosebery, memorandum, secret, 18 July 1886, FO65/1260.

87 Rosebery to Morier, telegram 150, 27 July 1886, FO65/1264.

88 Mundella to Rosebery, 22 April 1886, Rosebery Papers, 10085, ff.176–7.

89 Bryce to Rosebery, 14 July 1886, Rosebery Papers, 10086, f.19.

90 Hamilton Diary, 24 April 1886, Hamilton Papers, 48643, f.100.

91 Paget to Lascelles, private and confidential, 3 February 1886, Lascelles Papers, FO800/7.

92 Paget to Wharncliffe, 19 January and 6 May, 1893, Paget Papers, 51233.

93 Lascelles's minute of meeting with Rosebery in London, 5 August 1886, Lascelles Papers, FO800/7; Hamilton Diary, 4 March 1886, Hamilton Papers, 48643, ff.32–3.

94 Lascelles to White, private, 11 August 1886, Lascelles Papers, FO800/7.

95 Spring-Rice to Rosebery, 20 December 1888, Rosebery Papers, 10087, ff.301–3.

96 Hamilton Diary, 6 October 1886, Hamilton Papers, 48644, f.139.

97 Hamilton Diary, 8 December 1889, Hamilton Papers, 48652.

CHAPTER TWO

1 Hamilton Diary, 24 April 1886, Hamilton Papers, 48643, f.100.

2 Rosebery to Gladstone, 29 June 1886, Gladstone Papers, 44289, f.45.

3 Rosebery to Cooper, 20 April 1887 [never sent] Rosebery Papers, 10011, ff.173–6.

4 Rosebery to Gladstone, private and secret, 29 June 1886, Gladstone Papers, 44289, ff.45–7.

5 Rosebery to Cooper, 20 April 1887 [never sent] Rosebery Papers, 10011, ff.173–6.

6 Gilmour to Rosebery, 16 March 1887, Rosebery Papers, 10087, ff.64–71.

7 Hamilton Diary, 2 October 1887 and 1 January 1888, Hamilton Papers, 48647, ff.22–6 and 103–8.

8 Hamilton Diary, 27 May 1888, Hamilton Papers, 48648, f.103.

9 Hamilton Diary, 2 October 1887, Hamilton Papers, 48647, ff.22–6.

10 Rosebery to Gladstone, confidential, 15 January 1889, Gladstone Papers, 44289, ff.80–3.

11 Ibid.

12 Hamilton Diary, 18 October 1887, Hamilton Papers, 48647, ff.32–5; Hamilton Diary, 23 February 1888, Hamilton Papers, 48648, f.31.

13 See D.H. Hamer, *Liberal Politics in the Age of Gladstone and Rosebery* (Oxford 1972).

14 Bryce to Rosebery, 10 January 1890, Rosebery Papers, 10088, ff.125–6.

15 Harcourt to Gladstone, 19 June 1890, Rosebery Papers, 10024, ff.3–4. Gladstone sent a copy to Rosebery.

16 Bryce to Rosebery, 22 May [1890], Rosebery Papers, 10088, ff.189–90.

17 Harcourt to Gladstone, 19 June 1890, Rosebery Papers, 10024, ff.3–4.

18 Hamilton Diary, 27 June 1890, Hamilton Papers, 48653, ff.55–6.

19 Rosebery's memorandum, 4 July 1890, Rosebery Papers, 10176, ff.202–5; Harcourt to Gladstone, 19 June 1890, Rosebery Papers, 10024, ff.3–4.

20 Rosebery's memorandum, 4 July 1890, Rosebery Papers, 10176, ff.202–5.

21 Hamilton Diary, 21 September 1890, Hamilton Papers, 48653, f.127.

22 For a fuller discussion of Rosebery's relationship with his wife, see Rhodes James, *Rosebery*.

23 Randolph Churchill to Rosebery, 30 March 1891, Rosebery Papers, 10009, ff.30–2.

24 Bryce to Rosebery, 2 April 1891, Rosebery Papers, 10006.

25 Rosebery to Munro-Ferguson, 26 April 1891, Rosebery Papers, 10017, ff.230–2.

26 Rosebery to Gladstone, 16 July 1891, Gladstone Papers, 44289, ff.140–3.

27 Rosebery, *Pitt* (London 1891), 286.

28 Joseph Compton-Ricketts to Rosebery, strictly private, 3 July 1892, Rosebery Papers, 10090, ff.96–7; Hamilton Diary, 14 June 1892, Hamilton Papers, 48658, f.18.

29 Kimberley Journal, 13 July 1892 (extract by Rosebery), Rosebery Papers, 10186, f.276.

30 Prince of Wales to Rosebery, 14 August 1892, *The Letters of Queen Victoria, 1886–1901* (London 1930–2) (hereafter cited as *LQV*, 3rd ser.), 2: 144. Buckle to Rosebery, 14 August 1892, Rosebery Papers, 10090, ff.123–30.

31 Spencer to Rosebery, 4 August 1892, Rosebery Papers, 10062, ff.63–4.

32 Among the suspicious were the queen, and not a few historians. See, for

example, Cedric J. Lowe, *Salisbury and the Mediterranean* (London 1965), 92.

33 Gladstone to Rosebery, 26 August 1892, Rosebery Papers, 10024, ff.97-8.

34 Rosebery to Herbert Paul (copy), confidential, 21 January 1890, Rosebery Papers, 10202, f.58.

35 Rosebery to Gladstone, 27 August 1892, Gladstone Papers, 44289, f.181.

36 Currie to Rosebery, 18 August 1892, Rosebery Papers, 10132, ff.106-12. This encloses the memorandum by Salisbury.

37 Ibid.

38 Rosebery to Dufferin, private, 31 August 1892, Dufferin Papers, D107 H/10/3.

39 See Lowe, *Salisbury and the Mediterranean*, 73-6.

40 Solms to Caprivi, 18 August 1892, *Die grosse Politik der europäischen Kabinette 1871-1914* (hereafter cited as *GP*) 8, no. 1735; and see Calvin Roberts, "The Egyptian Question and the Triple Alliance, 1884-1904" (PHD thesis, University of New Mexico, 1973), 144-6.

41 Rosebery to Currie (copy) 8 September 1892, and Currie to Rosebery, 10 and 15 September 1892, Rosebery Papers, 10132, ff.115-16, 118, 123; Hatzfeldt to Caprivi, 11 September 1892, *GP* 8, no. 1740.

42 Report of Department of Military Intelligence and Department of Naval Intelligence, 18 March 1892, Salisbury Papers.

43 See A.J.P. Taylor, *The Struggle for Mastery in Europe*, 336-41.

44 Agatha Ramm, *Sir Robert Morier*, 359-60.

45 For the background of the incident see G.J. Alder, *British India's Northern Frontier, 1865-95*, 206-47.

46 Rosebery to Gladstone, 27 August 1892, Gladstone Papers, 44289, f.181.

47 Hamilton Diary, 29 August 1892, Hamilton Papers, 48658, f.124.

48 Gladstone to Rosebery, 3, 5, and 7 September 1892, Rosebery Papers, 10024, ff.105-6, 113-14, 123-4.

49 Morier to Rosebery, 28 September 1892, Morier Papers.

50 Morier to Rosebery, 23 November 1892, Morier Papers.

51 Morier to Rosebery, 12 September 1892, Morier Papers.

52 Morier to Brackenbury, 15 February 1892, Morier Papers.

53 Brackenbury to Morier, 20 March 1892, Morier Papers.

54 Brackenbury to Morier, 25 August 1891, Morier Papers.

55 Wolseley to Campbell-Bannerman, 6 December 1892, Campbell-Bannerman Papers, 41233, f.110-12; and see Adrian Preston, "Frustrated Great Gamesmanship: Sir Garnet Wolseley's Plans for War against Russia, 1873-80," *International History Review* 2 (1980): 239-65.

56 Chapman to Brackenbury, secret, 8 September 1892, Chapman Papers, WO16/106.

57 Chapman to Roberts, private and secret, 8 September 1892, Chapman Papers, WO16/106.

58 Lansdowne to Kimberley, 25 August 1892, FO65/1440; India Office Memorandum to Foreign Office, 14 October 1892, FO65/1442.

59 Kimberley to Lansdowne, 26 August 1892, Lansdowne Papers, Mss.Eur. D558/5; Hamilton Diary, 19 August 1892, Hamilton Papers, 48658, f.112.

60 Kimberley to Lansdowne, private, 13 October 1892, Lansdowne Papers, Mss. Eur. D558/5.

61 Ripon to Kimberley (copy), 26 August and 2 September 1892, Ripon Papers, 43526, f.76 and f.89.

62 Kimberley to Campbell-Bannerman, private, 7 October 1892, Campbell-Bannerman Papers, 41221, f.103.

63 Lansdowne to Kimberley, private, 23 November 1892, Lansdowne Papers, Mss.Eur. D558/5.

64 Lansdowne to Kimberley, telegram, secret, 25 August 1892, FO65/1440. The Afghans had driven the Chinese out of Somotash; see Sanderson's minute of 27 August 1892, FO65/1440.

65 Rosebery to Howard, no.154B, 26 August 1892, FO65/1440.

66 Lansdowne to Kimberley, 5 October 1892, Lansdowne Papers, Mss.Eur. D558/5.

67 Morier to Rosebery, private, 2 September 1892, Morier Papers.

68 Kimberley to Lansdowne, private, 8 September 1892, Lansdowne Papers, Mss.Eur. D558/5.

69 War Office Diary for July 1892, FO65/1441.

70 Lansdowne to Kimberley, private, 13 September 1892, Lansdowne Papers, Mss.Eur. D558/5.

71 Kimberley to Lansdowne, 6 October 1892, Lansdowne Papers, Mss.Eur. D558/5.

72 Lansdowne to Kimberley, 13 September 1892, Lansdowne Papers, Mss.Eur. D558/5.

73 Rosebery to O'Conor, no.198, 2 December 1892, and O'Conor to Rosebery, no.261, 24 December 1892, FO65/1444.

74 Lansdowne to Kimberley, 1 November 1892, private, Lansdowne Papers, Mss. Eur. D558/5.

75 Minute by Sanderson on memorandum from Foreign Office to India Office, 17 November 1892, FO17/1152.

76 Minutes by Currie and Rosebery on memorandum from India Office to Foreign Office, 24 November 1892; and memorandum from Foreign Office to India Office, 30 November 1892, FO17/1152.

77 Memorandum from India Office to Foreign Office, 10 December 1892, FO17/1152.

78 Minute by Currie on ibid.

79 Morier to Rosebery, 2 September 1892, Morier Papers.

80 Gladstone to Queen Victoria, 29 September 1892, LQV, 3rd ser., 2: 160; Gladstone to Rosebery, 21 September 1892, Rosebery Papers, 10024, ff.162–3.

81 Rosebery to Gladstone, 29 September 1892, Gladstone Papers, 44289, f.236.

82 On Anderson see, W.R. Louis, "Sir Percy Anderson's Grand African Strategy, 1883-1896," *English Historical Review* 81 (1966): 292-314.

83 Gladstone to Rosebery, 17 September 1892, Rosebery Papers, 10024, ff.144-6.

84 Currie to Anderson (with minute by Rosebery), 23 August 1892, FO84/2285.

85 Rosebery to Gladstone, 29 September 1892, Gladstone Papers, 44289, f.236.

86 See J.S. Galbraith, *Mackinnon and East Africa, 1878-95: A Study in the "New Imperialism,"* 218-19.

87 See, for example, Gladstone to Rosebery, 21 September 1892, Rosebery Papers 10024, ff.162-3; and Fowler to Rosebery, 23 September 1982, Rosebery Papers, 10132, f.139.

88 *Times*, 1 October 1892, p.6.

89 Salisbury produced a similar prospectus: "we must open new sources of consumption in the more untrodden portions of the earth." *Parliamentary Debates* (Lords), 25 (1894): 151.

90 Hamilton Diary, 3 February 1889, Hamilton Papers, 48650, f.47.

91 Harcourt to Morley, 21 September 1892, Harcourt Papers.

92 Harcourt to Loulou Harcourt, 22 September 1892, Harcourt Papers, box 1; Harcourt to Spencer, 26 September 1892, Harcourt Papers, box 27.

93 On Harcourt see Peter Stansky, *Ambitions and Strategies: The Struggle for the Leadership of the Liberal Party in the 1890s*, xiv-xv, 44-6.

94 John McLean, "Campbell-Bannerman: The New Imperialism and the Struggle for Leadership within the Liberal Party, 1894-1906" (PHD, University of Connecticut, 1974), 42.

95 Harcourt to Loulou Harcourt, 24 September 1892, Harcourt Papers, box 1.

96 Loulou Harcourt to Harcourt, 25 September 1892, Harcourt Papers, box 1; Ripon's memorandum (printed for cabinet distribution), 25 September 1892, Rosebery Papers, 10132, ff.156-7.

97 Harcourt to Loulou Harcourt, private, 24 September 1892, Harcourt Papers, box 1; Munro-Ferguson to wife, 22 October 1892, Munro-Ferguson Papers.

98 Harcourt to Spencer (copy), 11 October 1892, Harcourt Papers, box 27.

99 Harcourt to Rosebery, 13 September 1892, Rosebery Papers, 10035, ff.96-9.

100 Harcourt to Spencer (copy), 26 September 1892, Harcourt Papers, box 27.

101 Hamilton Diary, 31 October 1892, Hamilton Papers, 48659, f.23.

102 Rosebery to Harcourt, confidential, 19 October 1892, Harcourt Papers, box 23.

103 Hamilton Diary, 22 October 1892, Hamilton Papers, 48659, f.15; Harcourt to Rosebery, 18 October 1892, Rosebery Papers 10035, ff.138-41.

104 But even he regarded the proposal as a tactical manoeuvre. "If Uganda is to be retained - and it would be disastrous to let it go," he told Sir Percy

274   Notes to pages 87–98

Anderson, "it would have to be administered under the direct orders of Her Majesty's Government." 3 September 1892, Portal Papers.

105 Portal to Cawston, 2 October 1892, Portal Papers.

106 Rosebery to Portal, 1 December 1892, Portal Papers.

107 Ibid.

108 Esher Journal, 19 November 1892, Esher Papers.

109 Currie to Morier, 2 December 1892, Morier Papers.

110 Munro-Ferguson to Rosebery, 7 October 1892, Rosebery Papers, 10018, ff.186–91.

111 Ripon to Kimberley (copy), November 1892, Ripon Papers, 43526, f.139.

112 Gladstone to Harcourt, secret, 26 September 1892, Harcourt Papers, Box 23.

113 Morley to Gladstone, secret, 9 October 1892, Gladstone Papers, 44257, f.11.

114 Dufferin to Rosebery, private, 19 September and 4 October 1892, Dufferin Papers, D1071H/01.

115 Rosebery to Dufferin, private, 30 August 1892, Dufferin Papers, D1071H/02.

116 Gladstone to Rosebery, secret, 1 November 1892, Rosebery Papers, 10025, f.116.

117 Ibid.

118 Rosebery to Gladstone, secret, 4 November 1892, Gladstone Papers, 44290, f.41.

119 Rosebery to Gladstone, 7 November 1892, Gladstone Papers, 44290, f.47.

120 Gladstone to Rosebery, 4 November 1892, Rosebery Papers, 10025, ff.128–31.

121 Rosebery to Gladstone, 7 November 1892, Gladstone Papers, 44290, f.47.

122 Dufferin to Rosebery, private and personal, 2 November 1892, Dufferin Papers, D1071H/01.

123 Rosebery to Dufferin, "*Confidential* – nay, *Secret*," 1 November 1892, Dufferin Papers, D1071H/02.

124 Hardinge to Rosebery, telegram 150, confidential, 12 October 1892, FO78/4455.

125 Cromer to Rosebery, telegram 166, secret, 5 December 1892, FO78/4455.

126 Hamilton Diary, 15 September 1891, Hamilton Papers, 48656, f.82.

CHAPTER THREE

1 Rosebery to Gladstone, 16 July 1891, Gladstone Papers, 44289, ff.140–3.

2 Cromer to Rosebery, telegram 7, confidential, 7 January 1893, FO78/4517B.

3 White to Salisbury, private, 16 October 1888, FO364/1. On the background of the concession, see Colin L. Smith, *The Embassy of Sir William White at Constantinople*, 118–33; Bekir Silki, *Das Bagdadbahn-Problem 1890–1905* (Freiburg 1935); J.B. Wolfe, "The Bagdad Railway," *University of Mis-*

souri Studies 11 (1936); M.K. Chapman, "Great Britain and the Bagdad Railway, 1888–1914," *Smith Studies in History* 31 (1948).

4 On Siemens and the first phase of the Baghdad Railway see Karl Helfferich, *Georg von Siemens* 3 (Berlin 1923).

5 White to Salisbury, private, 16 October 1888, FO364/1.

6 See Engin Deniz Akarli, "The Problems of External Pressures, Power Struggles and Budgetary Deficits in Ottoman Politics under Abdulhamid II (1876–1909)" (PHD thesis, Princeton, 1976), 45–9; and also Ahmed Djemal Pascha, *Erinnerungen eines türkischen Staatsmannes* (Munich 1923), who argued that this was the motive behind the Turkish alliance with Germany in 1914.

7 See K.H.W. Hilborn, "British Policy and Diplomacy in the Near East during the Liberal Administrations: August 1892–June 1895" (D.Phil thesis, Oxford University, 1960).

8 Rosebery to Ford, telegram 79, 29 December 1892, FO78/4411.

9 Malet to Rosebery, no. 11, confidential, 12 January 1893, FO64/1293.

10 On the connection between "world policy" and commercial expansion see Bülow's memoirs: Prince Bernhard von Bülow, *Imperial Germany*, trans. Marie A. Lewenz (Toronto 1914), 26–31.

11 On this relationship generally see Theodore A. Bayer, *England und der neue Kurs 1890–1895: auf Grund unveröffentlicher Akten* (Tübingen 1955); Lillian M. Penson, "The New Course in British Foreign Policy, 1892–1902," *Transactions of the Royal Historical Society*, A ser., 25 (1943): 121–39; and Helge Granfelt, *Der Dreibund nach dem Sturze Bismarcks*, vol. 1, *England im Einverstandnis mit dem Dreibund, 1890–96* (Berlin 1962).

12 A good, although limited, introduction to writings on German policy in this period may be found in: Peter G. Thielen, "Die Aussenpolitik des deutschen Reichs 1890–1914, Literatur and Forschungsbericht für die Jahre 1945–60," *Welt als Geschichte* 22 (1962): 27–48; see also Fritz Fellner, *Der Dreibund europäische Diplomatie vor dem Ersten Weltkrieg* (Munich 1960); and the provocative article by Christopher Andrew, "German World Policy and the Reshaping of the Dual Alliance," *Journal of Contemporary History* 1 (1966): 137–51.

13 On the new course, see Norman Rich, "National Interest in Imperial German Foreign Policy: Bismarck, William II and the Road to World War I," in B. Mitchell Simpson III, ed., *War, Strategy, and Maritime Power* (New Brunswick 1977).

14 Cromer to Rosebery, telegram 7, confidential, 7 January 1893, FO78/4517B.

15 Cromer to Rosebery, telegram 13, confidential, 7 January 1893, FO78/4517B.

16 Rosebery to Cromer, telegram 7, 8 January 1893, FO78/4517A.

17 Rosebery to Ford, telegram 4, 9 January 1893, FO78/4485.

18 Minute by Sir Thomas Sanderson (head of the eastern department), on

Ford to Rosebery, telegram 5, 13 January 1893, FO78/4486.

19 Malet to Rosebery, no.8, confidential, 7 January 1893, FO64/1293.

20 Ibid. The German ambassador in London, Paul von Hatzfeldt, opposed the policy of forcing Rosebery to commit himself. Rosebery was Germany's best friend in the Liberal government, and they should not risk weakening his position. Hatzfeldt to Marschall, 24 November 1892, *GP 8*, no.1744, 93–6.

21 See Henry Cord Meyer, "German Economic Relations with Southeastern Europe, 1870–1914," *American Historical Review* 56 (October 1951): 77–90; and M.L. Flaningam, "German Eastward Expansion, Fact and Fiction: A Study in German-Ottoman Trade Relations, 1890–1914," *Journal of Central European Affairs* (January 1955).

22 See the minute by Sanderson on Cromer to Rosebery, telegram 12, confidential, 7 January 1893, FO78/4517B.

23 Rosebery to Malet, no.17A, secret, 12 January 1893, FO64/1291.

24 Rosebery to Ford, no.271, 29 December 1892, FO78/4411.

25 Rosebery to Ford, telegram 4, 9 January 1893, FO78/4485.

26 Ford to Rosebery, telegram 116, 26 December 1892, FO78/4419.

27 Ford to Rosebery, telegram 2, 9 January 1893, FO78/4486.

28 Ford to Rosebery, telegram 4, 13 January 1893, FO78/4486.

29 Ford to Rosebery, telegram 7, 16 January 1893, FO78/4486.

30 Malet to Rosebery, no.15, confidential, 14 January 1893, FO64/1293; and see the memorandum by Marschall in *GP* 14, pt. 2:455.

31 Rosebery to Malet, no.23, secret, 17 January 1893, FO64/1292.

32 Rosebery to Malet, no.17A, secret, 12 January 1893, FO64/1292.

33 Rosebery to Ford, telegram 8, 18 January 1893, FO78/4485.

34 Rosebery to Ford, telegram 15, secret, 25 January 1893, FO78/4485.

35 Cromer to Rosebery, telegram 177, confidential, 31 December 1892, FO78/4455.

36 Cromer to Rosebery, telegram 13, confidential, 7 January 1893, FO78/4517B.

37 Ford to Rosebery, telegram 111, secret, 12 December 1892. FO78/4419. Ford concluded that Ismail's advice was not directed against the British in Egypt.

38 Malet to Rosebery, private, 21 January 1893, Malet Papers, FO343/13; "and, of course, anything Ismail says is inspired by the Sultan," Cromer to Rosebery, private, 13 January 1893. Cromer Papers, FO633/7; The khedive's most influential adviser at this time was his Swiss teacher, Louis Rouiller, who had proclaimed when he landed in Egypt that his mission was to drive the British out. See Ann Elizabeth Mayer, "Abbas Hilmi II: The Khedive and Egypt's Struggle for Independence" (PHD thesis, University of Michigan, 1978), 90.

39 Cromer to Rosebery, telegram 19, 15 January 1893; and telegram 20, 16 January 1893, FO78/4517B.
40 Cromer to Rosebery, private, 13 January 1891, Cromer Papers, FO633/7.
41 Cromer to Rosebery, telegram 20, confidential, 16 January 1893, FO78/4517B.
42 Cromer to Rosebery, telegram 22, 17 January 1893, FO78/4517B. The khedive had also appointed new ministers of finance and justice.
43 Cromer to Rosebery, telegram 25, 17 January 1893, FO78/4517B.
44 Cromer to Rosebery, private, 22 January 1893, Cromer Papers, FO633/7.
45 Cromer to Rosebery, telegram 19, 15 January 1893, FO78/4517B.
46 Harcourt to Rosebery, secret, 17 January 1893, Rosebery Papers, 10035, ff.240–1.
47 Hamilton Diary, 17 January 1893, Hamilton Papers, 48659, f.85.
48 Gladstone to Queen Victoria, 16 January 1893, *LQV*, 3rd ser., 2: 203; Gladstone to Rosebery, immediate, 16 January 1893, Rosebery Papers, 10026, ff.3–4.
49 Cromer to Rosebery, telegram 19, 15 January 1893, FO78/4517B.
50 Hamilton Diary, 14 January 1893, Hamilton Papers, 48659, ff.81–2.
51 Journal of Jewis Harcourt, 17 January 1893, Harcourt Papers.
52 Cromer to Rosebery, 28 January 1893, Cromer Papers, FO633/7.
53 Rosebery to Cromer, private and confidential, 19 January 1893, Cromer Papers, FO633/7.
54 Ibid.; Rosebery to Queen Victoria, *LQV*, 3rd ser., 2: 207.
55 Rosebery to Cromer, telegram 16, secret, 17 January 1893, FO78/4517A; Cromer to Rosebery, telegram 28, 18 January 1893, FO78/4517B. The complete text of this telegram is reprinted in *LQV*, 3rd ser., 2: 205–6.
56 Rosebery to Cromer, private and confidential, 19 January 1893, Cromer Papers, FO633/7.
57 Rosebery to Cromer, secret, 27 January 1893, Cromer Papers, FO633/7.
58 Cromer to Rosebery, telegram 31, 19 January 1893, FO78/4517B.
59 Rosebery to Gladstone, secret, 19 January 1893, Gladstone Papers, 44290, f.80.
60 Rosebery to Queen Victoria, 20 January 1893, *LQV*, 3rd ser., 2: 208.
61 Gladstone to Rosebery, 1 November 1892, and 2 November 1892, Rosebery Papers, 10025, ff.114–15, 119–20.
62 Rosebery to Gladstone, 4 November 1892, Gladstone Papers, 42290, f.41; Gladstone to Rosebery, 4 November 1892, Rosebery Papers, 10025, ff.125–6.
63 Hamilton Diary, 20 January 1893, Hamilton Papers, 48659.
64 Ripon to Kimberley, 22 January 1893, Ripon Papers, 43526, f.157.
65 Campbell-Bannerman to Gladstone [sent on to Rosebery], 21 January 1893, Rosebery Papers, 10026, ff.47–9.
66 Cromer to Rosebery, telegrams 31 and 32, 19 January 1893, FO78/4517B;

Rosebery to Cromer, telegram 18, 20 January 1893, FO78/4517A; Cromer to Rosebery, telegram 36, 21 January 1893, FO78/4517B.

67 Rosebery to Queen Victoria, 22 January 1893, *LQV*, 3rd ser., 2: 211.

68 Rosebery to Dufferin, and all embassies, telegram 5, 23 January 1893, FO27/3122.

69 Rosebery to Malet, secret, 11 January 1893, Malet Papers, FO343/3.

70 Ibid.; Rosebery to Malet, no.23, secret, 17 January 1893, FO64/1292.

71 Rosebery to Malet, secret, 11 January 1893, Malet Papers, FO343/3.

72 Malet to Rosebery, no.31, confidential, 17 February 1893, FO99/311.

73 Kimberley to Lansdowne, private, 19 January 1893, Lansdowne Papers, Mss.Eur. D558/6.

74 Morier to Rosebery, no.24, 18 January 1893, FO65/1460.

75 Rosebery to Morier, no.19, 17 January 1893, FO65/1460.

76 Lansdowne to Kimberley, private, 11 January 1893, Lansdowne Papers, Mss.Eur. D558/6.

77 Lascelles to Rosebery, telegrams 173 and 174, 14 December 1892, FO65/1444; and memorandum by Godley, 1 February 1893, FO65/1461.

78 Lascelles to Lansdowne, private, 2 March 1893, Lansdowne Papers, Mss.Eur. D558/24.

79 Lansdowne to Kimberley, 11 January 1893, Lansdowne Papers, Mss.Eur. D558/6.

80 Rosebery to Morier, telegram 17, 21 February 1893, FO65/1448.

81 Roberts to Lansdowne, private, 2 February 1893, Lansdowne Papers, Mss.Eur. D558/24.

82 Sir West Ridgeway (special commissioner to Morocco) to Rosebery, private, 4 June 1893, Rosebery Papers, 10133, ff.84–90.

83 Eliot to Morier, private, 24 October 1892, Morier Papers.

84 Smith to Rosebery, no.171, confidential, 3 October 1892, FO99/296. In fact, the French were themselves divided on this issue. See L.M. Fozard, "Charles-Louis de Saulces de Freycinet: The Railways and the Expansion of the French Empire in North and West Africa, 1877–93" (PHD thesis, Boston University, 1975), 381–93.

85 Eliot to Rosebery, no.192, very confidential, 24 October 1892, FO99/296.

86 Eliot to Rosebery, no.198, very confidential, 31 October 1892, FO99/296.

87 Satow Diary, 28 October 1893, Satow Papers, 30 33/15/15.

88 On the Spanish role in Morocco, see Robert Chandler Bogard, "Africanismo and Morocco: 1830–1912" (PHD thesis, University of Texas at Austin, 1975).

89 Wolff to Rosebery, no.21, 19 January 1893, FO99/311; and see Wolff to Rosebery, secret and confidential, 24 January 1893, FO99/311.

90 Rosebery to Wolff, telegram 9, 27 January 1893, FO99/311.

91 Wolff to Rosebery, no.30, secret and confidential, 28 January 1893,

FO99/311; Rosebery to Wolff, no.24, confidential, 8 February 1893, FO99/311.

92 Rosebery to Gladstone, 16 July 1891, Gladstone Papers, 44289, ff.140–3.

93 Rosebery to Herbert Bismarck, private (copy), 2 October 1892, Rosebery Papers, 10201 (II), f.304.

CHAPTER FOUR

1 India Office memorandum to Foreign Office, 24 January 1893, FO17/1175.

2 Rosebery to Dufferin, no.87, 8 March 1893, FO17/1176.

3 Dufferin to Rosebery, no.122, 7 March 1893, FO17/1176.

4 Jones to Rosebery, telegram 4, 22 March 1893, and Rosebery to Jones, telegram 3, 22 March 1893, FO17/1176.

5 Foreign Office memorandum to India Office, immediate and confidential, 30 March 1893, FO17/1176.

6 Sanderson to Dufferin, private, 7 April 1893, FO17/1176.

7 Rosebery to Maha Yotha, 5 May 1893, FO17/1177.

8 Jones to Rosebery, telegram 16, 2 June 1893, FO17/1178.

9 Rosebery to Jones, telegrams 9 and 10, 4 and 5 June 1893, FO17/1178.

10 Jones to Rosebery, telegrams 17 and 23, 5 and 22 June 1893, FO17/1178.

11 Rosebery to Jones, telegram 20, secret, 12 July 1893, FO17/1179.

12 Phipps to Rosebery, telegram 42, 13 July 1893 (received by Foreign Office at 10 P.M.), FO17/1179.

13 Jones to Rosebery, telegram 32, 13 July 1893 (received by Foreign Office at 9:30 P.M.), FO17/1179.

14 Rosebery to Phipps, telegram 27, 14 July 1893, FO17/1179.

15 Rosebery to Jones, telegram 23, 15 July 1893, FO17/1179.

16 Foreign Office memorandum to Admiralty, immediate, 27 June 1893, FO17/1178.

17 Rosebery to Jones, telegram 24, 15 July 1893, FO17/1179.

18 Jones to Rosebery, telegram 36, 17 July 1893, FO17/1179.

19 Phipps to Rosebery, telegram 55, 19 July 1893; and Rosebery to Jones, telegram 26, confidential, 20 July 1893, FO17/1180.

20 Rosebery to Dufferin (unnumbered draft of instructions), 20 July 1893, FO17/1180.

21 Rosebery to Dufferin, no.251, 19 July 1893, FO17/1178.

22 Rosebery to Jones, telegram 29, 21 July 1893, FO17/1180.

23 Jones to Rosebery (unnumbered), 20 July 1893; and Colonial Office memorandum to Foreign Office, immediate and confidential, 22 June 1893, FO17/1180.

24 Rosebery to Jones, telegram 31, 22 July 1893, FO17/1180.

25 Satow Diary, 25 July 1893, Satow Papers, 30 33/15/15. Satow, the ministry's

leading expert on Siamese affairs, had recently been transferred from Brazil to Morocco. See Cecilia Osteen Jan, "The East Asian Diplomatic Service and Observations of Sir Ernest Mason Satow" (PHD thesis, Florida State University, 1976).

26 Rosebery to Dufferin, secret, 26 July 1893, Dufferin Papers, D1071/H/02/2.

27 Hamilton Diary, 23 July 1893, Hamilton Papers, 48661, f.1.

28 A.J.P. Taylor, *The Struggle for Mastery in Europe*, 343.

29 Rosebery to Dufferin, no.298A, confidential, 25 July 1893, FO17/1180.

30 See D.K. Fieldhouse, *The Colonial Empires* (New York 1965), 229.

31 This part of the conversation was not recorded officially. See the more candid account given in Rosebery to Dufferin, private, 25 July 1893, Dufferin Papers, D1071/H/02/2. The complete text may be found in Gordon Martel, "Documenting the Great Game: 'World Policy' and the 'Turbulent Frontier' in the 1890's," *International History Review* 2 (1980): 296–7.

32 Dufferin to Rosebery, private and personal, 23 July 1893, Dufferin Papers, D1071/H/01/3.

33 The French cabinet had agreed, on 25 July, to demand the occupation of Battambang and Angkor, but the next day "Develle had second thoughts, wanted to adjourn the occupation and seek instead an understanding with England." Christopher Andrew, *Théophile Delcassé and the Entente Cordiale* (London 1968), 33.

34 Rosebery to Dufferin, no.303A and no.311, confidential, 28 July 1893, FO17/1181.

35 Rosebery to Dufferin, private and confidential, 1 August 1893, Dufferin Papers, D1071/H/02/2.

36 Dufferin to Rosebery, telegram 82, 31 July 1893, FO17/1181.

37 Hamilton Diary, 24 July 1893, Hamilton Papers, 48661, f.3.

38 Gladstone to Rosebery, 18 September 1893, Rosebery Papers, 10027, ff.50–2.

39 See, for example, Taylor, *Struggle for Mastery*, 343.

40 Memorandum by Rosebery, 25 July 1893, Rosebery Papers, 10133, f.131.

41 Rosebery to Howard, telegram 92, 21 July 1893, FO65/1448.

42 Howard to Rosebery, no.203, confidential, 1 August 1893, FO65/1447.

43 Howard to Rosebery, no.194, secret, 25 July 1893, FO65/1447.

44 Morier to Currie, private, 6 June 1893, Morier Papers.

45 Rosebery to Gladstone, 10 August 1893, Gladstone Papers, 44290, ff.170–11. This judgment was certainly correct. The moderates, led by Develle, were constantly under attack from the colonial party, led by Delcassé. See Henri Brunschwig, "Le Parti colonial francais," *Revue française d'histoire d'outre-mer* 46 (1959), and Andrew, *Delcassé*, 32–42.

46 Kimberley to Lansdowne, private, 27 July 1893, Lansdowne Papers, D558/6; reproduced in Martel, "Great Game," 297.

47 Kimberley to Campbell-Bannerman, 7 October 1892, Campbell-Bannerman Papers, 41221, f.103.

48 Elgin to Rosebery, 7 July 1895, Rosebery Papers, 10105, ff.160–5.

49 Morier to Currie, private, 8 June 1893, Morier Papers.

50 Engin Deniz Akarli, "The Problems of External Pressures, Power Struggles and Budgetary Deficits in Ottoman Politics under Abdulhamid II (1876–1909)" (PHD thesis, Princeton University, 1976), 44–9.

51 Nicolson to Villiers, private, 5 June 1893, Nicolson Papers, FO800/22.

52 Vlangalay, the Russian ambassador to Italy, currently at St Petersburg on leave, was "gushing" in his appreciation of the speech. Morier to Rosebery, no.166, confidential, 21 June 1893, FO65/1447.

53 Friedrich Haselmayr, *Diplomatischen Geschichte des Zweiten Reichs*, Buch 4, *Ein Jahrzehnt Wechselvoller Kaiserlicher Politik, 1890–99* (Munich 1961), 135–58.

54 See Pierre Milza, "La politique étrangère francaise et l'Italie," *Rassagena storica toscana* 13 (1967): 47–80.

55 Howard to Rosebery, no.180, 5 July 1893, FO65/1447.

56 Paget to Rosebery, no.81, 13 May 1893, FO7, 1179.

57 H.W.V. Temperley and L.M. Penson, *Foundations of British Foreign Policy*, 473–4.

58 Malet to Rosebery, no.132, confidential, 9 June 1893, FO64/1293.

59 Rosebery's memorandum on his conversation with Deym, 27 June 1893, Rosebery Papers, 10133, ff.119–20. This is Rosebery's account of the conversation recorded by Deym and reproduced in Temperley and Penson, *Foundations*, 475–7. The conversation of 14 June, in which the issue of Salisbury's agreements had not been raised, Rosebery apparently considered not worth recording. His version of the 27 June meeting was kept absolutely secret; it was not shown even to Sir Philip Currie.

60 See Calvin Roberts, "The Egyptian Question and the Triple Alliance, 1894–1904" (PHD thesis, University of New Mexico, 1973), 140–4.

61 Rosebery to Gladstone, 10 August 1893, Gladstone Papers, 44290, f.170.

62 See T.B. Miller, "The Egyptian Question and British Foreign Policy, 1892–94," *Journal of Modern History* 32 (1960): 4–5.

63 Ford to Rosebery, telegram 89, secret, 10 June 1893; and Nicolson to Rosebery, telegram 116, secret, 9 July 1893, FO78/4486.

64 Nicolson to Rosebery, telegram 117, Secret, 9 July 1893, FO78/4486.

65 Nicolson to Rosebery, telegram 130, confidential, 16 July 1893, FO78/4486; Ann E. Mayer, "Abbas Hilmi II: The Khedive and Egypt's Struggle for Independence" (PHD thesis, University of Michigan, 1978), 311–14.

66 Nicolson to Rosebery, telegram 137, confidential, 20 July 1893, FO78/4486.

67 Nicolson to Rosebery, telegram 139, 21 July 1893, FO78/4486.

68 Rosebery to Hardinge (acting in Cromer's absence), private and secret, 28

July 1893, Cromer Papers, FO633/7.

69 Rosebery to Gladstone, confidential, 18 July 1893, Gladstone Papers, 44290, f.153.

70 Rosebery to Gladstone, 5 August 1893, Gladstone Papers, 44290, f.165.

71 Corbett to Rosebery, private, 14 August 1893, Corbett Papers, 26/124, f.88. Thoumian was one of the Armenian professors whom the British had managed to free.

72 See, for example, Prince Heinrich (ambassador at Vienna) to Caprivi, 1 May 1893, *GP* 9: 99–101.

73 The original proposal came from the Italians. See Edwardes to Rosebery, telegram 54, 9 July 1893, FO45/701; and Spencer to Rosebery, 29 July 1893, Rosebery Papers, 10062, ff.95–6.

74 Rosebery to Spencer, secret, 29 July 1893, Spencer Papers, Admiralty Box.

75 Rosebery to Campbell-Bannerman (copy), secret, 10 August 1893, Rosebery Papers, 10002, ff.98–9; Rosebery to Campbell-Bannerman, 26 August 1893, Campbell-Bannerman Papers, Add. Mss. 41226, f.148.

76 Rosebery to Campbell-Bannerman (copy), secret, 10 August 1893, Rosebery Papers, 10002, ff.98–9.

77 Ibid.

78 Chapman to Villiers, private, 29 July 1893, Rosebery Papers, 10133, ff.137–8.

79 Chapman to Villiers, private, 2 August 1893, Rosebery Papers, 10133, ff.143–4.

80 Copies were sent, or originals shown, to Rosebery as a matter of course. See Villiers to Rosebery, 12 August 1893, Rosebery Papers, 10133, ff.154–5.

81 Villiers to Rosebery, 12 August 1893, Rosebery Papers, 10133, ff.154–5

82 Campbell-Bannerman to Rosebery, secret, 22 August 1893, Rosebery Papers, 10002, ff.101–3.

83 Campbell-Bannerman to Spencer (copy), 17 August 1893, Campbell-Bannerman Papers, 41228, f.328.

84 Ibid.

85 See John McLean, "Campbell-Bannerman: The New Imperialism and the Struggle for Leadership within the Liberal Party, 1894–1906" (PHD thesis, University of Connecticut, 1974), esp. 1–72.

86 Chapman to Bridge (copy), private, 3 August 1893, Chapman Papers, WO16/106.

87 Chapman to Buller (copy), confidential, 5 August 1893, Chapman Papers, WO16/106.

88 Chapman to Villiers (copy), private and confidential, 12 August 1893, Chapman Papers, WO16/106.

89 Rosebery to Campbell-Bannerman, 26 August 1893, Campbell-Bannerman Papers, 41226, f.148. Rosebery had been informed of the results of the meeting by Chapman on 1 August. These included the Malta plan, which Chapman proposed to submit following Rosebery's approval. Chapman

to Rosebery, 1 August 1893, Rosebery Papers, 10133, f.140.

90 Chapman to Buller (copy), 5 and 9 August 1893, Rosebery Papers, 10133, ff.148–52.

91 Rosebery to Campbell-Bannerman, confidential, 1 September 1893, Campbell-Bannerman Papers, 41226, f.149; Campbell-Bannerman to Rosebery, 2 September 1893, Rosebery Papers, 10002, f.110.

92 Spencer to Rosebery, 3 October 1893, Rosebery Papers, 10062, ff.107–10.

93 Rosebery to Campbell-Bannerman (copy), confidential, 29 November 1893, Rosebery Papers, 10002, f.124.

94 Campbell-Bannerman to Rosebery, confidential, 4 December 1893, Rosebery Papers, 10002, ff.128–9.

95 Rosebery to Spencer and Campbell-Bannerman (copy), 14 December 1893, Rosebery Papers, 10133, f.246.

96 See the minute by Rosebery on Currie's memorandum of conversation with Chapman, 15 December 1893, Rosebery Papers, 10133. Francis Bertie was duly appointed as the Foreign Office representative on the committee. See also Rosebery to Campbell-Bannerman, 19 December 1893, Campbell-Bannerman Papers, 41226, f.152.

97 Hamilton Diary, 2 October 1887, Hamilton Papers, 48647, ff.22–6.

98 Harcourt to Rosebery, private, 14 December 1893, Rosebery Papers, 10036, ff.48–9.

99 Munro-Ferguson to wife, 27 August 1893, Munro-Ferguson Papers.

100 Hamilton Diary, 5 November 1893, Hamilton Papers, 48661, ff.114–15.

CHAPTER FIVE

1 H.C.G. Mathew, *The Liberal Imperialists: The Ideas and Politics of a Post-Gladstonian Elite*, 200.

2 Satow Diary, 22 August 1893, Satow Papers, 30 33/15/15.

3 Rosebery to Monham (chargé d'affaires at Madrid), no.129, 13 October 1893, FO99/311.

4 Satow Diary, 2 November 1893, Satow Papers, 30 33/15/15.

5 Rosebery to Satow, telegram 38, 6 November 1893, FO99/312; Satow to Maclean, 3 November 1893, Satow Papers, 30 33/14/4.

6 Hamilton Diary, 15 January 1893, Hamilton Papers, 48659, f.84.

7 Satow Diary, 12 December 1893, Satow Papers, 30 33/15/15.

8 Bonham to Rosebery, telegram 74, 5 November 1893, FO99/312; Satow to Currie (copy), private, 6 November 1893, Satow Papers, 30 33/14/4.

9 Satow to Rosebery, telegram 58, 8 November 1893, FO99/312.

10 Currie to Satow, private, 8 November 1893, Satow Papers, 30 33/3/3.

11 Wolff to Rosebery, telegram 83, secret and confidential, 13 November 1893, FO99/312; Currie to Satow, private, 15 November 1893, Satow Papers, 30 33/3/4.

12 Gosselin to Rosebery, telegram 18, secret, 16 November 1893; Monson to Rosebery, telegram 19, secret, 21 November 1893, FO99/312.

13 Wolff to Rosebery, telegram 118, secret and confidential, 24 December 1893, FO99/312.

14 Satow Diary, 6 January 1894, 30 33/15/15.

15 Rosebery to Malet, no.19, confidential; Rosebery to Wolff, telegram 5, 9 January 1894, FO99/323.

16 Malet to Rosebery, telegram 1, secret, 13 January 1894, FO99/323.

17 Rosebery's minute on ibid.

18 Satow Diary, 13 December 1893, 30 33/15/15.

19 Wolff to Rosebery, 10 November 1893, Rosebery Papers, 10133, ff.184-6.

20 Rosebery's memorandum on conversation with Hatzfeldt, Rosebery Papers, 10133, ff.241-4.

21 Ibid.

22 Ibid.

23 Ibid.

24 Malet to Rosebery, no.306, confidential, 20 December 1893, FO64/1294.

25 Ibid.

26 Ibid.

27 Gosselin to Rosebery, no.250A, confidential, 27 October 1893, FO64/1294.

28 Malet to Rosebery, no.308, confidential, 23 December 1893, FO64/1294.

29 Rosebery to Malet, private, 6 December 1893, Malet Papers, FO343/3.

30 Rosebery to Dufferin, private, 2 January 1894, Dufferin Papers D107 H/10/3.

31 Ibid.

32 Ibid.

33 *LQV*, 3rd ser., 2: 345.

34 Ibid., 344.

35 Swaine to Ponsonby, ibid., 345.

36 Rosebery to Campbell-Bannerman, secret, 15 January 1894, Campbell-Bannerman Papers, 41226, f.160.

37 *LQV*, 3rd ser., 2: 355.

38 Rosebery to Malet, private, 3 January 1894, Malet Papers, FO343/3.

39 Hatzfeldt to Holstein, 19 October 1893, in Norman Rich and M.H. Fisher, eds., *The Holstein Papers*, 4 vols. (Cambridge 1955-63), 2: 443.

40 Rosebery's memorandum on conversation with Deym, 31 January 1894, Rosebery Papers, 10135, ff.54-9.

41 Ibid.

42 Ibid.

43 Ibid.

44 Ibid.

45 Deym to Kálnoky, 7 February 1894, H.W.V. Temperley and L.M. Penson, *Foundations of British Foreign Policy*, 481.

46 Rosebery's memorandum on conversation with Deym, 1 February 1894, Rosebery Papers, 10135, 60-2.
47 Deym to Kálnoky, 7 February 1894, Temperley and Penson, *Foundations*, 487.
48 Rosebery's memorandum on conversation with Deym, 1 February 1894, Rosebery Papers, 10135, ff.60-2.
49 Rosebery's memorandum on conversation with Hatzfeldt, 14 February 1894, Rosebery Papers, 10135, ff.63-6. Hatzfeldt's account can be found in *GP* 9: 127-9.
50 Ibid.
51 Ibid.
52 Rosebery to Malet, telegram 1, 16 February 1894, FO64/1335.
53 Rosebery to Malet, no.150, 19 December 1893, FO64/1332.
54 Rosebery to Currie, telegram 9, confidential, 15 February 1894, FO78/4545.
55 Malet to Rosebery, telegram 1, 17 February 1894, FO64/1335.
56 Malet to Rosebery (copy), private, 17 February 1894, Malet Papers, FO343/13.
57 Phipps to Anderson, telegram, private, 3 March 1894, FO27/3188.
58 Rosebery to Malet, telegram 4, 24 February 1894, FO64/1335.
59 See chap. 6.
60 Kimberley to Malet, no.31, confidential, 19 March 1894, FO64/1332.
61 Kimberley to Malet, no.48A, 23 April 1894, FO64/1332.
62 Monson to Kimberley, telegram 21, secret, 30 March 1894, FO7/1216.
63 Ibid.
64 Rosebery's memorandum on conversation with Deym, 23 February 1894, Rosebery Papers, 10135, ff.67-70.
65 Rosebery's memorandum on conversation with Deym, 26 February 1894, Rosebery Papers, 10135, ff.71-5.
66 Ibid.
67 G.N. Sanderson, *England, Europe and the Upper Nile*, 107.

CHAPTER SIX

1 On the leadership contest see Peter Stansky, *Ambitions and Strategies*, 1-97 and Rhodes James, *Rosebery*, 294-329.
2 Rosebery to Munro-Ferguson, secret, 6 February 1894, Rosebery Papers, 10018, ff.209-10.
3 Sir Ian Malcolm, *Vacant Thrones* (London 1931), 13.
4 Kimberley's Journal (extract by Rosebery), 23 February 1894, Rosebery Papers, 10186, f.277.
5 Buckle to Rosebery, 4 March 1894, Rosebery Papers, 10092, ff.37-9.
6 Rosebery to Queen Victoria, 4 March 1894, *LQV*, 3rd ser., 2:374.
7 Queen Victoria's Journal, 9 March 1894, ibid., 378.

8 Rosebery to Ponsonby, 9 March 1894, ibid., 379.

9 Haldane to Rosebery, 6 March 1894, Rosebery Papers, 10029, ff.17–22.

10 *Speeches of Lord Rosebery* (London 1896), 154.

11 *Parliamentary Debates* (Lords), 4th ser., 22 (1894): 27.

12 Morley to Rosebery, 11 March 1894, Rosebery Papers, 10046.

13 Ellis to Rosebery, 13 March 1894, Rosebery Papers, 10092, ff.143–4.

14 Morley to Rosebery, secret, 16 March 1894, Rosebery Papers, 10046, ff.190–1.

15 Ellis to Rosebery, 16 March 1894, Rosebery Papers, 10092, ff.183–4.

16 Rosebery, *Speeches*, 182.

17 Ellis to Rosebery, 19 March 1894, Rosebery Papers, 10092, f.187.

18 Hamilton Diary, 3 March 1894, Hamilton Papers, 48663, f.9.

19 Harcourt Journal, 3 March 1894, Harcourt Papers.

20 Hamilton Diary, 21 February 1894. Hamilton Papers, 48662, f.123.

21 Munro-Ferguson to wife, 20 June 1892, Munro-Ferguson Papers.

22 Hamilton Diary, 5 April 1885, Hamilton Papers, 48639, f.126.

23 Hamilton Diary, 14 June and 11 August 1892, Hamilton Papers, 48658, ff.18 and 95.

24 Rosebery to Queen Victoria, 3 March 1894, *LQV*, 3rd ser., 2: 373.

25 Memorandum by Harcourt (in Loulou Harcourt's hand), 3 March 1894, Harcourt Papers, box 27.

26 Harcourt to Morley (copy), 4 March 1894, Harcourt Papers.

27 Stansky, *Ambitions and Strategies*, 94.

28 Memorandum by Harcourt (in Loulou Harcourt's hand), 3 March 1894, Harcourt Papers, box 27.

29 Quoted in Stansky, *Ambitions and Strategies*, 93.

30 Kimberley to Malet, no.31, confidential, 19 March 1894, FO64/1332.

31 G.N. Sanderson, *England, Europe and the Upper Nile*, 165.

32 Anderson to Phipps, telegram, private, 10 March 1894, FO27/3188.

33 See P.M. Holt, *The Mahdist State in the Sudan, 1881–98* (Oxford 1958), 197–203.

34 Rosebery memorandum, April 1885, Rosebery Papers, 10132, ff.42–9; Rosebery to Cromer, private and secret, 22 April 1895, Rosebery Papers, 10136, ff.190–5; Rosebery to Spencer, 21 March 1896, Spencer Papers.

35 Rosebery to Rodd, 5 March 1894, FO10/625.

36 Kimberley to Rosebery, 27 March 1894, Rosebery Papers, 10068, ff.83–4.

37 Kimberley to Harcourt (copy), secret, 28 March 1894, Rosebery Papers, 10143, f.5.

38 Harcourt to Kimberley (copy), 28 March 1894, Rosebery Papers, 10143, f.6.

39 Harcourt memorandum, 21 April 1894, Rosebery Papers, 10143, f.11.

40 Harcourt to Campbell-Bannerman, 22 April 1894, Campbell-Bannerman Papers, 41219, f.71.

41 Kimberley to Rosebery, 22 April 1894, Rosebery Papers, 10068, f.111.

42 Hamilton Diary, 23 April 1894, Hamilton Papers, 48663, f.81.

43 Harcourt Journal, 3 and 4 May 1894, Harcourt Papers.

44 Hamilton Diary, 23 April 1894, Hamilton Papers, 48663, f.81.

45 See A.G. Gardiner, *Life of Sir William Harcourt* (London 1923), 2: 315; Rhodes James, *Rosebery*, 348–9; Stansky, *Ambitions and Strategies*, 112–13; A.J.P. Taylor, "Prelude to Fashoda: The Question of the Upper Nile, 1894–95," *English Historical Review* 65 (1950): 57.

46 Kimberley's memorandum, 21 April 1894, Rosebery Papers, 10143, f.10.

47 Kimberley's memorandum to Cabinet, 28 April 1894, Rosebery Papers, 10143, f.21.

48 Kimberley to Rosebery, 2 May 1894, Rosebery Papers, 10068, ff.120–2.

49 Harcourt to Rosebery, 3 May 1894, Rosebery Papers, 10036, ff.83–4.

50 Kimberley to Harcourt, 3 May 1894, Rosebery Papers, 10143, f.25.

51 Memoranda by Harcourt and Morley (copies) 3 May 1894, Rosebery Papers, 10143, ff.22–3.

52 Asquith's memorandum (copy), 3 May 1894, Rosebery Papers, 10143, f.23; Ripon to Kimberley (copy), Ripon Papers, 43526, f.183.

53 Ripon to Kimberley (copy), Ripon Papers, 43526, f.183.

54 Rosebery to Queen Victoria, 4 May 1894, *LQV*, 3rd ser., 2:396.

55 Kimberley to Ripon, 6 May 1894, Ripon Papers, 43526, f.186.

56 Kimberley to Rosebery, 14 May 1894, Rosebery Papers, 10068, ff.144–5.

57 Gardiner, *Harcourt* 2: 317.

58 Harcourt to Kimberley (copy), 6 June 1894, Rosebery Papers, 10143, f.65.

59 Anderson's "Notes on the Belgian Negotiations," 15 April 1894, FO10/625.

60 Kimberley to Malet, no.72, 3 May 1894, FO64/1332.

61 Plunkett to Kimberley, telegram 7, 28 May 1894, FO10/618.

62 Kimberley to Plunkett, telegram 5, 29 May 1894, FO10/618.

63 Malet to Kimberley, telegram 9, secret, 11 June 1894, FO17/1335; see also Hatzfeldt to Caprivi, 1 June 1894, *GP* 8, no.2039.

64 Anderson's minute on Malet to Kimberley, 11 June 1894, FO 17/17335.

65 Kimberley's minute on ibid.

66 The phrase is G.N. Sanderson's, in *England, Europe and the Upper Nile*, 165.

67 Kimberley to Malet, no.41, 17 April 1894, FO64/1332.

68 Kimberley to Malet, no.48A, 23 April 1894, FO64/1332.

69 Kimberley to Malet, no.86, 11 June 1894, FO64/1332.

70 Hamilton Diary, 15 June 1894, Hamilton Papers, 48664, f.13.

71 Hamilton Diary, 19 June 1894, Hamilton Papers, 48664, f.17.

72 Rosebery's undated memorandum on Kimberley's manuscript memoirs, Rosebery Papers, 10186, f.252.

73 Kirk to Lugard, 16 June 1894, Lugard Papers, S.69, f.16a.

74 Harcourt to Kimberley (copy), 12 June 1894, Rosebery Papers, 10143, f.70.

75 Harcourt to Kimberley, 15 June 1894, Rosebery Papers, 10143, f.80.

76 Malet to Kimberley, telegram 12, 15 June 1894, FO17/1335; Plunkett to Kimberley, telegram 16, 15 June 1894, FO10/618; Alvensleben to Auswartige Amt, 15 June 1894, *GP* 8, no.2057.

77 Kimberley to Malet, private, 13 June 1894, Malet Papers, FO343/3.

78 Rosebery to Queen Victoria, 14 June 1894, *LQV*, 3rd ser., 2:404.

79 Monson to Kimberley, telegram 21, secret, 30 March 1894, FO17/1216; Eulenburg (ambassador in Vienna) to Auswartige Amt, 16 June 1894, *GP* 8, no.2159.

80 Malet to Kimberley, telegram 13, 16 June 1894, FO64/1335.

81 Kimberley to Rosebery, secret, 16 June 1894, Rosebery Papers, 10068, ff.166–7.

82 Malet to Kimberley, private, 30 June 1894, Malet Papers, FO343/13.

83 Kimberley to Rosebery, 2 June 1894, Rosebery Papers, 10068, ff.157–8.

84 Rosebery to Kimberley, 3 June 1894 (Rosebery's copybook, p.27), Rosebery Papers, 10130; Kimberley to Dufferin, no.187A, 5 June 1894, FO27/3182.

85 Rosebery's memorandum, 17 June 1894, Rosebery Papers, 10135, ff.116–18.

86 Kimberley to Dufferin, telegram 16, secret, 13 June 1894, FO27/3175

87 Monson to Kimberley, telegram 44, secret, 14 June 1894, FO27/1216; Kimberley to Malet, private, 13 June 1894, Malet Papers, FO343/3.

88 Satow to Kimberley, telegram 39, secret, 14 June 1894; and Kimberley to Satow, telegram 24, 15 June 1894, FO99/319.

89 Esher's memorandum, 24 February 1894, Esher Papers, 2/7.

90 Kimberley to Paget, no.61, 23 June 1894, FO46/434.

91 Kimberley to Rosebery, 30 July 1894, Rosebery Papers, 10068, ff.210–11.

92 Rosebery's memorandum, 30 July 1894, Rosebery Papers, 10134, ff.3–5.

93 Ibid.

94 Ibid.

95 French to Kimberley, telegram 73, 3 October 1894, FO46/440.

96 Sanderson to Rosebery, 19 September 1894, Rosebery Papers, 10097, ff.219–20.

97 O'Conor to Kimberley, telegram 85, 25 September 1894, FO17/1204.

98 Kimberley to Spencer, private, 26 September 1894, Spencer Papers.

99 Hart to Campbell, telegram, 30 September 1894 (enclosed in Murray [Rosebery's private secretary] to Rosebery, 1 October 1894), Rosebery Papers, 10134, f.17.

100 Rosebery to Kimberley (copy), confidential, 2 October 1894, Rosebery Papers, 10069, f.25.

101 Rosebery's minute on Murray to Rosebery, 16 October 1894, Rosebery Papers, 10134, ff.68–9.

102 Hart to Campbell, telegram, 5 October 1894 (enclosed in Murray to Rosebery, 5 October 1894), Rosebery Papers, 10134, f.41.

103 "Even poor Spencer, who is somewhere in the neighbourhood, has not

been able to get inside the gates." Murray to Rosebery, 1 October 1894, Rosebery Papers, 10049, ff.31–2.

104 Rosebery's minute on Murray to Rosebery, 16 October 1894, Rosebery Papers, 10134, ff.68–9.

105 Kimberley to French, no.109, confidential, 21 October 1894, FO46/434.

106 French to Kimberley, telegram 79, 23 October 1894, FO46/440.

107 O'Conor to Kimberley, telegram 105, confidential, 26 October 1894, FO17/1204.

108 Rendel to Rosebery, 4 November 1894, Rosebery Papers, 10134, f.90.

109 O'Conor to Kimberley, telegram 108, confidential, 3 November 1894, FO17/1204.

110 Kimberley to Rosebery, private, 4 and 8 November 1894, Rosebery Papers, 10069, ff.84–7.

CHAPTER SEVEN

1 Lascelles to Kimberley, no.281, 5 December 1894, FO65/1473.

2 Lascelles to Kimberley, no.291, 17 December 1894, FO65/1473.

3 See Kimberley's minute of 13 September 1894, on Macartney's Diary for June 15, transmitted from the India Office to the Foreign Office on 11 September 1894, FO65/1487; and Kimberley to Malet, private, 16 October 1894, Malet Papers, FO343/3.

4 Kimberley to Rosebery, private, 16 September 1894, Rosebery Papers, 10069, ff.11–12.

5 Kimberley to Rosebery, 28 September 1894, Rosebery Papers, 10069, ff.16–17.

6 Rosebery to Kimberley, 30 September 1894 (Rosebery's copybook, p.51), Rosebery Papers, 10131.

7 Kimberley to Ripon, 19 October 1894, Ripon Papers, 43526, f.238.

8 Ibid.

9 Kimberley to Sanderson, secret, 20 October 1894, Sanderson Papers, FO800/1.

10 Ripon to Kimberley, 21 October 1894, Ripon Papers, 43526, f.242.

11 Kimberley to Sanderson, secret, 20 October 1894, Sanderson Papers, FO800/1.

12 Rosebery to Kimberley (copy), secret, 21 October 1894, Rosebery Papers, 10069, ff.70–1.

13 Ibid.

14 Kimberley to Ripon, private and confidential, 22 October 1894, Ripon Papers, 43526, f.244.

15 Murray to Rosebery, 29 October 1894, Rosebery Papers, 10049, f.55.

16 Malet to Rosebery, 3 November 1894, Rosebery Papers, 10099, ff.27–32; for Hatzfeldt's summary of the state of Anglo-German relations, see Hatzfeldt

to Hohenloe, 11 November 1894, *GP* 8, no.2161.

17 Kimberley to Gosselin, no.316, secret, 19 November 1894, FO64/1324, Hatzfeldt to Hohenloe, 22 November 1894, *GP* 8, no.2163.

18 Ibid.

19 Kimberley to Malet, private, Malet Papers, FO343/3.

20 Kimberley to Currie, telegram 115, 6 December 1894, FO78/4545; Kimberley to Lascelles, telegram 112, 6 December 1894, FO65/1474; Kimberley to Dufferin, no.578, 13 December 1894, FO27/3169; Lascelles to Kimberley, no.293, 18 December 1894, FO65/1473.

21 Lascelles to Kimberley, no.275, confidential, 29 November 1894, FO65/1473.

22 Waters to Lascelles, confidential, 3 December 1894, FO27/3183.

24 Ford to Kimberley, no.250, most confidential, 2 December 1894, FO99/324.

25 Kimberley to Ford, no.288, confidential, 20 December 1894, FO45/715.

26 Monson to Kimberley, telegram 60, most confidential, 27 November 1894, FO7/1216.

27 Monson to Kimberley, telegram 68, most confidential, 4 December 1894, FO7/1216.

28 Kimberley to Harcourt, 7 December 1894, Rosebery Papers, 10143, f.183.

29 Malet to Kimberley, private, 15 December 1894, Malet Papers, FO343/13.

30 Malet to Rosebery, 22 December 1894, Rosebery Papers, 10134, ff.310–13.

31 Rosebery to Malet (copy), secret, 6 January 1895, Rosebery Papers, 10136, ff.10–11.

32 Rosebery to Queen Victoria (copy), 15 June 1894, Rosebery Papers, 10066, ff.75–6.

33 Rosebery to Malet, 6 January 1895, Rosebery Papers, 10136, ff.10–11.

34 Hamilton Diary, 29 January 1895, Hamilton Papers, 48666, f.1.

35 Bryce to Gladstone, 5 January 1895, Bryce Papers, 12, f.158.

36 On this subject see the excellent study by R.T. Shannon, *Gladstone and the Bulgarian Agitation, 1876* (Edinburgh 1963).

37 Kimberley to Rosebery, private, 3 January 1895, Rosebery Papers, 10069, ff.135–6.

38 Kimberley to Ripon, 13 January 1895, Ripon Papers, 43527.

39 Rosebery's minute on Dufferin to Kimberley, telegram 3, 8 January 1895, FO27/3234.

40 Kimberley to Rosebery, 26 January 1895, Rosebery Papers, 10069, ff.158–9.

41 Kimberley to Dufferin, no.99, 22 February 1895, FO17/1265.

42 Kimberley to Ripon, 9 September 1894, Ripon Papers, 43526, f.225.

43 Rosebery's memorandum, 19 February 1895, Rosebery Papers, box 97.

44 Ibid.; see also Rhodes James, *Rosebery*, 364–7.

45 Rosebery's undated note on entry in Kimberley's Journal for 19 February 1895, Rosebery Papers, box 97.

46 Kimberley's Journal, 19 February 1895, Rosebery Papers, box 97.

47 Malet to Kimberley, private, 19 January 1895, Malet Papers, FO343/3.
48 Kimberley's secret memorandum on conversation with Hatzfeldt, 7 February 1895, Sanderson Papers, FO800/1.
49 Monson to Kimberley, telegram 23, confidential, 1 March 1895, FO7/1230.
50 Kimberley's secret memorandum on conversation with Hatzfeldt, 9 March 1895, Sanderson Papers, FO800/1.
51 Ibid.
52 Kimberley's secret memorandum on conversation with Hatzfeldt, 13 March 1895, Sanderson Papers, FO800/1.
53 Kimberley to Malet, no.47A, 13 March 1895, FO64/1356.
54 Scott to Kimberley, telegram 12, 18 March 1895, FO17/1265.
55 Foreign Office memorandum to India Office, pressing and confidential, 19 March 1895, FO17/1266.
56 Kimberley to Rosebery, 26 March 1895, Rosebery Papers, 10069, ff.211–15.
57 Rosebery to Kimberley (copy), 27 March 1895, Rosebery Papers, 10069, ff.217–18.
58 Murray to Rosebery, 28 March 1895, Rosebery Papers, 10049, ff.159–60.
59 Kimberley to Rosebery, 28 March 1895, Rosebery Papers, 10069, ff.219–20.
60 Murray to Rosebery, 28 March 1895, Rosebery Papers, 10049, f.160.
61 Kimberley to Dufferin, no.111, 28 March 1895, FO27/3229; Viscount Grey, *Twenty-Five Years* (London 1925), 1: 19.
62 *Parliamentary Debates* (Commons), 32 (1895): 404.
63 Ronald Robinson and John A. Gallagher, *Africa and the Victorians*, 336.
64 Harcourt to Kimberley, 29 March 1895, Rosebery Papers, 10143, f.228.
65 Kimberley to Sanderson, 29 March 1895, Sanderson Papers, FO800/1.
66 Grey to Rosebery, 30 March 1895, Rosebery Papers, 10028, ff.12–14.
67 Kimberley to Rosebery, private, 29 March 1895, Rosebery Papers, 10069, ff.221–12.
68 See the memorandum by Wingate of 12 April 1895, drawn up at Rosebery's request. The document was enclosed in Cromer to Rosebery, 12 April 1895, Rosebery Papers, 10136, ff.142–55.
69 Rosebery to Cromer (copy), secret, 22 April 1895, Rosebery Papers, 10136, ff.190–5.
70 The secret report was conveyed to Sanderson from Colonel Chapman. Sanderson to Murray, private and confidential, 10 March 1895, Rosebery Papers, 10136, ff.83–96.
71 Rosebery to Wolff, 8 January 1895, Rosebery Papers, 10030 (copybook, p.89).
72 For the details of the settlement see G.J. Alder, *British India's Northern Frontier, 1856–95.*
73 Rosebery to Dufferin (copy), secret, 2 April 1895, Rosebery Papers, 10136, ff.130–1.

74 Dufferin to Kimberley, telegram 11, 5 April 1895, FO27/3234.
75 Harcourt to Kimberley (copy), 29 March 1895, Rosebery Papers, 10143, f.228.
76 Acland to Rosebery, secret, 30 March 1895, Rosebery Papers, 10102, ff.327–8; Rosebery to Queen Victoria, telegram, 30 March 1895, LQV, 3rd ser., 2: 491; Grey, Twenty-Five Years 1:19–20; Sanderson to Grey (copy), 30 March 1895, Rosebery Papers, 10028, ff.15–16.
77 Hamilton Diary, 30 March 1895, Hamilton Papers, 48666, f.78.
78 Harcourt to Kimberley (copy), 1 April 1895, Rosebery Papers, 10143, f.234.
79 Kimberley to Rosebery, 1 April 1895, Rosebery Papers, 10070, ff.1–5.
80 Rosebery to Kimberley (copy), 6 April 1895, Rosebery Papers, 10070, ff.21–2.
81 Kimberley to Rosebery, 6 April 1895, Rosebery Papers, 10070, f.23.
82 Rosebery to Kimberley (copy), secret, 7 April 1895, Rosebery Papers, 10070, f.33.
83 Lowther to Kimberley, telegram 33, 4 April 1895, FO46/456.
84 Kimberley to Rosebery, private, 6 April 1895, Rosebery Papers, 10070, ff.27–8.
85 Ibid.
86 Ibid.
87 Rosebery to Kimberley (copy), secret, 7 April 1895, Rosebery Papers, 10070, f.33; Rosebery to Queen Victoria (copy), 8 April 1895, Rosebery Papers, 10067, f.92.
88 Rosebery to Kimberley (copy), secret, 9 April 1895, Rosebery Papers, 10070, ff.35–6; Rosebery to Sanderson, 9 April 1895, Sanderson Papers, FO800/1.
89 Rosebery to Kimberley (draft copy), 10 April 1895, Rosebery Papers, 10070, ff.41–5.
90 Kimberley to Rosebery, 10 April 1895, Rosebery Papers, 10070, ff.46–7.
91 Sanderson to Rosebery, 10 April 1895, Rosebery Papers, 10034, f.116.
92 Rosebery to Kimberley (copy), secret, 11 April 1895, Rosebery Papers, 10070, ff.48–9.
93 Hamilton Diary, 12 April 1895, Hamilton Papers, 48667, f.93.
94 Rosebery to Lascelles (copy), 13 April 1895, Rosebery Papers, 10134, ff.133–4.
95 Rosebery to Kimberley (copy), confidential, 17 April 1895, Rosebery Papers, 10070, ff.68–9.
96 Harcourt to Kimberley (copy), 5 April 1895, Rosebery Papers, 10143, f.243.
97 Lascelles to Sanderson, private, 11 April 1895, Sanderson Papers, FO800/1.
98 Rosebery to Sanderson, 16 April 1895, Sanderson Papers, FO800/1.
99 Rosebery to Cromer (copy), secret, 22 April 1895, Rosebery Papers, 10136, ff.190–5.
100 Rosebery to Fowler (copy), confidential, 26 April 1895, Rosebery Papers, 10103, ff.175–6.

101 Lascelles to Rosebery, Private, 24 April 1895, Rosebery Papers, 10134, ff.145–6.

102 Rosebery to Kimberley (copy), confidential, 28 April 1895, Rosebery Papers, 10070, ff.89–90.

103 Lowther to Kimberley, telegram 49, 2 May 1895; and telegram 51, 6 May 1895, FO46/456.

104 Kimberley to Lowther, telegram 18, 7 May 1895, FO46/455; Lowther to Kimberley, telegram 52, 8 May 1895, FO46/456.

105 Kimberley to Dufferin, no.239, 10 May 1895, FO17/1267.

106 Kimberley to Dufferin, no.254, 25 May 1895, FO17/1267.

107 Bryce to Gladstone (copy), confidential, 3 May 1895, Bryce Papers, 12, f.165; Kimberley to Rosebery, 30 April 1895, Rosebery Papers, 10070, ff.92–3.

108 Rosebery to Kimberley (copy), 30 April 1895, Rosebery Papers, 10070, f.94.

109 Lascelles to Kimberley, no.124, confidential, 8 May 1895, FO65/1491.

110 Lascelles to Sanderson, 22 May 1895, Lascelles Papers, FO800/7.

111 White to Elgin (copy), 3 May 1895, White Papers, Mss.Eur. F108/20.

112 Elgin to Godley, 10 April 1895, Kilbracken Papers, Mss.Eur. F102/13.

113 On this, see Leonard K. Young, *British Policy in China, 1895*–1902 (Oxford 1970); and J.A.S. Grenville, *Lord Salisbury and Foreign Policy* (London 1964).

114 Rosebery to Elgin, private, "Waterloo Day" (18 June) 1895. Rosebery Papers, 10030 (copybook, p.135).

115 O'Conor to Kimberley (copy), telegram, private and secret, 18 May 1895, Rosebery Papers, 10134, f.200.

116 Rosebery's minute on Sanderson to Rosebery, 14 May 1895, Rosebery Papers, 10134, ff.183–4.

117 Kimberley to Lascelles, telegram 87, 21 May 1895, FO65/1493.

118 Kimberley to Rosebery, 18 May 1895, Rosebery Papers, 10070, ff.111–12.

119 Hart to Campbell, 18 May 1895 (enclosed in Rendel to Rosebery, secret, 26 May 1895), Rosebery Papers, 10134, ff.229–30.

120 Kimberley to Lowther, telegram 27, 7 June 1895, FO46/455.

121 Satow Diary, 31 May 1895, Satow Papers, 30 33/15/17.

122 Kimberley to Lowther, no.47B, 12 June 1895, FO46/449.

123 Rosebery Journal, 24 December 1874, Rosebery Papers, 10192, f.4.

124 Rosebery Journal, n.d. (September 1872), Rosebery Papers, 10189, f.71.

Bibliography

MANUSCRIPT SOURCES

Official Correspondence

Foreign Office Records, Public Record Office. Every letter, report, and memorandum that passed between London and the major capitals of Europe from January to July 1886 and from August 1892 to June 1895 has been read and used in the preparation of this book. The records pertaining to special questions such as the Moroccan, Burmese, and Siamese affairs have also been used in their entirety.

Private Correspondence

Public Record Office (London)
    Carnock Papers (Sir Arthur Nicolson, Baron Carnock)
    Chapman Papers (Sir Edward Francis Chapman)
    Corbett Papers (Sir Vincent Corbett)
    Cromer Papers (Sir Evelyn Baring, earl of Cromer)
    Grey Papers (Sir Edward Grey)
    Hardinge Papers (Sir Charles Hardinge, Baron Hardinge of Penshurst)
    Lascelles Papers (Sir Frank Lascelles)
    Malet Papers (Sir Edward Malet)
    Sanderson Papers (Sir Thomas Sanderson)
    Satow Papers (Sir Ernest Satow)
    Villiers Papers (Sir Francis Hyde Villiers)
    White Papers (Sir William White)
Public Record Office (Belfast)
    Dufferin Papers (Sir Frederick Temple Blackwood, marquess of Dufferin)

Scottish Record Office (Edinburgh)
    Munro-Ferguson Papers (Sir Ronald Munro-Ferguson)
India Office Library (London)
    Durand Papers (Sir Henry Mortimer Durand)
    Kilbracken Papers (Sir John Arthur Godley, Baron Kilbracken)
    Lansdowne Papers (Sir Henry Petty-Fitzmaurice, marquess of Lansdowne)
    Lyall Papers (Sir Alfred Lyall)
    General White Papers (Sir George Stuart White)
    Wolverhampton Papers (Sir Henry Hartley Fowler, Lord Wolverhampton)
British Library (London)
    Campbell-Bannerman Papers (Sir Henry Campbell-Bannerman)
    Dilke Papers (Sir Charles Dilke)
    Gladstone Papers (William Ewart Gladstone)
    Hamilton Papers (Sir Edward Hamilton)
    Paget Papers (Sir Augustus Paget)
    Ripon Papers (George Frederick Robinson, marquess of Ripon)
    Scott Papers (Sir Charles Scott)
National Library of Scotland (Edinburgh)
    Haldane Papers (Richard Burdon Haldane, Viscount Haldane)
    Kimberley Papers (John Wodehouse, earl of Kimberley)
    Rosebery Papers (Archibald Philip Primrose, earl of Rosebery)
Bodleian Library (Oxford)
    Bryce Papers (James Bryce, Viscount Bryce)
    Harcourt Papers (Sir William Harcourt and Lewis Harcourt, Viscount Harcourt
Balliol College Library (Oxford)
    Morier Papers (Sir Robert Morier)
Christ Church Library (Oxford)
    Salisbury Papers (Robert Arthur Cecil, marquess of Salisbury)
Rhodes House Library (Oxford)
    Lugard Papers (Frederick Lugard, Baron Lugard)
    Portal Papers (Sir Gerald Portal)
Cambridge University Library (Cambridge)
    Crewe Papers (Sir Robert Crewe-Milnes, Baron Houghton and marquess of Crewe)
Churchill College (Cambridge)
    Esher Papers (Sir Reginald Brett, Viscount Esher)
Private Collections
    Elgin Papers (Broomhall, Dunfermline)(Victor Alexander Bruce, earl of Elgin)
    Lyons Papers (Arundel Castle, Sussex) (Richard Lyons, Earl Lyons)
    Ridgeway Papers (Helmingham Hall, Stowmarket) (Sir West Ridgeway)
    Spencer Papers (Althorp, Northants) (John Poyntz Spencer, Earl Spencer)

SECONDARY SOURCES (Selected)

Alder, G.J. *British India's Northern Frontier, 1865-95.* London 1963.

Anderson, Pauline R. *The Background of Anti-English Feeling in Germany, 1890-1902.* Washington 1939.

Andrew, Christopher, "German World Policy and the Reshaping of the Dual Alliance." *Journal of Contemporary History* 1 (1966): 137-51.

Andrew, Christopher, and Kanya-Forstner, A. Sidney. "The French 'Colonial Party': Its Composition, Aims and Influence, 1885-1912." *Historical Journal* 14 (1971): 99-128.

Anstey, R.T. *Britain and the Congo in the Nineteenth Century.* London 1962.

Bayer, Theodore A. *England und der neue Kurs.* Tübingen 1955.

Berghahn, Volker R. "Zu den Zielen des deutschen Flottenbaues unter Wilhelm II." *Historische Zeitschrift* 210 (1970): 34-100.

Bickford, J.D., and Johnson, E.N. "The Contemplated Anglo-German Alliance, 1890-1901." *Political Science Quarterly* 13 (1927): 1-57.

Blanchard, Marcel. "Français et Belges sur l'Oubanghi, 1890-96." *Revue d'histoire des colonies* 37 (1950): 1-36.

Bourne, Kenneth. *The Foreign Policy of Victorian England 1830-1902.* Oxford 1970.

Bridge, Francis R. *From Sadowa to Sarajevo: The Foreign Policy of Austria-Hungary, 1866-1914.* London 1972.

Brown, Roger G. *Fashoda Reconsidered: The Impact of Domestic Politics on French Policy in Africa, 1893-98.* Baltimore 1969.

Calleo, David. *The German Problem Reconsidered.* Cambridge 1978.

Chapman, M.K. "Great Britain and the Bagdad Railway, 1888-1914." *Smith College Studies in History* 31 (1948).

Chastenet, Jacques. *Histoire de la Troisième République: La République triomphante, 1893-1906.* Paris 1955.

Collins, Robert O. *The Southern Sudan, 1883-98: A Struggle for Control.* New Haven 1962.

Conroy, Hilary. *The Japanese Seizure of Korea, 1868-1910.* Philadelphia 1960.

Cooke, James J. *New French Imperialism 1880-1910: The Third Republic and Colonial Expansion.* Hamden 1973.

Craig, Gordon A. *Germany, 1866-1945.* Oxford 1978.

Flournoy, F.R. "British Liberal Theories of International Relations, 1848-98." *Journal of the History of Ideas* 7 (1946): 195-217.

Galbraith, John S. "The 'Turbulent Frontier' as a Factor in British Expansion." *Comparative Studies in Society and History* 12 (1960): 150-68.

- *Mackinnon and East Africa, 1878-95: A Study in the "New Imperialism."* Cambridge 1972.

Ganiage, Jean. *L'expansion coloniale de la France sous la Troisième Répub-*

lique, 1871–1914. Paris 1968.

– "Un épisode du partage de l'Afrique: Les affaires du Bas-Niger, 1894–98." *Revue historique* 254 (1975): 149–88.

Geiss Immanuel. *German Foreign Policy, 1871–1914*. London 1976.

Gibbs, Norman H. *The Origin of Imperial Defence*. Oxford 1955.

Gillard, David R. "Salisbury and the Indian Defence Problem, 1885–1902." In *Studies in International History*, edited by Kenneth Bourne and Donald C. Watt. London 1967.

Greaves, Rose Louise. *Persia and the Defence of India, 1884–92*. London 1959.

– "British Policy in Persia, 1892–1902." *Bulletin of the School of Oriental and African Studies* 28 (1965): 34–60, 284–307.

Grupp, Peter. "Gabriel Honataux, le personnage et ses idées sur l'expansion coloniale." *Revue française d'histoire d'outre-mer* 58 (1971): 383–406.

Hargreaves, John D. *Prelude to the Partition of West Africa*. London 1963.

– *West Africa Partitioned*. London 1974.

Harris, Leslie. "A Scientific Frontier for India: Background to the Forward Policy of the Nineties." *Canadian Journal of History* 1 (1966): 46–71.

Heggoy, Alf Andrew. *The African Politics of Gabriel Hanotaux, 1894–98*. Athens, Ga. 1972.

Hirshfield, Claire. *The Diplomacy of Partition: Britain, France and the Creation of Nigeria, 1890–98*. The Hague 1979.

Hollingsworth, Lawrence W. *Zanzibar under the Foreign Office, 1890–1913*. London 1953.

Hornik, M.P. "The Anglo-Belgian Agreement of 12 May 1894." *English Historical Review* 57 (1942): 227–43.

Howard, Christopher. *Splendid Isolation*. London 1967.

Huttenback, Robert A. "The Siege of Chitral and the 'Breach of Faith Controversy': The Imperial Factor in Late Victorian Party Politics." *Journal of British Studies* 10 (1971): 126–44.

Iliams, T.M. *Dreyfus, Diplomatists and the Dual Alliance: Gabriel Hanotaux at the Quai d'Orsay, 1894–98*. Geneva 1962.

Ingram, Edward. "A Strategic Dilemma: The Defence of India, 1874–1914." *Militärgeschichtliche Mitteilungen* 6 (1974): 215–24.

James, Robert Rhodes. *Rosebery: A Biography of Archibald Philip, Fifth Earl of Rosebery*. London 1963.

Jelavich, Barbara. "Great Britain and the Russian Acquisition of Batum, 1878–86." *Slavonic and East European Review* 48 (1970): 44–66.

– "British Means of Offense against Russia in the Nineteenth Century." *Russian History* 2 (1974): 119–35.

Johnson, Franklyn A. *Defence by Committee*. Oxford 1962.

Kanamori, A. "The Siege of Chitral as an Imperial Factor." *Journal of Indian History* 46 (1968): 386–404.

Katzenellenbogen, S.E. "British Economic Activity in the German Colonies,

1884–1914." In *Great Britain and her World, 1750–1914*, edited by Barry M. Ratcliffe. Manchester 1975.

Kazemzadeh, Firuz. *Russia and Britain in Persia, 1864–1914*. New Haven 1968.

Kehr, Ekhardt. *Economic Interest, Militarism, and Foreign Policy*, edited by Gordon M. Craig. London 1977.

Kellas, James G. "The Liberal Party in Scotland, 1867–95." *Scottish Historical Review* 44 (1965): 1–16.

Kelley, Robert. " 'Midlothian': A Study in Politics and Ideas." *Victorian Studies* 4 (1960): 119–40.

Kennedy, Paul M. "Maritime Strategie probleme der deutsch: englischen Flottenrivalität." In *Marine und Marinepolitik im kaiserlichen Deutschland, 1871–1914*, edited by H. Schottelius and W. Deist. Düsseldorf 1972.

– *The Samoan Tangle: A Study in Anglo-German Relations, 1878–1900*. New York 1974.

– "Mahon versus Mackinder: Two Interpretations of British Sea Power." *Militargeschichtliche Mitteilungen* 16 (1974): 39–66.

– "Idealists and Realists: British Views of Germany, 1864–1939." *Transactions of the Royal Historical Society* 5th ser., 24 (1975): 137–56.

– *The Rise and Fall of British Naval Mastery*. London 1976.

– *The Rise of the Anglo-German Antagonism, 1860–1914*. London 1980.

Koch, Hans W. "The Anglo-German Alliance Negotiations: Missed Opportunity or Myth?" *History* 14 (1969) 378–92.

Koss, Stephen E. "Morley in the Middle." *English Historical Review* 82 (1967): 553–61.

Krausnick, H. "Holstein und das deutsch-englische Verhältnis von 1890 bis 1891." *Internationales Jahrbuch für Geschichtsunterricht* 1 (1951): 141–57.

Lademacher, Horst. *Die belgische Neutralität als Problem der europäischen Politik, 1830–1914*. Bonn 1971.

Lamb, Alistair. *Britain and Chinese Central Asia: The Road to Lhasa, 1767–1905*. London 1960.

Langer, William L. *The Franco-Russian Alliance, 1890–1904*. Cambridge 1929.

– *The Diplomacy of Imperialism, 1890–1902*. New York 1951.

Lederer, Ivo J., ed. *Russian Foreign Policy*. New Haven 1962.

Louis, William Roger. "The Anglo-Congolese Agreement of 1894 and the Cairo Corridor." *St Antony's Papers* 15 (1963): 81–100.

– "Sir Percy Anderson's Grand African Strategy, 1883–96." *English Historical Review* 81 (1966): 292–314.

Low, Donald Anthony. "British Public Opinion and the Uganda Question, October-December 1892." *The Uganda Journal* 18 (1954): 81–100.

Lowe, Cedric J. "Anglo-Italian Differences over East Africa, 1892–95, and Their Effects upon the Mediterranean Entente." *English Historical Review* 81 (1966): 315–36.

– *The Reluctant Imperialists*. London 1967.

Mackenzie, Kenneth. "Some British Reactions to German Colonial Methods, 1885–1907." *Historical Journal* 17 (1974): 165–75.

Malozemoff, Andrew. *Russian Far-Eastern Policy, 1881–1904*. London 1958.

Marder, Arthur J. *The Anatomy of British Sea Power: A History of British Naval Policy in the Pre-Dreadnought Era, 1880–1905*. New York 1940.

Marsden, Arthur. "Britain and the Tunis Base." *English Historical Review* 79 (1964): 67–96.

Martel, A. Gordon. "Documenting the Great Game: 'World Policy' and the 'Turbulent Frontier' in the 1890s." *International History Review* 2 (1980): 288–308.

– "The Near East in the Balance of Power: The Repercussions of the Kaulla Incident in 1893." *Middle Eastern Studies* 16 (1980): 23–41.

Mathew, H.C.G. *The Liberal Imperialists: The Ideas and Politics of a Post-Gladstonian Elite*. Oxford 1973.

Medicott, W.N. 'The Powers and the Unification of the Two Bulgarias, 1885." *English Historical Review* 54 (1939): 67–82, 263–84.

Miller, T.B. "The Egyptian Question and British Foreign Policy, 1892–94." *Journal of Modern History* 32 (1960): 1–15.

Newbury, Colin W. "The Development of French Policy on the Lower and Upper Niger, 1880–98." *Journal of Modern History* 31 (1959): 16–26.

– "Victorians, Republicans and the Partition of West Africa." *Journal of African History* 3 (1962): 493–501.

– "The Tariff Factor in Anglo-French West African Partition." In *France and Britain in Africa*, edited by Prosser Gifford and William Roger Louis. New Haven 1971.

Nicholls, Anthony J. *Germany after Bismarck: The Caprivi Era, 1890–94*. New York 1968.

Nish, Ian H. *The Anglo-Japanese Alliance: The Diplomacy of Two Island Empires, 1894–1907*. London 1966.

Obichere, Boniface I. *West African States and European Expansion*. New Haven 1971.

Penson, Lillian M. "The New Course in British Foreign Policy, 1892–1902." *Transactions of the Royal Historical Society* 4th ser. 25 (1943): 127–38.

Perham, Margery. *Lugard: The Years of Adventure*. London 1956.

Pierce, Richard A. *Russian Central Asia, 1867–1917*. Berkeley 1967.

Platt, Desmond Christopher M. *Finance, Trade and Politics in British Foreign Policy, 1815–1914*. Oxford 1968.

Pogge von Strandmann, Hartmut. "Nationale Verbände zwischen Weltpolitik und Kontinentalpolitik." In *Marine und Marinepolitik in kaiserlichen Deutschland, 1871–1914*, edited by H. Schottelius and W. Deist. Düsseldorf 1972.

Ramm, Agatha. *Sir Robert Morier, Envoy and Ambassador in the Age of Imperialism, 1876–93*. Oxford 1973.

Reuss, Martin. "Bismarck's Dismissal and the Holstein Circle." *European Studies Review* 5 (1975): 31–46.

Rich, Norman. *Friedrich von Holstein.* 2 vols. Cambridge 1965.

Robbins, Keith. *Sir Edward Grey.* London 1971.

Robinson, Ronald, and Gallagher, John A. *Africa and the Victorians.* London 1961.

Röhl, John Charles G. *Germany without Bismarck: The Crisis of Government in the Second Reich, 1890–1900.* London 1967.

– ed. *Kaiser Wilhelm II: New Interpretations.* Cambridge 1982.

Sanderson, G.N. *England, Europe and the Upper Nile, 11882–99.* Edinburgh 1965.

Semmel, Bernard. *Imperialism and Social Reform: English Social-Imperial Thought, 1895–1914.* Cambridge 1960.

Shannon, Richard T. *The Crisis of Imperialism, 1865–1915.* London 1976.

Singhal, Damodar P. *India and Afghanistan, 1876–1907: A Study in Diplomatic Relations.* St Lucia 1963.

Skrine, C.P., and Nightingale, P. *Macartney at Kashgar: New Light on British, Chinese and Russian Activities in Sinkiang, 1890–1918.* London 1973.

Smith, Colin L. *The Embassy of Sir William White at Constantinople, 1886–91.* Oxford 1957.

Smith, Woodruff D. "The Ideology of German Colonialism, 1840–1906." *Journal of Modern History* 46 (1974): 461–62.

Sontag, Raymond J. *Germany and England: Background of Conflict, 1848–94.* New York 1964.

Stansky, Peter. *Ambitions and Strategies: The Struggle for the Leadership of the Liberal Party in the 1890s.* Oxford 1964.

Steinberg, Jonathan. *Yesterday's Deterrent.* London 1965.

Steiner, Zara S. *The Foreign Office and Foreign Policy.* Cambridge 1969.

– *Britain and the Origins of the First World War.* London 1977.

Stengers, Jean. "Aux origines de Fachoda: L'expedition Monteil." *Revue belge de philologie et d'histoire* 36 (1958): 436–50; 38 (1960): 1040–65.

– "L'imperialisme coloniale de la fin du XIXe siècle: Myth ou réalité?" *Journal of African History* 3 (1962): 569–91.

Stribny, Wolfgang. *Bismarck und die deutsche Politik nach siner Entlassung.* Paderborn 1977.

Taden, B.N. "The British Policy towards the Maintenance of the Territorial Integrity and Independence of Iran, 1875–1900." *Indo-Iranica* 16 (1963): 50–60.

Taylor, A.J.P. "Prelude to Fashoda." *English Historical Review* 65 (1950): 52–80.

– "British Policy in Morocco, 1886–19092." *English Historical Review* 66 (1951): 342–74.

– *The Struggle for Mastery in Europe.* Oxford 1954.

Tessieres, Yves de "Un épisode du partage de l'Afrique: La mission Monteil de

1890–92." *Revue française d'histoire d'outre-mer* 59 (1972): 345–410.

Thornton, A.P. "Rivalries in the Mediterranean, the Middle East and Egypt." In *The New Cambridge Modern History*, vol. 12, *The Shifting Balance of World Forces, 1898–1945.* Cambridge 1968.

Trainor, Luke. "The Liberals and the Formation of Imperial Defence Policy, 1892–95." *Bulletin of the Institute of Historical Research* 52 (1969): 188–200.

Uzoigwe, G.N. *Britain and the Conquest of Africa.* Ann Arbor 1974.

Vagts, Alfred. "Wilhelm II and the Siam Episode." *American Historical Review* 65 (1940): 834–40.

Warhurst, Philip R. *Anglo-Portuguese Relations in South-Central Africa, 1890–1900.* London 1962.

Wehler, Hans-Ulrich. *Das deutsche Kaiserreich, 1871–1918.* Göttingen 1973.

Willequet, Jacques. *Le Congo Belge et le Weltpolitik, 1894–1914.* Paris 1962.

– "Anglo-German Rivalry in Belgian and Portuguese Africa?" In *Britain and Germany in Africa,* edited by Prosser Gifford and William Roger Louis. New Haven 1967.

Wittram, R. "Bismarcks Russlandpolitik nach der Reichsgründung." *Historische Zeitschrift* 186 (1958): 261–84.

Index